Freud and His
Self-Analysis

DOWNSTATE PSYCHOANALYTIC INSTITUTE
TWENTY-FIFTH ANNIVERSARY
SERIES

Mark Kanzer, M.D., General Editor

Freud and His
Self-Analysis

Volume I
Downstate Psychoanalytic Institute
Twenty-Fifth Anniversary
Series

edited by
Mark Kanzer, M.D., and Jules Glenn, M.D.

New York • Jason Aronson • London

COMMENTARY

Freud and His Self Analysis complements the two major bio-graphies, Ernest Jones' *The Life and Work of Sigmund Freud* and Max Schur's *Freud: Living and Dying*, going beyond the bare chronological facts of Freud's life. The authors, members of the faculty of the Downstate Psychoanalytic Institute, examine Freud's analysis of himself and supplement his efforts. This volume is also a companion piece to *Freud and His Patients* for it sets the stage for relating Freud's brilliant clinical and theoretical innovations to his persistent and relentless self-analysis.

The reader follows Freud from one palpable experience to another; his discovery of his unconscious, likened by him to a demon; his successful attempts to extricate himself from his transference attachments to Wilhelm Fliess, aided by his gradually recognizing his mentor's grievous mistreatment of the famous patient, Irma (Freud's dream about Irma is the first he fully analyzed); his identifications with Biblical heroes and his memories of his oedipal love for his mother as he analyzed himself in the course of writing the Dream Book; his excitement and depersonalization when he reached the Acropolis after years of travel phobia. The book also includes revealing analyses of Freud's relationships with his colleagues after he emerged from scientific isolation.

This volume creates an indelible portrait of Freud as a poignantly human genius, a devoted man who dared look into the unconscious mind of himself, his patients and his colleagues, and thus make his revolutionary discoveries.

PREFACE TO THE SERIES

Freud's royal road to the unconscious was the dream. However, as the father of psychoanalysis, his legacy to all included a far broader royal road, psychoanalysis itself, which pointed the way to the understanding of the psychology of man. Could even Freud himself have envisioned the complex routes taken by the discipline he fathered, its influences upon the arts and social sciences as well as practically every form of psychotherapy? Could he have foreseen the many tasks required of psychoanalytic institutes and psychoanalytic educators?

Psychoanalytic education with its many demands could well be a full-time job, yet it has so far been able to enjoy the wise luxury of requiring that its educators also have a firm footing in clinical psychoanalysis; that its teachers also be, often full time, clinical practitioners. The benefits of this somewhat anachronistic tradition have been considerable, but the price has been high. Psychoanalytic teachers must attend to their patients and then search for precious hours with which to plan, organize, and accomplish their teaching mission. Is it a mission in the full sense? Perhaps not, but it can be a most compelling and fulfilling aspect of one's career, as it has been for those of us who have been part of the Downstate Psychoanalytic Institute.

The Institute, founded by Drs. Howard Potter and Sandor Lorand, and itself parent to, and later in some respects child of, the Psychoanalytic Association of New York, has been shameless in its demands on the time and energy of its members. And yet it has become a part of us, a structuring part of our professional identity, of our self systems, and, by extension, an important and loved foundation of our professional family ties.

Absorbed in this demanding relationship, we were surprised to discover that this parent-child to us all, so warmly and ambivalently loved, in the sense that all such love is ambivalent, would in 1974 celebrate its twenty-fifth birthday.

We had a new task: to determine how a twenty-fifth anniversary of a psychoanalytic institute should most appropriately be acknowledged. There were to be, of course, the usual celebrations and testimonials. But these excellent occasions, relatively private gatherings, occur and become memories.

Perhaps more important are the desirable group self-observations and developmental evaluations. A psychoanalytic institute should, first and foremost, educate graduates who are able practitioners of psychoanalysis. But while this may be a necessary and wholesome criterion of adequate accomplishment, by itself it scarcely represents excellence. For it is always a hope that among the graduates will be some with the creative spark enabling them to make original scientific contributions. Even this is not enough: a healthy institute must also provide the systems and structures which enable its teaching programs to continue and develop, constantly supplementing courses and faculty with new ideas and new people. Ultimately, older faculty members will retire, and new teachers must be available. Finally, the institute must be able to take its place, as well as should its members individually, within the scientific and professional community.

Evaluating these steps according to a rough timetable, one could say that by age ten a psychoanalytic institute should be able to point to a growing body of graduates beginning to participate scientifically and organizationally on local levels and beyond. From years ten to twenty the institute's own graduates should be able to form the core first of the teaching faculty and then of the training analysts of the institute. Eventually, the administrative positions of the institute should be filled by its own graduates, who by this time have had the the chance to gain experience at these tasks. At twenty-five, Downstate has completed these steps, though happily without the parochial rigidity which might otherwise have precluded a welcome to talented and congenial colleagues from other programs who wished to join and enrich us.

We of the Downstate Psychoanalytic Institute are pleased with the quality of our programs and our graduates. We believe that we have accomplished these goals while creating a cohesive psychoanalytic group with a shared commitment to ideals which in no way detracts from the individual styles of its members. We hope that we are not complacent in our judgment that the goals for the first twenty-five years have been achieved well.

After all the anniversary celebrations, there was still the feeling that something more should be done. For this we have turned, through these volumes, to our colleagues, that we might share with them through their work an affirmation of our ideals as analysts—as observers, seekers of knowledge, enlighteners, and helpers. We hope that these four Anniversary Volumes will, through the work of the members of Downstate Psychoanalytic Institute, provide a glimpse of what we all treasure so much about our Institute: an atmosphere where we can work together pursuing our common goals individually and collectively, inspiring one another and enriching the creative capacity of all. The Downstate Institute has offered such an atmosphere. In return we offer these volumes as an expression of our gratitude for its existence and its excellence.

There are many people to whom we are indebted for their work on these volumes; only a few can be singled out for their contributions. Dr. Mark

Kanzer, General Editor, comes first. He has been not only a wise editor but a stimulator of new ideas and contributions. The only problem was to limit his efforts, for his quest for excellence and his productivity know no bounds. Dr. Jules Glenn was his able assistant overall and co-editor with him for Volumes I and II. Drs. Shelley Orgel and Bernard Fine were co-editors for Volume III, Dr. Joseph Coltrara editor for Volume IV. Each of them gave many hours of enlightened editorial advice to authors and fellow editors alike. It was a pleasure to work with all of them

We are grateful to the Department of Psychiatry of the Downstate Medical Center for providing our Institute its home, and to Drs. Howard Potter and those after him who chaired the Department of Psychiatry during these twenty-five years.

Special thanks are due to Drs. Robert Savitt, Merl Jackel, and Samuel Lanes, Presidents of the Psychoanalytic Association of New York during the years that these volumes were in preparation. It was the understanding sponsorship of the Psychoanalytic Association of New York that allowed this project to get under way. More than special thanks are due also to Drs. Howard Potter and Sandor Lorand for their instrumental role in the formation of the Downstate Institute, and to Drs. Sylvan Keiser, Mark Kanzer, Sidney Tarachow, William Console, Maurice Friend, Leonard Shengold, and Roy Lilleskov, and to Miss Vera Krassin and all those others who have worked so hard to help the Institute grow and prosper. Finally, we are indebted to all of the candidates and to all of the faculty members who, collectively, made the Downstate Institute such a wonderful place to work, to teach, and to learn.

Alan J. Eisnitz, M.D.
Director, Downstate Psychoanalytic Institute 1972–1975
Chairman, Editorial Board, 25th Anniversary Series

Postscript: After these volumes were completed and the above preface written, an important change occurred to our Institute. As conditions in Brooklyn, and more specifically at the Downstate Medical Center, no longer favored the continued development of psychoanalytic education there, it was decided to move.

On July 1, 1979 The Psychoanalytic Institute transferred its affiliation to the New York University Medical Center. This entailed moving the offices and classes to Bellevue Psychiatric Hospital in Manhattan. While we now have a new name—The Psychoanalytic Institute at New York University

Medical Center—and a new home, the candidates, faculty, and administration remain the same. We are still the same psychoanalytic institute.

To extend Dr. Eisnitz's developmental analogy further, we can say that the Institute had achieved the degree of independence and autonomy which permitted it to leave home when that departure was indicated. We now look forward to our new affiliation with New York University in hopeful anticipation that our spirit and our accomplishments will continue as before.

In a sense, therefore, these volumes not only celebrate the anniversary which occasioned their preparation, but are also a tribute to our thirty years at the Downstate Medical Center.

Roy K. Lilleskov, M.D.
Director, Downstate Psychoanalytic Institute 1978–1979
Director, The Psychoanalytic Institute
at New York University Medical Center

CONTENTS

ACKNOWLEDGMENTS

Many of the chapters have been previously published. We are grateful to the journals and publishers for their kind permission to reprint these articles:

Kanzer, M. (1961). Freud and the Demon. *Journal of Hillside Hospital* 10:190–202.

Shengold, L. (1966) The Metaphor of the Journey in *The Interpretation of Dreams*. *American Imago* 23:316–331.

Shengold, L. (1961). Freud and Joseph. In *The Unconscious Today*, pp. 473–494. M. Kanzer, Editor. New York: International Universities Press.

Schur, M. (1966). Some Additional "Day Residues" of "The Specimen Dream of Psychoanalysis." In *Psychoanalysis—A General Psychology*, pp. 45–85. R. M. Loewenstein et al., Editors. New York: International Universities Press. (This article has been somewhat abridged in the present volume.)

Schur, M. (1969) The Background of Freud's "Disturbance" on the Acropolis. *American Imago* 26:303–323.

Stamm, J. (1969). The Problems of Depersonalization in Freud's "Disturbance of Memory on the Acropolis." *American Imago* 26:364–72.

Kanzer, M. (1971). Freud: The First Psychoanalytic Group Leader. In *Comparative Group Psychotherapy*, pp. 32–46. H. Kaplan and B. J. Sadock, Editors. Baltimore: The Williams and Wilkins Co.

Shengold, L. (1976). Book Review: The Freud/Jung Letters; The Correspondence between Sigmund Freud and C. J. Jung. W. McGuire, Editor. *Journal of the American Psychoanalytic Association* 24:669–683. (This article has been expanded for publication in this volume.)

Kanzer, M. (1969). Sigmund and Alexander Freud on the Acropolis. *American Imago* 26:324–354.

Shengold, L. (1972). A Parapraxis of Freud's in Relation to Karl Abraham. *American Imago* 29:123–159.

Kanzer, M. (1972). Discussion of Leonard Shengold's (1972) Paper. *American Imago* 29:160–164.

Kanzer, M. (1976). Freud and his Literary Doubles. *American Imago* 33:231–243.

Blum, H. P. (1977). The Prototype of Preoedipal Reconstruction. *Journal of the American Psychoanalytic Association* 25:757–785.

The *American Imago* is published by the Wayne State University Press.
The International Universities Press published the *Journal of Hillside Hospital* and publishes the *Journal of the American Psychoanalytic Association*.

Chapter 1

INTRODUCTION: A Map of a Psychoanalytic Journey

MARK KANZER, M.D.

The present volume, *Freud and His Self-Analysis*, and the forthcoming *Freud and His Patients* are part of a series prepared to mark the twenty-fifth anniversary of the Division of Psychoanalytic Education, a unit of the Department of Psychiatry of the Downstate Medical Center of the State University of New York. This institution, founded in 1949, was an enterprise pioneered to demonstrate the feasibility of training analysts in a university to meet the standards of the American Psychoanalytic Association. The experiment has proved eminently successful and has served as a model for others of its kind.

The original independence of psychoanalytic institutes from medical schools was largely involuntary and reflected early doubts by the latter as to the scientific validity of the teachings and procedures of psychoanalysis. These often were used as a cloak for prejudices toward its doctrines about sexuality and the unconscious. Moreover, psychoanalysis was rooted in conceptions of the personality that far transcended the relatively narrow boundaries of therapy. It became increasingly apparent that medical psychology and psychotherapy could not ignore psychoanalysis; the situation changed when medical students, residents, and psychiatrists were unable to secure the training they required either in the university or the limited facilities of psychoanalytic institutes.

It was under such circumstances, during the boom in psychoanalysis which followed the Second World War, that Dr. Howard Potter, chairman of the Department of Psychiatry at the Long Island College of Medicine (later incorporated into the State University of New York), approached two noted analysts, Dr. Sandor Lorand and Dr. Richard L. Frank, and laid the foundations for the Division of Psychoanalytic Education.

The idea for the present study derived from the many contributions that had been made by the Downstate faculty members in the past. Max Schur had been Freud's personal physician during his last years and, in the two papers republished here, laid the foundations for his important biography, *Freud: Living and Dying* (1972). William G. Niederland's investigations (1974) of the early background of Dr. Paul Schreber, whose reminiscences had provided Freud his classical concepts concerning paranoia, uncovered new material which will remain both a permanent contribution to the literature of the relationship between childhood experiences and subsequent mental symptoms and an indispensable reference for an understanding of the Schreber case. Important studies by other members of the faculty brought out new data and placed the classical cases in modern frameworks essential for the contemporary reader. These contributions suffered, however, from scattered presentation in a variety of journals over the years, and they acquire great value merely by being collected and placed in juxtaposition. Two focal points of interest emerged: Freud's scientific work in relation to his self-analysis; and the application of modern frameworks to his case histories. We have supplemented these spontaneous trends with editorial commentary and with new articles written especially for the volumes by the original group and other members of the faculty.

What is offered therefore now includes: (1) material relevant to Freud's personal analysis as carried out by himself and others; (2) material relating to interactions between Freud's personality and that of his patients; and (3) commentaries viewing Freud's case histories in retrospect, elaborating upon them, and fitting them into modern frameworks. Our goals are modest; we offer annotations of our subjects rather than complete surveys. This first volume is devoted to the first of the three categories listed; a second volume will treat the second and third categories.

Leonard Shengold, Director of the Division of Psychoanalytic Education from 1975–1978, sounds an appropriate keynote in his essay "Freud and the Idea of a University" (chapter 2). We find the man and his work assumed their historical functions in a university setting—until the academic tradition offered psychoanalysis neither precedent nor shelter. Then, forced to find his pathway through uncharted terrain, Freud—at times consciously comparing himself to Columbus and other explorers—found problems and solutions in treating the mentally ill, thereby comprehending areas of psychology the university considered inadmissible aberrations. In time Freud reestablished a limited degree of contact with his former associates, but it was their need for him and for psychoanalysis—not his for them—that was the basis of the relationship. Psychoanalysis has now become an integral and reciprocally beneficial part of the university in the United States.

Even during the examinations that would lead to his admission to the University of Vienna, the seventeen-year-old Freud gave evidence of a remarkably lucid and original mind. Thus he wrote to Emil Fluss (nomen est omen!), a friend his own age, on June 16, 1873, that the examination in Greek had come off well—it had consisted of passages from *Oedipus Rex* which "I had also read on my own account, and made no secret of it" (E. Freud 1960, pp. 3–6). After some soul-searching in which he expresses a fear that he may come to a mediocre end, he extols the advantages of introspection and self-knowledge: "I don't mean to suggest that if you find yourself in a doubtful situation, you should mercilessly dissect your feelings, but if you do you will see how little about yourself you are sure of. The magnificence of the world rests after all on the wealth of possibilities, except that it is unfortunately not a firm basis for self-knowledge."

Freud's career would be built on his own proclivity to mercilessly dissect his own feelings and then to help the Emil Flusses do the same. Our ability to learn how he did this is based to no small extent on the thousands of letters he wrote in his lifetime, one avenue by which the introspective may reach out to others for a needed sharing of minds. The material offered in this volume will depend especially on the published Fliess letters, the correspondence with Carl Jung, Karl Abraham, Arnold Zweig, and assembled letters made available through Ernst Freud (1960). A most valuable portion of the latter is made up of the courtship letters to his fiancée, Martha Bernays, during four years of separation (1882–1886). There are thousands of other documents, published and unpublished, and our picture of Sigmund Freud will gain clarity as the unpublished part reaches his public.

The characteristics that appeared in the letter to Emil Fluss are further developed in the beautiful love letters to Martha Bernays from the young neuropathologist pursuing his studies in Vienna and Paris. Freud shows a rich vein of poetry and imaginativeness (almost invariably he addresses her as "my princess") which touches everything he reads and sees. There is also keen observation of both himself and others—Don Quixote is subjected to psychological appraisal in a "book review" written for her alone, while the suicide of a friend is transformed into a perceptive and compassionate evaluation of the processes that led to that end. Freud's very considerable literary abilities were to be absorbed into his later analytic insights and style.

The letters are also studded with phrases and concepts that would become familiar ingredients of his later analytic works—for example, humanity's pursuit of pleasure and avoidance of pain (the pleasure principle), the ability to find enjoyment and perform work (practical criteria of analytic success), and recurrent references to the Sphinx, to which this particular Oedipus seemed drawn. Soon after his engagement to Martha, this extraordinary neuropathologist was reporting on his "unruly dreams" and by 1883 was collecting them in notebooks which unfortunately seem to have been lost. It is thus erroneous to believe, as some do, that Freud's interest in dreams arose from the communications of his patients. More correctly, his own introspective disposition, already turning into self-analysis, taught him that dreams were meaningful, disposed him to make similar discoveries with his patients and enabled him to unite the two sources of observation into a "royal road to the unconscious."

Even in the letters to Martha Bernays, Freud went beyond merely reporting and collecting his dreams. His efforts to understand them showed that already he did not regard them as nonsense but as subjects for serious scientific study. His notes contain familiar elements of his later teachings—that dreams represent continuations of incomplete actions of the previous day, that they reflect predominant waking interests, experiences of frustration, etc. Foreshadowings of his later travel neurosis are also found in the dreams, as are typical examination dreams. Thus Jones reports a "blissful dream of landscape 'which according to this private notebook on dreams which I have composed from my experiences indicates travelling' " (symbolism was being discovered empirically!) and another of harbors—though Freud is not aware of their sexual symbolism as he describes them to his beloved. Their frustrated need for each other finds more direct representation, however, in recurrent dreams which, in one instance, "I was fighting some one for your sake and had the disagreeable feeling of being paralyzed just when I wanted to strike a blow." The unseen oedipal opponent intrudes into another field when "interference comes at the place of the dream when I still have to pass my doctor's examination, a task which has tormented me for years" (Jones 1953, pp. 351–352). It was a task which, as in fairy tales, was a necessary precondition to marriage. Thus travel inclinations and inhibitions, examination fears and frustrated aggressive and sexual inclinations coalesced to turn attention to dreams, the escape hatch for fantasied solutions of real life problems.

One pleasing introspective interpretation was arrived at in 1886 as though it came from without. "You know what Breuer told me one evening? . . . that hidden under the surface of timidity there lay in me an extremely daring and fearless human being. I had always thought so, but never dared tell anyone. I have often felt as though I had inherited all the defiance and all the passions with which our ancestors defended their Temple and could gladly sacrifice my life for one great moment in history. And at the same time I always felt so helpless and incapable of expressing these ardent passions even by a word or a poem. So I have always restrained myself, and it is this, I think, which people must see in me" (E. Freud, 1960, p. 202). Inhibited aggression and inhibited sexuality would form keystones of psychoanalytic doctrine.

Freud understandably soon became receptive to Breuer's idea that neuroses arose from strangulated affects which could undergo therapeutic catharsis through the verbalization of forgotten memories hidden in the unconscious. Repeatedly, Freud himself showed an extraordinary dichotomy between his descriptions of strangulated aggression and his ability to formulate aggression in theoretical terms. Nevertheless, it was from such inhibitions that self-observations and self-understanding grew—as well as the ability to observe and empathize with others. In his work on "Aphasia" (1891), the last of his purely neurological writings, he empathized with patients who were supposedly suffering from organic defects alone. Meditating upon the fixations of some of them on the last scenes and activities before trauma struck, he became definitely self-analytic as he recalled "having twice been in danger of my life, and each time the awareness of the danger occurred to me quite suddenly. On both occasions I felt 'This is the end,' and while otherwise my inner language proceeds with only indistinct sound images and slight lip movements, in these situations of danger I heard these words as if somebody were shouting them into my ears, and at the same time I saw them as if they were printed on a piece of paper floating in the air" (Freud 1891, p. 62).

It was not surprising that Freud, unlike his other neurological colleagues, insisted that an understanding of aphasia required a theory of not only cerebral localization but also normal psychological functions of language. Later he would require an understanding of the normal functions of the personality as well. Organic paraphasia graded into slips of the tongue, asymbolia into difficulties in recalling names. We do not know more about the interesting experiences he records here, which involve ego splitting, derealization and the dissociation of language into visual and auditory components. We do know of at least two recorded dreams in which a similar dissociation took place—the "specimen dream" (Freud 1900) which initiated him into the secrets of the dream, and the "Hella" dream described as his self-analysis was getting under way (Freud 1954, p. 206). Both were clearly oedipal. In both the verbal portion was not shouted but recorded in heavy type—a visual equivalent, perhaps—which almost certainly conveyed a superego warning against emergent libidinal wishes. On the Acropolis, a similar split would cause him to doubt the reality of what he saw; the return of the denied with a claim also resulted in experiences of déjà vu to which he was prone.

Freud's introspective tendencies and creative solutions never permitted him to follow slavishly in the footsteps of tradition—a characteristic which he some-times regarded as part of his Jewishness and the status of his people as a permanent minority. In the neuropathology laboratory, he introduced an original staining technique which drew much recognition. He discovered the extraor-dinary properties of cocaine and was one of its first unwitting addicts. The independence of his own thinking about aphasia was not devoid of conscious aggressive satisfactions against his superiors; as he told Fliess in a letter, "I have been very cheeky in it [the "Aphasia" book] and have crossed swords with your friend Wernicke, as well as with Lichtheim and Grashey, and have even scratched the high and mighty idol Meynert" (Freud 1954, Letter 8, p. 61). The paralysis experienced in his dreams in the face of ambition was turning into dreams and realities of conquest in everyday life.

In these letters to Fliess, he was finding an ally who was aiding in this transition and enabling him to turn their correspondence into an instrument which developed the first psychoanalysis. Both behind and before him lay a pattern that he was only partly to understand and resolve—the need for a "high and mighty idol" whom he would place upon a pedestal and then demolish. Thus to a certain extent aggression would always be acted out rather than analyzed. Destiny would have it that Freud himself became a high and mighty idol, sensitive to the intentions of admirers who nurtured in their idolatry the same ultimate plans for him.

In my "Freud and the Demon" (chapter 3), I have made extensive use of the Freud-Fliess correspondence (1887–1902) which coincides with the deepest pe-riod of estrangement between Freud and the intellectual world of his time. The notion of the demon arises in connection with his reactions, as his experiences with treatment, first in association with Joseph Breuer (the cathartic technique) and then independently, taught him to plumb the unconscious and to discover the underworld demons of sexuality and aggression which lurked beneath the surface of logic and culture. Freud was in every respect a middle-class family man who guided his own life by logic and culture. The demons shocked him but he insisted on confronting them rather than running away as did his collab-orator Breuer. Anxiety states developed but his gifts for transforming them into poetry and imagination supplemented his disposition to apply insight. "Demon" or "daimon" came to signify in psychoanalysis, as it had for Plato, an instinctual urge which, confronting the rational mind, threatens to wrest from it control over its faculties and will (Freud 1920, p. 36). The essence of psychoanalysis became in fact the summoning forth of the demon, forcing it to disclose its name and intentions, and taming it so as to serve the rest of the personality.

Leonard Shengold (chapter 4) continues with later stages in the Freud-Fliess correspondence and especially with "the metaphor of the journey" that finds its way into basic theoretical formulations of psychoanalysis. Speaking of his proposed arrangement of the *Interpretation of Dreams*, Freud explains to his friend: "The whole thing is planned on the model of an imaginary walk. First comes the dark wood of the authorities (who cannot see the trees), where there is no clear view and it is easy to go astray. Then there is a cavernous defile through which I lead my readers—my specimens dream with its peculiarities, its details, its indiscretions, and its bad jokes—and then, all at once, the high ground and the prospect, and the question: 'Which way do you want to go?' " (1954, p. 290).

Shengold explores the imagery of this psychic quest in terms of the self-analysis of a man with a travel phobia who has recently begun to dredge up the memories that will help cure the disorder. Prominent among these memories was the trip to Vienna from his birthplace when at the age of three he first saw his mother nude, an event associated in his mind with the first glimpse of gaslights that reminded him "of souls burning in hell" (p. 237). One aspect of analysis would enable him to continue the journey without fear and enable him to look down from the seven hills of Rome and the legendary Acropolis. Another insight that derived from his study of dreams, however, would be summed up autosymbolically in the mental apparatus that he constructed at the end of the volume, the intellectual "high ground" at the end of the "walk." Shengold makes an intriguing comparison between the topographically conceived mental apparatus and the structure of the womb from which all travellers begin their journeys and to which in the end they return.

In a follow-up study, Shengold (chapter 5) traces the life-journey of Sigmund Freud from its incipience to its end through his identifications with the Biblical figures of Joseph and Moses. The former was also a famous dream-interpreter and his family structure had a remarkable similarity to Freud's—each with a father named Jacob who had many children through a plurality of wives. Well-known factors in Freud's life receive new scrutiny—the role of the nursemaid who was a second mother, the death of the little brother Julius which left the older one with a permanent sense of guilt, and the advent of the youngest brother Alexander who was to become his "Benjamin."

The Moses identification gained significance in Freud's later years when he had become, like this prototype, the head of the analytic movement and had led his people toward a promised land. The "Moses of Michelangelo" (Freud, 1914a), written after disheartening desertions by former followers, is commonly regarded as symbolic of his own resolve that he must control his resentment and preserve the tables of the law. In his last years, when the Jews of Austria were endangered, when Freud's books were publicly burned and exile loomed for himself and other analysts, he occupied himself with a very original history of

Moses and monotheism (1939) which is widely regarded as a personal "family romance" of great interest.

The letters to Fliess, the part played by the latter in the dreams and self-analysis of Freud, and a bitter quarrel in 1904 that took the place of their former intimacy, furnish the texts for two major studies by Max Schur. In the first, "Some Additional 'Day Residues' of 'The Specimen Dream of Psychoanalysis' " (1966; chapter 6), he brings new and hitherto unpublished letters to Fliess into conjunction with "The Dream of Irma's Injection" (Freud 1900), which, according to Freud himself, taught him the secret of dreams on July 24, 1895. It has always been apparent—and Freud acknowledged this—that he did not share with his readers all these secrets. Through Schur, we learn the most important of them: Irma (actually Emma), one of Freud's analytic patients, was operated on for a sinus condition by Fliess. Very grave complications arose which nearly cost her life. A second operation brought to light a piece of gauze that Fliess had left in the wound.

Never did Freud reveal the secret that reflected on his friend and shook his confidence at a crucial point in the "analysis" he was undergoing with him. Schur points out the obvious influence of Irma's operation on the dream and gives us more data about her as a patient. An additional study of mine (unpublished) indicates the important part played by "Irma" in the period of transition from cathartic to analytic therapy, as a continuing figure in Freud's analysis with Fliess, and a factor in their ultimate estrangement.

The Freud-Fliess relationship figures in the background of an uncanny experience that Freud sustained on a vacation visit to the Acropolis in 1904 and was rooted in a residue of the travel neurosis he had largely overcome with his own self-analytic method. Schur (chapter 7) explores the continuing undercurrent of hostility to Fliess in Freud's dreams even when they seemed on affectionate terms (the latent negative transference).

Two of Fliess's theories held an ambivalent attraction for Freud—those of bisexuality and "periodicity," the latter of which, in a semi-mystical fashion, predicted dates of death. Just before leaving for the 1904 summer vacation, the "demon" Fliess rose from the past to direct vitriolic criticisms against Freud for alleged plagiarism with respect to the theory of bisexuality and for unprofessional conduct in communicating that theory to a patient, with the result that it appeared in print without acknowledging Fliess's priority. Unfortunately there was some truth to these assertions, which the unhappy Freud explained as due to an amnesia for Fliess's views. There is little reason to doubt this explanation, especially with Schur's analysis of the death wishes in Freud's dreams which were directed against the former analyst. Nevertheless Freud was depressed, and experienced on the Acropolis a state of depersonalization—doubting the reality of the matchless scene before him. Schur points to evidence that in this negation of the pleasures of surveying the view from the Acropolis, as well as in throwing doubt upon the efficacy of his self-analysis in curing his travel neurosis, Freud's guilt was active in turning the death-wishes toward Fliess against himself. In this instance Freud accepted the theory of periodicity and saw it as foretelling his own death. The data is curious and interesting; Julian Stamm (chapter 8) and William G. Niederland (1969), in a symposium, have supported Schur's views. (We shall have occasion to return to the Acropolis experience in another context.)

Harold P. Blum, in an essay on "The Prototype of Preoedipal Reconstruction" (chapter 9), applies current views on the earliest years of life to bring together Freud's reminiscences and self-analysis of this "prehistoric period," predominantly before the age of three, and its subsequent influence on his personality development. As Blum points out, such reconstructions include not merely the events themselves but also the reactions associated with them. He takes the opportunity to discuss contemporary differences of opinion as to the uses of preoedipal material in the analysis of adults and reminds us that Freud did precisely this.

He examines Freud's dreams, his smoking habits and biographical data to confirm Mahler's observation that "certain configurations persist in transference and acting-out patterns which seem to be the outcome of unresolved conflicts in the separation-individuation process of the preoedipal period" (1971, p. 415). Of special interest is the evidence which Blum offers that Freud's article on "Constructions" in 1937 utilized material related to preoedipal memories of his infant brother Julius that had been dredged up at an early stage of his self-analysis just forty years earlier and about eighty years after the death of the child.

Blum observes that Freud's very first reconstruction was of the preoedipal period. In 1897 Freud wrote to Fliess that he had, at two years of age, suffered the "seed of self-reproach" on the death of his brother Julius. Blum expresses the opinion that Freud's wording reflected certain distinctions we now make between the "depressively tinged basic mood" of the child of the rapprochement subphase and the guilty feelings of the child whose superego has developed. He described his reactions to Julius' death as the "seed of self-reproach" rather than "guilt." The latter, as he later observed, appears following the oedipal period.

Of considerable interest too is Blum's surmise that early memories of a "constant companion" of the preoedipal and early oedipal phases, John, really related to Freud's mother.

The two-person relationship through which we view Freud's behavior and self-analysis in his correspondence with Fliess gives way to a broader and more objectively oriented study made available by the publication of the *Minutes of the Vienna Psychoanalytic Society* (4 volumes) by Herman Nunberg and Paul Federn (1962–1975). In 1901, after the publication of the *Interpretation of Dreams*, disciples gradually gathered about Freud, meeting on Wednesday evenings and ultimately forming the Vienna Psychoanalytic Society. After 1906, records were kept by Otto Rank—the most important member during the subsequent proceedings up to 1914, when the first World War drew him into military service. In an article on "Freud: The First Psychoanalytic Group Leader" (chapter 10), I suggest that the meetings—which became the scenes of analyses, often wild and spiteful, of members by each other, and increasingly of Freud himself by dissident members—were in fact phenomena of group analysis that were only partly recognized and controlled. An interesting polarization took place when Alfred Adler, closest to Freud in mental stature of any in the group, and the only one destined to put forward a coherent conception of therapy which drew upon and yet departed from psychoanalysis, offered both himself and his ideas to the group in competition with Freud. Adler actually succeeded for a while in ousting Freud from the leadership of the society! These experiences were probably operative in suggesting to Freud the revolt of the sons against the primal father which he postulated in *Totem and Taboo* (1913) and, with variants, in "The Moses of Michelangelo" (1914a) and "The History of the Psychoanalytic Movement" (1914b).

Adler's bold attempts at assuming dominance occurred at a time when Freud was contemplating transfer of the leadership of the psychoanalytic movement to Carl Jung. Freud was planning to have the "Aryan" Swiss with their more prestigious academic status become the guardians of psychoanalysis and to diminish the importance of his Viennese colleagues. In fact, Freud intended to surrender the presidency of the Viennese group, which in turn rebelled against him and his plans. Adler, like Freud, retained unresolved ambivalence toward siblings and their surrogates; he offered a program that would replace Freud's administrative and intellectual leadership in Vienna with his own. A compromise resulted in Adler as the president and Freud as the scientific chairman of a newly formed local psychoanalytic society which replaced the Wednesday evening society. With this division of leadership, psychoanalysis ceased to function as a one-man discipline; the society became a congregation of scientists rather than an assemblage of students. In a few months, however, when a rebellious lack of caution impelled Adler to proclaim views carrying him far from the Freudian school, the society, whose members suffered guilt over deposing Freud, forced Adler to resign. After a period of self-scrutiny, Freud returned to the group which received him gladly. Nevertheless, the departure of Stekel and some followers lay ahead.

Until the *Interpretation of Dreams* and the phase in his self-analysis when he could dispense with Fliess as mentor, Freud would characteristically attach himself to an older man who was at first treated with reverence and toward whom he developed a dependent relationship (Meynert, Bruecke, Charcot, Breuer). Often they were to be demolished in his own mind. (Fliess, it may be noted, was actually two years younger but treated as though senior.) After the *Interpretation of Dreams*, it was Freud himself who became the father figure in the Oedipal dyad and the "sons" who, first attaching themselves to him, sought in time to demolish him. It would be an oversimplification to state, as is sometimes done, that Freud tolerated only docile sons. He seems to have had a decided preference for amusing albeit rebellious sons, like Wittels, over stodgy but loyal ones like Abraham.

Freud was greatly stimulated by Carl Jung who came into his life in 1906 when he was fifty and the younger man thirty years of age. The eight-year correspondence that followed showed Jung traversing the course which had been Freud's in the past by first idolizing the father figure and then breaking with him in a state of mounting negative transference which Freud could now understand but not change. The latter's own countertransference analysis was advancing, but was not yet sufficiently developed to master the intricate personal and intellectual problems that the Swiss Calvinist—in some respects an externalized ideal—presented to the Viennese Jewish identity of Freud and most of his followers.

Shengold (chapter 11) has reviewed the important and fascinating exchange of letters between the two men (McGuire 1974). He compares them, naturally enough, to the earlier Fliess correspondence (as indeed did Freud and Jung themselves). Jung was by no means the likely candidate for the psychoanalytic succession that Freud insisted on finding him to be. A mutual infatuation developed which held for Freud the fairly obvious seeds of disillusionment which perhaps he craved, and for Jung a need to assert his ego identity and masculine independence. The ostensible issue that drove them apart—the repudiation by Jung of the sexual aspects of the Oedipus complex which, he insisted, were merely "symbolic" of deeper mental forces and inherited memories—was merely a cover for incompatibility of age, temperament, religion, and a personal involvement that Jung, and perhaps Freud as well, had to escape. When their infatuation ended, the high intellectual levels of debate were left behind and Jung provided Freud with "personal analyses" that were vitriolic, unfair—and sometimes correct. In chapter 12 I examine the letters Jung's wife Emma wrote in an endeavor to defuse the impending crisis between the two men. Her attempts to analyze both of them (by no means without insight) were not at all welcomed by the founder of psychoanalysis and she ended with an equally fruitless offer to establish with him a patient-doctor relationship. She found Freud prematurely resigned to old age and urged him to permit his spiritual sons to grow without imposing on them the guilt for what seemed to her his concomitant dwindling. Though Emma Jung was relegated to the background role that wives of analysts usually played, an analysis of her husband's dreams by Freud himself indicated that she was far more involved with them along historically familiar oedipal lines than any of them realized.

Carl Jung was the first president of the International Psychoanalytic Society from 1910 until it became clear in 1914 that he needed to retire. He was succeeded by Karl Abraham who held the office until his death in 1925. If Jung was the patriarchal favorite son, his hold depending on obscure affections, Abraham was the sensible older son and was respected but was not permitted into the inner citadels of Freud's devotion. There was a lengthy correspondence between them (1907–1925) which Shengold reviews in his analysis of "A Parapraxis of Freud's in Relation to Karl Abraham" (chapter 13). In the early years, Abraham apparently sought to find his way into Freud's personal good graces by showing an interest in Egyptian antiquity and particularly by writing a monograph on the monotheistic pharaoh Akhenaten, who repudiated the name and religion inherited from his father and insisted that his reluctant priests accept the worship of a single invisible god. The subject was indeed calculated to arouse Freud's enthusiasm, and extensive collaboration occurred until the paper appeared in 1912. A coolness ensued when Abraham repeatedly warned Freud against Jung—and especially after he was proven right. Another disturbing factor developed when Abraham, living in Berlin, struck up a close friendship with Fliess. Before Abraham's death there were two direct clashes between himself and Freud: one in which he protested the favors the latter still bestowed on a favorite, Otto Rank, despite his increasingly heretical position; another over the issue of whether the Berlin Psychoanalytic Institute should cooperate in a venture with the motion picture industry to popularize Freud's teachings.

The problem that Shengold raises takes its departure from the circumstance that Freud, in discussing Akhenaten in *Moses and Monotheism* (1939), failed to mention Abraham's contribution on the subject. Shengold sees here not only a residue of unresolved resentment toward Abraham but also a complement to the view of Moses that Freud developed: the Hebraic figures of Abraham, Isaac and Jacob (!) as ancestors of the Jewish people were eliminated, and Moses given their place as the virtual father and lawgiver to a slave people whom he liberated and taught the monotheism of Akhenaten. Support for the notion of a continuing hostile cross-fire between Freud and Abraham despite a predominantly respectful friendship is found in my essay (chapter 14) which examines the images that passed between them in their writings (for example, the "rescue of the father fantasy" which Abraham discovered to arise in death wishes). While Lilleskov (chapter 15) emphasizes the affectionate and cooperative relationship between the two men, he suggests that Freud had serious difficulties in accepting ideas ("impregnation") from another person. Self-analysis found its limits here and indeed in the "bedrock" that Freud conceived as a limiting factor in analysis, the inability of one man to accept a gift from another. Lilleskov also takes note of Freud's state of perturbation as well as an octogenarian's forgetfulness during the writing of *Moses and Monotheism*.

Even as Freud was approaching eighty, however, he made one of his last and most enlightening contributions to his own self-analysis. With the life voyage—and certainly the use of Vienna as a "port of call"—approaching its end, Freud rather reluctantly accepted an invitation to contribute an article to a *Festschrift* to honor his close friend, Romain Rolland, on the occasion of his seventieth birthday. He chose to analyze the parapraxis on the Acropolis in 1904, whose background in a contemporary controversy with Fliess we have already mentioned. Chapter 16 offers my view of the meaning of the reminiscence from the standpoint of Freud's feelings in 1936 when the self-analysis took place.

Freud's article is a remarkable demonstration of his continued acuity as a self-analyst despite his own protestations that he was losing his mental powers (an apparent but not absolute contradiction). His associations take the form of a letter to Rolland in which the latter quickly disappears as a person and is replaced by Alexander Freud, the younger brother who had accompanied Freud on the trip to the Acropolis and was exactly Rolland's age, that is, ten years younger than himself.

What emerges is a remarkable illumination of the role that this "Benjamin" had played in his brother's life. Many analysts, including Freud himself, have stressed the guilt that he experienced but never quite resolved after the death of his infant brother Julius. As is so often the case, however, the especially affectionate relations with the next and last-born brother received little attention. For many years, it is noted, Alexander was his brother's constant companion on the semi-mystical summer pilgrimages that Freud undertook almost every year. They were together when the travel neurosis was seemingly conquered as Freud pushed on to Rome and three years later at Athens, when residues of the neurosis were apparently revived by the unpleasant state of affairs with Fliess, a revenant (returned ghost) of Julius, according to Schur.

The agoraphobic often can venture forth only in the company of a specially trusted person who, as analysis discloses, is really the recipient of death wishes. Many scattered references to Alexander in Freud's works suggest that their apparent affection similarly covered the older brother's wishes to do away with him as he had once done in his unconscious with Julius. There seem to have been two layers to the travel phobia in which the younger brother figured—to do away with him at the end of the journey (a death symbol), but also to give birth to him in identification with the mother. As Freud approached eighty and was so visibly further along on the "journey" as compared to Alexander and Rolland, an envious wish for an exchange of identities is seen as motivated by a desire to gain the decade of renewed powers while the younger brother is advanced that much closer to the end. A Faustian pact with the demons!

I propose that Freud, in suggesting the name of Alexander, after the Greek conqueror, for his younger brother, mitigated sibling rivalry by becoming his "father." In *Moses and Monotheism*, it is Moses who becomes the spiritual ancestor of the Jewish people while the legendary ancestors are eliminated. At this same time Freud was becoming obstinately dedicated to the proposition that the very obscure Earl of Oxford was the real author of Shakespeare's plays. A general trend appears recognizable here and may shed light on the background to charge of plagiarism which intermittently insinuated itself into Freud's problems. It may be that a desire to deprive another of his works becomes a substitute for depriving the father of his powers. Relatedly, Freud was repetitively bemoaning his own real and creative loss of potency and hailing (especially with Jung) the younger man who would replace him.

It is along these lines that the subject of "Freud and His Literary Doubles" (chapter 17) is explored. Freud's feelings of affinity for creative writers was often attested. His own ability as a creative writer is apparent and won him the Goethe Prize. Rather remarkably, he kept insisting that the writers were in an enviable position since they knew seemingly effortlessly from within much about mental processes that the analyst could acquire only laboriously from without. Freud seems to have been disavowing here his own effortless recourse to empathy and intuition, to poetic imagination, and to a remarkable literary skill in the presentation of his ideas. As he began to fall under the sway of self-analysis and permitted free association to take the place of reason in his observations and writings, he spoke of himself as a budding poet and commented that his case histories read like short stories. Critics sometimes agreed with him in a less than flattering fashion. He also remarked that he obtained more pleasure from his semi-literary works about "Gradiva" (1906), "Leonardo" (1910), and *Moses and Monotheism* (1939) than from his more clinical and theoretical discussions.

A key to the puzzling denial of the gifts of a writer is to be found, it is suggested, in Freud's treatment of certain literary men like Arthur Schnitzler and Romain Rolland as "doubles," as uncanny alter egos whom he admired but strove to keep at a distance. The "double" is an omen of death, as Freud indicated; in a psychological sense, he absorbs the personality of the "twin" and does away with him. This signifies a need to repress the oedipal strivings which the poet may freely express; as a scientist, Freud could admit this to consciousness only in the trappings of logic and laborious research which satisfied the superego.

Further clues about these literary doubles are found in the congratulations which Freud regularly sent to them on their birthdays. These congratulations tended to be rather dubious; Freud usually found reasons, as illustrated by the Rolland letter, to limit the expression of congratulations and turn the further course of the communication to himself and his own activities. Thomas Mann and Arnold and Stephen Zweig may be cited among the literary figures who, later in Freud's life, sought out the older man with veneration for the reciprocal fascination that he exerted upon them. Arnold Zweig was in fact a much-valued auditor for Freud's ideas about *Moses and Monotheism* while this "historical novel" was being written. He did research for Freud and his agreements were prized—his disagreements less appreciated. He was probably the last of the Fliesses in the long list that Freud had gathered. What the Freud-Zweig correspondence reveals above all is the autobiography of a creative idea.

The final linking of Freud with his doubles follows the route of the self-analytic letter to Romain Rolland and finds that the model of the relationship is much like that of the older brother-younger brother relationship with Alexander. A number of Freud's commentaries on that subject are collected and presented in this essay, detailing a picture consistent with a personal "family romance:" the younger brother is the mother's favorite, thus making him enviable and prone to success; the older brother, though the father's favorite, has a more difficult life. The younger brother becomes a poet and hero and may even be chosen to succeed the father after the latter is slain by the brother band. In *Moses and Monotheism*, where the family romance is given much sway, the older brother, as favored son of the father-God, becomes the prototype of the Jew; the younger son, still the mother's beloved, becomes the Christian. Freud himself, it may be noted, was long the youngest son in the family into which he was born—a position he regained after the brief "reign" of Julius but finally lost forever to Alexander.

In the final paper (chapter 18), Glenn discusses narcissistic aspects of Freud's doubles. It has been demonstrated clinically that the double derives from the symbiotic relationship when self- and object-representations are poorly differentiated and primitive narcissism prevails. Glenn contends that mature development of narcissism and regression to earlier states are essential for creativity. Duplication can also be used defensively, especially against primal scene traumata such as Freud experienced in early childhood when his family occupied a single room (Schur 1972). Glenn distinguishes between the defensive and creative aspects of Freud's disposition to admire writers as doubles.

The family romances described in chapter 16 were islands that could largely be spared self-analysis. Nevertheless, in projected form they permit much to be discovered. The continuation of the analytic process by Freud's successors will complete for his science, though of course not for himself, the superhuman problem he left unfinished. In our second volume of essays, concerning Freud's relationship to his patients, the same "follow-up" task will be undertaken in a different setting.

References

Abraham, K. (1912). "Amenhotep IV: A psychoanalytic contribution towards the understanding of his personality and the monotheistic cult of Aton." In *Clinical Papers and Essays on Psycho-Analysis*, pp. 262–290 London: Hogarth Press, 1955.

Freud, E., ed. (1960). *Letters of Sigmund Freud*. New York: Basic Books

————(1970). *The Letters of Sigmund Freud and Arnold Zweig*. New York: Harcourt, Brace and Wald.

Freud, S. (1891). On aphasia. New York: International Universities Press (1953).

———— (1900). The interpretation of dreams. *Standard Edition* 4/5.

———— (1906). Delusion and dream in Jenson's "Gradiva." *Standard Edition* 9:7–95.

———— (1910). Leonardo da Vinci and a memory of his childhood. *Standard Edition* 11:63–137.

———— (1913). Totem and taboo. *Standard Edition* 13:1–161.

———— (1914a). The Moses of Michelangelo. *Standard Edition* 13:211–238.

———— (1914b). The history of the psychoanalytic movement. *Standard Edition* 14:7–66.

———— (1939). Moses and monotheism. *Standard Edition* 23:7–137.

———— (1950). The Origins of Psychoanalysis. New York: Basic Books (1954).

Jones, E. (1953–57). *The Life and Work of Sigmund Freud*. New York: Basic Books.

Mahler, M. (1971). A study of the separation-individuation process: and its possible application to borderline phenomena in the psychoanalytic situation. *Psychoanalytic Study of the Child* 26:403–424.

McGuire, W., ed. (1974). *The Freud/Jung Letters*. Bollingen Series XCIV. Princeton: Princeton University Press.

Niederland, W. G. (1974). *The Schreber Case. Psychoanalytic Profile of a Paranoid Personality*. New York: Quadrangle/The New York Times Book Co.

Nunberg, H. and Federn, E. (1962–1975). *Minutes of the Vienna Psychoanalytic Society*. Volumes 1–4. New York: International Universities Press.

Schur, M. (1972). *Freud: Living and Dying*. New York: International Universities Press.

Chapter 2

FREUD AND THE IDEA OF A UNIVERSITY

LEONARD SHENGOLD, M.D.

Universities began developing in Italy at the end of the eleventh century and at Paris and Oxford in the twelfth. The establishment of universities was part of the movement toward the renaissance of the ancient Greek and Latin cultures. The term "university" was applied to collegiate societies of learning because their aim was to teach the *universitas literarum* (the entire range of literature): arts, theology, law, languages, science. The idea of learning everything is an expression of the unconscious wish for omniscience, part of infantile fantasy connected with the wish to re-experience the bliss and feeling of omnipotence of some primal fusion with the mother. To be able to know everything seemed much more possible in those times when the conception of an omnipotent God ruling a limited universe was a general assumption. Recent centuries have brought the decline of religion and the development of a science of infinite complexity. As man has lost his central position in the universe, the *realistic* promise of attaining omniscience, or contacting omniscience, has disappeared; but in unconscious fantasy the wishes retain their power.

In his paper, "Education or the Quest for Omniscience" (1958), Bertram Lewin draws a parallel between the rise of universities and the development of psychoanalytic institutes. Both universities and psychoanalytic education, Lewin says, developed in three different phases (and forms). For psychoanalysis these are:

(1): independent, empiric and informal private teaching—the period of the individual seeker for knowledge; (2): loosely formal instruction ranging from individual instruction to simple society regulation; which developed into (3): formal institutionalized instruction—the institutes of today. [1958, p. 461]

Lewin believes the desire for omniscience is a basic drive in the development of all institutions of learning. When an attitude of omniscience gets institutionalized it inevitably operates against free inquiry and the advancement of knowledge. The medical schools and the official psychiatry of Freud's student days "purported to rest on unimpeachable evidence" supplied by materialistic scientific assumptions "and by inference to supply the means of professional omniscience. . . . one can readily understand the resistance to (Freud's) complete rethinking of assumptions. . . . that challenged the omniscience of the medical profession" (1958, p. 469). Lewin describes a struggle in which institutionalized conservative forces fight to retain power and the right to declare what is there and what is true by isolating the challenger of the established order and suppressing his ideas. Lewin is also aware of the struggle within institutions and within individuals for and against authority and omniscience.

In the 1850s, John Henry Newman published a series of discourses and sketches (later published as *The Idea Of A University* and *University Sketches*) that attempted to define a university—its history, purpose and philosophy. He pictured an historical continuity starting from education in Athens—"the home of the intellectual and beautiful"—to the European higher learning of his own time. In the essay "What is a University?" Newman sketches his ideal of what a university should be. He begins with the old definition of a university as a "school of universal learning. . . . a school of knowledge of every kind, consisting of teachers and learners from every quarter. . . . in its essence, a place for the communication and circulation of thought, by means of personal intercourse. . . ." (1852, p. 6). These assemblies of learning started in great cities like Athens. Students were drawn to the cities like a contemporary "young artist who aspires to visit the great Masters in Florence and in Rome." Newman eloquently describes the promise of the university and links it with the promise of the great cities of history: "A university is a place of concourse, whither students come from every quarter for every kind of knowledge. You cannot have the best of every kind everywhere; you must go to some great city or emporium for it. There you have all the choicest production of nature and art all together, which you find each in its own separate place elsewhere. . . . In the nature of things, greatness and unity go together; excellence implies a centre. Such then. . . . is a university" (1852, p. 15). Newman sees the university as the place for the display of the wonderful, the search for truth, and the attainment of greatness:

It is the place for seeing galleries of first-rate pictures, and for hearing wonderful voices and miraculous performers. It is the place for great preachers, great orators, great statesmen. . . . it is the place to which a thousand schools make contributions; in which intellect may safely range and speculate, sure to find its equal in some antagonistic activity, and its judge in the tribunal of truth. It is a place where inquiry is pushed forward, and discoveries verified and perfected, and rashness rendered innocuous, and error exposed, by the collision of mind with mind and knowledge with knowledge. It is the place where the professor becomes eloquent, . . . a missionary and preacher of science, displaying it in its most complete and winning form, pouring it forth with the zeal of enthusiasm, and lighting up his own love of it in the breasts of his hearers. . . . It is a place which attracts the affections of the young by its fame, wins the judgement of the middle-aged by its beauty, and rivets the memory of the old by its associations. It is a seat of wisdom, a light of the world, a minister of the faith, an Alma Mater of the rising generation. [1852, pp. 15–16]

It is unlikely that Freud, anglophile and accomplished reader of English though he was, read Newman's essays; he would have shared the ideal of a university as a means toward universal knowledge, following the tradition of the Greeks.*

Freud had a lifelong bent toward philosophy: Freud told Jones that in his youth his attraction toward philosophical speculation was so strong he had to check it "ruthlessly" (Jones 1953, p. 29). It was hearing Goethe's essay on Nature read aloud that occasioned Freud's decision to study medicine. In this essay Nature is portrayed as a bountiful mother who allows a favorite child the privilege of solving her "riddles." Alma Mater (literally "fostering mother") is an institutionalized and attenuated version of Goethe's Nature.

Freud's 1919 paper, "On the Teaching of Psycho-Analysis in Universities," is a realistic appraisal of the effects that would follow an official establishment of analytic teaching at a university. The idea of a university assumed by Freud is similar to Newman's. Acceptance by a university meant to Freud an official acknowledgement of his right to explore Nature's secrets and acceptance by the Establishment of his solutions. Apart from its practical significance, a link with

*Of Vienna University toward the beginning of the 20th century Esslin writes: "Medical students and doctors would be hotly engaged in veritable battles which raged about the music of Wagner between the conservatives and the innovators, while classical scholars, having had to pass their *matura* in higher mathematics and physics as well, were still able to get excited about the theories of Einstein or Max Planck" (1972, p. 45). This paper was originally prepared for the Conference on Psychoanalytic Education and Research (COPER) sponsored by the American Psychoanalytic Association in 1974.

the university had complex and many-layered personal meanings for Freud. To start at the surface, Freud's idea of a university was connected not only with the Western cultural tradition stemming from Plato and the Greeks but also with his heritage as a Jew of the study of Hebrew holy writings: "My early familiarity with the Bible story (at a time almost before I had learnt the art of reading) had, as I recognized much later, an enduring effect upon the direction of my interests" (Freud 1925, p. 8). This alternative tradition involved a lonely scholar, or a group of scholars under a Master, studying the Torah, the Talmud, the Zohar and the Kabbala (see Bakan 1958). There is a well-known nineteenth century quotation from Thomas Carlyle that applies to this model: "The true University of these days is a Collection of Books" (1840, p. 390). Freud was, of course, a passionate reader.

In his professional life, Freud was first associated with the university, then retreated from it, and edged back toward it late in life. After his undergraduate and medical training came those most creative years of the 1890s when he was a lonely "conquistadore" of the mind—an isolated scholar with an audience of one: Fliess, whom he lost. Then came a gathering of students and followers—Abraham, Jung and the others—and the beginnings of official societies for psychoanalysis. Later came increasing recognition by the intellectual world and even some grudging official notice from universities.

Freud's longing to be accepted by the Western humanist and scientific tradition as embodied in the university was tinged with ambivalence, and kept at a distance by his pride and his sense of reality. His real struggle with medical authorities brought out both Freud's impulses to be part of the university "parental" establishment and to strike out against it for independence. In his *Autobiographical Study* (1925) Freud wrote:

When in 1873, I first joined the University I experienced some appreciable disappointments. Above all, I found that I was expected to feel myself inferior and an alien because I was a Jew. I refused absolutely to do the first of these things. I have never been able to see why I should feel ashamed of my descent or, as people were beginning to say, of my "race". . . . These first impressions at the University, however, had one consequence which was afterwards to prove important; for at an early age I was made familiar with the fate of being in the Opposition and of being put under the ban of the "compact majority." The foundation was thus laid for a certain degree of independence of judgement. [1925, p. 9]

Freud then quotes Ibsen and identifies with his hero Dr. Stockmann, the "enemy of the people," who is rejected by the authorities and by the "compact majority" because he stands for the truth, whatever the consequences; and who, sadly, discovers "the strongest man in the world is he who stands most alone."

Both what he said and what he did kept Freud "alone" and an outsider, especially in his home city of Vienna. Here again, his Jewishness is relevant. His family was among the increasing number of Jewish immigrants who settled in Vienna in the second half of the nineteenth century. Not only many Viennese gentiles but many aristocratic Viennese Jews looked down on the newcomers from the east with disdain and alarm. To these unwanted immigrants, education for their children meant everything. This was a continuation of their cultural tradition; the University was the main gateway to knowledge, power and success in Vienna.

Newman's stress on the appeal of great cities was shared by Freud. Like Alma Mater, the city refers (as symbol) to the mother. In late adolescence Freud turned away from his early military ambition to be a conqueror like Hannibal, the would-be taker of Rome, toward the exploration and understanding of the mind. He intended to conquer with his intellect (like his fellow dream-interpreter, Joseph). After his university studies, he did become a traveler to great cities. In his letters, we read of *his* struggle to reach Rome, and of his Hannibal-like feeling of triumph when he finally arrived there. He wrote a paper in his old age describing the symptoms that arose in 1904 when he visited Athens and climbed the hill of the Acropolis—a feeling of unreality at the thought of going further than his father had. Paris was the site of a postgraduate pilgrimage to study with Charcot. But it was his home city, Vienna, that all Freud's life evoked the deepest ambivalent feelings. As a child, he felt lured by Vienna with the promise of its University; he would study law and become a cabinet minister, or take up science and discover the secrets of nature. The concourse with the great paternal figures of the Professors would give him access to their power with which he could conquer Alma Mater and the city of Vienna.

Jones tells of a fantasy of Freud's that connects the ambition to be a professor at the University of Vienna with his oedipus complex. In 1906, to mark his fiftieth birthday, Freud was presented with a medallion depicting Oedipus and the Sphinx. It was inscribed with a line from Sophocles' *Oedipus Tyrannus*: "Who divined the famed riddle and was a man most mighty." Freud turned pale when he saw his disciples' gift; he was stricken with a sense of the uncanny. "He disclosed that as a young student at the University of Vienna he used to stroll around the great arcaded court inspecting the busts of former famous professors of the institution. He then had the phantasy, not merely of seeing his own bust there in the future, which would not have been anything remarkable in an ambitious student, but of it actually being inscribed with the identical words he now saw on the medallion" (1955, pp. 13–14).

Freud's rivalry with his siblings was also a force in his feelings about the University of Vienna and the prospect of a professorship. Sigmund was the indisputable family favorite. His older half-brothers were no longer at home as he grew up. All of his younger sisters and his brother Alexander were expected to sacrifice to give Sigmund the means for a university education. He was the only child to have his own room so that he could study in peace.

The ambitious wish to be the favorite sibling with the highest possible title and attainment—part of Freud's acknowledged identification with the biblical Joseph (see Shengold 1970)—emerged in competition with his youngest sibling, Alexander: Freud's Benjamin. Freud documents his concern about the prospect of Alexander's reaching the goal of professorship first in a letter to Fliess in 1899: "Alexander has a lectureship on tariffs at the Export Academy, and after a year will have the title and rank of professor extraordinary—long before me, in fact . . ." (Freud 1887–1902, p. 292). What is more, Alexander would come first in the eyes of their mother (sibling rivalry draws much of its deadly power from the displacement onto the brother of the rivalry with the father *for the mother*; this was markedly true for Freud): ". . . our mother expressed her surprise that her younger son was to become a professor before her elder" (Freud 1901, p. 108; see Kanzer [1969] for more about this and other meanings of brother Alexander for Freud).

Toward the end of the nineteenth century, Newman's idea of a university had become part of the zeitgeist; this was apparent in Vienna. Esslin states that in Vienna:

[the] ideal of a universally educated man. . . . inspired the curriculum of the Austrian educational system, particularly in the "middleschool" (between the elementary and the university levels); the Gymnasium or grammar school (was) mainly classical but natural science and mathematics were also taught very thoroughly. . . . the examination which gave access to the University, the *Matura* [maturity examination] had to be taken in humanist and science subjects. Moreover so powerful was the ideal of universal culture [*Allgemeinbildung*] that even those who, on entering university, specialized in subjects like law or medicine, continued to regard it as incumbent on them to show their appreciation of the humanities by an interest in music, painting and literature. [1972, pp. 46–47]

Freud had done brilliantly in Gymnasium and he entered the University of Vienna as a medical student in the autumn of 1873 at the age of seventeen. Statistics of the year 1869 show that there were 40,227 Jews in Vienna, comprising 6.3 percent of the population. In that same year (1869), 30 percent of the medical faculty of the University was Jewish. By 1889, the ratio of Jews on the medical faculty had increased to 48 percent (Heer 1972). As the number of Jewish immigrants to Vienna grew, and as the Jewish proportion of University faculty (especially in medicine and law) rose, anti-Semitism increased. The Jews themselves were divided; both the upper class Jews and the left wing Jewish Social Democrats, for example, were for the most part opposed to Zionism. Many of those in the Jewish Establishment who had thrived under the predominantly tolerant rule of the Habsburgs feared the influx of Jews from the East and they resented any notoriety that was associated with Jewishness—such as Freud's ideas about sexual motivation which were the subject of much gossip in the 1890s. Viennese anti-Semitism stemmed from clerical and right wing aristocratic circles (where it was rationalized on ideologic German nationalist grounds), and also from the lower middle class where it began to flourish—seemingly for economic reasons.

> [Anti-Semitism] fed on the bitterness caused by the great slump of 1873 and the identification of share-pushers, stock exchange jobbers and ruthless profiteers with well-known Jewish capitalists, and swept the lower middle class along for the starkest economic reasons. It was fast becoming a powerful political factor, but cultured Viennese tended to despise and underrate it as mere rabble-rousing, even when it found allies in the clerical and conservative-aristocratic parties. [Barea 1966, p. 300]

Toward the end of the century, a political blend of upper and lower classes was achieved under the leadership of the rabble-rousing, anti-intellectual Karl Lueger, who founded the anti-Semitic Christian Social party; in 1900 he became Mayor of Vienna and retained the position until his death in 1910, to the disgust both of Freud and of Kaiser Franz Josef.

It was in 1873, the year of the "great slump," that Freud began his medical studies at the University. Following the University ideal of the universally educated man, Freud took courses in philosophy under Felix Brentano, together with scientific subjects. (A three year course in philosophy had been obligatory for medical students up until 1872.) One of Freud's courses outside the immediate medical curriculum was "Biology and Darwinism" given by the zoologist Clause. He also took a course under Professor Brücke, the great man in whose laboratory he was to work, on the physiology of voice and speech. In 1876, after two and a half years as a student, he began to do research in the University laboratories—an unsuccessful attempt to find the testes of the eel. Freud later wrote:

> During my first three years at the University I was compelled to make the

discovery that the peculiarities and limitations of my gifts denied me all success in many of the departments of science into which my youthful eagerness had plunged me. Thus is learned the truth of Mephistopheles' warning: "It is in vain that you range from science to science; each man learns only what he can." At length in Ernst Brücke's Physiology Laboratory I found rest and satisfaction—and men, too, whom I could respect and take as my models: the great Brücke himself and his assistants Sigmund Exner and Ernst von Fleischl-Marxow. [1925, p. 9]

Brücke was the epitome of the great professor for Freud. He had been the friend and co-worker of Helmholtz. In his "non vixit" dream, Freud recalled the overwhelming reproach of Brücke's "terrible blue eyes" (Freud 1900, p. 422) when the young man came late one day to the Professor's laboratory. In his account of that dream, Freud describes his identification with Brücke; he grants himself the power of the basilisk—to cause death with his eyes. One might describe Freud's superego as possessing Brücke's steel-blue eyes, which, according to Jones, would "appear at any moment when he might be tempted to any remissness in duty or to any imperfection in executing it scrupulously" (1956, p. 39). Like Freud's father Jacob, Brücke was 40 years older than Freud. After his father's funeral, Freud dreamt: "I found myself in a shop where there was a notice up saying: 'You are requested/To close the *eyes*' " (my italics; Freud 1887–1902, p. 171) which Freud says was an expression of *reproach*. Brücke was not only a figure who condemned any straying from scientific virtue; he was also an ideal who inspired Freud to emulate his standards and his eminence. The ambitious young Freud had to deal with the desire to surpass the great man and take his place (as with his father Jacob). Brücke was the living representative of the school of physiological thought associated with the name of Helmholtz that dominated late nineteenth century medicine; its creed was that all forces in the living organism were to be regarded as determined by physical and chemical factors. Freud was to serve and to rebel against this narrow determinism. Freud was to re-introduce some of the "vitalistic" ideas of Johannes Müller, which had been repudiated by Müller's students Brücke and Helmholtz (going back to a grandfather figure to transcend fathers). After all, his choice of medicine had been made under the influence of Goethe, a contemporary of Müller. Goethe was an amateur scientist as well as an artist. He, like his hero Faust, aimed at understanding everything—again *universitas literarum*—an ideal that was challenged by the reductionist materialistic assumptions of official science at the end of the nineteenth century. One can glimpse conflicts and shifts in Freud between vitalistic ideals (derived from the German philosophical movement called *Naturphilosophie*) and materialistic ones. These ideals would seem to have maternalistic (Mother Nature) as against paternalistic (Professor Brücke) auras and were connected with Freud's oedipus complex.

In 1881 Freud received his medical degree and left Brücke's laboratory to go into private practice. He had appointments in the University hospital, first as *aspirant* (equivalent to intern), and then as *Sekundarzt* (equivalent to junior resident). After stints in surgery and medicine, the latter under Nothnagel—a believer in physiologically based medicine and in treating the whole human being and not just the illness (see Rosen 1972)—Freud was appointed *Sekundarzt* in 1883 in the Department of Psychiatry headed by Theodore Meynert. Later in the year he switched to *Sekundarzt* in neurology, although he continued to work in Meynert's laboratory until 1885. During all these post-student years he was doing neurological and physiological research.

Freud had to make a living through private practice and was anxious to receive an official University appointment which was so highly regarded by the Viennese. In 1885, Freud was appointed a *privatdozent*—"a rank in German and Austrian medical schools that has no exact counterpart in America or Britain. A *privatdozent* has no right to attend faculty meetings and has no salary but he can give a certain number of classes on topics outside the regular curriculum—it was necessary to attain it for university advancement and it enjoyed high prestige with the general public" (Jones 1953, p. 70). Freud did give classes (he had attained a European reputation in neurology), and Wilhelm Fliess was for a short time one of his pupils. But to be really successful in Vienna one had to be a professor; there was medical snobbishness in the capital "and the cream of medical practice went to those doctors with the envied title of Professor" (Jones 1953, p. 339).

Freud was to remain a *privatdozent* for the long period of twelve years. Kris feels the delay was due to "the anti-Semitic tendencies in the Vienna Medical Society, the Medical faculty and the academic administration" (1954, p. 11). In 1897 there was serious prospect of his appointment. He was at that time absorbed in his ideas about seduction by parents and the role of sexuality in dreams and pathology. The struggles over the wish to become a Professor can be followed in Freud's letters to Fliess.

At first it appeared he would be ignored by the medical faculty. He wrote to Fliess on January 14, 1897, of a rumor: "I am left cold by the news that the board of professors have proposed my younger colleagues in my specialty for the title of professor, thus passing me over, if the news is true. It leaves me quite cold but perhaps it will hasten my final break with the university" (Freud 1887–1902, pp. 190–191). Shortly after this Freud was proposed to the Medical Faculty Board for the position of Associate Professor. On June 6, 1897, the Board voted by a majority for Freud to be awarded the title. But he was not appointed. In his favor was the high quality of his work as a neurologist, but his reputation had been damaged by his sexual theories. Kris attributes the delay "solely to the (anti-Semitic) policy of the Ministry of Education" (1954, p. 200). In the annual ratifications Freud and his group were passed over in 1897, 1898, and 1899. In 1900 all the others were appointed—but not Freud.

At first Freud expected the appointment to come through. On June 12, 1897, he wrote Fliess, "At our next congress you shall call me 'Herr Professor'—I mean to be a gentleman like other gentlemen" (Freud 1887–1902, p. 210). On February 9, 1898, he wrote a letter which hints at the oedipal connotations of the appointment: "There is a rumour that we are to be invested with the title of professor at the Emperor's jubilee on Dec. 2. I do not believe it, but I had a fascinating dream on the subject; unfortunately it is unpublishable, because its background, its deeper meaning, shuttles to and fro between my nurse (my mother) and my wife. . . ." (1887–1902, p. 245). For Alma Mater, he was fighting with the authorities—perhaps with the Emperor.

The professorship finally came in 1902. The determination to get it came after Freud had achieved his long wished-for visit to Rome, and after the break with Fliess—so painful for Freud but so necessary to cast off subjection and become his own man.

Although their regular correspondence had ceased, Freud wrote Fliess of the appointment and received a letter of congratulations from him. He then replied (March 11, 1902): "Just think what an 'excellency' can do! He can even cause me again to hear your welcome voice in a letter. But as you talk about such grand things in connection with the news—recognition, mastery etc.—my usual compulsion to honesty makes me feel it incumbent on me to tell you exactly how it came about. It was my own doing, in fact. When I got back from Rome, my zest for life and work had somewhat grown and my zest for martyrdom had somewhat diminished" (1887–1902, p. 342). Here is victorious Hannibal who has conquered his inhibitions and taken the city. The work Freud had accomplished in his splendid isolation had solidified his identity; his self-analysis helped him to come to terms with oedipal triumph. His ambition was again stirred and he resolved to go on to *take* the professorship and Vienna:

> I found that my practice had melted away and I withdrew my last work from publication because in you I had recently lost my only remaining audience. I reflected that waiting for recognition might take up a good portion of the remainder of my life, and that in the meantime none of my fellow-men were likely to trouble about me. And I wanted to see Rome again and look after my patients and keep my children happy. So I made up my mind to break with my strict scruples and take appropriate steps, as others do after all. One

must look somewhere for one's salvation, and the salvation I chose was the title of professor. [1887–1902, p. 342]

Freud called on his old teacher Exner who treated him rudely and suggested that he try to use influence on the Minister of Education. He enlisted his old friend Frau Gomperz who approached the Minister. He pretended to know nothing about it and said a new recommendation was needed. The old one was renewed, but nothing happened until one of Freud's patients, the wife of a diplomat, heard about the situation and, by donating a picture by Böcklin to a new municipal gallery in which the Minister was interested, got him to forward the appointment to be signed by the Emperor. At the end of his letter (his last letter to Fliess) Freud ironically portrays the professor-worship of the Viennese:

> So one day she came to her appointment beaming and waving an express letter from the Minister. It was done. The *Weiner Zeitung* has not yet published it, but the news spread quickly from the Ministry. The public enthusiasm is immense. Congratulations and bouquets keep pouring in, as if the role of sexuality had been suddenly recognized by His Majesty, the interpretation of dreams confirmed by the Council of Ministers and the necessity of psycho-analytic therapy of hysteria carried by a two-thirds majority in Parliament. I have now obviously become respectable again, and my shyest admirers now greet me from a distance in the street. [1887–1902, p. 343]

Jones says that Freud's practice took a permanent turn for the better, but "the change in the title made no intrinsic difference in Freud's academic position. As before when he was a *privatdozent*, he was allowed to give lectures at the University, but was not obliged to. Only a full Professor (Professor Ordinarius) who was a member of the Faculty had that responsibility" (1953, p. 341).

In 1908, Carl Jung sent Freud a draft for the title page of a new psychoanalytic journal he was editing. He apologized (perhaps not without some malicious enjoyment in the pitting of one father-figure against another): "Naturally it went against the grain to put Bleuler's name before yours; I did so only because Bleuler has the advantage of being Professor publicus ordinarius (full professor)" (Freud/Jung 1974, p. 187). Bleuler, who was Jung's chief at Zurich, had apparently wanted his name to appear below Freud's. Freud responded that Bleuler's modesty might "hurt us both. It is easy to see that if his name comes first this reflects not an order of rank but an alphabetical order, as is customary in such publications. For the same reason it would be an order of rank and highly objectionable if my name were to come first." Freud's suggestion was to put both names on the same line. Jung accepted this:

DIRECTED BY
PROF. DR. E. BLEULER and PROF. DR. SIGM. FREUD

So the siblings were made equal, or almost equal. But for Freud not coming first in the order of professorial rank remained bothersome. He added in his letter that his suggested change "has to do with titles and *is designed to conceal my nakedness*" (1954, p. 188; my italics; not being a full professor made Freud the helpless infant). "My 'professor' is only a title and cannot be put in anywhere else" (1954, p. 188). Freud wanted to show himself as professor.

After Freud began to gather a following, there was official recognition from a university—in America! Stanley Hall, the president of Clark University in Massachusetts, invited Freud to give a course of lectures on the occasion of the twentieth anniversary of the foundation of the university. Ferenczi and Jung were also invited. In September, 1909, Freud gave five lectures there. He met William James who told him that he felt the future of psychology belonged to Freud's work. "A particularly affecting moment was when Freud stood up to thank the University for the Doctorate that was conferred on him at the close of the ceremonies. To be treated with honor after so many years of ostracism and contempt seemed like a dream, and he was visibly moved when he uttered the first words of his little speech: 'This is the first official recognition of our endeavors' " (Jones 1957, p. 57).

Freud used his right to give lectures at the University of Vienna, continuing up to the time of the First World War. His *Introductory Lectures* (1916–17) are derived from talks he gave extemporaneously at the University. In 1920 he was finally granted the title of Professor Ordinarius, "but being in independent private practice, he was not made a member of the Faculty or given charge of a Department. So, strictly speaking, Freud was never a regular academic teacher" (Jones 1957, p. 341).

The professorial appointment was a wish fulfilment for Freud. In 1914, after the breaks with Jung, Bleuler and the other academic Swiss, he had written to Abraham: "I do not know if I have already told you that Rank has brilliantly solved the problem of Homer. I want him to make it his thesis for admission to the faculty. I still want to see him, you and Ferenczi as university lecturers in order to enable psycho-analysis to survive the bad times ahead" (Freud and Abraham, 1907–25, p. 207). By 1919 Freud felt much less urgency. In 1919 when a Bolshevik government took over in Hungary, Ferenczi was installed as Professor of Psycho-Analysis at Budapest. This was a reaction to pressure from medical students there in 1918. In response to the Hungarian situation, Freud wrote a paper, "On the Teaching of Psycho-Analysis in Universities" (1919). It is a reserved statement; he does not show enthusiasm for acceptance by universities, saying that they would stand to gain more than the analysts from the ties. At the same time "the inclusion of psycho-analysis in the University would no doubt be regarded with satisfaction by every psycho-analyst" (1919, p. 171). Analysts do not need the connection, he says, since they can acquire understanding of theory from reading (the solitary path to omniscience), as well as from meetings of psychoanalytic societies (their own learning-groups). Analysts can be independent because the experience vital to the training of an analyst comes from his own analysis and from supervision by more experienced colleagues. Psychoanalytic societies were formed specifically because the universities excluded psychoanalysis. Freud describes the benefits that learning psychoanalysis would confer on physicians who sometimes show a lack of interest in the most absorbing problems of human life. All future physicians could be taught the importance of mental and emotional factors in human physical functioning, and in illness and the treatment of illness. This could be accomplished by introductory courses on the relation between mental and physical life, and on basic psychoanalytic principles. For those who go on to a career in psychiatry, more advanced and specialized courses would be needed to supply the understanding of mental illness "furnished by depth-psychology" (1919, p. 171).

But Freud was not exclusively or even primarily interested in medical training since psychoanalysis has a bearing on problems in "art, philosophy, religion, history of literature, mythology, history of civilization, philosophy of religion" (1919, p. 171). A general course in psychoanalysis should be available for students in these branches of learning. Freud here echoes Newman's ideal: "the fertilizing effects of psycho-analytic thought on these other disciplines would certainly contribute greatly toward forging a closer link in the sense of a *universitas literarum*, between medical science and the branches of learning which lie within the spheres of philosophy and the arts" (1919, p. 173).

Freud's estimate of the consequences of university affiliation is modest and realistic. There are no signs that the unconscious wishes involved with the promise of a university are distorting his judgment. He is aware that the university has much to offer the analysts in supplying them access to out-patient departments for neurotic patients, and to mental hospital wards for the study of other psychiatric conditions. This access would facilitate psychoanalytic research. As for the medical student and the general university student, the object would not be to teach the practice of psychoanalysis. Teaching for these groups would have to be done "in a dogmatic and critical manner, by means of theoretical lectures. . . . for the purposes we have in view it will be enough if [these students] learn something *about* psycho-analysis and something *from* it (1919, p. 173).

Freud, whose first psychoanalytic books had more acceptance from artists and literary critics than from official medical and academic circles, was not convinced that medical training was needed to be an analyst. Max Graf, the music critic and father of the patient, had been his co-worker in treating "little Hans," and Otto Rank and Hanns Sachs, who were not physicians, became important colleagues. In October 1910, Jung wrote to Freud that his Zurich Psychoanalytic Society had adopted "a rule that only holders of academic degrees can be accepted as members" (Freud/Jung 1907–1925, p. 363). Jung favored the rule; he cited with disapproval the invitation that Ferenczi had tendered to a "stage director" (*Theaterregisseur*) who had given a lecture to the Budapest Society. Freud answered that such restrictions personally displeased him. Zurich was free to adopt the measure according to the rules of the International Psycho-Analytic Association, but in Freud's opinion the spirit of the International's statutes ". . . does not tend toward such exclusiveness. . . . In Vienna it [would be] impossible, if only because we should then have to exclude our secretary of many years [Rank]. It would also be a pity to exclude several new and very hopeful student members. Finally such a 'regressive' measure is not really appropriate in the era of *University Extension*" (1907–25, pp. 367–368). The last two words were written in English. This suggests that if he had not read Newman, at least his ideas about the university came from English writers. Certainly education toward becoming an analyst was not thought of by Freud as primarily utilitarian, aiming at professional competence, but as directed toward something like Newman's goal of the extension of universal knowledge.

The increasing doubts Freud had in later life about the need for medical training for analysts are presented (with a linking of the doubt to a description of his own path to analysis) in the postscript to his work "The Question of Lay Analysis" (1927). This is Freud's last statement that has bearing on the idea of a university; I will quote from it extensively. Again he repudiates the limited area of medical knowledge in the service of the ideal of universal knowledge:

> [It is still violently disputed but] I have assumed. . . . that psycho-analysis is not a specialized branch of medicine. I cannot see how it is possible to dispute this. Psycho-analysis is a part of psychology; not of medical psychology in the old sense, not of psychology of morbid processes, but simply of psychology. It is certainly not the whole of psychology, but its substructure and perhaps even its entire foundation. The possibility of its application to medical purposes must not lead us astray. Electricity and radiology also have their medical applications, but the science to which they belong is none-the-less physics. [1927, p. 252]

> My main thesis [is] that the important question is not whether an analyst

possesses a medical diploma but whether he has had the special training necessary for the practice of analysis. . . . what is the training most suitable for an analyst? My own view was and still remains that it is not the training prescribed by the University for future doctors. What is known as medical education appears to me to be an arduous and circuitous way of approaching the profession of analysis. No doubt it offers the analyst much that is indispensable to him. But it burdens him with too much else of which he can never make use, and there is a danger of its diverting his interest and his whole mode of thought from its understanding of psychical phenomena. A scheme of training for analysts has still to be created. It must include elements from the mental sciences, from psychology, the history of civilization and sociology, as well as from anatomy, biology and the study of evolution. . . . it is easy to meet this suggestion by objecting that analytic colleges of this kind do not exist and that I am merely setting up an ideal. An ideal, no doubt. But an ideal which can and must be realized. And in our training institutes, in spite of all their youthful insufficiencies, that realization has already begun. [1927, pp. 251–252]

Freud's ideal here would seem to be a kind of specialized psychoanalytic university, although it could also fit a psychoanalytic unit in an established university.

Freud continues, discussing his own career: I should like to consider the historical argument a moment longer. Since it is with me personally that we are concerned, I can throw a little light, for anyone who may be interested, on my own motives. After forty-one years of medical activity, my self-knowledge tells me that I have never really been a doctor in the proper sense. I became a doctor through having been compelled to deviate from my original purpose; and *the triumph of my life lies in my having, after a long and roundabout journey, found my way back to my earliest path.* . . . In my youth I felt an overpowering need to understand something of the riddles of the world in which we live and perhaps even to contribute something to their solution. [1927, p. 253; my italics]

Here, with his favorite metaphor of a journey (with all its own preoedipal and oedipal connotations; see Shengold 1966), Freud speaks of the triumph of returning to the promises of Mother Nature—the favorite child possessing her breast with the timeless peace of the omniscience that follows solution of all her riddles; and also the possessor of her body, having displaced the paternal authorities and the fraternal rivals. Freud's triumph had not been conferred by the

Establishment as embodied in the University. The old Conquistador has made his own way: not only has he influenced Western thought so that psychoanalysis invades the medical schools and universities despite the hostility of some of the professors, but he can design his own university.

Summary

Freud both furthered the Western humanist tradition—carrying on the torch of the Enlightenment—and rebelled against it—a lonely rebel like Prometheus, bringing fire to light up the underworld. Both roles expressed and were motivated by Freud's psychological conflicts; his rivalry with his father and brothers and his desires for his mother figured in his ambivalent attitudes toward the universities of his time, especially toward the University of Vienna. But to the idea of a university—a place for the fullest exploration of science and the highest manifestations of art—he had an unwavering devotion. The ideal of *universitas literarum* was part of Freud's concept of the highest morality: to discover and to stand for the truth.

References

Bakan, D. (1958). *Sigmund Freud and the Jewish Mystical Tradition*. New York: Shocken.

Barea, I. (1966). *Vienna*. New York: Knopf.

Carlyle, T. (1840). *On Heroes, Hero-Worship and the Heroic in History*. New York: Dutton, 1908.

Esslin, M. (1972). Freud's Vienna. In *Freud: The Man, His World, His Influence*, ed. J. Miller, pp. 42–54. Boston: Little, Brown.

Freud, S. (1887–1902). *The Origins of Psychoanalysis*, ed. M. Bonaparte, A. Freud, E. Kris. New York: Basic Books, 1954.

———— (1900). The interpretation of dreams. *Standard Edition* 4/5. London: Hogarth Press, 1953.

———— (1901). The psychopathology of everyday life. *Standard Edition* 6. London: Hogarth Press, 1960.

———— (1913). The claims of psycho-analysis to scientific interest. *Standard Edition* 13:165–190. London: Hogarth Press, 1955.

———— (1916–1917). Introductory lectures on psycho-analysis. *Standard Edition* 15 and 16. London: Hogarth Press, 1963.

———— (1919). On the teaching of psycho-analysis in universities. *Standard Edition* 17:169–173.

———— (1925). An autobiographical study. *Standard Edition* 20:7–76. London: Hogarth Press, 1959.

————— (1927). The question of lay analysis. *Standard Edition* 20:183–258. London: Hogarth Press, 1959.

Freud, S., and Abraham, K. (1907–1925). *The Letters of Sigmund Freud and Karl Abraham*, ed. H. Abraham and E. Freud. New York: Basic Books, 1965.

Freud, S., and Jung, C. (1906–1923). *The Freud/Jung Letters*, ed. W. McGuire. Princeton: Princeton University Press, 1974.

Heer, F. (1972). Freud, the Viennese Jew. In *Freud: The Man, His World, His Influence*, ed. J. Miller, pp. 2–20. Boston: Little, Brown.

Ibsen, H. (1882). *An Enemy of the People*, tr. W. Archer. New York: Scribners, 1912.

Jones, E. (1953). *The Life of Sigmund Freud. Volume One*. New York: Basic Books.

————— (1955). *The Life of Sigmund Freud. Volume Two*. New York: Basic Books.

Kanzer, M. (1969). Sigmund and Alexander Freud on the Acropolis. *American Imago* 26:324—354. (Chapter 16 of this volume).

Kris, E. (1954). Introduction to *The Origins of Psycho-Analysis*, ed. M. Bonaparte, A. Freud, and E. Kris. New York: Basic Books.

Lewin, B. D. (1958). Education or the quest for omniscience. In *Selected Writings of Bertram D. Lewin*, ed. J. Arlow, pp. 459–491. New York: Psychoanalytic Quarterly Press.

Newman, J. H. (1852). *The Idea of a University*. Garden City: Image Books, 1959.

————— (1856). *University Sketches*. Staten Island: St. Paul Publications.

Rosen, G. (1972). Freud and medicine in Vienna. In *Freud: The Man, His World, His Influence*, ed. J. Miller, pp. 56–71. Boston: Little, Brown.

Shengold, L. (1966). The Metaphor of the journey in "The Interpretation of Dreams." *American Imago* 23:316—331. (Chapter 4 of this volume).

————— (1970). Freud and Joseph. In *The Unconscious Today*, ed. M. Kanzer, pp. 473—494. New York; International Universities Press. (Chapter 5 of this volume)

Chapter 3

FREUD AND THE DEMON

MARK KANZER, M.D.

Seen in the perspective of the history and philosophy of science, Freud's foremost contribution may have been the extension of rational understanding to the phenomena of the irrational. His immediate background in the medical climate of Vienna during the 1880s was that of the "physical physiology" of Helmholtz, Du Bois-Reymond, and Brücke, which sought to establish the study of the mind on a "truly" scientific basis in contrast to the mysticism of the vitalists, who left scope for the supernatural in their concepts of biology. In the formulation of Du Bois-Reymond, "No other forces than the common physical chemical ones are active within the organism" (Bernfeld 1944).

In striving for scientific rationality, however, the Helmholtz group tacitly nurtured its own mysticism when confronted with psychological data. No aspects of human mentality were deemed worthy of serious scientific consideration unless they could be studied in the laboratory and offered prospects of ultimate localization in the brain—a very narrow basis from which to operate. In all justice, it must be remembered that the mapping of the brain was making great progress at the time, and the need to dispel the influence of vitalism was both immediate and important as anti-Darwinians sought to combat a materialistic science. Nevertheless, a pattern was set for all subsequent critiques of psychoanalysis by scientists whose chosen fields of observation and methods of technique carefully eliminated the essential complexities of human psychology.

Other scientific approaches to behavior were available to Freud even in the 1880s, such as the application of hypnosis to clinical disorders. It was a momentous and fortunate turn of affairs when he had to realize that circumstances would interfere with his ambition to follow in Brücke's footsteps as a neuropathologist and that he must master a field in which treatment called for flexibility and inventiveness rather than exactness of technique. A new attitude, not merely a new subject, was necessary to become a psychiatrist. Man's inner mental functioning had to be observed, both in the patient and in oneself (as in empathy), but experience showed how difficult it was to maintain in that case the objective and dispassionate viewpoint which was thought to be the true essence of science.

The traditional scientist is an externalizer, in contrast to the poet, the philosopher, the religious mystic, and the moralizer, whose interests are introspective. Helmholtz and Brücke dealt with the irrational by excluding it, Charcot and Breuer by treating it as an alien and presumably localized symptom of brain disorder. Only Freud discovered that the irrational was part of normal mental functioning, in himself as well as in others, and succeeded in demonstrating it with the same detachment and objectivity as with any other natural process. To be sure, this was not achieved at once, and in his self-explorations Freud encountered inner veins of poetry, philosophy, and religion which seduced him momentarily from objectivity—but which he eventually harnessed to reason so that they became contributors, not obstacles to science. These elements, especially as they emerged in the letters to Fliess, will be the subject of our present discussion.

The background of the problem, both in its personal and psychiatric aspects, was Freud's growing recognition that sexuality, especially in its infantile origins, was of fundamental importance in the development of neuroses. At first, his explanations followed the "externalizing" course so familiar to the scientist. Thus sex was approached in terms of physical practices and their effects on the body (actual neuroses) or of seduction at different ages, with resulting memories and impulses which required discharge. His "Project for a Scientific Psychology" (1895) represented a last almost desperate attempt to establish a common frame of reference for "physical physiology" and the new data and methodology arising from clinical experience. Not only was there no guidance to be found among the teachers and contemporaries he most respected, but his findings and ideas were rejected by them contemptuously and without scientific tests. Insight and courage had to sustain him in continuing his research as a lonely pioneer; the self-knowledge that he gained in this way was not only a recompense but a key to the understanding of mental processes generally.

Wilhelm Fliess emerged during this period as a tolerant figure who seemed to grant external sources of reference both for validating scientific inferences and for giving personal encouragement: the respected scientific teacher cherished by the younger man. To a considerable extent, Fliess fulfilled this role only in an illusory fashion as demanded by Freud's needs; by the end of the correspondence, which lasted from 1887 to 1902, Freud had outgrown the need of illusions and the uncertain friendship of Fliess. Concomitantly, he had made the transition from "physical physiology" to psychoanalysis. In Letter 5 of the one-sidedly recorded correspondence, there is already a significant resonance in Freud when he notes that Bernheim's theory of suggestion as a cause of hysteria exerts a greater "charm" for him than the more physiological orientation of Charcot. In Letter 18 (May 21, 1894), Freud's progress toward analysis was already well advanced and had involuntarily brought about his isolation from contemporary scientists. The strain showed in his comments: "I am pretty well alone here in tackling the neuroses. They regard me rather as a monomaniac, while I have the distinct feeling that I have touched on one of the great secrets of nature."

An inner, not merely external conflict about his activities was revealed in ensuing letters. In Letter 24 (May 25, 1895) he complains that the work imposed upon him is "inhuman"; in strong language, psychology is described as a "plague" and a "tyrant," which nevertheless "has always been my distant beckoning goal." Self-analysis enters into the observation that a man of his own temperament requires a "hobby-horse, a consuming passion." Such personal masochism, obscured beneath the techniques and principles of the dedicated scientist, does not often become the subject of the scientist's own study, as it did with Freud. There is here an element of religious zeal, which was both a sustaining force and an emergent one as inner boundaries against the irrational began to be effaced under the combined pressure of external difficulties and inwardly turned curiosity.

By Letter 27, the "charm," the "tyrant," the "hobby-horse" assume the form of a demon which seeks to control Freud's mind. Actually, it heralds insight into the unconscious as a driving force in all men. "This psychology is really an incubus," Freud writes. In Letter 29, something of the struggle against the demon seems to have been given up, and Freud, like the oracles of ancient days, listens to a "still small voice" within himself which judges the value of his ideas. "Inner struggles" are resumed, however, accompanied by irritability and somatic complaints, until release is found in the promulgation of a scientific thesis, the "Project," conceived during a period of "painful discomfort during which my mind works best" (Letter 32). In this connection, he uses a notable image in apologizing for his slow progress, namely, commenting that it is no sin to limp when one cannot fly. This image, drawn from the Biblical story of Jacob wrestling with the Angel, was one that appealed to Freud and he used it again on later occasions.

Psychology did not long remain an angel; Letter 35 again refers to it as a tyrant and by Letter 36, the "Project" seems a remote and unsatisfactory product of a mental stage which Freud himself could no longer understand. Mood swings continued and systems of scientific hypotheses rose and fell with them. The "Project" was hailed again in a New Year's flood of optimism (January 1, 1896), when it seemed a gateway through which "a number of obscure and ancient medical ideas acquire life and importance." In more than one sense Freud was experiencing a sense of contact with the past that placed the boundaries of current reality testing under a strain; he referred to his outline of "The Neuroses of Defense" as a "Christmas fairy tale" (Letter 39).

At this point, a disposition to indulge a literary side of himself became manifest, apparently granting his creative imagination scope while protecting his scientific tenets from being flooded by emergent fantasies that were prestages of new theories. Letter 42 contains a literary reference to G. Keller's *Der grüne Heinrich* to convey an idea, and in Letter 43 he compares himself to a "budding poet" in contemplating the future works on the neuroses into which he must put himself with his "entire soul." In Letter 44, he notes that "when I was young, the only thing I longed for was philosophical knowledge, and now that I am going over from medicine into psychology I am in the process of attaining it. I have become a therapist against my will."

Freud, regressively in search of a new science, elaborated for himself the fiction that it was "fate" directing his footsteps toward a goal which he himself was actively seeking. This familiar mechanism of the inspired serves to allay guilt (Kris 1939); Oedipus, who also limped, concocted a similar explanation for his particular way of solving the riddle of the Sphinx. Freud's discovery of the Oedipus complex was in fact drawing near, and Erikson (1955) has justly observed that every step of Freud's search for insight into himself as well as into mental treatment led him further into oedipal guilt and hubris (the challenge of man to the gods which plays such an important role in Greek tragedy).

Letter 49 tells of the death of Freud's father Jacob (who also wrestled with the Angel). Letter 50 again continues the literary theme, with Freud seeing himself as "Pegasus yoked to the plow" and comparing his case histories to "gruesome horrible old wives' psychiatry." Letter 51 finds him daydreaming about chapter headings for the great works that he was to write on the neuroses. They reveal a remarkable preoccupation with Heaven and Hell, with gods, ghosts, and demons. For hysteria, the motto was to be: "*Introite et hic dii sunt* [Enter, here too are gods]"; for summation: "*Sie treiben's toll, ich fürcht' es breche, nicht jeden Wochenschluss macht Gott die Zeche* [They drive madly, I fear a break; God does not present a reckoning at the end of each week]"; for symptom formation: "*Flectere si nequeo superos Acheronta movebo* [If I cannot bend the gods, I shall stir up the river of the underworld]"; for resistance:

"Mach' es kurz! Am jüngsten Tag ist' nur ein—[Cut it short! On doomsday, it will not be worth a—]."

Letter 54 continues the same theme with uncharacteristic boastfulness: "When I am not afraid, I can take on all the devils in Hell." The chapter headings continue the same note of exploring other worlds—for sexuality: "From Heaven through the world to Hell"; for therapy: *"Flavit et dissipati sunt* [He blew and they were scattered]"—an allusion to the motto referring to the destruction of the Armada, but with the acknowledgment of God's help "inadvertently" omitted. In the proposal with which the letter ends, namely, that Fliess, his substitute father, meet him at Prague (near his birthplace) during Easter, there is perhaps a related note of religion and of thoughts of resurrection which are part of the mourning of the dead father that underlies the preceding excursions of thought.

By Letter 56, interest in the supernatural is even more marked and has been brought into connection with research into the neuroses. Freud had become intrigued with medieval theories about the "possession" of witches by the Devil, in which he recognized an analogy to his own idea about seduction by the father as the cause of hysteria. The views of the ecclesiastical courts coincided in their own language "with our theory of a foreign body and the splitting of consciousness." The victims were always represented as sexually used by the Devil, and their confessions, extracted under torture, were "very like what my patients tell me under psychological treatment." At this time, Freud's methodology called for actively prodding patients to reveal the memories which he assumed they more or less deliberately withheld—a procedure which he acknowledged to be "tormenting." Not only the problem of the victim but that of the inquisitor challenged the relentlessly honest investigative drive of Freud, who recognized that the torturer was reliving in common with the tortured a period of infantile memories (possibly the first instance of analysis of the countertransference on record).

The parallel thus established led to a burst of insight in Letter 57 which broadened the study of the neuroses to include a glimpse into cultures and religions as age-old patterns for holding in check the same instinctual forces which Freud observed in his patients and in himself. Thus he postulated in the perversions "the remnants of a primitive sexual cult, which in the Semitic East may once have been a religion." Germinating in this idea are the analytic concepts of polymorphous perversion, totemistic thought, the inheritance of memories, and also the Egyptian Moses of Freud's later years.

Freud now allowed himself to be possessed by the demon of psychology rather than to struggle against it—the true beginning of the free association technique. In Letter 62, he reported an "obscure" feeling that something vital

within himself was emerging; elsewhere (9) he reminisced, "following an obscure presentiment, I decided to exchange hypnosis for free association." No
matter what he started with, his mind was forced to turn to psychology. "Inside
me there is a seething ferment and I am only waiting for the next surge forward."
Like the oracle, he received a message from the gods and felt "impelled to start
writing about dreams"—the traditional vehicle of divine utterances to men. In
keeping with this role, Freud compared himself to Puck, the Celtic imp, and
was glad that no man's eyes had penetrated his disguise—i.e., that he himself
alone could feel at home in the world of dreams.

Self-analysis was indeed advancing (May 16, 1897), though others place the
date later. The next surge from the unconscious (Letter 64) reveals unconscious
sexual feelings toward his daughter who is here named "Hella" (Hell, not
Hellas, as he interprets it?). "The dream of course fulfills my wish to pin down
a father as the originator of neurosis," he concludes. The inner voice, the oracle,
thus has a definite contribution to make to science; self-analysis is making
untenable the externalizing seduction theory and preparing the way for the libido
theory, which transfers responsibility to man's own constitution. Insight, however, is still tinged with poetry, and there are references in the letter to Titania
and Oberon and to the justice of Shakespeare's observation that poetry and
madness are inherently related. Science translates this, however, into a dictum
of psychoanalysis: "The mechanism of creative writing is the same as that of
hysterical fantasies."

Resistance and regression followed this triumph of insight gained from within,
and the door to the unconscious genie's abode was kept tightly closed for a
while as Freud complained of "intellectual paralysis" and a feeling that "every
line I write is a torture." He sought diversion at this point by making a collection
of Jewish stories, another aspect of the self-analysis and search for the past
which was in time to yield scientific treasure in his work on wit. The spell of
the demon passed off; in Letter 68, Freud notes: "My handwriting is more
human again"—but the respite was only temporary. In Letter 69, he is comparing
himself to Hamlet, the moody prince, and literary allusions again serve as
prodromes to analytic insights.

Letter 70 (October 3, 1897) marks a break-through in self-analysis to memories
of his nurse, who "told me a great deal about God and Hell" and to other
crucial memories of his early years. Letter 71 brings confirmatory memories
from Freud's mother, who recalls that the nurse was always taking him to
church, from which he returned to preach to the family "and tell us all about
how God conducted His affairs." Thoughts go on to the birth of siblings, and
there is the momentous introduction of the Oedipus legend into analytic
thinking—mythology and literature had been uncovered not as untrustworthy

fantasies but as storehouses of science. Analyzing the appeal of Sophocles' play (and thus launching the science of analytic aesthetics), Freud finds a basis of sympathy with the Greek hero in the thought that "our feelings rise against any arbitrary individual fate"—a line strikingly reminiscent of a rebellion of his own against the "tyranny of suggestion," which played its part in the obscure urges that induced him to substitute free association for hypnosis in research and therapy (1921). With free association, men may claim a greater share in shaping their own destinies!

Destiny, in the form of past memories, rose up like a ghost before Freud in Letter 72 and pointed to a relationship between neurotic symptoms and the repressed masturbation of childhood. With Letter 75, this insight evolved into the libido theory, which he hailed with the homage due to a new Messiah born when "the sun was in the eastern quarter and Mercury and Venus in conjunction"—poetry and religion providing the membranes for a scientific infant. However, these myth-making proclivities were themselves translated into science in Letter 78 with the observation that "endopsychic myths are the dim inner perception of one's own psychic apparatus" as projected outward to create a belief in "immortality, retribution, the world after death." The membranes were definitely to be cast off!

The gods were still permitted to exist for a while, but only as useful servants of literature subordinated to the interests of science. "The Gods" are described as assembling a discouraging mass of literature on dreams for Freud to master (Letter 107). With the main portion of the dream book finished, "The ancient gods still exist" and he purchases a Janus who looks two-headedly into the past and the future (Letter 111). "My grubby old gods, of whom you think so little, take part in my work as paper weights," he informs Fliess in Letter 113. Yet the Gods reclaim their power in Letter 134, where Freud reports that he is engaged in "arduous wrestling with the demon." Guilt and castration threats have mounted in connection with the dream book, and the "inner voices to which I am accustomed to listen" suggest only a modest evaluation of the work and predict that as "a fitting punishment for me none of the unexplored regions of the mind in which I have been the first mortal to set foot will ever bear my name or submit to my laws." Identifications with (Father) Jacob and Moses, ancestors who dared to challenge God and were punished, emerge at this point (Kanzer, in preparation). There are secrets that are not to be discovered with impunity, as Oedipus had learned. With a mood swing in the opposite direction, Freud pronounces the dream book to be his claim for immortality (Letter 137).

In Letter 138 (July 10, 1900), Freud is again suffering in "an intellectual Hell, layer upon layer of it, with everything fitfully gleaming and pulsating, and the outline of Lucifer-Amor coming into sight at the darkest center." After a summer's rest, he forces the devils to usher in *The Psychopathology of Everyday Life* with the motto, "Now the air is so full of sprites," that is, the tricksters from the unconscious who bewitch men and cause confusion between intention and deed have been reduced to psychic forces that are ruled by inescapable laws of scientific determinism. Freud's own inner escape from the demons proceeds concomitantly with conquests over those in the outer world: the ensuing letters report the completion of Dora's analysis, the overcoming of the travel phobia that had long prevented him from reaching Rome, and the attainment of the professorship which had been withheld from him for many years. Toward the end, he was emboldened to criticize and psychologically separate himself from his unwitting analyst, Dr. Fliess, and terminated the correspondence appropriately enough with a picture postcard from the temple of Neptune, which was marked by a single line: "Cordial greetings from the culminating point of the journey!"

Discussion

During the transitional phase when Freud was seeking a psychological understanding of the neuroses and evolving the psychoanalytic technique, his explorations of his patients and his introspective observations brought him into contact with traditional manifestations of the unconscious which had long been familiar to poets and religious mystics but not to the neuropathologists of his era. He was probably giving an account of the resultant findings and thoughts when, at a later date, he followed anthropologists in postulating three systems of thought which marked the evolution of human society (*Totem and Taboo*). The most primitive, or animistic system, which coincides with the stage of magic omnipotence of the ego, practices sorcery to control reality, "influencing spirits by treating them like people. . . . The first theoretical accomplishment of man was the creation of spirits" through which he delegated his sense of freedom of the will to external powers, a stage in the development of reality testing. Religion, the next advance in thought, represents a systematized effort to restore to life the parricidally destroyed father in whom the magic of the spirits has become centrally vested—that is, it is the mythology of a later stage of ego maturation in which the father serves as model for the organized and coercive nature of the forces in the external world (superego). Ultimately, in the scientific stage of thought, the progressive acknowledgement of external reality has decreased further the scope of man's omnipotence, even when symbolized by his father, and with this comes, as Freud stressed, a resignation to the inevitability of death. Even in the consoling reliance of the scientist on "the power of the human spirit which copes with the laws of reality, there still lives on a fragment of this primitive belief in the omnipotence of thought.'' Science, and psychotherapy based on reason, may cure neuroses but do not insure happiness. Freud always made it clear that courage and the love of truth were not only the sustaining forces but perhaps also the rewards of successful analysis.

In making contact with animism, the demoniacal world of primitive thought that is so close to the processes of the unconscious, Freud inevitably groped his way to the magical sources of mental healing, and it is interesting to compare his discoveries with the concepts of demons held by different cultures in the past and in primitive societies of the present. Typically, demons are considered as beings with powers intermediate between those of men and gods (transition from the animistic to the religious stage!), not seldom arising from the souls of the dead. In this respect, they are allied to ghosts and inspire a sense of dread and of the uncanny, such as men experience when confronted with their own unconscious. The demon, persisting as a more archaic deity in the age of gods, often becomes a messenger of the gods and a herald of the divine will and of destiny, as in filling and speaking through the mouths of oracles.

In the severely monotheistic Jewish religion, the demon was regarded with abhorrence as unclean and a manifestation of evil. Bans were placed on traffic with demons in the form of sorcery or necromancy. The battle against demons was further exacerbated by their supposed constant attempts to occupy human bodies to satisfy their desires, since they had no bodies of their own (the Dybbuk). In analytic terminology, they represented repressed instinctual desires that sought repossession of the physical channels from which they were barred. Illness, not unnaturally, was frequently ascribed to demonic possession, and the tribal medicine men and magicians thrived on their ability to expel the power of evil, displaying in the process a considerable degree of psychological insight. At times, demons might be regarded as good spirits, akin to guardian spirits and angels; a sociological element might convert the gods of a defeated tribe into the demons of the conquerors.

The Greeks, less repressed than the Jews, were more tolerant to demons and disposed to study them psychologically. As early as 500 B.C., Heraclites observed that a man's character is his demon and destiny. Socrates used the term ''*daemon*'' as the equivalent of intuition or inner voice (just as did Freud), while Plato, in the *Symposium*, regarded demons as spiritual forces that mediated between men and gods, especially in the state of sleep. The man who was wise in dealing with God was himself demonic—that is, participated in the nature of divinity.

The ancient and intuitive wisdom, purged of the mystical and interpreted psychologically, was placed at the disposition of science by Freud. ''What in those [seventeenth-century] days were thought to be evil spirits to us are base and evil wishes," he declared (1923). Foreign to our own consciousness, they inspire us as a "counterwill" (1893) which, finally acknowledged as part of ourselves, "disappear like a wandering spirit returning to rest" (Breuer and Freud 1895). The perception of a demoniacal counterwill constitutes the oldest root of conscience and morality (Freud 1913), perpetuating the vengeful spirit of parents whose death we desired because they opposed our wishes. Ultimately Freud defined the demon metapsychologically as the repetition compulsion (1920), the death drive itself, which takes precedence over the pleasure principle as the regulator of human destiny. In the course of ego development, the demonic lure of the past retains its hold on a successive series of introjects, beginning with the animistically conceived image of the parent and extending ultimately to "that dark supremacy of Fate, which only the few among us are able to conceive impersonally" (1924).

Analytic therapy, as conducted with its established goals and technique, respects the limitations of reason in establishing control over the instincts, or realm of the demons. The wise physician may use technique, but Freud admonishes him to learn from the French physician who felt it was God that cured (1910–1919). Indeed, the psychiatrist, like the priest of old, is able to serve as a fit instrument for his dedicated purpose only after he first submits to his own "purification" by a psychoanalytic purging of desires. Toward this end, Freud warned the would-be analyst against a number of "temptations" that lie in his pathway:

1.   the "temptation" to inject his own personality into the proceedings rather than to accept a neutral position;
2.   the "temptation" to develop therapeutic ambition for the patient;
3.   the "temptation" to belittle the free excursions of fantasy in favor of the rational (as is usual in science);
4.   the "temptation" to yield to the patient's demand for love—in which case, Freud suggested, he might find himself in the position of the pastor who undertook to convert the atheistic insurance man but succeeded only in being sold an insurance policy.

For psychoanalysis, he declared, "is founded on truthfulness . . . It is dangerous to depart from this sure foundation. When a man's life has become bound up with the analytic technique, he finds himself altogether at a loss for the lies and the guile which are otherwise so indispensable to a physician. Since we demand strict truthfulness from our patients, we jeopardize our whole authority if we let ourselves be caught by them in a departure from the truth." Abstinence is a driving force in the analytic work and Freud notes, with respect to this problem, that he is "in the happy position of being able to put the requirements of analytic technique in the place of a moral decree without any alteration in the results." Ultimately it is "faith in one's theoretical principles" upon which the analyst relies, and he must curb his conscious and rational impulses to the end that he does not "compete with the guidance of the unconscious" which manifests itself in the apparently accidental connections in the chain of mental events. With a little rewording, the rules set up for the analyst might not differ too much from the Ten Commandments transmitted by Moses, with whom Freud was so prone to identify himself (Jones 1955).

In retrospect, it may be said that Freud, who broadened science to include the irrational and who drew the techniques of poetry and the dream into the therapeutic armamentarium of the analyst, likewise included religion in certain of its aspects, viz., faith, courage, and love of truth. He deprived these qualities of their supernatural aspects, to be sure, and found that they were vital psychological forces which must be recognized and used in dealing with mental illness and health. Yet this enlightened viewpoint inevitably extends into a sphere where uncertain boundaries between intellectual knowledge and feeling, between tested experience and personal values, constitute dangers to which rationalists and mystics each in their own way succumb. It is the merit of psychoanalysis that, following in the footsteps of Freud, self-scrutiny of its own techniques and assumptions is unending, thus providing the best safeguard against the persistence of the demons of the irrational in any guise except as instincts in the service of the ego—an ego, of course, that is committed in turn to the healthy service of the instincts in their social setting.

References

Bernfeld, S. (1944). Freud's earliest theories and the school of Helmholtz. *Psychoanalytic Quarterly* 13:341–362.

Breuer, J., and Freud, S. (1893–1895). Studies on hysteria. *Standard Edition* 2.

Encyclopaedia Americana (1947). s.v. "Demon."

Erikson, E. H. (1955). Freud's *The Origins of Psychoanalysis*. *International Journal of Psycho-Analysis* 36:1–15.

Freud, S. (1887–1902). *The Origins of Psychoanalysis*. New York: Basic Books, 1954.

——— (1893). A case of successful treatment by hypnotism. In *Collected Papers*, vol. 5, pp. 33–46. London: Hogarth Press, 1950.

——— (1910–19). Papers on technique. In *Collected Papers*, vol. 2, pp. 285–402. London: Hogarth Press, 1924.

——— (1913). Totem and taboo. *Standard Edition* 13:1–162.

————— (1914). On the history of the psychoanalytic movement. In *Collected Papers*, vol. 1, pp. 287–359. London: Hogarth Press, 1949.

————— (1920). *Beyond the Pleasure Principle*. London: Hogarth Press, 1922.

————— (1921). *Group Psychology and the Analysis of the Ego*. London: Hogarth Press, 1948.

————— (1923). A neurosis of demoniacal possession in the seventeenth century. In *Collected Papers*, vol. 4, pp. 436–472. London: Hogarth Press, 1949.

————— (1924). The economic problem in masochism. In *Collected Papers*, vol. 2, pp. 255–268. London: Hogarth Press, 1949.

Jones, E. (1955). *The Life and Work of Sigmund Freud*. Vol. 2. New York: Basic Books.

Kanzer, M. (in preparation). Imagery in Freud's writings.

Kris, E. (1939). On inspiration. In *Psychoanalytic Explorations in Art*. New York: International Universities Press, 1952.

Chapter 4

THE METAPHOR OF THE JOURNEY IN

The Interpretation of Dreams

LEONARD SHENGOLD, M.D.

Dreams, Freud was fond of repeating, provide a royal road to the unconscious activities of the mind. In his masterpiece, *The Interpretation of Dreams*, Freud makes consistent use of the metaphor of a journey. The discoverer himself guides the reader along the road he has made through *terra incognita*. Freud describes his journey specifically enough so that a "map" can be drawn. I want to examine his *journey*, in particular to concentrate on a point of transition, the place where Freud turns from the study of the dream (based largely on verifiable clinical observation) to the hypotheses (called "paths that will end in darkness") that are meant to account for all psychic structure and psychic functioning: the three pages of introduction to Section A of the seventh chapter of *The Interpretation of Dreams*.*

"At this point," Freud says, there is a dream "which has special claims upon our attention." Its source, he says, is not known to him, but was told him by a woman patient who had heard it in a lecture on dreams, and who proceeded to "re-dream it, thereby making it her own." We can assume that, whatever its source, Freud makes the dream *his* own: he interpolates it at the crucial turning point of his *journey*.

*I am indebted to Dr. Mark Kanzer for several helpful suggestions concerning this paper.

The Dream of the Burning Child

A father, whose sick child had just died, left an old man to watch over the boy's body, leaving the door open to go to sleep in the next room. He had a dream: his child was standing beside his bed, and caught him by the arm, whispering reproachfully, "Father, don't you see I'm burning?" The father awoke to find that the old man had fallen asleep, a candle had overturned, and one of the child's arms was burning. Freud says that the words spoken by the child must have been made up of words actually said in his lifetime. "I'm burning" was probably spoken during his last illness, as well as earlier. "Father, don't you see" would have unknown connections with past events. Freud interprets the preconscious dream wish (the distinction between preconscious and unconscious wishes is yet to be made) as bringing the child back to life. Later in the chapter, Freud uses the dream to illustrate the preconscious wish to sleep.

This dream leads to an announcement about the rest of the journey. At this point, we are apparently on a hill, about to descend into darkness: "But before starting off on along this new path, it will be well to pause and look around, to see whether in the course of our journey up to this point we have overlooked anything of importance. For . . . the easy and agreeable portion of our journey lies behind us. Hitherto . . . all the paths along which we have traveled have led up towards the light—towards elucidation and fuller understanding. But as soon as we endeavour to penetrate more deeply into the mental processes involved in dreaming, every path will end in darkness . . ." (Freud 1900).

The purpose of this essay is to examine some of Freud's imagery in *The Interpretation of Dreams*. The warp of its fabric will be supplied by the metaphor of a journey and the related image of a place on the road. The recurrent interconnected threads to be woven in as the woof are many (most can be found in the Dream of the Burning Child): fire and ambition; vision and insight; Freud's self-analysis; his relation to his parents; sin, Hell and Dante; gods and heroes.

The Journey

According to Freud, a journey symbolizes death, the last journey. Death is psychologically reducible to a going away from the mother and to castration; both are traumatic separations. Traffic and travelling, however, symbolize sexual intercourse. There is condensation in the symbol of a journey of both halves of the Oedipus complex (the sexual possession of one parent and the getting rid of the other) as well as the castrative punishment for these "wishes that arise from a veritable Hell" (Freud 1916–1917). Since it can connote this core of a man's nature, the image of a journey is often found in patients' associations and their dreams. Freud tells of a specific allusive use of this image: "It is not surprising that a person undergoing psychoanalytic treatment should often dream of it and be led to give expression in his dreams to the many thoughts and expectations to which the treatment gives rise. The imagery most frequently chosen to represent it is that of a journey . . .'' (Freud 1900).

The beginning and the course of the journey in the first part of *The Interpretation of Dreams* was first described by Freud in a letter to his friend, his "only audience," and the chief transference-figure in his self-analysis (that is, journey), Wilhelm Fliess: "The whole thing is now arranged on the analogy with a stroll in the forest. At the outset the dark wood of authors (who can't see the trees), without any outlook, and full of blind alleys. Then a concealed path along which I conduct the reader—my specimen dream with its peculiarities, details, indiscretions, bad jokes [the Irma Dream]—and then suddenly the heights, the prospect, and the inquiry: where should you like to go from here?'' (Freud 1887–1902).

In *The Tangled Bank*, Stanley Edgar Hyman compares *The Interpretation of Dreams* with other literary works constructed around a journey, such as Dante's *Divine Comedy*. The *Comedy* begins: "In the middle of the journey of my life I came to myself in a dark wood where the straight way was lost.'' Then follows the meeting with Virgil and the exploration of the *Inferno*.

Freud was in the middle of the journey of his life when he was writing *The Interpretation of Dreams*. He was 41 when his father died in October of 1896 ("the most important event, the most poignant loss, in a man's life"). After writing the book, Freud said that he recognized it as a reaction to the death of his father. His first recorded allusion to the book is in a letter to Fliess of May 16, 1897, when he was, according to Jones, "certainly under the influence of the motives that led him to undertake . . . self-analysis" (Jones 1953). The work is, in many respects, a censored record of Freud's self-analysis, in that it contains many of his own dreams and discoveries, such as the Oedipus complex. The self-analysis was a truly heroic journey—a pioneer effort of painful discovery made by the man who called himself not "really a man of science . . . nothing but by temperament a *Conquistador*'' (Jones 1953). In the Dream Book and in the letters to Fliess, he makes many allusions to the great figures who fired his boyhood imagination—conquerors and travellers along royal roads, such as Hercules, Hannibal, Columbus, Caesar, Cromwell, Massena, Napoleon, and, of course, Oedipus. The epic ages, the battles over Troy, Thebes, Athens, and Rome are evoked.

The Journey, Sin and Hellfire

One of the main symptoms of Freud's neurosis, as he revealed to Fliess, was a "travelling phobia" (Jones 1954), and this was the subject of much work in his self-analysis. Freud loved to travel, despite his neurosis. At twenty-nine he wrote, "The delight of the first moments in a strange place is overpowering" (Jones 1954). Later, he experienced that mixture of intense pleasure and anxiety which frequently accompanies the fulfilment of an infantile wish. Journeys and travel had always been occasions for passion: "When he was five years old, his father presented him and his little sister with a book, a narration of a journey through Persia, with the mischievous suggestion that they amuse themselves by tearing out its coloured plates . . . Freud traced to this episode the earliest passion of his life—that of collecting and possessing books, but he also called it a 'screen memory' for something more primitive" (Jones 1953). Surely the "earliest passion" would be for his mother, here symbolized by a book. And this particular book about a journey links up with another early passion—the passion for travel.

We can also connect Freud's earliest *memories* of travel with the desire for his mother. When he was three, according to Jones, there was a "fateful" train journey in the course of the family's long move from Moravia to Vienna. On the way to Leipzig, the train passed through Breslau, where Freud saw gas jets for the first time: "they made him think of souls burning in Hell" (Jones 1953). The "ugly, old nurse" who was his "first instructress in sexual matters" had told him "a great deal about God and Hell" (Freud 1887–1902). Thus, Freud's discovery and exploration of his "Inferno" had already begun at three. He dated his "travelling phobia" from this journey: "susceptibility to attacks of acute anxiety at the moment of embarking on a journey" (Jones 1954), from which he suffered for about a dozen years (from age thirty-one to forty-three). "Even after (his analysis) it left a residue in the form of a slightly undue anxiety about catching trains" (Jones 1953). Jones writes further about Freud's childhood journey from Moravia: "On the journey from Leipzig to Vienna, a year later, Freud had occasion to see his mother naked: an awesome fact which forty years later he related in a letter to Fliess—but in Latin! Curiously enough he gives his age then as between two and two and a half, whereas he was in fact four years old on that journey. One must surmise that the memories of two such experiences had got telescoped." Following Jones' surmise then, the light of the gas jets, evoking souls burning in Hell, was blended with the sight of his mother's naked body ("Father, don't you see I'm burning"). Jones tells of another oedipal journey, a short one (from one room to another like the journey in the Dream of the Burning Child). Some time in his first six years he "penetrated into his parents' bedroom out of (sexual) curiosity and (was) ordered out by an irate father" (Jones 1953).

Dante

Sin and hellfire evoke Dante. The motto on the title page of *The Interpretation of Dreams* is taken from the Aeneid by Virgil (Dante's guide through the *Inferno* and part of *Purgatorio*)· *Flectere si nequeo superos, Acheronta movebo* ("If I cannot bend the Higher Powers, I will move the Lower Regions"). This motto of a conquistador with its sexual implications is again stated in Chapter Seven.

A fascinating study could be made of parallels between Dante and Freud, between the *Commedia* and the *Interpretation of Dreams*. Both masterpieces are composed by men in their early forties, writing of themselves when younger; the works describe a pilgrimage towards knowledge—towards the exploration of man's potential for good and evil. Both works are, and are about, journeys of the soul. Each man is essentially alone, guided by the great minds of the past. Both journeys are full of similar imagery: woods and clearings, holes and valleys, hills and mountains, darkness and light, fire. Both men are proud, both eagerly and consciously seek fame. Both are "good haters," as Freud called himself. Both, aware of their limitations, are driven to the fullest exploration of truth of which they are capable, no matter what the inner or outer danger. Many commentators have pointed out Dante's identification with the great traveller Ulysses, perhaps the most heroic figure in the Inferno—a man being punished in Hell for making a journey forbidden by God (like Prometheus). The penalty for his striving after knowledge is envelopment in eternal flame ("Father, don't you see I'm burning"!).

I am indebted to Dr. Harry Slochower for pointing out to me the fascinating parallel between the passage of the soul through the Purgatorio and a psychoanalysis: In the Inferno, there is no hope, but in Purgatory change and salvation are possible; thus, Purgatory most resembles life on Earth. Here Dante can see his shadow which marks him as a living being. The soul in purgatory relives its sins, but does so *symbolically* ("verbally"), accepts punishment, repeats and transcends temptations. Instead of punishment being imposed from without, as in Hell, the sufferer wills to re-experience his sin and torment in order to change—to be purged—and gain Paradise. Indeed the entire *Commedia*, the entire journey from Inferno to Paradiso, represents the process of purification—a process that Dante wanted to teach all men, but—as with Freud and the Dream Book—the journey is at the same time a record and a representation of his own attempt at self-analysis.

According to Jones, Freud was reading Dante during the years he was writing *The Interpretation of Dreams*. His conscious purpose was to help prepare himself for a journey, the source of great enterprise and pleasure for him, the exploration of his beloved Italy.

Italy was a longed-for and forbidden object: Freud mentions a dream of travel (riding on horseback) that he had when suffering from a boil in the perineal area—"Furthermore the dream had derived some of its elements from my travels in Italy; the street in the dream was composed of impressions of Verona and Siena. A still deeper interpretation led to sexual dream thoughts, and I recalled the meaning which references to Italy seem to have in the dreams of a woman patient who had never visited that lovely country: gen Italien (to Italy) = Genitalien (genitals)" (Freud 1900).

The letters to Fliess during these years are full of references to Italy, the "promised land" (as he called it, identifying himself with the two great leaders, Moses and Hannibal) "that he was not to see until he was 40" (Jones 1954). In his study of Freud's use of the image of the demon, Kanzer cites the frequent mention of Hell and devils in the Freud-Fliess letters (Kanzer 1961; chapter 3 of the present volume). Dante is mentioned specifically several times in the correspondence. In a letter of April 14, 1898, Freud describes his exploration of the caves of St. Cangian in Italy: "The caves . . . are a horrifying freak of nature—a subterranean river running through magnificent vaults, with waterfalls and stalactites and pitch darkness, and a slippery path guarded by iron railings. It was Tartarus itself. If Dante saw anything like this, he needed no great effort of the imagination for his Inferno." The cave, he says, "after three and a half hours spewed us all out into the light again." This involved a penetration, a descent into darkness, and a coming forth into light, as part of a journey of exploration. Freud's awareness of the sexual implications of the expedition is evidenced by his quoting the boastful guide whose "*conquistador* exploits (I recognized) as an erotic equivalent," and who had said of penetrating into the caves: "It's like with a virgin: the farther the better" (Freud 1887–1902).

The Journey Metaphor and Oedipus

The image of the journey is first used in *The Interpretation of Dreams* just after the exposition of the Irma dream which brought Freud so much insight. Its analysis was completed on July 24, 1895, and Freud half-humorously thought of putting up a plaque to immortalize that date. The wishes adduced in connection with the Irma dream are surface preconscious wishes. One feels, however, that Freud was quite aware of deeper layers, including the wish to possess and explore his mother's body. It is not until Chapter Seven that Freud presents the significance of the primal unconscious wishes; he leads up to this and withholds it until near the end of the book, thereby making the reader repeat with him, step by step, the journey of his discovery. After recounting the analysis of the Irma dream, Freud describes a high "place" on the road, as surrounded by light. Here, it is not hellfire, but bright sunlight that illumines. Oedipus, young and resplendent, has just solved the riddle of the Sphinx: "We find ourselves in the full daylight of a sudden discovery . . . when, after passing through a narrow defile, we suddenly emerge upon a piece of high ground, where the path divides and the finest prospects open up on every side, we may pause for a moment and consider in which direction we may turn our steps" (Freud 1900).

From here, there are paths traversed back and forth to this place "where the path divides" (a fork in the road like the one where Oedipus killed Laius; the fork in the road may also represent the maternal genitals [cf. Abraham 1923]). The first descent into the "veritable Hell" of the unconscious—the exploration of childhood sexuality and the Oedipus complex—is reached in the fifth chapter. There, Freud's synopsis of the myth evokes Oedipus as the traveller: "On the road leading from what he believed was his home, he met King Laius and slew him in a sudden quarrel. He came next to Thebes and solved the riddle set him by the Sphinx who barred his way. Out of gratitude, the Thebans made him their King and gave him Jocasta's hand in marriage" (Freud 1900). The action of the play, Freud says, "can be likened to the work of a psychoanalysis." It is Freud's self-analysis. He is re-tracing the path of Oedipus, having started from the death of his father.

Father, Don't You See I'm Burning

Of the symbolism of this journey through a landscape, Hyman (1962) says, "All of these dark woods, narrow defiles, high grounds and deep penetrations are unconscious sexual imagery and we are exploring a woman's body, that of Freud's mother." The Dream of the Burning Child involves the fire that, as hellfire, was linked with the sight of his mother's naked body in Freud's early travel experiences. If we look at the dream as Freud having "made it his own," we note a reversal: Freud had lost his father; and so, it is the son who watched over the dead father. The dream depicts a son standing at the father's bedside, as Freud had done in childhood. Actually, Freud had a dream on the night after his father's funeral about which he wrote to Fliess—"I found myself in a shop where there was a notice up saying:

> You are requested
> To close the eyes.

. . . the phrase on the notice board has a double meaning. It means 'one should do one's duty towards the dead' in two senses—an apology, as though I had not done my duty and the conduct needed over-looking, and the actual duty itself. The dream was thus an outlet for the feeling of self-reproach which a death generally leaves among the survivors" (Freud 1887–1902). The dream specifically enjoins Freud *not to see*. "Father, don't you see I'm burning," says Freud, refers to repressed childhood wishes. The child Freud was once, as he stood by the parental bed, burning with desire for his mother. (*Je brûle*, says Racine's Phèdre of her incestuous passion.) He was also burning with ambition—ambition to fulfill his erotic wishes and to replace his father. "Mein goldener Sigi," the mother had called her favorite child who was born with a caul and of whom a fortune teller had predicted great things. "A man who had been the indisputable favorite of his mother," wrote Freud of Goethe, "keeps for life the feelings of a conqueror ('I am . . . a conquistador'), that confidence of his success that often induces real success" (Freud 1917).

Freud's great ambition, we know from his remarks on another dream in *The Interpretation of Dreams*, is connected with a scene at his father's bedside when he was seven years old that led to another "Father, don't you see." "One evening before going to sleep I disregarded the rules which modesty lays down and obeyed the call of nature in my parents' bedroom while they were present. In the course of his reprimand my father let fall the words: 'the boy will come to nothing.' This must have been a frightful blow to my ambition, for references to this dream are still constantly recurring in my dreams and are always linked with an enumeration of my achievements and successes, as though I wanted to say: 'You see, I have come to something!'." The dream in question was one in which an old blind man (You are requested to close the eyes) was micturating in front of Freud, reversing the humiliating scene of childhood. Freud tells of still another dream connected with the scene at his father's bedside: "a long stream of urine washing everything clean . . . Hercules cleaning the Augean Stables—this Hercules was I." He was the conqueror and man of journeys, Hercules. Freud then refers to another famous traveller, bringing in the theme of fire: "It was in that way that Gulliver extinguished the fire in Lilliput, observed by the tiny king and queen" (1900). Ambition, and fire and burning as symbols for urination, link the scene at seven and these dreams with the Dream of the Burning Child and identify Freud as the child, becoming aware of his own phallic (urinary and sexual) sensations.

The Acquisition of Power over Fire

Several times in his writings (1900, 1932a, 1932b) Freud connects fire, urination and ambition. He interprets the myth of Prometheus, who had defied the gods by bringing fire "hidden in a hollow stalk" down from the heavens to Man (*Flectere si nequeo superos, Acheronta movebo*) as a theft of phallic power from the father. "In order to gain control over fire, men had to renounce the homosexually tinged desire to put it out with a stream of urine." The sexual organ of the male has two functions and "man quenches his own fire with his water" (1932b). The sexual burning aroused in the seven-year-old Freud through the primal scene was easily extinguished by the father; it was expressed and renounced by the boy's exhibitionistic urination. Like Prometheus, the adult Freud has challenged the gods and hellfire to bring a gift to mankind—the gift of vision, the power to light up dark places. He dares explore the body of his mother and is aflame once more; but this time he is the conqueror. The child's attempt to pass off sexual excitement ("I'm burning") through urination has now become a display of phallic power ("Father, don't you see"). The child who was supposed to come to nothing is showing his father how much he has achieved. He is burning with the blazing light of his intellect. Of *The Interpretation of Dreams* Freud was to say, "Insight such as this comes to one's lot but once in a lifetime" (1900).

On the Heights —the Hills of Athens and Rome

Another set of images identifies the mother's genitals with the *place* at the beginning of Chapter Seven. Here, Freud *again* conducts the reader to the "high prospect" (it has been déjà vu; of *déjà vu* in relation to a locale in dreams, Freud says, "these places are invariably the genitals of the dreamer's mother" [1900]). This "hill" from which he is going to descend and penetrate has symbolic and allusive reference to Freud as the oedipal conqueror. Freud says of a landscape dream in the Dream Book, "what is called a hill in the dream is also called one in anatomy—the Mons Veneris." Freud loved mountains and was passionately fond of climbing them, especially the Dolomites in Northern Italy (*gen Italien*). From that vantage point, he writes to Fliess during the years when the Dream Book is hatching, he admires the *view*. In letter after letter, he expresses a longing to see Rome; he clearly recognizes that this represents a childhood wish, and he dreams of it: "I dreamt I was in Rome . . . incidentally my longing for Rome is deeply neurotic. It is connected with my schoolboy hero-worship of the Semitic Hannibal, and in fact this year (1897) I have no more reached Rome than he did from Trasimene" (1887–1902). Hannibal, too, had stood on the "high prospect" of the Alps before descending into Italy. Later, Freud did descend and explore Rome, *Roma virum genitrix* ("Rome the mother of men"). "It is better not to begin about this divine city," he writes to Jones (1955). When he was eighty, Freud writes about a similar conquest of a longed-for city,

Athens, that he had first visited twenty years after Rome (Freud 1936). He had climbed the *hill* of the "Acropolis and cast my eyes around the landscape" and then experienced "a peculiar disbelief in the reality" of what was before his eyes. He attributes this to the influence of the forbidden wish to excel his father in achievement; he cannot believe that he is in a position to visit *such a wonderful place*. But the concomitant and even more forbidden wish to possess the mother (Athens, "the city, our mother," says Sophocles) is, curiously enough, not mentioned directly. An identification with the mother is implied—Freud compares his disbelief with that of a "girl (who) learns that the man she has secretly loved has asked her parents for leave to pay his addresses to her." Here, we have a hint of Freud's negative Oedipus complex, so important in his relationship to Fliess. Freud wrote to Fliess: "I am busy thinking about something which would cement our work together and put my column on your base . . ." (Freud 1887–1902). The desire to have the mother expressible by "I'm burning," is evoked in terms allusive to his "earliest passion" and the book of the journey through Persia: ". . . I recall the passionate desire to travel and see the world by which I was dominated at school and later, and how long it was before that desire began to find its fulfilment." The mother is also brought in with another symbol, the sea, and there is another allusion to the conquistador: "I had long seen clearly that a great part of the pleasure of travel lies in the fulfilment of . . . early wishes—that it is rooted, that is, in dissatisfaction with home and family. When first one catches sight of the sea, crosses the ocean and experiences as realistic cities and lands which for so long have been distant unattainable things of desire—one feels like a hero who has performed deeds of improbable greatness" (1936). Freud had written many years after the experience, in 1926, that "the amber coloured columns of the Acropolis were the most beautiful things that he had ever seen in his life" (Jones 1955). One wonders if the sight of his mother's body as seen lit up by gaslight (amber coloured?) did not provide an unconscious determinant for this aesthetic judgment.

At the end of his paper about being in Athens, Freud writes movingly of himself at eighty, in terms that are reminiscent of that other traveller nearing the end of his road, a royal road, near Athens—Oedipus, at Colonos, "And now you will no longer wonder that the recollection of this incident on the Acropolis should have troubled me so often since I myself have grown old and stand in need of forbearance and can travel no more."

The Mental Apparatus as a Place

Even in his construction of the mental apparatus, set forth in Chapter Seven, Freud is influenced by the metaphor of a journey through space. The concept of a place to be explored is first brought in when Freud presents Fechner's view that "the scene of action of dreams is different from that of waking ideational life." He wrote to Fliess that this established the idea of "the psychical territory on which the dream process is played out . . . It has been left to me to draw the first crude map of it . . ." (1887–1902). Freud calls his schema "depth psychology," and in the Dream Book and other works brings in imagery from archaeology which involves travel in an up-and-down direction, and establishes the "place" as a hole. "Father, don't you see" is evoked by the comparison of the mind to a compound optical instrument in Chapter Seven, and by the importance of visual memories and visual hallucinations to the working of the mental apparatus.

In Chapter Seven, Freud begins by mapping out the psychic systems spatially, with arrows indicating the directions taken by psychical processes. Later, Freud says that the progression of mental contents through the system probably doesn't take place in a spatial sequence at all, but rather in a temporal one. He dissociates himself from the spatial hypothesis ("What we have in mind here is not the forming of a second thought situated in a new place . . . and the notion of forcing a way through into consciousness must be kept carefully free from any idea of change of locality") in favor of an economic explanation in which the systems "*Pcs* and *Ucs*" imply two kinds of "processes of excitation or modes of discharge." The passage from the *Ucs* through the *Pcs* is then really not at all like a journey through a landscape but "a matter of the receiving and withdrawing of cathexes." "Nevertheless," says Freud, "I consider it expedient and justifiable to make use of the figurative image (that is, the 'map') of the two systems." He notes that many of his images concerning mental processes are "derived from a set of ideas relating to a struggle for a piece of ground" (potentially then alluding to a conquistador). Freud says that he wants to retain the spatial metaphor to help the reader picture—see—the functioning of the mental apparatus, and this didactic reason is convincing. One might, however, call this an "anagogic" explanation, following Silberer's usage for a "higher" meaning that Freud alludes to in Chapter Seven. For the analytic interpretation of the misleading spatial imagery we return to the symbolism involved. The dream is presented repeatedly as a result of mental processes travelling back and forth through space, from the *Pcs* to the *Ucs* and back again: "What happens in reality is no doubt a simultaneous exploring of one path and another, a swinging of the excitation now this way and now that. . . ." Finally the regressive path back to the *Ucs* and the *Pcpt* system is taken, and then a turning forwards again towards consciousness. All this traffic back and forth, following the "penetration" into the depths, symbolizes intercourse. I would speculate that the spatial concept is held to unconsciously because of its use in the symbolic process to represent the maternal genitals. This is the "place" which the burning child had seen on his first journey, and it is the source of the hypothetical space for the scene of action of the dream, and of all mental functioning: "the unexplored region of the mind in which I have been the first mortal to set forth."

Genetic View of the "Place"

In order to account for the scene of action of the dream, Lewin (1946, 1953) has introduced the concept of the dream screen, a one-dimensional backdrop to the dream hypothetically derived from the maternal breast. The derivation from the breast allows for a flat segment of a curved surface—the curve bringing in the possibility of more than a one-dimensional representation in a dream. There would be great confusion about dimensional representation at the very early time when the infant is unable to separate inside from outside, self from the breast. In and out, here and there, up and down—all have to be established, and this must occur in a piecemeal fashion concurrent with the differentiation between *breast* and *me* out of *breast: me*. (The Isakower phenomena would represent a regressive reversal of developmental events.) The emerging experience of a projection and a cavity (breast and mouth) would, after the establishment of inside and outside, be basically involved in the possibility of maintaining the concept of a three-dimensional place—a space. Lewin (1953) presents material demonstrating that the inside of a hollow space or concavity may represent the breast, complementing this in a footnote with Rogawsky's comment that the earliest impression of the mouth would serve as a prototype of all later ideas of body cavities. The dream screen would then be an early one-dimensional representation of the "place"—the mind's eye—where dreaming occurs.

We are most familiar clinically with the use of a space or place to represent the female genitals, developmentally the mother's genitals. But how this representation is arrived at is not clearly known. There must be a developmental "journey" from the idea of space as breast:mouth to the idea of space as cloacal or vaginal cavity—not completely mapped out, but involving a complicated series of introjections and projections. There is room here for ontogenetic and phylogenetic speculation. Clinically, we find that the undiscovered vagina is a hypothetical three dimensional place for children of both sexes. The establishment of the reality of this "place" is achieved only with a relatively successful passing through of the oedipus complex. Keiser (1962) has demonstrated the thinking defects that can accompany the unconsummated concept of internal cavities.

It is possible that the internal conception of the basic movements—in-and-out, up-and-down, back-and-forth—that characterize most dreams and make for a full three dimensional representation is not arrived at until after the development of some degree of exploratory and locomotor ability. The predominantly passive experiences in relation to the breast (involving separation) would in time be supplemented by active experiences of explorations of the mother's and the infant's own body. This maturational separation from the mother includes the anal stage of libido development where the "travel" is partly inside and partly outside the child's body with increasing active use of the will. On the oedipal level, where possession of the mother is aimed at after the child is no longer part of her, the in-and-out, back-and-forth, up-and-down movements (all involving travel) symbolize intercourse. It is clear that the image of a journey, in addition to its connotations of the oedipus and castration complexes, stands for preoedipal involvement: separation from the breast; the establishment of inside and outside, penetration and expulsion; and the ability to walk away from the mother that marks the dissolution of the symbiotic ties that is so important in establishing identity. A successful journey, a successful exploration, means the achievement of potential mastery of one's own body and of the environment.

The End of the Journey

Several years after the completion of his self-analysis and of the Dream Book, Freud sent a final communication to his "unwitting analyst" (Kanzer 1961), Fliess. It was a picture postcard from the temple of Neptune in Paestum, south of Rome. He had gone further south than Hannibal, was at the site of an archaeological treasure, was with the god of waters who could extinguish fire, and he separated himself from the father-figure with the one line message: "cordial greetings from the culminating point of the journey" (1887–1902).

Discussion

We have seen that the "journey" and the "place" are multi-determined symbols—basically evoked, like all symbols, from the body of the mother and the infant. I have tried to document the importance to Freud of the metaphor of a journey, especially (as the road of the "Burning Child") in his self-analysis and in the construction of his masterpiece, *The Interpretation of Dreams*, through which it runs as the "royal road to the unconscious activities of the mind." In his writings the royal road appears as the road of the conquistador, the taker of cities, the aspirer to kingship. It is the road of Hannibal, going on further than that hero did to Rome, "mother of men." It is the road of Prometheus, who defied Zeus and brought down fire from Olympus to mankind. It is the road toward Phocis, where Oedipus struck down Laius—the road to Thebes, the

Sphinx and the solving of the mystery—the road to Jocasta and the crown—and finally the road toward Athens and Colonos—a road through incest and blindness to insight and transfiguration.

The reductive interpretations in relation to *The Interpretation of Dreams* concerning the mother's genitals and the exhibitionistic display of the son's phallic power only increase one's awe of Freud's achievement. Like Oedipus, his dedication to the truth regardless of any obstacles became his determining motivation, driving him on to finish his journey of exploration. And like Oedipus, his insight was achieved not only in spite of, but in relation to, his incestuous strivings. His heroic and unparalleled struggle, the agony and joy which can be glimpsed in the letters to Fliess, and its glorious outcome, mark Freud as one of the greatest of conquistadors.

References

Abraham, K. (1923). Two contributions to the study of symbols. In *Clinical Papers and Essays on Psycho-Analysis*. London: Hogarth Press, 1955.

Erikson, E. H. (1955). Freud's *The Origins of Psychoanalysis. International Journal of Psycho-Analysis* 36:1–15.

Freud, S. (1887–1902). *The Origins of Psychoanalysis*. New York: Basic Books, 1954.

———— (1900). The interpretation of dreams. *Standard Edition* 4/5.

———— (1916–17). Introductory lectures on psychoanalysis. *Standard Edition* 15/16.

———— (1917). A childhood recollection from *Dichtung und Wahrheit. Standard Edition* 17:145–156.

———— (1932a). New introductory lectures on psychoanalysis. *Standard Edition* 22:3–184.

———— (1932b). The acquisition and control of fire. *Standard Edition* 22:187–196.

———— (1936). A disturbance of memory on the Acropolis. *Standard Edition* 22:239–248.

Hyman, S. (1962). *The Tangled Bank*. New York: Atheneum.

Jones, E. (1953). *The Life and Work of Sigmund Freud*. Vol. 1. New York: Basic Books.

———— (1954). Freud's early travels. *International Journal of Psycho-Analysis* 35:81–84.

———— (1955). *The Life and Work of Sigmund Freud*. Vol. 2. New York: Basic Books.

Keiser, S. (1962). Disturbances of ego functions of speech and abstract thinking.

Journal of the American Psychoanalytic Association 10:50–73.

Lewin, B. (1946). Sleep, the mouth, and the dream screen. *Psychoanalytic Quarterly* 15:419–434.

——— (1953). Reconsideration of the dream screen. *Psychoanalytic Quarterly* 22:174–199.

Shengold, L. (1963). The parent as sphinx. *Journal of the American Psychoanalytic Association* 11:725–151.

Sophocles. *Oedipus at Colonus*. Trans. R. Jebb. London: Cambridge University Press, 1928.

Chapter 5

FREUD AND JOSEPH

LEONARD SHENGOLD, M.D.

After reading Thomas Mann's *Joseph in Egypt* (1938), Freud wrote the author: "I keep wondering if there isn't a figure in history for whom the life of Joseph was a mythical prototype, allowing us to detect the phantasy of Joseph as the secret daemonic motor behind the scenes of his complex life. I am thinking of Napoleon I" (E. Freud 1960, p. 432). What Freud goes on to say of Napoleon as Joseph, and of Napoleon's relation to his older brother, Joseph, provides a fascinating way of looking at the Emperor. In this paper, I try to show Freud, too, living out a Joseph fantasy; I hope to add dimension to our view of a great and complex man.*

Mann (1936), in his essay on Freud, agrees with and quotes "a Viennese scholar of the Freudian school" (I am indebted to Dr. Samuel Abrams for the information that this analyst was none other than Ernst Kris) who spells out Mann's "fundamental motif" in the Joseph novels (1938, 1948) of an individual living out the life of a mythical character type—"precisely this idea of the 'lived life,' life as succession, as a moving in other's steps, as identification" with figures from the past. This concept implies the importance of great men—spiritual fathers and brothers from myth and history—for the formation of the ego ideal.

*I thank Drs. Max Schur and Mark Kanzer for their advice and encouragement which contributed so much to the writing of this paper.

Freud identified himself passionately with some of the great leaders and heroes of the actual and mythical past; we know of Moses, Oedipus, Hannibal, Julius Caesar, and Napoleon from his writings, especially from *The Interpretation of Dreams*. There, Freud (1900) presents himself as Joseph for the first time and documents his involvement with the Biblical Joseph and other people of that name: "It will be noticed that the name Josef plays a great part in my dreams (cf. the dream about my uncle [Josef]). My own ego finds it very easy to hide itself behind people of that name, since Joseph was the name of a man famous in the Bible as an interpreter of dreams (1900, p. 484n)." But Freud's interest in Biblical heroes had started much earlier, and in his *Autobiographical Study* (1925) he mentions this as a determinant of his curiosity about human beings and his ultimate choice of a life's work: "My deep engrossment in the Bible story (almost as soon as I had learnt the art of reading) had, as I recognized much later, an enduring effect upon the direction of my interest" (1925, p. 8). Even earlier, his Catholic nurse, whom he called the "primary originator" of his neurosis, had deeply impressed him with her stories "about God and Hell" (Freud 1887–1902).

As a child, Freud's specific interest in the Biblical tale of Joseph must have been very great because it reflected his own family situation (Eissler 1963, p. 1104). Similarity and identity of names always impressed Freud. His own father's name was also Jacob; this Jacob, too, had had two wives; Sigmund, like Joseph, was the eldest child of the beloved younger wife. Jacob Freud was born in 1815 and married when he was seventeen. His first son, Emmanuel (father of Freud's childhood companion, John), was born in 1832 or 1833. His second son, Phillip, was born in 1836 and was therefore twenty years older than Sigmund. Jacob Freud married again when he was forty. He and Amalie Nathanson (*his* Rachel) had eight children. Sigmund was the eldest; then a little less than a year later, came Julius who died at eight months. Ten years after Sigmund, the youngest child, Alexander, was born. In between were five girls.

Jones (1953) has described how Freud's unusual family constellation gave spur to his curiosity and facilitated his later discovery of the universality of the Oedipus complex. The relations between father and brothers (with concomitant relations to mothers and sisters) in the Joseph story parallel those of Freud. Joseph was the favorite son, not only of the doting Rachel, but also of Jacob who had eleven others. Sigmund was Jacob's pride and joy and was, of course, the first born and lifelong favorite of his mother. Freud (1917) says of Goethe what is equally applicable to Joseph and to himself: ". . . if a man has been his mother's undisputable darling, he retains throughout life the triumphant feeling [Freud uses the German word *Eroberergefühl*: literally, feeling of a *conqueror*], the confidence in success, which not seldom brings actual success with it" (1917, p. 156).

Freud was ambitious; when already dedicated to scientific and medical study, he wrote to his friend, Wilhelm Fliess: "I am not really a man of science . . . nothing but by temperament a *conquistadore*" (Jones 1953, p. 348). As a child, he identified with many great heroes. Ambition, the natural heritage of a gifted "indisputable" family favorite (young Joseph's strength as well as the sin that led him to the pit), is attested to by Joseph's dreams. He dreams first that his sheaf stands up and remains upright, while those of his brothers gather around and bow low to it; then he dreams that the sun, the moon, and eleven stars bow down to him. The first dream is of phallic ascendancy over his brothers—to be first in the eyes of the parents. Zeligs (1955) interprets these dreams of ambition as defensive—the greatness compensatory to the feelings of the weaker younger brother vis-à-vis his hostile stronger older brothers.

Joseph's second dream has him also ruling over his parents. Jacob reproaches him, "Are we to come, I and your mother and your brothers, and bow low to you to the ground" (Genesis 37:10); Joseph's brothers are infuriated by his dreams.

Freud (1900) writes of his own fraternal rivalries. We learn most about his relations with his much older half-brother, Phillip; his younger brother, Julius, who lived such a short time; his nephew, John (Emmanuel's son), who was a year older than Sigmund. Phillip was old enough to be—and was confused with—a father; Julius was a younger brother; John's role was that of an older brother. We read of warm and loving feelings toward the ten-year-younger Alexander (Sigmund's *Benjamin*).

Fratricide as a Displacement of Parricide

If, as Freud hypothesized, and work with patients suggests, the primal crime (as "felt" by the superego) is parricide,* the biblical myth portrays a displacement in the murder of Abel by Cain. The father is defied in the eating of the forbidden fruit, but the first murder is that of brother by brother, out of jealousy for the father's love: "The Lord paid heed to Abel and his offering, but to Cain and his offering he paid no heed" (Genesis 4:45). Here is the parallel in the Joseph story: "Now Israel [Jacob] loved Joseph best of all his sons, for he was the child of his old age, and he had made him a coat of many colors. And when his brothers saw that their father loved him more than any of his brothers, they hated him . . ." (Genesis 37:3, 4).

---

*"If the Son of God was obliged to sacrifice his life to redeem mankind from original sin, then by the law of talion, . . . that sin must have been a killing, a murder. . . . And ᵂif ᴱ the original sin was an offense against God the Father, ᵂthen ᴱ the primal crime of mankind must have been a parricide, the killing of the primal father of the primitive human horde, whose mnemic image was later transfigured into a deity" (Freud 1915, pp. 292–293).

Genesis is full of stories of hatred and rivalry between brothers: Cain and Abel; Isaac and Ishmael; Esau and Jacob. In every instance the father is spared, and rage is turned against the brother. Jacob, with the connivance of his mother, Rebekah, steals by trickery his older brother's birthright and his belssing. The paternal blessing not only passes on the goods and power of the father, it also confers the privilege of carrying on the Covenant with God—that special relationship with God the Father (the primal parent) which led to Cain's murder of Abel. It is largely the not-unwarranted expectation that Joseph will be the recipient of Jacob's blessing that rouses the older brothers' hatred and fear of the young boy. Reuben, the eldest and the natural heir (like Esau), had offended against his father by seducing his father's concubine Bilhah. Mann portrays Reuben as partly motivated toward the incest by his jealous rage at the prospect of the young Joseph (then seven) being preferred over him. It is when Joseph is seventeen, following the telling of his overweening dreams, that the brothers attempt to kill him, thereby venting their fury against their father. Joseph is first cast down into the pit and then, Reuben having managed to dissuade the more zealous from murder, sold into slavery. He again descends—to Egypt, called by Mann Hell or the Lower World. He rises by becoming the steward of Potiphar, again is cast down—this time into prison—because of the accusation of Potiphar's wife. His power of dream interpretation enables him to rise again. He gains Pharaoh's trust and becomes his overseer. He is the highest in all the land, save Pharaoh himself. (These descents and ascents, from the lower regions to the upper world, are reminiscent of Freud's imagery in *The Interpretation of Dreams*; see Shengold 1966, chapter 4 of the present volume.) Joseph, through his ability to leave his father and transcend his dependency on him, finally attains a position from which he can become the father to his father and his brothers.

The displacement from father-murder to brother-murder is also seen in *Hamlet* (III, iii) where Claudius says of his crime: "O, my offense is rank, it smells to heaven. / It hath the primal eldest curse upon't, / A brother's murder." The play, though, is about the paralysis that murderous wishes toward the father bring out. Freud comments on this in the momentous letter to Fliess announcing his discovery of the Oedipus complex, and in so doing, he provides, by way of a slip, the counterpart of his own father-to-brother displacement. It is the letter of October 15, 1897, written a year after his father's death that launched the great task of his self-analysis. Hamlet, Freud (1892–1899) says, hesitates to avenge his father by killing his uncle because of his unconscious feeling of guilt, for he himself "had meditated the same deed against his father from passion for his mother." It is not characteristic of Hamlet, Freud adds, to avoid aggressive action, considering that "he is the same man, who sends his courtiers to their deaths without a scruple, and who is positively precipitate in killing Laertes." Hamlet, of course, is not "precipitate" in killing Laertes; he does it unwittingly, having no knowledge of the poison that makes his slight scratching of Laertes fatal. But he does precipitately kill Polonius, Laertes' father, whom he hears behind the arras in his mother's bedchamber. That Freud made a slip is confirmed by the parallel passage in *The Interpretation of Dreams*: ". . . Hamlet is far from being represented as a person incapable of taking any action. We see him doing so on two occasions: first in a sudden outburst of temper, when he runs his sword through the eavesdropper behind the arras, and secondly in a premeditated and even crafty fashion, when, with all the callousness of a Renaissance prince, he sends the two courtiers to the death that had been planned for himself." In both passages he couples the killing of Rosencrantz and Guildenstern with that of Polonius, and his writing *Laertes* (Freud 1887–1902) represents a slip of the pen, the dispensable brother figure (Phillip, Julius, John) replacing the needed and beloved Jacob whose loss Freud was mourning at that time. Polonius is especially important in the play as the father-figure that Hamlet can kill freely (Claudius is dispatched only when Hamlet is already dying). Polonius can evoke the murdered father. Freud even refrains from naming him in the above quoted passages.

James Joyce in *Ulysses*, that novel of fathers and sons in which the hero searches for and finds a maternal father (as Mann characterizes Jacob), also shifts the focus of hatred away from the father onto the mother and the brothers. Joyce's theory, stated by Stephen Daedalus in the Scylla and Charybdis episode of *Ulysses*, is that the play, *Hamlet*, represents Shakespeare's reaction to his having been cuckolded by his brothers Edmund and Richard, Shakespeare portraying himself in the play as both old Hamlet, the murdered father, and young Hamlet, the dispossessed son (paralleling Joyce who represents himself as both Stephen and Bloom in his novel). Joyce also states that Shakespeare wrote Hamlet immediately after his father's death. This may not be true, but it parallels the timing of Freud's writing about Hamlet after *his* father's death. Joyce emphasizes *Hamlet* as evidence of Shakespeare's obsession with the theme of the "false, or usurping, or adulterous *brother*" (Blamires 1966, p. 90; my italics).

Freud and His "Brother" John

Jones (1953) considers John "the most important person in Freud's early childhood . . . next to his parents." In trying to account for the aggressive ambition which colored his boyhood preoccupation with the military heroes,

Hannibal and (Napoleon's) Marshal Masséna,* Freud (1900) says, "[Perhaps] the development of this martial ideal is traceable still farther back into my childhood: to the times when, at the age of three, I was in a close relation, sometimes friendly but sometimes warlike, with a boy a year older than myself [John], and to the wishes which that relation must have stirred up in the weaker of us" (1900, p. 198). The relationship was intense and ambivalent:

> Until the end of my third year we had been inseparable. We had loved each other and fought each other; and this childhood relationship, as I have already hinted, had a determining influence on all my subsequent relations with contemporaries. Since that time my nephew John has had many re-incarnations. . . . my warm friendships as well as my enmities with contemporaries [go] back to my relations [with John]. . . . My emotional life has always insisted that I should hav an intimate friend and a hated enemy. I have always been able to provide myself afresh with both, and it has not infrequently happened that the ideal situation of childhood has been so completely reproduced that friend and enemy have come together in a single individual . . . [Freud 1900, pp. 424–483 *passim*]

Freud wrote this at a time when he had, at least in large part (Schur, *Freud: Living and Dying*, 1972), come to terms with the then-current revenant of John, Wilhelm Fliess. Fliess was a kind of analyst for Freud and, as in most important relationships in life, including the one to the analyst, was kaleidoscopically invested with transferences of all Freud's important early love objects, including brothers and father.

Freud and Phillip

Freud had another important ambivalent, although perhaps more consistently hostile, relationship with his much older half-brother, Phillip, who was the same age as Freud's mother. In his oedipal fantasies, Freud spared the beloved, feared, and respected Jacob, focusing instead on Phillip as his rival. When Freud was two and a half and just after his sister Anna was born, his nurse was dismissed

---

*One of Napoleon's generals who was, Freud believed, like Hannibal, of Semitic origin. That Masséna was born a hundred years to the day earlier than Freud furthered the boy's sense of identification with him. Freud thought that Masséna was a variant of the Jewish name Manasseh. The first Manasseh was the eldest son of Joseph. In Jewish lore, stemming from the times of the Roman occupation of Palestine, it is written that the first Messiah would be a warrior, preparing the way for the spiritual Messiah-ben-David who would rule forever; this military hero Messiah was expected to come from the seed of Joseph. This eventual "conquistadore" was alternatively called Messiah-ben-Joseph, or, from Joseph's sons, Messiah-ben Ephraim or Messiah-ben-Manasseh (Bakan 1958). Here was material for young Sigmund's fantasies of military glory.

for stealing. Freud asked Phillip where she had gone. He took literally Phillip's joking answer, *Sie ist eingekastelt* ("She has been put into a chest"), and confused it with his pregnancy fantasies. According to Jones, Freud had the fantasy that "his half-brother and his mother, who were of the same age, had cooperated in producing the usurping Anna" (1953, p. 10). This made Phillip the hated rival, bypassing Jacob. The attribution of the paternal role to Phillip is at least unconsciously implicit in relation to an incident following the birth of Freud's youngest sibling, Alexander, when Sigmund was ten. Jacob had asked the boy to choose a name, and he had suggested calling the infant Alexander after one of his conqueror heroes, Alexander the Great, son of *Philip* of Macedon (Jones 1953).

Freud's Philippic fantasies are evident in one of his dreams which is only dimly interpreted in *The Interpretation of Dreams* (1900). He calls it an anxiety dream from his seventh or eighth year in which "*I saw my beloved mother, with a peculiarly peaceful, sleeping expression on her features, being carried into the room by two (or three) people with birds' beaks and laid upon the bed*" (1900, p. 583). Freud associates to illustrations of Egyptian gods in *Phillippson's* Bible. He does not mention brother Phillip, but tells of a namesake who also had supplied sexual information—the son of a concierge named Philipp who told him the vulgar word for intercourse—*Vögeln*, derived from *vögel* ("bird"). Freud had awakened from the dream screaming and had awakened his parents. He traces the anxiety back "to an obscure and evidently sexual craving that had found appropriate expression in the visual content of the dream" (1900, p. 584). The dream links incest, Phillip (not Jacob) as the rival, and Egypt—here connoting, as for Mann's Joseph, the underworld, the sexual world, the land of the dead.

Freud and Julius; the Sin of Cain

His younger brother Julius figured large in Freud's personal mythology. Freud was nineteen months old when the eight-month-old Julius died. He tells Fliess (Freud 1887–1902), "I welcomed my one-year-younger brother (who died within a few months) with ill-wishes and real infantile jealousy, and . . . his death left the germ of guilt in me" (1887–1902, p. 219). The theme of self-reproach, founded not only on guilt for oedipal wishes, but on the fulfilled wish to get rid of Julius, is dealt with in terms of the many Joseph-meanings (as well as in relation to many Josephs) in another famous dream of Freud's: the "non vixit" dream (Freud 1900). I am indebted to Max Schur for pointing out to me the importance of Julius for this dream.

The dream is full of Josephs; it deals mainly with death wishes and reproaches for death wishes. The main contemporary object of the hostile wishes was Fliess, who can be seen as a current incarnation of Julius. Fliess had for many years been Freud's closest friend and the "only audience" for his ideas. It is in connection with the "non vixit" dream that Freud writes of the series of "revenants" of John in whom "friend and enemy have come together in a single individual" (1900, p. 198). As had happened before with others, the close relationship with Fliess was heading for a break-up (still several years away), partly because Freud's self-analysis rid him of his dependency needs, partly because of Fliess' intolerance of dissent.

"The central feature of the dream," which is too long to be reproduced here, was, Freud says, "a scene in which I annihilated [Josef Paneth] with a look" (1900, p. 422). Josef Paneth, younger than Freud, had been his successor at Brücke's Physiological Institute. One of the reasons Freud had left Brücke's laboratory was because he had little chance of advancement there; both the capable Sigmund Exner and the gifted, tragic Ernst Fleischl being senior to him. Freud reproached himself for contributing to Fleischl's death by his well-meant attempt to cure the older man's morphine addiction with cocaine. Freud had been shocked at Josef Paneth's open wish to have the seriously-ill Fleischl out of the way, but was honest enough to realize that he himself had had the same wish when he was a demonstrator in Brücke's laboratory, "but, as was to be expected, the dream punished my friend [Josef P.] and not me, for the callous wish" (1900, p. 484) At the time of the dream, both Josef Paneth and Fleischl (who had also appeared in the dream) were dead, as was the Emperor Josef II from whose monument the dream had borrowed the words *non* and *vixit*.

The dream is full of ghosts who return, and Freud had felt while dreaming that "*people of that kind only existed as long as one liked and could be got rid of if someone else* [!] *wished it*" (1900, p. 421). Freud's death wishes gave him the lethal power of the basilisk, to be able to kill with a look, reversing the scene from the past in which the father-figure Brücke had crushed him with an unforgettable piercing look of reproach from "his terrible blue eyes" (1900, p. 422). After his own father's death, Freud had dreamt of a sign that read: "You are requested to close the eyes" (Freud 1887–1902, p. 171) which obviously involves Oedipus' symbolic talion punishment of blindness.

The dream occurred during a time when Fliess was about to undergo an operation. Freud was worried about him, and "the dream thoughts now informed me that I feared for my friend's life" (1900, p. 481). Freud recognized the hostile wish toward Fliess and connected it with desires to get rid of a series of "revenants," especially John and Fleischl, older-brother figures: "I had replaced one Josef by another in the dream and found it impossible to suppress the similarity between the opening letters of the name 'Fleischl' and ('Fliess') (1900, p. 486).

The dream is a demonstration of the hostility toward the father (Brücke, Emperor Josef) being displaced onto brother figures. Another Josef in the dream was Josef Breuer who had been like a father to Freud, helping him with advice and money. With their joint work on hysteria, Breuer became more of an older brother. As Freud began to outstrip Breuer in the sweep of his imagination, increasing hostility arose between the two, especially on Freud's part (Jones 1953). "Freud's intellect is soaring at its highest. I gaze after him as a hen at a hawk," Breuer had written to Fliess. There came a time when the hawk began to attack the hen; Jones feels that Freud was chiefly at fault. This Joseph, Breuer, had become a revenant of John as the enemy, and the closeness between the two men became "violent antipathy" (Jones 1953, p. 255) on Freud's side, during the last years of the friendship with Fliess.

But the dream also alludes to brother Julius. Freud associates to Brutus's speech of self-justification in Shakespeare's *Julius Caesar* (III, ii): "as he was ambitious, I slew him." (This was the brothers' response to Joseph's dreams of ambition.) Sigmund had acted the part of *Brutus* to John's *Caesar* as a child. The dream also said, "My friend [Fliess] came to Vienna in July" (1900, p. 421), and Freud associates to July's being named after Julius Caesar. Fliess, to whom Freud had looked up as a leader for so many years, was actually younger than Freud, about as much younger as Julius had been. There can be no doubt of the tremendous effect of the death wish toward that first Julius which actually had coincided with his having been "got rid of." (Schur, *Freud: Living and Dying*, 1972).

The Fliess family had asked Freud not to mention Fliess' illness to anyone. The implication that his discretion was not taken for granted annoyed him, for it implied he could not keep a secret:

I was very disagreeably affected by the veiled reproach because it was—not wholly without justification. . . . [At an earlier time] I caused trouble between two friends . . . by quite unnecessarily telling one of them, in the course of conversation, what the other had said about him. At that time, too, reproaches had been levelled at me, and they were still in my memory. One of the two friends concerned was Professor Fleischl; I may describe the other by his first name of 'Josef' [Breuer]—which was also that of P. [Josef Paneth], my friend and opponent in the dream." [Freud 1900, pp. 481–482]

This reproach for being a tattle-tale foreshadows the final quarrel between Fliess and Freud about Freud's unauthorized talking of Fliess's ideas of bisexuality to an analysand. It also connects Freud with Joseph, who was reproached by his brothers for being a tale-bearer: "And Joseph brought bad reports of them [his brothers, the sons of Bilhah and Zilpah] to their father" (Genesis 37:2).

It is in connection with the *non vixit* dream that Freud makes the statement about his own ego "hiding behind" people named Joseph. Freud has taught us that any figure in a dream can stand not only for the dreamer himself, but also for any of the important people in his life. Parents, siblings, mate, children, friends—all can be Joseph. If Fliess, in dream or in life, was a "revenant", he could represent for Freud at various times Julius, John, Phillip, or Jacob. The combinations and complications made by trying to delineate object relations and identifications with each of the above (not to mention the possible representation of mother and sisters by a male figure) show the constantly changing complexity of human identity. *To be* Joseph, then, means being many other people at the same time. One can see the oversimplification involved in the (nonetheless breathtaking) insight contained in Freud's comment to Fliess, "And I am accustoming myself to the idea of regarding every sexual act as a process in which four persons are involved" (Freud 1887–1902, p. 289). To see clarity amidst these complications is the analyst's daily task. This is done in large part by the awareness of the predominant role the patient is transferring onto the analyst at any given time. It is to be remembered that Freud made use of Fliess as a kind of analyst during the years of his heroic self-analysis.

Uncle Josef

Hostility to brothers is also evident in Freud's "Uncle Dream" (1900). The hostility is disguised by being transferred to his father's generation. This also allows for the expression of ill-will toward his father who had suffered from the misconduct of his ne'er-do-well brother Josef. The dream took place at a time when Freud had been recommended for appointment as Professor, so again ambition is involved. The dream led to thoughts disparaging two colleagues who had not been appointed to professorship, supposedly for reasons that would leave Freud's hopes untouched. Freud dreamed: ". . . My friend R. was my uncle—I had a great feeling of affection for him." And here are his associations:

> "*R. was my uncle.*" What could that mean? I never had more than one uncle—Uncle Josef. [Freud adds a footnote here: ". . . my memory . . . was narrowed at this point. . . . Actually I have known five of my uncles, and loved and honoured one of them . . .".] There was an unhappy story attached to him. Once—more than thirty years ago,—in his eagerness to make money, he allowed himself to be involved in a transaction of a kind that is severely punished by the law, and he was in fact punished for it. My father whose hair turned grey from grief in a few days, used always to say that Uncle Josef was not a bad man but only a simpleton. . . . [1900, pp. 137–138].

Freud goes on to show that the feeling of affection in the dream was really hypocritical; his dream had contained a slander against R. and "in order that I might not notice this, what appeared in the dream was the opposite, a feeling of affection for him" (1900, p. 141). The "Uncle Dream" expresses hatred in a competition for the lordly position (in Vienna) for Professor. And is it too fanciful to speculate that here Freud is himself the uncle Josef (he *was* an uncle to the beloved enemy, John), not only putting himself in a position to turn his father's hair grey again, but also reducing the five brothers to the one Josef? Could not the missing four brothers be Emmanuel, Phillip, Alexander, and Julius, leaving Freud "standing erect" as in the Biblical Joseph's first dream of ambition?

Joseph as Father: the Emperors Josef II and Napoleon

Kings and emperors symbolize the father, illustrating the power and majesty of the head of the household as seen from the cradle. Freud (1936) tells an anecdote about Napoleon when that ruler invoked *his* original ruler: "Napoleon, during his coronation as Emperor in Notre Dame, turned to one of his brothers—it must no doubt have been the eldest one, Joseph—and remarked: 'What would *Monsieur notre Père* have said to this, if he could have been here today?' " (1936, p. 247).

Freud wrote this in the course of describing to Romain Rolland a peculiar feeling of unreality he had when, in fulfillment of his infantile wish to travel, he climbed the hill of the Acropolis accompanied by his brother, Alexander. He described the symptom as the result of his feeling guilty for having gone further (and seen more!) than his father. Implicit is the conquest of the mother, symbolized by climbing the hill. Joseph's climbing to the pinnacle of power in Egypt also meant the fulfillment of the forbidden wish of ruling over his father and family; he was able to take care of them, showing *his* father how far *he* had come.

Wittels (1924) speaks of the influence the name Joseph had for Freud and stresses the effect of the Freud family's many years of residence in the Kaiser Josef Strasse when Sigmund was growing up. The nineteenth century regarded Emperor Josef II (1741–1790) of the Holy Roman Empire as a kind of philosopher-king, contrasting his attempt to fulfill the ideals of liberty and equality of the enlightenment philosophers by benevolent despotism with the repressive regime of the later Hapsburg Kaisers. The attitude was expressed by Austria's greatest poet, Grillparzer, who in his poems would periodically trot out Josef II to give paternally reproachful lectures to his successors (Barea, 1966). Josef II had abolished serfdom, curtailed the feudal privileges of the nobles, clashed openly and rudely with the Pope, built many hospitals (preparing Vienna for her role as center of medical education), and published an Edict of Toleration for Protestants and Jews.

We know that Freud was influenced by Emperor Josef II. He appears in the *non vixit* dream, and Freud in his writings often expresses the wish for the therapeutic power of Emperor Josef: "the benevolent interference of a powerful personage before whose will people bow and difficulties vanish" in order to fight neurosis by alleviating the misery imposed by the realities of poverty and oppression (Freud 1916/17, p. 432; see also 1919, p. 167).

The childhood wish to be emperor appears in an anecdote told by Jones. Once, when Freud (having attained the rank of Professor Extraordinarius) was giving a lecture at the University, "Abraham, Ferenczi, Rank, Sachs, and myself [Jones] were seated in the front row, he made a graceful little bow, waved his hand towards us, and murmured [as Napoleon had in the theater at Erfurt]: 'Un parterre de rois' " (1953, p. 342). (See also Grotjahn 1967, p. 15).

That Josef II had not only granted equal civil rights to the Jews but also equal duties—he was the first monarch in Europe to make Jews liable for service in the Army (Palmer and Colton 1965)—must have been particularly important to young Sigmund, whose alter egos were military heroes of Semitic origin. Freud (1900) wrote: "I can still remember sticking labels on the flat backs of my wooden soldiers with the names of Napoleon's marshals written on them. And at that time my declared favorite was already Masséna (or, to give it its Jewish form, Manasseh)" (1900, p. 197). To be son of an emperor is to be Manasseh, son of the powerful vizier of Egypt. Freud had bitterly contrasted his father who had allowed a Christian to force him into the gutter and knock his hat off with "Hamilcar Barca, [who] made his boy swear . . . to take vengeance on the Romans" (1900, p. 197). Hannibal, a "Semitic general," was the favorite hero of Freud's later schooldays. To be the emperor Josef himself would mean that no anti-Semite would dare to force *his* father, Jacob, into the gutter again; he too could be Joseph, savior of Jacob. Napoleon was the son (not the oldest) who became the savior of his entire family—lifting them all up to partake of his power.

Hostility Displaced onto the Brothers

Thomas Mann makes obvious what is implicit in the Bible: that for all his hostility, the young Joseph loves his brothers. Joseph is easily able to suppress his hatred because he has had the experience of successful narcissism. He assumes the superiority conferred both by his great natural gifts of beauty and intelligence and by the favoritism of his parents. But when his pre-eminence is threatened, his hatred shows. He wants his brothers out of the way if there is any hint that one of them might obtain the blessing of the parent-god. His hatred is evident in his telling his dreams and of the gift of the coat of many colors to his brothers. It is evident in his tale-bearing, a fault allied to his curiosity. The defensive nature of his assertions of supremacy is obvious: the smaller brother must suppress the murderous hostility that pits him against the frightening superior strength of the older brothers. Freud says of Napoleon:

> His eldest brother was called Joseph . . . the elder brother is the natural rival; the younger one feels for him an elemental, unfathomable deep hostility for which in later life the expressions "death-wish" and "murderous intent" may be found appropriate. To eliminate Joseph, to become Joseph himself, must have been Napoleon's strongest emotion as a young child. It is strange no doubt and yet it has been correctly observed that just these excessive, infantile impulses tend to turn into their opposites—the hated rival becomes the loved one. This was the case with Napoleon. We assume that he started out with an ardent hatred of Joseph, but we learn later on he loved him more than any other human being and could hardly find a fault with this worthless, unreliable man. Thus the original hatred had been overcompensated, but the early aggression released was only waiting to be transferred to other objects. Hundreds of thousands of unknown individuals had to atone for the fact that the little tyrant had spared his first enemy. [E. Freud 1960, p. 432]

We are reminded of Freud's own excessive admiration and love for Fliess in the years before the publication of *The Interpretation of Dreams*; the man looked up to as a kind of "Messiah" in the early letters (Freud 1887–1902) is finally broken with—"a brutal personality," as Freud wrote of him in 1906.

Hatred for the usurping younger brother is also suppressed. Benjamin had taken Joseph's place as *the* son of Rachel, and, worse, his birth had caused her death. Yet Joseph truly loved Benjamin, as Freud was apparently truly fond of Alexander. Freud's hatred for Julius was especially pathogenic because he had actually died at a time when no working over of the original impulses was possible. But siblings are relatively dispensable; hatred of the vitally-needed parents is much more frightening. In his explanation of Napoleon's career of conquest and slaughter, Freud, the discoverer of what he for so long called the "father complex," strangely leaves the great man's hatred of his father out of account, although Napoleon was sixteen when his father died.

A child's primal hatred must first of all be directed outward to the mother (or the mothering figure; Anna Freud (1965) says infants at the beginning of life choose their objects on the basis of function, not of sex) who is at the same time gradually being distinguished from the self. The caretaking mother earns hostility as what Anna Freud calls "the first external legislator" (1965, p. 168). Hostility is displaced from the mother onto others: the father and siblings. The father is cathected early as "a symbol of power, protectiveness, ownership of the mother" (1965, p. 186). Sexual differentiation of the object becomes important in the phallic phase, and the "oedipus complex itself . . . is based on the recognition of sex difference" (1965, p. 187). It is during the phallic phase, under the impact of the castration complex, that the boy must fully and frighteningly feel hostility for the father. His power to protect and his presence as a focus for masculine identification make him appear indispensable to the young boy.

The son, like Joseph or Sigmund, turns this access of oedipal hatred toward the unwelcome brothers who have already been resented as rivals for the parent's care and love. The stories of Cain and Abel (with God preferring Abel) and Joseph show that the hostility to the sibling exists chiefly in relation to the parent. A parent with small children can observe daily that the previously peaceful siblings begin to quarrel *after* the parent enters on the scene.

A man, involved professionally in treating psychologically disturbed patients, had a brother who was several years his senior (as was his analyst, whose age he had looked up in a medical directory). At the beginning, the hostility expressed in the analysis was that of a sibling rival for the love of a parent; this parent was Fortune or Fate as with Oedipus. (This is Oedipus's last heroic, ironically pathetic attempt at denial. As he is about to be crushed by Fate, he claims Fate as a loving parent. Why should he care who his parents are, he says, when "I am Fortune's child, not man's; her mother face hath ever smiled above me.") God had smiled on the analyst who must have been lucky enough to have the right contacts and who earned more, lived better, and was happy. The hatred was intense and genuinely rooted in the relationship to his brother. His parents had always played one child off against the other, training them, as it were, to become Cain and Abel. This level of hatred was rather easily voiced. In contrast, appearing later in the analysis was a terrifying and paralyzing hatred for the analyst as parent: the preoedipal "bad" mother merging into the oedipal father. In dealing with the analyst as father, castration anxiety brought out the full terror of the fury that he expressed with relative freedom in life in his rather successful competition with brother figures. He would always beat a brother, but in any competition with fathers he had to lose.

For Freud, it was terrible to want to get rid of John, but at least John could fight back. It is the power of the older brother that makes hating him dangerous, evoking fear of retaliation and punishment. To want to get rid of Julius was worse; it is the vulnerability of the younger brother, the fear of one's own aggression, that makes hating him more dangerous. But to want to get rid of Jacob was unthinkable and yet it is man's fate to think of it; the full force of the guilt associated with the Oedipus complex is involved with fear of both the power of, and the punishment for, one's own aggressive wishes. Freud always emphasized the phylogenetic impact of the phallic phase and of the castration complex. Clinically it would seem that, whatever the explanation, the intensity of hostile feeling for the father is more than can be accounted for by ontogenetic experience. The necessary search for substitutes to hate instead of the father begins with the rival brothers. This was the essence of the story of Joseph for Freud.

The Sublimation of the Drive for Power

In his middle seventies, Freud again became involved with the Bible stories, no doubt partly as a reaction to the Nazi persecution of the Jews. In 1934 he began to write his last book—on Moses. Moses had long been (like Joseph) an engrossing mythopoeic figure for Freud, appearing often in his writings (1900, 1914, 1939), now as a "formidable father-image" (Jones 1957), now as Freud himself. Moses, like Joseph, was associated with Egypt, had a messianic role in relation to the Jewish people, a covenant with God. But his story lacked the element of conflict with the brothers: Aaron appears only once in *Moses and Monotheism*; Freud even casts doubt on the fraternal relationship by describing him as "Aaron, *called* (Moses') brother" (my italics).

By 1934 Freud had come a "long way from the child who devoured Thiers' story of Napoleon's power and who identified himself with the Marshal Masséna" (Bernfeld 1946, p. 163). Joseph was seventeen when, after expressing his overweening ambition to his brothers, he was cast into the pit to begin his struggle for greatness. Greatness came only after he had left his father Jacob. The dreams of glory and worship were fulfilled in Egypt; conquest was achieved not by killing, but by Joseph's charm and especially his wisdom, specifically his ability to interpret dreams. Seventeen marked an important turning point for Freud too. Adolescence meant a reawakening of hostility for the father, and a renewed need to turn the oedipal wishes away from the parents onto contemporaries—brothers; but here too, naked aggression is sublimated. Both Bernfeld and Jones set Freud's renunciation of military and political ambition at seventeen: "shortly after his graduation from high school, Freud suddenly retreats from his search for power over men" (Bernfeld 1949, p. 169). Freud, like Joseph, "perceived that the ultimate secret of power was not force, but understanding" (Jones 1953, p. 53). In his forties, and only after *he* had lost *his* father Jacob, Freud began his self-analysis, accomplished largely through *his* ability to interpret dreams. The exploration of his own past led to mastery, to the attempt at conquest of that "unexplored region of the mind in which I have been the first mortal to set forth" (Freud 1887–1902). He emerged as the successful "conquistador," not by blood and killing, but by understanding. It was the discovery of the Oedipus complex and his acknowledgement of his own murderous and incestuous wishes that made it possible for him to come to terms with Jacob and with his brothers, by way of altered identifications and object relationships. Fratricide and parricide had been transmuted to psychic analysis; incest and the sexual probing of his mother's body to the exploration of the human mind.

Egypt: the Journey West

I have remarked on the Egyptian setting of Freud's dream about his mother. Egypt had always fascinated Freud, as it had Napoleon, of whose Egyptian campaign Freud wrote, asking "where else could one go but Egypt if one were Joseph and wanted to loom large in the brothers' eyes?" (E. Freud 1960, p. 433). He loved to collect antiquities; his consulting room was filled with Egyptian statuettes. This collection was "his only extravagance" (Jones 1957, p. 297). Freud, like Oedipus, was the solver of the riddle of the sphinx, that fabulous monster of Egyptian origin. During his last five years, the heroic, cancer-ridden man had Egypt in the background of his still active and creative mind—Egypt as a kind of ground bass against which the themes of Joseph and Moses could play in counterpoint. Freud was writing and revising his Moses book in the years 1934–1938. Moses, according to Freud's idea, was—like Joseph, like Freud himself—a Jew and yet not a Jew. Freud had him an Egyptian, as Joseph had become an Egyptian. In the family romance fantasy, the child tries to evade his impulses toward his own parents by claiming another, usually a royal or divine, parentage. Moses was "found" by Pharaoh's daughter. Thus Pharaoh, and not Jacob, is the father to be reckoned with. The ambivalence inherent in the father-son confrontation, deflectable onto the struggle between siblings, figures in the Hebrew myths as the struggle between Egyptians and Jews. When Freud's book appeared in 1939, it was resented by many Jews because it attributed to an Egyptian the lineage and ideas of the greatest of Jewish cultural heroes. Moses, the godlike father-figure, was presented as the spiritual son of the Pharaoh Akhenaten!

Like Joseph, Freud had even had an Abraham who preceded him to Egypt. In his study of Amenhotep IV (Arhenaten), Abraham (1912) anticipated some of the things Freud was to say in *Moses and Monotheism*. It is so absolutely uncharacteristic of Freud not to mention Abraham's study (which Freud surely had read) in the Moses book, that one can only assume this represented a slip, and the forgetting was based on the hostility unconsciously associated with rivalry brought out by things Egyptian. Abraham was twenty years younger than Freud—the age difference that separated Freud from his older brother, Phillip. Abraham had died (in 1925) and therefore could also be a "revenant" of dead younger brother Julius.

Egypt had another ambivalent meaning for Freud during these years. It was both the place of refuge and plenty, and the land of exile and persecution. The Nazi invasion of Austria finally forced the old "conquistador," who in his life and in the imagery of his books was so often indulging his "earliest passion" (Freud 1887–1902) for travelling, to take his penultimate great journey to England. We know from his letters that he was thinking of earlier flights west—from Israel into Egypt. (According to Altman (1959) *west* symbolizes death; so, Freud (1900) says, does a *journey*.) His forebears had been forced to flee from Palestine to Bessarabia to Cologne to Bohemia; and when he was two, his father Jacob had chosen, because of anti-Semitic outbursts, to leave Sigmund's birthplace, Freiburg, for Leipzig and finally for Vienna. Now the escape to England could be seen as both a journey into, and a journey out of, Egypt. Egypt had been a haven offering sustenance—for Joseph fleeing from his persecuting brothers, for Jacob and his sons fleeing from famine. Up to the time of Moses, Egypt is represented in the Bible as a place for the Jews to go and live in freedom, thanks to Joseph and his providing for them the land of Goshen. But Egypt was also a land of exile and persecution. Moses led his people out of Egyptian bondage into the promised land of Canaan. And when he did so, the Bible says (Exodus 13:19) "Moses took with him the bones of Joseph who had exacted an oath from the children of Israel, that they would take his body back to the land of Jacob." For Freud, England had long been a promised land, but it was also a land of exile away from the city of Vienna, so often described in his letters to Fliess as detested and detestable: "I hate Vienna with a positively personal hatred, and, just the contrary of the giant Antaeus I draw fresh strength whenever I remove my feet from the soil of the city which is my home" (1887–1902, p. 311). Later it had become a "beloved prison." His feelings were most ambivalent; for all his threats of leaving and mutterings of hatred, he finally had to be forced to leave the city by his children, friends, and pupils, even after the Nazi takeover had made the hatred eminently justifiable. Not only was he leaving behind the many, many years of his past, he was also separating himself from the bones of his parents. The grave evokes the womb. For Joseph, this meant the cave of Machpelah where he could lie at peace with the bones of his ancestors. But Joseph never was buried with either Rachel or Jacob. His tomb lies apart, as does Freud's, and that of Oedipus who was not permitted burial in Athens but only at nearby Colonus. The city is a symbol for the mother, and to finally come to terms with that first object of hostility and love is to return to earth in a hallowed spot. It was perhaps in this sense that Freud longed for Vienna.

Freud was very ill, very aware of his old age and of his identity as father and patriarch. He was no longer Joseph going to Egypt to triumph over his brothers. He had come to terms with, and now again identified with, a greater and older rival, Jacob. The Biblical Jacob had gone to Egypt to be reunited with his lost son, Joseph, and was to die there in exile. It is as Jacob that Freud, awaiting emigration in Vienna, writes to his son, Ernst, in England: the role of Jacob that can coalesce himself as father, his own father, Jacob, the Biblical Patriarch, Jacob, and the Wandering Jew: "Two prospects keep me going in these grim times: to rejoin you all and—*to die in freedom* [last four words in English]. I sometimes compare myself with the old Jacob who, when a very old man, was taken by his children to Egypt, as Thomas Mann is to describe in his next novel. Let us hope it won't be also followed by an exodus from Egypt. It is high time that Ahasuerus [the Wandering Jew—forced, like Oedipus, to travel for his sins]came to rest somewhere" (E. Freud 1960, p. 442). He was going to England to die:

> To go back to the earth in London
> An Important Jew who died in exile. [Auden 1945, p. 163]

The great road from childhood to paternity had been completely traversed, the drive for power over father and brothers had been transcended. He had himself become a patriarch, the undisputed leader of a new school of thinking about, and helping, human beings:

> To us he is no more a person
> Now but a whole climate of opinion. [Auden 1945, p. 167]

And just before crossing the channel into England, the ambition of Joseph shows itself again. The old man dreams of himself as William the Conqueror! The wish to be the "conquistador," Messiah-ben-Joseph conquering the promised land, still stirred as he was about to embark on the last journey.

References

Abraham, K. (1912). Amenhotep IV: psycho-analytic contributions towards the understanding of his personality and of the monotheistic cult of Aton. In K. Abraham, *Clinical Papers and Essays on Psycho-Analysis*, pp. 262–290. London: Hogarth Press, 1955.

Altman, L. (1959). "West" as a symbol of death. *Psychoanalytic Quarterly* 28:236–241.

Auden, W. H. (1945). In memory of Sigmund Freud. *The Collected Poetry of W. H. Auden.* New York: Alfred A. Knopf.

Bakan, D. (1958). *Sigmund Freud and the Mystical Tradition.* Princeton: Van Nostrand.

Barea, I. (1966). *Vienna.* New York: Alfred A. Knopf.

Bernfeld, S. (1946). An unknown autobiographical fragment by Freud. *American Imago* 4:3–19.

———— (1949). Freud's scientific beginnings. *American Imago* 6:163–196.

Blamires, H. (1966). *The Bloomsday Book.* London: Methuen.

Eissler, K. R. (1963). *Goethe: A Psychoanalytic Study.* Detroit: Wayne State University Press.

Freud, A. (1965). *Normality and Pathology in Childhood.* New York: International Universities Press.

Freud, E. L., ed. (1960). *The Letters of Sigmund Freud.* New York: Basic Books.

Freud, S. (1887–1902). *The Origins of Psychoanalysis: Letters, Drafts and Notes to Wilhelm Fliess.* New York: Basic Books, 1954.

———— (1892–1899). Extracts from the Fliess papers. *Standard Edition* 1:175–289.

———— (1900). The interpretation of dreams. *Standard Edition* 4/5.

———— (1914). The Moses of Michelangelo. *Standard Edition* 13:211–236.

———— (1915). Thoughts for the times on war and death. *Standard Edition* 14:274–300.

———— (1916–1917). Introductory lectures on psychoanalysis. *Standard Edition* 15/16.

———— (1917). A childhood recollection from *Dichtung und Wahrheit.* Standard Edition 17:146–156.

———— (1919). Lines of advance in psycho-analytic therapy. *Standard Edition* 17:158–168.

———— (1925). An autobiographical study. *Standard Edition* 20:3–74.

———— (1936). A disturbance of memory on the acropolis. *Standard Edition* 22:239–248.

———— (1939). Moses and monotheism. *Standard Edition* 23:3–137.

Grotjahn, M. (1967). Sigmund Freud and the art of letter writing. *Journal of the American Medical Association* 200:13–18.

Jones, E. (1953). *Sigmund Freud, Life and Work,* 1. New York: Basic Books.

———— (1957). *Sigmund Freud, Life and Work,* 3. New York: Basic Books.

Joyce, J. (1934). *Ulysses.* New York: Random House.

Mann, T. (1936). Freud and the future. In T. Mann, *Freud, Goethe, Wagner*, pp. 3–45. New York: Alfred A. Knopf, 1937.

———— (1938). *Joseph in Egypt*. New York: Alfred A. Knopf.

———— (1948). *Joseph and His Brothers*. New York: Alfred A. Knopf.

Palmer, R., and Colton, J. (1965). *A History of the Modern World*. New York: Alfred A. Knopf.

Schur, M. (1972). *Freud: Living and Dying*. New York: International Universities Press.

Shengold, L. (1966). The metaphor of the journey in *The Interpretation of Dreams*. *American Imago* 23:316–331.

Sophocles (1943). Oedipus King (tr. Murray). In *Ten Greek Plays*. New York: Oxford University Press.

Wittels, F. (1924). *Sigmund Freud. His Personality, His Teaching and His School*. London: Allen and Unwin.

Zeligs, D. F. (1955). The personality of Joseph. *American Imago* 12:47–67.

Chapter 6

SOME ADDITIONAL "DAY RESIDUES" OF "THE SPECIMEN DREAM OF PSYCHOANALYSIS"

MAX SCHUR, M.D.

On June 12, 1900, following the publication of *The Interpretation of Dreams*, Freud wrote to Wilhelm Fliess:

> Life at the Bellevue [a house situated on a hill in one of the suburbs of Vienna, where Freud and his family were spending the summer, as they had also done the summer of 1895] is turning out very pleasantly for everyone. The evenings and mornings are enchanting; the scent of acacia and jasmine has succeeded that of lilac and laburnum, the wild roses are in bloom, and everything, as even I notice, seems suddenly to have burst out. [The translations in this essay differ somewhat from the published versions since they were made by Dr. Schur himself.]

Was it this expansive mood, a response to witnessing the miracle of spring, which made it possible for Freud to continue as follows:

This paper was supported in part by a grant from the Foundation for Research in Psychoanalysis, Berkeley, California. I am also indebted to the Sigmund Freud Copyright, Ltd. for permission to use certain of the unpublished letters of Sigmund Freud to Wilhelm Fliess. The article which appears here has been somewhat abridged. We have omitted an introductory section which is not germane to the paper's point and, in addition, have omitted the original German of many of the letters quoted.

Do you actually suppose that some day this house will have a marble plaque
with the inscription:

> "Here, on July 24, 1895, the mystery
> of dreams revealed itself to Dr. Sigm.
> Freud."

Or were there still other determinants?

This letter was written after Freud had overcome the letdown following the
feverish effort of completing *The Interpretation of Dreams*. It had been the kind
of letdown which frequently had certain characteristics of a depressive mood.
He had by then also mastered his disappointment over the almost total neglect
of the book by both the professional and the general public. (According to J.
Strachey's introduction to *The Interpretation of Dreams*, only 351 copies were
sold in the first six years after this book's publication!) Once before, in a letter
written on May 21, 1894, when his cardiac episode was at its height (see Schur
1966), Freud had expressed a similarly exuberant evaluation of his work, saying:
"I have the distinct feeling of having touched upon one of the great mysteries
of nature."

On the one hand, the letter of June 12, 1900, clearly indicates that Freud was
unshaken in the firm conviction, held throughout his life, that *The Interpretation
of Dreams* represented his *magnum opus*. On the other hand, it points to the
fact that his interpretation of the Irma dream ("of July 23rd–24th, 1895")
represented an important milestone in the development of his work.

We can trace Freud's interest in dreams to his betrothal letters (Freud 1960;
Jones 1953–1957; Eissler 1964). In a footnote to his first case history in the
Studies on Hysteria (1895), Freud reports his attempts to understand some of
his own dreams. This effort was necessitated in part by the more and more
frequent reporting of dreams on the part of patients in the course of their associations. In a letter to Fliess of March 4, 1895, Freud not only reports to Fliess
about the dream of Rudi Kaufmann (Rudolf Kaufmann, who later became one
of Vienna's leading cardiologists), indicating that he had already formulated the
wish-fulfillment hypothesis of dreams (1900, p. 125; 1950, Letter 22), but also
alludes to the "dream psychosis" of one of his patients, Emma, about whom
we shall hear quite a lot later in this paper. This passage in his letter indicates
that Freud had already concluded that there were certain analogies between the
dream and neurotic and psychotic symptom formation.

Freud indicates in a footnote to the preamble of the Irma dream that this was
the first dream he had submitted to a "thorough interpretation." The letter
quoted at the beginning of this paper also claims that the secret of the dream
had been unveiled to Freud on the occasion of his analysis of the Irma dream.

This statement has been tacitly accepted in the psychoanalytic literature (see, for example, Erikson 1954). We may assume, however, that this *systematic* dream interpretation was only the culmination of an ongoing process, which must have lasted for quite some time.

The previously quoted remarks from the Fliess correspondence indicate that by that time Freud took it for granted that dreams were meaningful and could be understood. He tried to understand the dreams of his patients and to relate them to the latter's symptomatology. In 1914 he stated that *The Interpretation of Dreams* had to a great extent been finished by 1896. In the book itself (1900, p. 104) he mentions that he has "analyzed over a thousand dreams" of his neurotic patients. The reference to the dreams of Rudi Kaufmann (a nephew of Breuer) indicates that Freud's friends and colleagues must have been aware of his interest in dreams and were "collecting" them for him. Even if Freud's recollection that *The Interpretation of Dreams* was practically finished in 1896 (with the exception of Chapters Six and Seven) proved to be not entirely accurate, as shown by the Fliess correspondence, he must have partly analyzed an ample number of his own and his patients' dreams in those earlier years.

What Freud may have been attempting for the first time with the Irma dream was the systematic application of free association to every single element of the manifest dream, after which he connected these associations until a meaningful trend emerged. While the meaningfulness of dreams and their importance in our mental life were already familiar to Freud, this systematic analysis alone enabled him to discover the mechanism of the "dream work," which was of course the unveiling of a mystery, the stripping off of one of the "seven veils."

The Fliess correspondence points to an additional reason for Freud's interest in his own dreams. He reveals his increasing awareness that progress in understanding the intricacies of neurotic symptoms would have to be paralleled by an understanding of normal phenomena, all of which he could achieve in part by self-analysis. The letters to Fliess indicate that Freud's systematic self-analysis began some time in the spring of 1897, when the crucial importance of the first years of life had become apparent to him.

This *systematic* self-analysis, however, was preceded by a prolonged introductory phase, during which Freud had to develop the tools necessary for this effort. This was analogous to the prolonged phase of dream interpretation which had preceded the *systematic* attempt to interpret the Irma dream. During this introductory phase of Freud's analysis, the interpretation of his own dreams probably played an important part, as it did to an even greater extent after he had "unraveled the mystery of the dream" by analyzing the Irma dream.

This introductory phase showed many of the aspects common to the unfolding of the analytic situation so familiar to us through the treatment of our patients and students and our own firsthand experience with analysis. The most important ingredient of this preliminary phase was what we would recognize in the light of present-day concepts as full-fledged transference phenomena, which in Freud's unique case manifested themselves to a large extent in his relationship to Fliess. Certain aspects of this transference situation were apparent during Freud's cardiac episode, the most severe symptoms of which preceded the Irma dream (for a detailed discussion, see Schur 1966).

The material to be presented will make apparent the manner in which these transference phenomena manifested themselves in an episode preceding the Irma dream, influenced the content of that dream and Freud's associations to it, and probably also interfered to some extent with his interpretation.

Freud indicates in several passages of his interpretation of the Irma dream that he will not pursue a certain train of thought any further. In the last paragraph of the chapter dealing with the Irma dream, Freud says:

> I will not pretend that I have completely uncovered the meaning of this dream or that its interpretation is without a gap. I could spend much more time over it, derive further information from it and discuss fresh problems raised by it. I myself know the points from which further trains of thought could be followed. But considerations which arise in the case of every dream of my own restrain me from pursuing my interpretative work. If anyone should feel tempted to express a hasty condemnation of my reticence, I would advise him to make the experiment of being franker than I am. [p. 120–121]

Many passages of the dream lend themselves to speculation about additional meanings. An ingenious "supplement" to Freud's interpretation of the Irma dream was attempted by Erikson (1954), who used this "dream specimen" to elaborate on some of his theoretical concepts. I shall refrain from speculation and limit myself to comparing and contrasting some additional day residues of the Irma dream with Freud's associations and the interpretations derived from them.

On the assumption that the Irma dream (his dream is frequently called the dream of Irma's injection, thus singling out one element to represent the whole) is sufficiently familiar to the reader, I shall omit a verbatim quotation of the whole dream and Freud's associations (see 1900, pp. 106–121 and 292–295).

Freud gives us the following background for this dream (the italicized portions pertain to the supplementary information supplied in the hitherto unpublished material).

Freud was spending the summer of 1895 at the Bellevue, slowly recovering from a severe cardiac episode which had started in the fall of 1893 and had reached a critical phase in the spring of 1894. He had recently resumed smoking in defiance of Fliess's strict orders (see Freud 1950, Letter 25 of June 12, 1895). His wife, who had arranged a party for her birthday on July 26, was in the fourth month of her sixth pregnancy.

Freud had broken off for the summer months the treatment of his patient Irma, who had shown partial improvement. *At that point the concepts of resistance and working through had not yet occurred to Freud,* so that he had been blaming Irma for not accepting his "solution" to her symptoms. He was aware (as opposed to Breuer) of the importance of a positive, sexualized transference in the treatment of hysterics, *but was not yet familiar with the intricacies of the transference neurosis* and the difficulties inherent in its dissolution, especially under the contaminated circumstances of a close social relationship.

Freud was faced with a special dilemma, which had haunted all succeeding generations of analysts. Irma was still suffering from certain (gastric) somatic symptoms; *were they due to an unresolved element of her neurosis or to an organic condition? Was he blaming her unjustly for not accepting his interpretations and thereby preventing her own full recovery, when in reality she was suffering from an organic illness?* (Freud added a footnote in 1909 stating that Irma's "unresolved" gastric pains were forerunners of gallstones, thus indicating his ongoing concern about this matter.) He had the impression of mild reproof from a remark made with reference to Irma by his friend "Otto" (Dr. Oskar Rie, one of Freud's oldest and most devoted friends, the pediatrician of Freud's children, and the future brother-in-law of Fliess), *and he had sat down that evening and written a long report to M.* (Breuer), who had obviously referred Irma to Freud for treatment, "in order *to justify himself.*"

Freud's relationship to Breuer had been quite strained during the year 1894, but in a letter to Fliess of May 25, 1895, Freud emphasized that Breuer had changed his attitude completely and had fully accepted Freud's theory of sexuality.

I quote below first the pertinent facts from the Irma dream, and later Freud's associations. I shall italicize what seem to me the salient features. (Throughout this essay *all* italics in quotations are mine. To distinguish them from Freud's italics in the original, mine will be designated by asterisks.)

A large hall—numerous guests, whom we were receiving —Among them was Irma. I at once took her on one side, as though to answer her letter and to *reproach her for not having accepted my* "solution" yet. I said to her: "*If you still get pains, it's really only your fault.*" She replied: "If you only knew what pains I've got now *in my throat* and stomach and abdomen—it's choking me"—I was alarmed and looked at her. She looked pale and puffy.

I thought to myself that after all I must be missing some organic trouble. I took her to the window and looked down her throat, and she showed signs of recalcitrance. . . . *She then opened her mouth properly* and on the right I found a big white patch; at another place I *saw extensive whitish grey scabs* upon some remarkable curly structures which were *evidently modelled on the turbinal bones of the nose.—I at once called in Dr. M., and he repeated the examination and confirmed it. . . . My friend Otto was now standing beside her as well*, and my friend Leopold was percussing her through her bodice and saying: "She has a dull area low down on the left." . . . M. said: "There's no doubt it's an infection, but no matter; dysentery will supervene and the toxin will be eliminated." . . . *We were directly aware, too, of the origin of the infection.* Not long before, when she was feeling unwell, *my friend Otto had given her an injection* of a preparation of propyl, propyls . . . propionic acid . . . trimethylamin (and I saw before me the formula for this printed in heavy type). . . . *Injections of that sort ought not to be made so thoughtlessly. . . . And probably the syringe had not been clean.* [1900, p. 107]

The chain of Freud's associations to the individual elements of the dream led him far afield. They brought back painful memories of situations in which he could not have failed to feel self-reproach. This applied, above all, to the episode involving Fleischl, Freud's admired friend and brilliant senior colleague, a man of high social standing and wealth, endowed with unusual physical and intellectual qualities. Fleischl had been a victim of his profession and succumbed to the consequences of what had first been a morphine addiction and then, as Freud had tried to cure him by cocaine, a cocaine addiction even more tragic than the original (see Jones 1953, pp. 78–97).

Freud was also reminded of the patient who had actually died of *toxicity* from the sulphonal he had prescribed for her.

However, all of his associations led Freud to the interpretation that he had succeeded in displacing all blame to others—his friend Otto (Rie), Dr. M. (Breuer), Irma, who would not accept his solutions, other female patients, even his pregnant wife. The hostile associations were directed mainly against Otto, who had given Irma the injection with a dirty syringe, and Dr. M., who as a consultant had to some extent made a fool of himself by confusing dysentery and diphtheria. They were also directed against Irma and most of the other females he associated with her.

Freud summarizes the wish fulfillment of the Irma dream as follows:

The conclusion of the dream . . . was that *I was not responsible for the* *persistence of Irma's pains, but that Otto was.* Otto had in fact annoyed me by his remarks about Irma's incomplete cure, and the dream gave me my revenge by throwing the reproach back on to him. The dream acquitted me of the responsibility for Irma's condition by showing that it was due to other factors—it produced a whole series of reasons. The dream represented a particular state of affairs as I should have wished it to be. *Thus its content was the fulfilment of a wish and its motive was a wish.**

Thus much leapt to the eyes. But many of the details of the dream also became intelligible to me from the point of view of wish-fulfilment. Not only did I revenge myself on Otto for being too hasty in taking sides against me by representing him as being too hasty in his medical treatment (in giving the injection); but I also revenged myself on him for giving me the bad liqueur which had an aroma of fusel oil. . . . This did not satisfy me and I pursued my revenge further by contrasting him with his more trustworthy competitor. I seemed to be saying: "I like *him** better than *you."** But Otto was not the only person to suffer from the vials of my wrath. I took revenge as well on my disobedient patient by exchanging her for one who was wiser and less recalcitrant. Nor did I allow Dr. M. to escape the consequences of his con- tradiction but showed him by means of a clear allusion that he was an ig- noramus on the subject. ("*Dysentery will supervene,** etc.") Indeed I seemed to be appealing from him to someone else with greater knowledge (to my friend who had told me of trimethylamin) just as I had turned from Irma to her friend and from Otto to Leopold. . . . The groundlessness of the re- proaches was proved for me in the dream in the most elaborate fashion: *I** was not to blame for Irma's pains, since she herself was to blame for them by refusing to accept my solution. *I** was not concerned with Irma's pains, *since they were of an organic nature and quite incurable by psychological treatment.* . . . Irma's pains had been caused by Otto giving her an incautious injection of an unsuitable drug—a thing *I** should never have done. Irma's pains were the results of an injection with a dirty needle. . . . [1900, p. 118–121]

This friend "with greater knowledge" was, of course, Fliess, who entered the chain of Freud's associations to the dream in connection with the word "trimethylamin" and also with the association of "pyemia":

What was it, then, to which my attention was to be directed in this way by trimethylamin? It was to a conversation with another friend who had for many years been familiar with all my writings during the period of their gestation, just as I had been with his. He had at that time confided some ideas to me on the subject of the chemistry of the sexual processes, and had mentioned among other things that he believed that one of the products of sexual metabolism was trimethylamin. [p. 116]

I began to guess why the formula for trimethylamin had been so prominent in the dream. So many important subjects converged upon that one word. Trimethylamin was an allusion not only to the immensely powerful factor of sexuality, *but also to a person whose agreement I recalled with satisfaction whenever I felt isolated in my opinions. Surely this friend who played so large a part in my life must appear again elsewhere in these trains of thought. Yes. For he had a special knowledge of the consequences of affections of the nose and its accessory cavities*; and he had drawn scientific attention to some very remarkable connections between the *turbinal bones* and the female organs of sex. (Cf. the three curly structures in Irma's throat.) *I had had Irma examined by him to see whether her gastric pains might be of nasal origin.* But *he suffered himself from suppurative rhinitis, which caused me anxiety*; and no doubt there was an allusion to this in the *pyaemia* which vaguely came into my mind in connection with the metastases in the dream. [1900, p. 117]

Freud returns to this part of his associations in his discussion of the process of condensation in dreams:

On the one hand we see the group of ideas attached to my friend Otto, who did not understand me, who sided against me, and who made me a present of liqueur with an aroma of amyl. On the other hand we see—linked to the former group by its very contrast—the group of ideas attached to my friend in Berlin [Wilhelm Fliess], who *did* understand me, who would take my side, and to whom I owed so much valuable information, dealing, amongst other things, with the chemistry of the sexual process.

The recent exciting causes—the actual instigators of the dream—determined what was to attract my attention in the "Otto" group; the amyl was among these selected elements, which were predestined to form part of the dream-content. The copious "Wilhelm" group was stirred up precisely through being in contrast to "Otto," and those elements in it were emphasized which echoed those which were already stirred up in "Otto." All through the dream, indeed, I kept on turning from someone who annoyed me to someone else who could be agreeably contrasted with him; point by point, I called up a friend against an opponent. [1900, p. 294–295]

We may therefore add to Freud's summation that his associations and interpretations reaffirm the exalted position of his friend Wilhelm Fliess, who *knows better* than Otto or M. and *understands Freud fully*.

After this lengthy introduction, I come now to the supplementary background material for the Irma dream which will constitute, so to speak, a preamble to Freud's preamble.

We are accustomed to applying the term "day residues" to material originating during the few days preceding a dream. We know, however, that preconscious material resulting from events of previous weeks can actually influence both the manifest and the latent contents of a dream if, on the one hand, more recent events provide the means for representing such preconscious material, and, on the other hand, this preconscious material contains id derivatives of sufficient intensity to press for discharge through representation in the dream (see also Fisher 1954).

In the course of preparing another publication (Schur 1966), I studied the unpublished letters of Freud to Fliess. From a series of these letters the following facts emerged: Freud had treated a female patient, Emma, for hysteria. In the correspondence, this patient is first mentioned in the previously quoted letter of March 4, 1895. Like Irma, Emma had been examined by Fliess, at Freud's request, to determine if there was a partly "nasal origin" of her somatic symptoms. (Fliess, who had started his medical career as a nose and throat specialist, claimed on the grounds of his clinical observations that the application of cocaine to nasal mucous membranes and the performing of certain surgical procedures on the turbinate bone and the nasal sinuses could favorably influence a wide variety of symptoms such as migraine, Ménière's syndrome, neuralgias not restricted to the head, gastrointestinal disorders, and, above all, disturbances of various sexual functions. He coined the term *nasal-reflex neurosis*, and on Freud's suggestion published in 1897 a monograph entitled *Die Beziehungen zwischen Nase und weiblichen Geschlechtsorganen in ihren biologischen Bedeutungen dargestellt* ("Representation of the Relationship Between the Nose and the Female Sex Organs in their Biological Significance"). For further details and bibliography, see Freud 1950.) Fliess had come to Vienna, recommended surgery (apparently of the turbinate bone and one of the sinuses—compare the Irma dream), and had operated on her there, returning to Berlin a few days later.

The letter of March 4, 1895 begins with the following passages:

Dearest Wilhelm,

We really can't be satisfied with Emma's condition; persistent swelling, going up and down "like an avalanche," pain to the point where morphine is indispensable, poor nights. The purulent secretion has somewhat decreased since yesterday. The day before yesterday (Saturday) she had a massive hemorrhage, probably because a bone chip the size of a penny had come loose; there were about two bowlfuls. Today we encountered some resistance on irrigation, and because the pain and edema had increased, I let myself be persuaded to call in G. [Gersuny, a prominent Viennese surgeon]. (By the way, he greatly admired an etching of "The Isle of the Dead" [by Böcklin].) He stated that the access [to the cavity] had considerably contracted and was insufficient for drainage. He inserted a rubber tube and threatened to break it [the bone] open if this didn't stay in. To judge by the smell, all this is probably right. Please send me your authoritative advice. I don't look forward to new surgery on this girl. . . .

On March 8, 1895, Freud wrote to Fliess:

Dearest Wilhelm,

Just received your letter and am able to answer it immediately. Fortunately I am finally seeing my way clear and feel reassured about Miss Emma, about whom I can give you a report which will probably upset you as much as me; but I hope you will also get over it as fast I have.

I wrote you that the swelling and bleeding wouldn't let up, and that suddenly a foetid odor set in along with an obstacle to irrigation (or was the latter new?). I arranged for Gersuny to be called in, and he inserted a drain, hoping that things would work out if discharge were re-established. Otherwise he behaved in a rather rejecting way. Two days later I was awakened early in the morning—quite profuse bleeding had started again, with pain, etc. I got a telephone message from G[ersuny] that he could come only in the evening, so I asked R. [an ear, nose and throat specialist. Cf. the Irma dream: "I at once called in Dr. M."] to meet me [at Miss Emma's apartment]. This we did at noon. There was moderate bleeding from the nose and mouth; the foetid odor was very bad. R. cleaned the area surrounding the opening, removed some blood clots which were sticking to the surface, and suddenly pulled at something like a thread. He kept right on pulling, and before either of us had time to think, at least half a meter of gauze had been removed from the cavity. The next moment came a flood of blood. The patient turned white, her eyes bulged, and her pulse was no longer palpable. However, immediately after this he packed the cavity with fresh iodoform gauze, and the hemorrhage stopped. It had lasted about half a minute, but this was enough to make the poor creature, who by then we had lying quite flat, unrecognizable. In the meantime, or actually afterwards, something else happened. At the moment the foreign body came out, and everything had become obvious to me, immediately after which I was confronted with the sight of the patient, I felt sick. After she had been packed I fled to the next room, drank a bottle of water, and felt rather miserable. The brave Frau Doktor then brought me a small glass of cognac [cf. the liqueur of the Irma dream], and I felt like myself again.

R. remained with the patient until I arranged to have both of them taken to the Loew Sanatorium [a private hospital] by S. Nothing more happened that evening. The following day, i.e., yesterday, Thursday, the operation was repeated with the assistance of G. The bone was broken wide open, the packing removed, and the wound curetted. There was hardly any further bleeding. She had not lost consciousness during the severe hemorrhage scene [the literal translation of *Verblutungsszene* would be "the scene of bleeding to death"], and when I returned to the room somewhat shaky, she greeted me with the condescending remark: "This is the strong sex."

I don't think I had been overwhelmed by the blood; affects were welling up in me at that moment. *So we had done her an injustice. She had not been abnormal at all, but a piece of iodoform gauze had gotten torn off when you removed the rest, and stayed in for fourteen days* [There is hardly a more sickeningly foetid odor than that of iodoform gauze left in a wound for fourteen days. There is also an absorption of iodoform with *toxic* effects (cf. associations to the Irma dream: sulphonal, cocaine toxicity; the poisonous, smelly fusel oil).], interfering with the healing process, after which it had torn away and provoked the bleeding. [There is a subtle slip in the wording of this sentence; Freud does not say: *sie wurde losgerissen, was die Blutung provociert hat*—"it [the gauze] was torn away, which provoked the bleeding." In Freud's wording, the gauze tore away, thus becoming the sole culprit! Here begins the displacement operative in the Irma dream, of which we shall see further evidence.] The fact that this mishap should have happened to *you*, how you would react to it when you learned about it, what others would make of it, how wrong I had been to press you to operate in a foreign city where you couldn't handle the aftercare, how my intention of getting [Freud's use of the word *anzuthun* from *anthun* is quite ambiguous. The correct translation is "inflict"—used prevalently in the sense of inflicting violence, pain, etc.] the best for the poor girl was insidiously thwarted, with the resultant danger to her life—all this came over me simultaneously. I have worked it off [see bracketed material following "assimilated" in the next paragraph] by now. *I was not sufficiently clear-headed to think of reproaching R. at that moment.* [Now R. had become the culprit. The displacement operative in the Irma dream is continuing full force.] That occurred to me only ten minutes later; he should have thought immediately. "There is something there; don't pull it out or you'll start a hemorrhage; stick some more in, take her to Loew and do the cleaning and widening [of the opening to the cavity—obviously the sinus] at the same time. [Freud's medical reasoning is also highly subjective at this point. The need for displacement still holds sway. The removal of the old iodoform gauze would inevitably have been followed by a hemorrhage, even if done in the hospital, and R. must have had things quite well under control if the hemorrhage lasted only half a minute and he had another packing ready. However, at the end of the paragraph, Freud is somewhat more charitable with poor R.] But he was just as surprised as I was.

Now that I have assimilated [Freud's use of the word *verarbeiten* ("assimilate") here, and of the word *aufarbeiten* ("work off") in the paragraph above, indicates that he was going through progressive phases of a process to which he later assigned the term *durcharbeiten* ("working through"), an important technical concept of psychoanalysis] all this, nothing remains but sincere compassion for my "child of sorrow" [*Schmerzenskind*]. Indeed, I shouldn't have tortured you, but I had every reason to entrust you with such a matter and with even more than this. You handled it as well as possible. The tearing off of the iodoform gauze was one of those accidents [Freud had not yet written *The Psychopathology of Everyday Life!*] that happen to the most fortunate and cautious of surgeons. . . . G[ersuny] mentioned that he had had a similar experience, and that he therefore used iodoform wicks instead of gauze (you must remember this from your own case). [Apparently Fliess had been operated on by Gersuny. This is about as far as Freud goes in expressing a veiled reproach: "Why didn't *you* use wicks on Emma instead of gauze, as G. did with you?"] Of course no one blames you in any way, nor do I know why they should. [Freud did not yet know that such protestations and negations stood for their opposite!] And I only hope that you will come as quickly as I did to feel only pity. [Freud's use of the word *Bedauern* is also ambiguous. While it can be used in the sense of pity, commiseration, the common meaning is that of regret.] Rest assured that I felt no need to restore my trust in you. I only want to add that I hesitated for a day to tell you all about it, and that then I began to be ashamed, and here is the letter.

In view of all this, any other news had obviously faded into the background. As far as my condition is concerned, you are certainly right. In some peculiar way I'm never more productive than when I have mild symptoms like these. So I've been writing page after page of "The Therapy of Hysterias."

There is a peculiar idea of a different kind that I'll confess to you only after we have Emma off our minds.

> With cordial greetings,
> Your
> Sigm.

However, this was not the end of the Emma affair. Nearly three weeks later, Freud writes:

Vienna, March 28, 1895

Dearest Wilhelm,

I know what you want to hear first: *she* is doing tolerably well, completely calmed down, no fever, no hemorrhage. The packing which was inserted six days ago is still in, and we hope to be safe from new surprises. Of course, she is starting to develop new hysterias from this past period, which then are being dissolved by me.

I must take it in my stride that you are not quite so well either. I hope this won't be for long. I suppose you will work your way out of it pretty soon. . . .

My own condition is not especially bad, but keeps me out of sorts. A pulse as irregular as that seems after all to preclude well-being. The motoric insufficiency was intolerable for several days. [For a discussion of Freud's cardiac symptoms, see Schur (1966). As far as the Irma dream is concerned, I shall mention only that Freud himself was uncertain whether he was suffering from an organic heart condition or nicotine toxicity.] I would like to accept your proposition, but the present time is obviously not propitious. Besides this, my practice is particularly poor at the moment, and as far as my mood is concerned, I'm mostly quite useless.

April 2. [Freud only rarely allowed a letter to remain unposted for several days.] These past days I have really felt abjectly unconcerned. Writing has been difficult; at such times I am unbearable; the slightest indications of fluctuating changes of mood. Now I'm of a piece again, and also "strong of heart," but wildly thirsty to enjoy some of the spring. Perhaps it is not so important how I felt or feel. But I have little that is important to report . . . .

In general I miss you badly. Am I really the same person who was overflowing with ideas and projects as long as you were within reach? When I sit down at my desk in the evening, I often don't know *what** I would work on. [This is the kind of mood which Freud frequently described in 1897, during the time of his *systematic* self-analysis, indicating clearly that he had already been "in analysis" well before that year.]

She, Miss Emma, is doing well; she is a nice, decent girl who does not blame either of us in this affair, and who speaks of you with high esteem.

Keep quite well; give me detailed reports about yourself and don't take me to task this time. Another time I'll swamp you with letters and enclosures. *You are steady; I am not.*

Cordially your
Sigm.

The calm did not last long. After two weeks Freud reports again:

Vienna, April 11, 1895

Dearest Wilhelm,

Gloomy times, unbelievably gloomy. Mainly this business with Emma which is rapidly deteriorating. I reported to you last time that G. had inspected the cavity under general anesthesia, palpated it, and declared it satisfactory. We indulged our hopes and the patient was gradually recovering. However, eight days ago she began to bleed with the packing in place, something which had not happened before. She was packed again. The bleeding was minimal. Two days ago a new hemorrhage, again with the packing in place, and by now more than ample. New packing, renewed helplessness. Yesterday, R. wanted to re-examine the cavity. A new hypothesis about the source of the hemorrhage after the first operation (the one performed by you) had by chance been suggested by Weil. [Another ear, nose and throat specialist. While Freud was protesting adamantly that no one could accuse Fliess of any negligence, his hint about Weil's remark had far-reaching repercussions (see below).] As soon as the packing was partly out, there was a new, highly dangerous hemorrhage, which I witnessed. It didn't spurt, [Cf. Irma's injection: *Es spritzte nicht*] but it surged, something like a [fluid] level rising exceedingly fast and then overflowing everything. It must have been a large vessel; but which one, and where? We of course couldn't see anything, and were glad that the packing was inside again. Add to this the pain, the morphine, the demoralization resulting from the obvious medical helplessness, and the whole air of danger, and you can picture the state the poor girl is in. We don't know what can be done. R. has been resisting the suggestion that he perform a ligation of the carotid artery. The danger that she will start to run a fever is also not far off. [Cf. the Irma dream: "there is no doubt it is an infection"; the association: pyemia might set it; the allusion to Fliess's suppurative rhinitis.] I'm really quite shaken that such a misfortune can have arisen from this operation, which was depicted as harmless. [This is a less disguised but still not conscious accusation of Fliess.]

I am not sure that I should attribute exclusively to this depressing business the fact that my cardiac condition is so much below par for this year of my illness. [Freud's worst attack of anginal pain with paroxysmal tachycardia had occurred just one year before this letter was written (Schur, 1966).] After an interruption of several months I have started to take strophantus [a digitalislike drug] again so as to have a less miserable pulse, but I have not yet succeeded. Mood and strength are very low. I shall spend Easter with Rie ["Otto"] on the Semmering, and perhaps pull myself together there. . . .

With cordial regards to you and your dear wife,

Your
   Sigm.

Fliess must have been quite offended by Weil's remark as reported to him by Freud (see letter of April 11, 1895). The immediate consequence was that Fliess probably demanded some kind of "testimonial" from Gersuny (who was the more renowned surgeon) that the latter did not share Weil's belief in the connection between Emma's continuing hemorrhage and the operation performed on her by Fliess. To this demand Freud replied with the following letter:

Vienna, April 20, 1895

Dearest Wilhelm,

The Easter trip and one day in Abbazia have delayed my answer to your letter. I shall mail to you today the proofs of the second part of our book [Breuer and Freud: *Studies on Hysteria* (1893–1895)], do not be bothered by the misprints. I am delighted that for once I can write about something [other] [the word "other" (*anderen*) which obviously belongs here was omitted, raising a doubt about what Freud really wanted to say] than the two tedious states of health. Your health is fortunately no longer on the agenda. We are so ungrateful; how hesitant we were about surgery and all the dangers it entailed. [Fliess had had to undergo some surgery.] Now we hardly say a word about it having been successful and your being able to work again. I want to rejoice out loud, and I now wait to hear about your scientific discoveries.

Of course I immediately informed R. of your suggestions concerning Emma. Naturally things look different from close up, for example, the hemorrhage. I can assure you that for the surgeons, to sit around and wait would have been out of the question. It was bleeding as though from the carotid artery. Within half a minute she would have bled to death. However, she is doing better now. The packing was carefully and gradually removed. There was no mishap, and she is now in the clear.

The writer of this is still very miserable, but is also quite offended that you should deem it necessary to have a testimonial from G. for your rehabilitation. Even if G. should have the same opinion of your skill as Weil, for me you remain the healer, the prototype of the man into whose hands one confidently entrusts one's life and that of one's family. I wanted to tell you of my misery, perhaps ask you for some advice about Emma, but not reproach you for anything. *This would have been stupid, unjustified, in clear contradiction to my feelings. . . .*

With this letter Freud probably reached the high watermark of his transference relationship to Fliess. It also tells us why his positive feelings were so strong. In this letter Freud is addressing not only Fliess the "mentor," the substitute analyst, but the healer who is also his physician. (In another unpublished letter, Freud even begins with the salutation *Lieber Zauberer*—"Dear Magician".) The last sentence of this letter clearly illustrates the "transference" situation. Freud stresses that any doubt about Fliess's skill would be in clear contradiction to his *feelings*. "Transference" is mainly an expression of "feelings" and not of logical thinking.

The last letter referring to the Emma episode prior to the Irma dream was written on May 25, 1895. Emma's condition was finally stabilized and the bleeding had stopped. She was convalescing and continuing with her treatment. An epilogue with a "happy ending" followed about a year later and will be quoted further on.

The link between the Emma episode and the Irma dream is self-evident, and I shall single out only a few links to the manifest dream content and to Freud's associations, as reported by him.

Here was a patient being treated by Freud for hysteria who *did* have an organic, largely "iatrogenic" illness; who had narrowly escaped death because a physician really had committed an error; whose pathology was located in the nasal cavity; whose case had confronted Freud with a number of emergencies requiring him urgently to call in several consultants, all of whom had been helpless and confused; Emma's lesion had a foetid odor (propylamyl); Freud had had to look repeatedly into her nose and mouth.

The most pertinent link is to be found in Freud's attitude toward Fliess, reflected in his letters about the Emma affair, his associations about Fliess in connection with the manifest dream content, and his final interpretation of the dream.

The second letter of March 8th already contains the whole conflict: Freud was shocked by the outcome of Emma's symptoms, the severe hemorrhage, and the "slip" of Fliess. In his letter Freud attributes his spell of faintness not to the impact of Emma's hemorrhage but to the affects which were welling up in him at that moment. "So *we* had done her an *injustice*." Hence, the first, overwhelming affect was guilt, because "we"—Freud and Fliess—shared in the responsibility. To accuse both himself *and* Fliess was apparently intolerable; hence his spell of weakness, after which the process of displacement began. [In later years, Freud had two fainting spells in the presence of Fliess and two in the presence of Jung (see Jones 1953, p. 317; 1955, pp. 55, 146). Freud himself linked the last of these fainting spells (in 1912) to Fliess and to the death of his younger brother when Freud was about two years old. This brother had died in 1858—the year Fliess was born (Schur 1966).] Freud had hesitated for an entire day about telling Fliess of the complication. However, within a matter of ten minutes he had already, at least tentatively, displaced all his reproaches first to the gauze and then to R. Compare this with the Irma dream, in which his dear friend Otto became the culprit. At that time Freud did not yet know that negations of reproaches, solemn protestations of trust, can only mean a defense against their opposite. When Freud confesses his shame about hesitating to write the letter to Fliess, he is confessing his guilt for actually having blamed Fliess.

This letter, which expresses such painful emotions, is full of contradictions arising from largely unconscious conflicts between positive and highly critical—hence hostile—feelings. Showing clearly the very mechanisms that Freud was soon to detect as the elements of the dream work (for example, displacement, condensation, etc.), it reads like a record of an analytic session. [The Fliess correspondence, especially some of the unpublished letters, contains many similar examples.] The explanation is obvious. Freud was by that time already "in analysis," at a stage where the "material" was pouring out in free associations. While Freud was in the main his own analyst, he was manifesting at this stage in his relationship with Fliess what we would now call transference phenomena, and he could not yet afford to abandon his positive "transference" to Fliess.

Only after the death of his father in 1896, which occurred at a time when he had already been engaged for a year and a half in *systematically* analyzing his own dreams and those of his patients, and when the crucial importance of early childhood events had begun to dawn on him, could he also begin what was to be his most heroic feat—his *systematic* self-analysis. This led to the reconstruction of early infantile material; the discovery of the oedipus complex, anality, and other aspects of early infantile fantasies; and eventually to the dissolution of this "transference" relationship to Fliess.

And this brings us back to the beginning of this paper, and Freud's challenging, proud letter about the Irma dream. That letter was written on June 12, 1900.

A study of the Fliess correspondence (including the unpublished letters) indicates clearly that while the actual final break in the relationship between Freud and Fliess did not occur until their last meeting, during the summer of 1900, the change in Freud's attitude was a gradual one, with many ups and downs (Schur 1966). Freud's letter of March 23, 1900 (1950, Letter 131) represents one of the final turning points in his inner relationship to Fliess. [See Kris's introduction to Freud (1950), and his footnote to Letter 138 of July 7, 1900.]

Could the triumphant letter referring to the Irma dream have been an (unconscious) challenge to Fliess, telling him, in essence: "One part of me thinks in terms of *ere perennius*—lasting fame—and that part of me already knew at the time of the Irma dream who had committed an error and whom I really had to protect because the other part of me was not yet as strong, sure, and *steady* [see letter of March 28, 1895] as it is now"? Could this episode have been the first step, therefore, in the direction of loosening the "transference"?

The two letters that followed, especially the second, indicate some of Freud's doubts: was the hemorrhage connected with something which had happened during the first operation, apart from the "lost" gauze packing? Are operations of this kind really necessary, especially if they are not all that harmless? We may also speculate that another doubt arose at this point: is the theory of the nasal origin of abdominal, and more especially, genital symptoms really cogent? Should I really have all my patients examined by Fliess? Should I constantly treat my own nose with cocaine?

And what of Fliess's symptoms? Why does he have such persistent headaches and nasal suppurations?

Is the defiance of Fliess (the resumption of smoking [see Freud 1950, Letter 25 of June 12, 1895]) another indication of the growing conflict? And the praise of Breuer in the preceding letter of May 25, 1895?

However, none of this could have reached consciousness in 1895. In the Irma dream Fliess had again to be put in the exalted role of the knowing, understanding, superior friend. The blame had to be displaced to Rie (Otto), while M. (Breuer) had to be ridiculed.

Does this addition detract from the historical importance of the Irma dream? In no way. In the interpretation of the Irma dream Freud first used the systematic analysis of each individual element of the dream. He discovered such mechanisms of the dream work as condensation, displacement, overdetermination, multiple representation, the wish-fulfillment function of dreams, etc. He had thus unveiled most, but not all, of the mysteries of the dream. He was, for example, not yet aware of the transference implication of dreams. Freud was right in claiming that the wish fulfillment of the Irma dream was a displacement of his responsibility for any failure with his patients, and a disclaimer that he had not been conscientious. Moreover, the complex process of displacement, which had started during the traumatic scene of Emma's hemorrhage, had freed Freud at least temporarily from guilt, thereby facilitating a similar displacement in the Irma dream.

But it was not only his own exculpation that he achieved; it was the need to exculpate Fliess from responsibility for Emma's nearly fatal complications that was probably the strongest (immediate) motive for the constellation of this dream. Why was this so?

Fliess was not only Freud's admired friend, his sounding board and therefore a substitute analyst; he was also the only one who not only believed in Freud's theories but also took the repeated changes of Freud's tentative formulations for granted, encouraged any new discovery, however revolutionary, and provided Freud's only "audience," his only protection from complete isolation.

Fliess was even more than this. Freud was just emerging from a severe cardiac episode which had started in the fall of 1893 and reached its culmination in April, 1894. During this period one of Fliess's roles was that of trusted physician, the source of constant support. Nothing describes this role better than a passage of what was in a sense Freud's (unpublished) farewell letter to Fliess, written on June 9, 1901, at a time when the break between them had in essence already taken place.

You have reminded me of that beautiful and difficult time when I was forced to believe that I was very close to the end of my life, and when it was your confidence that kept me going. I certainly did not behave either very bravely or very wisely then. I was too young, my instincts still too hungry, my curiosity still too great to be able to remain indifferent. However, I have always lacked your optimism. It is certainly foolish to want to banish suffering and dying from the earth, as we do in our New Year's wishes, and it was not for this that we did away with our dear Lord God, only to shift both of these things from ourselves and our dear ones to strangers.

I am thus more humble now, and more ready to bear whatever may come. There is no doubt that not all wishes can be fulfilled. Many a thing for which I have striven ardently is today no longer possible; why shouldn't I be obliged to bury some new hope each year? If you don't agree, this may be an attempt to soothe me, or it may be an appraisal led astray by friendship.

It is true that it is hard to tolerate complainers. This, too, I have learned to understand. I have been quite pleased with my mood for many weeks now.

I hope to have good news about you and yours soon and greet you cordially.

Your,
   Sigm.

This letter is made even more meaningful by the fact that it, too, opens with the theme of an injection.

Vienna, June 9, 1901

Dear Wilhelm,
   I am taking advantage of this strange Sunday to write to you once again.

It is the first Sunday I have been completely free, with nothing to remind me that at other times I am a physician. My aged lady, whom I have been visiting twice a day at fixed hours, was taken to the country yesterday, and I have been looking at my watch every fifteen minutes to see whether I am not keeping her waiting too long for her injection. *Thus we still feel the shackles even after they are removed, and do not really know how to enjoy our freedom.*

How clearly the last sentence of this paragraph expresses the pain of being "free!" Gratitude for what Fliess had done for him persisted long after the dissolution of the transference and left Freud with an unresolved feeling of guilt (Schur 1966).

For all these reasons Freud was still obliged in 1895 to exculpate Fliess, because only by keeping Fliess strong and "steady" could he preserve both his ego ideal and his own security.

However, we find at one point in Freud's associations a highly aggressive wish against Fliess, *disguised as concern*: the association that Fliess "suffered himself from suppurative rhinitis, which caused me anxiety; and no doubt there was an allusion to this in the pyaemia which vaguely came into my mind in connection with the metastases in the dream." Here Fliess *is* being punished for Emma's fate!

For all these reasons, both the Emma episode and the Irma dream were important milestones. With the discovery of the necessary tools and the concepts for dream interpretation, Freud took another important step not only toward the understanding of psychic phenomena, but toward his own liberation—ultimately inescapable—from the necessity for his "transference" relationship to Fliess.

The following question might be raised: is it possible that Freud was aware of this meaning of the Irma dream which I have just discussed, specifically when he referred to certain omissions of material because of the limits to be placed on divulging associations pertaining to his innermost secrets?

Freud certainly was aware of *omissions* in his discussions of the Irma dream (see, for example, 1900, p. 113; p. 105, n. 2; p. 118, n. 2, added in 1909). However, the highly complimentary associations and interpretations pertaining to Fliess in the Irma dream were not *omissions* but *positive* conclusions involving one of the main elements of the dream. Knowing as we do that Freud wrote the final version of *The Interpretation of Dreams* in 1899, and knowing his superb honesty, we must assume that by that time any connection between the Irma dream and the Emma episode had been even more thoroughly repressed than before. Moreover, Freud did not change any of these passages after his break with Fliess in any of his many revisions of *The Interpretation of Dreams*.

One further question might be raised in connection with the history of the

Irma dream. Careful readers of the Fliess correspondence and of J. Strachey's introduction to *The Interpretation of Dreams* are aware of the fact that Fliess closely scrutinized and even "censored" the manuscript and proofs of *The Interpretation of Dreams*. There is a somewhat cryptic passage in Freud's letter to Fliess of October 23, 1898 (Letter 99), which Strachey quotes (p. xix): "Freud writes that the book 'remains stationary, unchanged; I have no motive for preparing it for publication, and the gap in the psychology [that is, Chapter VII] as well as the gap left by removing the completely analysed sample dream [Chapter II] are obstacles to my finishing it which I have not yet overcome.' "

Strachey's translation "sample" dream for the German *Beispiel*, rather than the more correct "example," and his insertion of the reference to Chapter II (which contains the Irma dream), added to his remark (p. xx) that Fliess seems "to have been responsible for the omission (evidently on grounds of discretion) of an analysis of one important dream of Freud's own" would seem to indicate that Strachey believes the dream omitted on Fliess's recommendation to have been the Irma dream. (See Strachey's translation of the heading of Chapter II as "specimen" dream [*Traummuster*], a term much closer to "sample" than to "example.") This opinion is shared by a number of others.

However, there are various indications that the Irma dream was not the one "censored" by Fliess and withdrawn by Freud.

First, of course, is the fact that the Irma dream *does* appear in *The Interpretation of Dreams*. If it had been withdrawn on Fliess's objections and subsequently restored before publication, it is likely that some indication of this change of decision on Freud's part would have appeared in his correspondence with Fliess, but in fact none does.

Secondly, Freud never referred to the Irma dream as a "*completely*" (*zu Grunde*) analyzed dream. Instead, he spoke of it as the first dream subjected to a "thorough" (*eingehend*) analysis.

Most important is the evidence found in a number of letters to Fliess, pointing to an entirely different dream which in fact *was* (regretfully) removed by Freud and replaced by several others.

On June 9, 1898 Freud writes (in an unpublished portion of Letter 90):

I also thank you cordially for your criticism. I am aware of the fact that you have undertaken a very thankless task. I am reasonable enough to recognize that I need your critical help, because in this instance I myself have lost the feeling of shame required of an author. So this dream is condemned. However, now that the sentence has been passed, I would like to shed a tear for it and confess that I regret it and that I cannot hope to find a better one as a substitute. You must know that a beautiful dream and no indiscretion do not go together. At least write me to which topic you took exception, and where you feared an attack by a malicious critic. Was it my anxiety, or Martha, or the *Dalles* [a Jewish word for poverty, frequently used colloquially by Viennese Jews], or my being without a fatherland? [Please let me know] so I can omit the topic you designate in a substitute dream, because I can have dreams like that to order. . . .

This is the first mention of the rejected dream which I found in the Fliess correspondence.

Of the topics mentioned by Freud as possibly objectionable in Fliess's opinion, only the reference to his wife applies also to the Irma dream. No special anxiety and no allusion to Freud's poverty or his lack of a fatherland can be found in the Irma dream. Nor is there any reference to Fliess which might be offensive to the latter.

In an unpublished paragraph of his letter of June 20, 1898 (Letter 91), Freud writes:

My mourning for the lost dream is not yet over. As if in spite I recently had a substitute dream in which a house constructed of building blocks collapsed (we had built a *staatliches* [The words in parentheses represent one of Freud's associations. The word *staatliches* is a pun combining the two words: *stattlich*—stately, imposing, grand; and *staatlich*—pertaining to the state, to public affairs, to politics.] house); this dream, therefore, because of that reference, cannot be used either.

This letter and dream on the one hand express Freud's resentment and regrets in a characteristically witty way. On the other hand—and this is of course much more important to my topic—the pun indicates that the main bone of contention in the rejected dream must have been something "political," probably connected with Freud's allusion in the previous letter to "being without a fatherland." The collapsed house could, of course, pertain to Freud's relationship with Fliess as well as to the collapse or threatened collapse of other hopes and expectations.

The next reference to the rejected dream is the passage in the letter of October 23, 1898 (Letter 99) where Freud for the first time speaks of the *completely analyzed* example. At that time Freud had already "discovered" the oedipus complex and other aspects of infantile sexuality. It is therefore most unlikely that he would still consider the Irma dream to be a *completely* analyzed dream. For this reason Freud himself later referred to the Irma dream as the first one subjected to a "thorough" analysis. (Freud's letters written between January 3 and March 3, 1899 [1950, letters 101–107] explain the actual reasons for the long interruption in the progress of *The Interpretation of Dreams*.)

The Dream Book was put aside until Freud caught up with his self-analysis and his new understanding of the material of his patients. In May, 1899, one of his periods of feverish activity began, and after only two months he was able to announce to Fliess that the first chapter had gone to the printer. Fliess was now regularly receiving the manuscripts and first galleys of each chapter.

In a letter of August 1, 1899 (Letter 113), Freud again mentions the omitted dream:

The gap made by the big dream which you took out is to be filled by a small collection of dreams (innocent and absurd dreams, calculations and speeches in dreams, affects in dreams). Real revision will only be required for the last, psychological chapter [VII]. . . .

This letter clearly indicates that "the" dream actually was left out, and was replaced by others. Early in October, 1899, *The Interpretation of Dreams* was published with the Irma dream included. We may therefore safely claim that the omitted dream was not the Irma dream.

Among the many other possible links between the Emma episode and the Irma dream I shall mention only two.

Freud's need to exculpate Fliess and also, indirectly, himself resulted in a displacement of hostile accusations to the person of his innocent friend "Otto." But there were also hostile associations directed against Irma and other female figures. If the reproaches against "Otto" were meant as a displacement from Fliess (hence belonging to the category of what Freud later described as "hypocritical" dreams), could the hostility expressed against Irma also have been a displacement from Emma?

Emma had certainly caused Freud a great deal of trouble and concern. She had shaken Freud's trust in Fliess—even though he had denied this at the time—and this trust was absolutely essential for Freud's equilibrium. But she had done even more. She had seen Freud at a weak moment and mocked him with her remark: "This is the strong sex." Is it possible that Freud, who at the time of the Irma dream was recovering from his cardiac episode and was enjoying his stay at the beautiful villa (which he described so vividly in his letter of June 12, 1900) as a sign of beginning prosperity, who had resumed smoking in defiance of Fliess, who had realized that he was on the threshold of "touch[ing] upon one of the great mysteries of nature" (Letter 18, May 21, 1894), and, last but not least, whose wife was pregnant with her sixth child, was "getting even" with the "weak woman" who dared to doubt his interpretations and even to mock him? Was he "getting even," too, with the "recalcitrant" girl friend of Irma's who had "shown herself strong enough to master her condition without outside help" (1900, p. 110)? Was he in fact retaliating against "brave women''—the "brave Frau Doktor" of the Emma episode and the "Frau Professor," his courageous wife, against whom he directed his somewhat deprecatory associations to the Irma dream?

Finally, in the preamble to the Irma dream, Freud indicated his annoyance over a passing remark of his friend O. (Dr. Oskar Rie) in which he "fancied" he detected skeptical reproof about his therapeutic results in the Irma case (1900, p. 106). Freud thought that M. (Breuer), "at that time the leading figure in our circle," might share this skepticism, and that same evening he wrote out Irma's case history with the idea of giving it to Breuer in order to justify himself. In his letter of April 11, 1895, Freud had *told* Fliess about a similarly critical remark of Weil's, to which Fliess had taken strong exception, necessitating in turn a rather humble apology from Freud. I have already mentioned the far-reaching repercussions which Freud's *"telling"* had for him. This theme of "telling" on or about someone was one of the main motives of another of Freud's most revealing dreams, which he reported in *The Interpretation of Dreams*—the "non vixit" dream. It played a decisive role in the final break between Freud and Fliess, especially in the latter's accusation against Freud in connection with Otto Weininger's publication (see Freud 1950, p. 41).

That the Irma dream—like any other—was overdetermined, that its latent content comprised genetic material from Freud's childhood, that it had sexual connotations is self-evident. Erikson, for example, in his 1954 study, tried to reanalyze this "specimen dream of psychoanalysis" by using biographical data on Freud's early childhood obtained from various sources.

I have deliberately refrained from attempting any such reinterpretation of the "deeper" sources of the dream, and restricted myself to the use of material presented in Freud's own words, which quite obviously represented the background residuum both for the manifest dream and for the most important associations and interpretations given by Freud. I have also refrained from tracing *all* the links between the Emma material and each single element of the Irma dream—something that can easily be done but seems superfluous for the purposes of this paper.

The background material and the use made of it by Freud throw important light on the earlier stages of Freud's self-analysis and on the role which his "transference" phenomena, reflected in his relationship to Fliess, played in the "specimen dream," as well as in his progressive unveiling of the secrets of the mind. The whole Emma episode also throws an important and more intimate light on the period of trial and error through which Freud's therapeutic technique had to pass. It explains why Freud eventually had to stress the role of abstinence in the transference situation. But all this was contingent upon Freud's progress in his self-analysis and the concomitant dissolution of his transference relationship.

In his introduction to the Irma dream, Freud quotes the French psychologist Delboeuf: "Every psychologist is under an obligation to confess even his own weaknesses, if he thinks that it may throw light upon some obscure problem" (1900, p. 105).

Freud certainly followed this exhortation, and did not hesitate to divulge in *The Interpretation of Dreams* a number of intimate details about his own life and the life of those around him. To do this in the service of science was not "weakness" but courage and strength. We are all inclined to look upon Freud as the incarnation of strength, wisdom, and courage. But Freud could not have been Freud without being intensely human, and this condition included deep suffering.

Nothing shows this quality better than his letters. K. R. Eissler (1964) could therefore have chosen no better title for his review of Freud's collection of letters than "Mankind at Its Best."

In my discussion of a small segment of Freud's development, I have chosen to speak of his "transference phenomena." In so doing I wished to demonstrate, on the one hand, how intensely human Freud showed himself to be even in this phase which included severe physical illness, and how, on the other hand, Freud was able to emerge from this period of conflict and suffering having accomplished one of his greatest feats—the discovery of the secret of the dream.

Epilogue

And now we come to the denoucment and epilogue of the drama, which illustrate Freud's ability even at that early stage to achieve therapeutic results and arrive at new insights in a case which confronted him with many seemingly insurmountable obstacles.

On April 16, 1896, approximately one year after the last-quoted letter about Miss Emma, Freud wrote to Fliess upon his return from one of their periodic meetings:

Vienna, April 16, 1896

Dearest Wilhelm,

I felt the same way. With my head full of periods and hunches about summations [this word probably pertains both to Fliess's theories on periodicity, to which Freud was thus paying somewhat tongue-in-cheek lip service, and to his own feeling that his ideas and concepts were starting to fall into place], proud of having achieved some recognition, and with a bold feeling of *independence* [does the use of this term in the context of his expansive mood herald Freud's gradual shift from a "transference" relationship to a more independent one?], I came back with a real sense of well-being, and have been quite lazy ever since, because that state of semi-misery [Freud had remarked repeatedly in his correspondence that he was most creative during periods of mild physical distress (Schur 1966). This mood was also characteristic of periods in which new material was coming up in his self-analysis and in the treatment of his patients.] which is essential for intensive work won't re-establish itself. I have only some sparse hunches to set down about the "in-between realm" [Freud coined the term *Zwischenreich*, combining *zwischen* ("between," "in-between") and *Reich* ("realm," "state," "empire"). This probably refers to the "Unconscious" and also to his self-analysis.] which have come out of my daily work, plus a general reinforcement of the impression that *everything** is the way I have surmised it to be and that everything will thus become clear. Among all these things is a quite surprising explanation of Emma's hemorrhages, which will give you great satisfaction. I have already guessed what the story is, but I shall wait to communicate it until the patient herself has caught up with it. . . .

In a letter of April 26, 1896, Freud provides more specific information:

with regard to Emma, I shall be able to prove to you that you were right; her hemorrhages were hysterical, brought on by *longing,** probably at the "sexual period" [Freud is apparently using the awkward word *Sexualtermine* instead of *Menstruation*, in accordance with Fliess's theory about the link between periodicity and menstruation] (out of sheer resistance that *Frauenzimmer* [literally, "woman's apartment." The word is very often used in German as a slightly derogatory synonym for "woman." See Strachey's note in *Standard Edition* 15:162.] has not yet given me the dates). . . .

This letter is full of hidden ambiguities obviously related to Freud's increasing ambivalence toward Fliess, which also expresses itself in doubts about Fliess's theory of periodicity. On the one hand, he is giving Fliess credit by agreeing that Emma's hemorrhages were hysterical, thus exculpating Fliess even more than heretofore. He also refers to Fliess's theory of periodicity. On the other hand, he asserts that Emma's hysterical hemorrhages were based on an unconscious (sexual) wish, and therefore on an emotional conflict. What Fliess expected was an unconditional acceptance of his theory that periodicity was the main cause of pathology. (See Kris's footnote to Freud's Letter 43 and Chapter IV of his introduction to Freud 1950.)

In a letter of May 4, 1896, Freud finally divulges the analytic material underlying his assumption that the hemorrhages were hysterical in origin:

Vienna, May 4, 1896

Concerning Emma, about whose history I am making notes to send you, I know so far that she was bleeding out of *longing*.* She had been a bleeder all along, whenever she cut herself, etc. As a child she suffered from severe nosebleeds. During her prepuberty years [she] started to have headaches, which were interpreted to her as malingering, which in fact had been due to [auto]suggestion, so that she greeted her intense menstural bleeding with pleasure, as a proof of the genuineness of her illness, a proof which was even accepted as valid. She had [the image of] a *scene* from her fifteenth year, where she suddenly starts to bleed from the nose, with the wish to be treated by a particular young physician who was present at the time (and also appears in the dream). When she became aware of my deep emotion during her first hemorrhage while in the hands of R., she experienced the realization of an old wish to be loved in her sickness, and during the next few hours, despite her danger, felt happy as never before. Then in the sanatorium, during the night, she began to feel restless out of unconscious longing and the intention of drawing me to her side. And since I did not come during the night, she renewed the hemorrhage as an unfailing means of reawakening my affection. She bled spontaneously three times, and each hemorrhage lasted approximately four days, which must be significant. She still owes me details and specific dates.

My heartfelt greetings to you and do not forget to write as often as your head permits. [Fliess was suffering from persistent headaches which he attributed to his nose, for which he had undergone repeated surgery.]

Yours,
Sigm.

Nowadays we would of course expect a careful hematological work-up to establish what kind of "bleeder" Emma was. But in this letter Freud was—without mentioning it—continuing with the exculpation of Fliess! The iodoform gauze was buried and forgotten! However, Freud had obviously also conceived of the possibility of "hysterical" nose-bleeding and probably of vicarious menstrual nasal bleeding as well, a step from the concept of conversion to that of "resomatization" (Schur 1955).

On January 17, 1897, Freud wrote Fliess a letter, most of which was published in *The Origins of Psychoanalysis* (Letter 56). This letter is remarkable for many reasons. It introduces, among other points, the link between the symptomatology

of hysterics and the accusations of possession by the devil made by the Inquis-
ition. (See Kris's footnote to this letter.)

In the unpublished portion of the letter Freud writes:

> Emma has a scene [in mind] where the *Diabolus* sticks pins into her finger
> and puts a piece of candy on each drop of blood. As far as the blood is
> concerned [meaning the hemorrhage. Now Fliess has been completely vin-
> dicated, even of having left the iodoform strip in the wound!], you are al-
> together innocent! As a counterpart to this: the fear of needles and pointed
> objects from the second psychic period. [At that time Freud already distin-
> guished several periods of mental development.] As for cruelty in general:
> the fear of hurting someone with a knife or in some other way [an allusion
> to what Freud later described as the sadistic component of phallic strivings].

The allusions to Emma continue, this time with a reminder of Fliess's surgery!
In an unpublished part of Letter 57, written on January 24, 1897, Freud
writes:

> Think of it; I have been given a scene [The use of the word "scene" here
> and in the two previous letters is very significant. We know from Freud's
> correspondence with Fliess that he still believed in the "seduction etiology"
> of hysteria. However, in the published portion of this letter and the preceding
> one he clearly describes what he later called fantasies. This holds true for
> Emma's "scenes." It would therefore seem that Emma was one of the first
> patients who offered Freud a clue to the crucial realization that what his
> patients had described to him as actual seduction episodes were fantasies. As
> we know, this realization opened the way to the discovery of early infantile
> sexuality and its manifestations in infancy.] about the circumcision of a girl,
> involving the cutting off of a piece of one of the labia minora (which is shorter
> even now) and the sucking off of the blood, after which the child got to eat
> a piece of the skin. This child at the age of thirteen once claimed that she
> could swallow a piece of an earthworm, which she actually did. And an
> operation once performed by you had to come to grief from a hemophilia
> based on all this. . . .

This is the last reference to the case of Emma I was able to find in Freud's
correspondence with Fliess. (I plan at a later date to study once again the originals
of this correspondence, because some of the letters still have to be transcribed.)
One more attempt has been made here to exculpate Fliess. The further—post-
Irma-dream—additions pertaining to the case of Emma confirm my elaboration
of the interpretations of that dream. Moreover, the little snatches of material,

when put together, give us a fascinating clinical vignette of those early cases of hysteria treated by Freud. On the one hand, these sparse portions of a case history add to our satisfaction that the correspondence between Freud and Fliess has been preserved (see Kris's Introduction to Freud [1950]; Schur [1965]). On the other hand, they add to our feeling of loss that so many of Freud's early case histories—for example, that of Emma, about whom Freud was obviously writing to Fliess—have remained unknown to us.

Summary

The material of this essay gives us a fascinating glimpse into the "workshop" of a genius during a heroic and dramatic phase of his struggle to unveil the mysteries of the mind.

Giving us an insight into the early phases of Freud's unique analytic situation, this material provides an unusually vivid example of how a transference relationship can almost simultaneously reach its climax and show the signs of its incipient dissolution. The material provides highly illuminating examples of displacement *in statu nascendi*; these found their way into a dream which took place more than three months later. We find a confirmation of the hypothesis that the "day residue" includes elements originating much earlier than the day immediately preceding the dream. Finally, it provides a brilliant example of the transition from fantasy to conversion and resomatization through the interplay of psychopathology, "somatic compliance," and traumatization.

References

Breuer, J., and Freud, S. (1893–1895). Studies on hysteria. *Standard Edition* 2.

Eissler, K. R. (1964). Mankind at its best. *Journal of the American Psychoanalytic Association* 12:187–222.

Erikson, E. H. (1954). The dream specimen of psychoanalysis. *Journal of the American Psychoanalytic Association* 2:5–56.

Fisher, C. (1954). Dreams and perception. *Journal of the American Psychoanalytic Association* 2:389–445.

Freud, S. (1900). The interpretation of dreams. *Standard Edition* 4/5.

——— (1950). *The Origins of Psychoanalysis*. New York: Basic Books, 1954.

——— (1960). *Briefe 1873–1939*. Frankfurt: Fischer.

Hartmann, H. (1948). Comments on the psychoanalytic theory of instinctual drives. In H. Hartmann, *Essays on Ego Psychology*, pp. 69–89. New York: International Universities Press, 1964.

———— (1956). The development of the ego concept in Freud's work. In *Essays on Ego Psychology*, pp. 268–296. New York: International Universities Press, 1964.

Jones, E. (1953). *The Life and Work of Sigmund Freud*. Vol. 1. New York: Basic Books.

———— (1955). *The Life and Work of Sigmund Freud*. Vol. 2. New York: Basic Books.

———— (1957). *The Life and Work of Sigmund Freud*. Vol. 3. New York: Basic Books.

Schur, M. (1955). Comments on the metapsychology of somatization. *Psychoanalytic Study of the Child* 10:119–164.

———— (1965). Editor's Introduction. In *Drives, Affects, Behavior* 2:9–20. New York: International Universities Press.

———— (1966). *The Problem of Death in Freud's Writings and Life*. New York: International Universities Press, in preparation. (This volume appeared in 1972 under the title *Freud: Living and Dying*.)

Strachey, J., ed. (1963). *Standard Edition* 15:162n.

Chapter 7

THE BACKGROUND OF FREUD'S "DISTURBANCE" ON

THE ACROPOLIS

MAX SCHUR, M.D.

In my Freud Lecture delivered to the New York Psychoanalytic Society in 1964, I presented a condensed over-view of Freud's evolving attitude towards death, from his persistent preoccupation with the idea that he might die at certain ages to the supreme serenity and heroism with which he faced sixteen years of suffering from cancer, and, ultimately, his own death. I indicated then that the clue to our understanding of this evolution could be found in Freud's self-analysis, and therefore in that phase of his life generally known as the "Fliess period." My paper on "Some Additional 'Day Residues' of 'The Specimen Dream of Psychoanalysis' " (chapter 6, this volume), published in the Heinz Hartmann *Festschrift*, dealt with one episode of this period. Because this pre-sentation is intrinsically a continuation of that paper, I will begin with a brief summary of it.

On July 24, 1895, Freud carried out the first *systematic* interpretation of one of his own dreams, known as "the dream of Irma's injection." The months preceding this dream had given rise to the first crisis in his relationship to Fliess. By that time, Fliess had developed his hypothesis of the "nasal reflex neurosis," which claimed that a host of physical symptoms were caused by pathology of

This is one of Max Schur's last papers before his death on October 12, 1969. This paper was presented before the New York Psychoanalytic Society on January 14, 1969. It appeared in *American Imago* 26:303–323. (Eds.)

the nose and the sinuses and could be cured either by surgery or application of cocaine to the nasal mucosa.

Freud was in the habit of sending many of his analytic patients who suffered from such symptoms to Fliess for examination and treatment. In February of 1895, Fliess came to Vienna to operate on a patient of Freud's named Irma. Subsequently she developed pain, nosebleeds, fever, and a putrid secretion. Freud finally called in a consultant, who discovered to everyone's horror that Fliess had left a large packing of iodoform gauze in the wound. After its removal, the patient collapsed and nearly bled to death. For many weeks the outcome was in doubt, but finally she recovered. The previously unpublished correspondence of these months revealed Freud's desperate attempts to deny any realization of the fact that Fliess had committed a nearly fatal error.

Reading these letters, I became aware of the unmistakable link between the details of this episode and the "Irma" dream. Freud designated his need to exculpate *himself* for the persistent pain of his patient Irma, and for the death of his friend Fleischl, as well as the need to express his anger against Breuer, who was skeptical about his therapeutic results, as the main precipitating factors of the "Irma" dream. I realized that this was mainly a displacement of Freud's desperate need to deny his ambivalence towards Fliess, who emerged in his associations to the dream as an exalted figure with superior knowledge.

My paper dealt with this episode and the new light it throws on the intricate conflict in Freud's relationship with Fliess. On further study, it became apparent that this applied to many of Freud's other dreams reported in *The Interpretation of Dreams*.

It was therefore a logical follow-up to scrutinize such dreams including Freud's interpretations and to correlate them with his correspondence. The correlation of Freud's behavior in everyday life and his letters and works, which I attempt in my book, *Freud: Living and Dying* (International Universities Press, 1972), permits us a glimpse into the intensive struggle and the adaptive mechanism which enabled Freud to initiate the psychological revolution and also to achieve his ultimate attitude towards illness and death.

Today we are concerned with one phase of this struggle. In 1896, Freud had recovered from a cardiac episode, which, I assume, was a small, well-localized myocardial infection suffered in 1894. During these two years, Fliess's support literally kept Freud going. Fliess insisted, however, without lasting success, that Freud abstain from smoking. Thus Fliess became the trusted healer, but also the frustrator.

Fliess had by then already formulated his theory of periodicity, which claimed the predictability of specific dates in the periodic cycles which predetermine birth, illness, and death. As is characteristic of a fantastic hypothesis of this kind, it provided in a magical way for the evasion of a fateful date, substituting, for example, a less severe illness for a fatal one.

On October 26, 1896, Freud reported to Fliess that his father had died on October 23rd. The published part of this letter ends with the remark that "*it all happened in my critical period.*"* In the unpublished part, Freud wrote that he had only just learned that Fliess's birthday was October 24th.

Freud's next letter indicates that his self-analysis was well on its way and how it was influenced by the death of his father. He wrote: "By one of the obscure routes behind the official consciousness the old man's death affected me deeply. By the time he died his life had long been over, but of course one's whole past is awakened within one by such an event." He also referred to a short dream he had had the night after his father's funeral, indicating that his family had been displeased over the very simple funeral arrangements he had made and over his tardy arrival on that occasion, following a long wait at his barber's. Freud's interpretation held that the dream was "an outlet for the feeling of self-reproach which a death regularly leaves among the survivors."

The year following his father's death was perhaps the most dramatic one in Freud's life. His self-analysis led him then to the reconstruction of specific memories from his early childhood, culminating in the discovery of the oedipal conflict and infantile sexuality. On October 3, 1897, he reported to Fliess:

> I welcomed my one-year-younger brother (who died within a few months) with ill wishes and real infantile jealousy, and his death left a germ of guilt in me. I have long known that my companion in crime between the ages of one and two was a nephew of mine, who is only a year older than I am.

This nephew was the son of Freud's oldest brother Emmanuel, who moved with his family to Manchester when Freud was a little boy.

> We seem occasionally to have treated my niece, who was a year younger, shockingly. *My newphew and younger brother determined not only the neurotic side of all my friendships but also their depth.*

We must wonder: What was Fliess's reaction to this last sentence? Let me add here that Fliess was two years younger than Freud, having been born around the time when this younger brother of Freud, Julius, died at the age of eight months.

In a letter written three and a half weeks later, Freud, who was not yet aware

---

*I have italicized what seem to me the salient features in the extracted material.

of the meaning of parapraxes, remarked nonchalantly that because of his preoccupation with his self-analysis he had forgotten to congratulate Fliess on his "not-yet-fortieth" birthday. The pertinence of this "forgetfulness" will become apparent.

A meeting at the end of 1897 brought into the open the first serious controversy between the two men. It arose over Fliess's new addition to his theory of bisexuality—the concept of bilaterality, which meant that the various determinants of periodicity and sexual dominance were, so to speak, distributed on different sides of the body. This Freud could not swallow. And yet, for reasons to be discussed later, this break between the two men was soon patched up.

Fliess' wild theories were published in book form in 1897. In April, 1898, a Viennese medical journal ran a devastating review, quoting extensive passages and speculating on the sanity of the author. Freud angrily withdrew from the editorial board of the journal, informed Fliess of the review, but refused to send him a copy, dismissing it as a piece of nonsense. Shortly afterwards, Freud had a dream, an analysis of which appeared in *The Interpretation of Dreams* and also in his essay "On Dreams" published in 1901, from which I am quoting:

> An acquaintance, Herr M., has been attacked in an essay with unjustifiable violence by no less a person than Goethe. Herr M. was crushed by the attack. *I tried to throw some light on the chronological data*, which seemed to me improbable. Since Goethe died in 1832, Herr M. must have been quite a young man at the time of the attack. *I was not quite sure, however, what year we were actually in*, so that my whole calculation melted into obscurity.

Freud's interpretation of the dream included the following points:

> A medical journal had published a "crushing" criticism by a *youthful* reviewer of a book by my friend Fliess. This was the true source of the dream. The unfavorable reception of my friend's work had made a profound impression on me. It contained, in my opinion, a fundamental biological discovery, *which is only now—many years later—beginning to find favor with the experts.* Behind my own ego in the dream content lay concealed my friend who had been so badly treated by the critic. "*I tried to throw some light on the chronological data.*" My friend's book dealt with the chronological data of life and among other things showed that the length of Goethe's life was a multiple of numbers that has a significance in biology. But this ego was compared with a paralytic: "*I was not quite sure what year we were in.*" Thus the dream made out that my friend was behaving like a paralytic.

Freud escaped this conclusion by the following twist:

> The dream-thoughts were saying ironically: "Naturally, it's *he*, my friend Fliess, who is the crazy fool, and it's *you*, the critics, who are the men of genius and know better. Surely it couldn't be the *reverse*?" There were plenty of examples of this *reversal* in the dream.
>
> In fact, the ego in the present dream does not stand only for my friend but for myself as well. I was identifying myself with him, because the fate of his discovery seemed to foreshadow the reception of my own findings. [*Standard Edition* 5:664]

In this dream we can discern Freud's dilemma: Was Fliess crazy or a genius? And what about the validity of his own discoveries? Even while writing the essay "On Dreams," when the break with Fliess was already an accomplished fact, Freud still needed to cling to the fiction that Fliess's speculations about periodicity were valid.

Several months later, in October, 1898, Freud had what has come to be called the "non vixit" dream:

> I had gone to Brücke's laboratory. The late Professor Fleischl came in with some strangers and sat down at his table. This was followed by a second dream. My friend Fliess had come to Vienna in July. I met him in the street in conversation with my deceased friend Joseph Paneth. Fliess spoke about his sister and said that in three quarters of an hour she was dead. As Paneth failed to understand him, Fliess turned to me and asked me how much I had told Paneth about his affairs. I tried to explain to Fliess that Paneth could not understand anything because he was not alive. But what I actually said was "NON VIXIT." I then gave Paneth a piercing look. He turned pale; his form grew indistinct and finally he melted away. I was delighted and realized that Fleischl, too, had been no more than an apparition, a "revenant", and it seemed to me quite possible that people of that kind only existed as long as one liked and could be got rid of if someone else wished it.

Freud's interpretation reported two main sets of associations, each of them linked to each other as well as to events of the past.

The first was the unveiling of a memorial to Fleischl, on October 16, 1898. Fleischl had been an associate of Freud's teacher, the physiologist Brücke. A brilliant, rich aristocrat, Fleischl was destined for a rapid academic career which Freud could never hope to match. However, after an infected injury to his hand during an experiment, he had undergone the amputation of several fingers, resulting in causalgia with intolerable pain, and addiction to morphine. When Freud discovered the anesthetic quality of cocaine, he had tried to cure Fleischl's addiction by the oral administration of cocaine, not realizing its addicting quality. After an initial success, the morphine addiction had been replaced by a cocaine addiction with even more disastrous symptoms. Freud was haunted by guilt feelings for years afterwards. These guilt feelings, moreover, had additional determinants. The number of associate appointments was limited, and Freud was aware of occasional death wishes directed against Fleischl, whose life was in any event a constant torture. Furthermore, Fleischl, a man of means, had most generously and tactfully lent Freud money at various times, when Freud was literally destitute. Without his support Freud could never have managed to study in Paris with Charcot on the meager stipend he had been allotted.

The second "revenant" of the dream was Joseph Paneth, one of Freud's oldest friends, one year his junior. Paneth had succeeded to Freud's position at the Brücke Institute. Knowing that his life span was limited because of an illness, he did not hide his wishes for Fleischl's early demise. As it happened, he died in 1890, one year before Fleischl.

Paneth, also a wealthy man, was even more generous to Freud that Fleischl. Aware of Freud's hopelessly prolonged courtship, he had set aside a sum of money, the interest on which had permitted Freud to visit his fiancee from time to time, while the principal had helped the young couple to hasten the date of their marriage.

There was more to the day-residues of the dream than these details, however. Freud gave as the main precipitating cause the fact that Fliess had had to undergo surgery and that his post-operative condition was far from reassuring.

Here are some additional data:

In 1898, Freud had started to work with utmost intensity on his *The Interpretation of Dreams*. For this he needed Fliess desperately. Fliess was not only Freud's admired friend, his sounding board and therefore a substitute analyst; he was also the only one who believed in Freud's theories, who encouraged any new discovery, however revolutionary. Fliess read all the drafts and galleys of the Dream Book, praised and criticized, even insisting on the omission of one dream which Freud considered to be the only one he had completely analyzed. For all these reasons, Freud could "forget" his doubts, which were so clearly manifested in the "Goethe" dream.

They met in July, 1898, Freud reading to Fliess drafts of his dream book and Fliess bombarding him with formulas. Freud responded with boundless admiration, calling Fliess the Kepler of biology. But he was obviously also quite bewildered.

This dual response was evidenced in Freud's letters written in August. He expressed his delight that Fliess was coming closer to a solution of the riddles of life and the universe, but also cautioned his friend to bear in mind how incapable he, Freud, was of understanding Fliess's new geometric formulas or remembering much of anything his mentor had taught him.

In October Fliess's letters must have indicated severe headaches; they played a great role in the correspondence of these two men. At first they were attributed to migraine. Later, after Fliess had formulated his nasal reflex neurosis theory, he attributed them to pathology of the nose and sinuses. Consequently, he underwent several surgical procedures, one rather radical, in the late summer of 1894. Freud was angry at Fliess's illness and doubtful about the necessity of this operation. Torn between a sense of obligation to rush to his friend's side and a wish to go away on vacation with his wife, he chose the latter course, feeling quite guilty for failing his friend. When Fliess later developed his periodicity theory, he attributed attacks of migraine and of sinusitis to "critical periods."

But now, in October, 1898, Fliess was approaching what was for *him* his most "critical" date—his fortieth birthday. And this was the period he chose for even more radical surgery than in 1894!

This time Freud did not forget his friend's birthday. His letter, intended to reach Fliess on "the date that is most important of all to you," was, however, couched in a style lacking Freud's usual elegance. He wished Fliess the acquisition of new possessions, children, and knowledge, and then expressed the hope that Fliess would be "spared every trace of suffering and illness beyond that which a man requires to increase his powers and stimulate his enjoyment of the good by comparison with the bad."

A few days after this birthday letter, Freud learned from Fliess's sister-in-law that his friend had undergone surgery. Only then did Freud realize that Fliess had *previously* alluded in a letter to this forthcoming surgery. Freud now reproached himself for having expressed his birthday greetings in such "sober terms," instead of wishing that Fliess could be spared *all* suffering. He countered this idea in an unpublished letter written on October 30th, by remarking that this reproach was actually nonsensical because wishing could not become rational "through any correction." What Freud meant was that no wishes had magical powers. This was Freud's ambivalent mood at the time of the "non vixit" dream which we can date now as having occurred some time between October 24th and October 30th, 1898.

I will now return to Freud's interpretation. From the correspondence with Fliess we have reason to believe that Freud was here following a method he utilized for many of his dreams. First, he made notes about the manifest dream

and the immediate set of associations. At a later date, he completed his interpretation. He must have done this with the ''non vixit'' dream during the summer
of 1899, when he was completing the Dream Book:

> The dream thoughts informed me that I feared for my friend's life. His only
> sister, whom I had never known, had died in early youth after a very brief
> illness. (*In the dream, Fliess said that his sister was dead in three quarters
> of an hour.*) I must have imagined that his constitution was not much more
> resistant than his sister's and that, after getting worse news of him, I would
> make the journey after all—and arrive *too late*, for which I might never cease
> to reproach myself. It was this phantasy which so insistently demanded ''non
> vivit'' instead of ''non vixit'': You have come too late, he is no longer alive.

Freud then explained that he had not been able to rush to Fliess's bedside
(a situation comparable to that of 1894) because he was at that time ''the victim
of a painful complaint which made movement of any kind a torture,'' referring
to a furuncle on his scrotum which came up in another of his dreams.

This remark was part of the later interpretation because to Freud's embar-
rassment, Fliess, when reading the proofs of this part of the book, called his
attention to the fact that in reality this furuncle had developed somewhat later
on!

Fliess's sister, mentioned in Freud's associations, had been named Pauline.
So was Freud's niece, the sister of that nephew John whom he had described
as the model of all his friendships and enmities. But just a few weeks before
the ''non vixit'' dream, Fliess's wife had given birth to a girl, who was
named—Pauline. On that occasion, about two weeks before the birthday letter,
Freud had written to Fliess, in an unpublished letter: ''You will see how soon
Paulinchen reveals herself to you as the *reincarnation* of your sister.'' Here we
have the ''revenant'' element of the dream!

This was one of the many links between the Fleischl–Paneth themes and the
Fliess theme. But it was also the first ''dipping'' of the associations into early
infantile material.

Freud's interpretation next dealt with his associations to a ''slight present-day
anger'' he felt towards Fliess. Freud had been hurt over the warning given him
not to mention Fliess's operation to anyone. While he was consciously offended,
the associations to the dream brought back memories of times when he had
really been indiscreet; he had created trouble between Breuer—a Joseph like
Paneth—and Fleischl, by ''carrying tales,'' and as a child he had ''told'' on his
playmate John to his father.

Thus two new figures were added to the dream. Freud's associations had led him beyond the rivalries of the Brücke period deep into his early childhood. They actually repeated the reconstruction achieved in his self-analysis that his relationship to John had "a determining influence on all his subsequent relationships with contemporaries."

There was one important omission in Freud's associations, however. When Freud had reported his reconstruction in October 1897, he had spoken about his jealousy of his brother Julius and of the germ of guilt which the latter's early death had left in him. Brother Julius was not mentioned in Freud's interpretation of the "non vixit" dream, although he linked an association of Julius Caesar to the phrase of the manifest dream content: "My friend Fliess came to Vienna in *July*." Here again, it is to be noted, that Fliess was born around the time when Julius died. Thus, Fliess too was a revenant of Freud's brother, as Fliess's daughter was a revenant of his sister who died in infancy, and of Freud's niece. I recently obtained proof that this interpretation is justified.

In 1912, Freud met with Jung in Munich, in a last attempt to resolve their differences. He suffered there a fainting spell, the analysis of which he reported in letters to Jones and Ferenczi. In the first letter, Freud linked the spell to his relationship with Fliess, to "similar symptoms" he had had during a meeting with the latter, and to "some unruly homosexuality at the root of the matter."

In a later unpublished letter, the transcript of which I obtained from Dr. M. Balint, Freud wrote: "I have dealt well analytically with the spell in Munich—and even started on the long avoided third level of correlation. All these attacks point to the impact of early experienced death, in my case a brother who died very young, when I was somewhat over one year old. This reconstruction *did* reach the deepest, dynamically crucial point."

Nephew John was also a "revenant." He came to Vienna for a visit in 1870 when he was fifteen and Freud fourteen, and mysteriously disappeared in 1872. During this visit, Freud had acted the role of Brutus and John of Julius Caesar before an audience of children. Freud continued his associations by quoting Brutus's speech of self-justification in Shakespeare's tragedy: "As Caesar loved me, I weep for him; as he was valiant, I honor him! but as he was ambitious I slew him."

However, the roles which John and Freud had played were not from Shakespeare's play but from Schiller's tragedy *The Robbers*, in which this scene appears as a play within a play. The main theme of Schiller's work is a vicious, murderous rivalry between two brothers, which culminates in the death of all the main characters. This makes the omission of Freud's brother in his associations even more pertinent.

Freud mentioned still another Shakespearian figure, Prince Hal, who "could not, at his father's sick bed, resist the temptation of trying on his crown." Freud then stated "wherever there is rank and promotion the way lies open for wishes that call for repression." Freud himself admitted to such wishes, but "the dream punished my friends, not myself."

Freud had "slain" most of his friends in this dream, including Fliess, and the dead appeared as ghosts—"revenants." But what about Breuer? Freud had never failed to acknowledge Breuer's role in the development of psychoanalysis. Breuer had been following the unfolding of Freud's ideas with a mixture of skepticism and awed admiration. He once wrote in a letter to Fliess: "Freud's intellect is soaring. I struggle along behind him like a hen behind a hawk." But there was also frequent underhand criticism expressed to third parties. Breuer was left alive in the dream, and yet in the associations was included among the "revenants." He was one who has been *left by the wayside*.

It was an earmark of Freud's genius that the stimulus he received from others could become a nucleus of the psychological revolution he was to institute. Himself a source of inspiration for so many, he was on the receiving end with regard to certain people in his life. One of these was Breuer; another was Fliess.

In his interpretation, Freud gave full expression to his death wishes against Fliess. "No one is irreplacable. How many people I have followed to the grave already. I am left in possession of the field." Freud admitted that, having such a thought at a time when he was afraid of not finding Fliess alive if he made the trip to Berlin, meant that he was delighted because Fliess and not he had died.

Faced with this failure of repression, Freud asked himself what had become of the dream censor. Freud got around this question by emphasizing "with what fond feelings he had thought about Fliess," claiming that he had "gained a friend who meant more to him than ever the others did." Freud attributed to infantile affection *only* the reinforcement of his "contemporary and justified affection" for Fliess, but assigned his death wishes *entirely* to "infantile hatred" of his playmate and rival, his nephew John, which had succeeded in getting itself represented due to his "slight present-day anger" at Fliess.

The relationship of Prince Hal to his father, Henry IV, and of Brutus to Caesar, which had come up previously in Freud's associations, were both prime examples of the oedipal conflict. However, Freud presented these associations only as examples of conflicts of rivalry and ambition.

Some further details might explain the latter denial. I noted that the "non vixit" dream took place sometime during the week of October 24th–30th. Two years earlier, *during the same week*, Freud's father had died, been buried, and Freud had the dream referring to the guilt of the survivor.

Freud was able to show in his dream book that virtually every dream expressed certain infantile wishes and the conflicts precipitated by them. What he did not know at the time was the importance of what we call anniversary reactions. More important, he had not yet realized that occasionally *the emphasis on infantile material can be used successfully as a defense against recent conflicts, in particular, those which arise in the transference relationship*. This phenomenon manifests itself in every analysis. Only a thorough analysis of the transference can then unravel the intricate interweaving of present-day and infantile conflicts, in this instance the Cain and oedipal conflicts.

If we are to understand fully the "non vixit" dream and the repercussions which its conflicts had in Freud's later life, we must understand this dream in the context of Freud's relationship to Fliess.

In the "Irma" dream, Freud's hostility to Fliess was displaced on to others. In the "Goethe" dream, Freud questioned Fliess's sanity. In the "non vixit" dream, his death wishes against Fliess were undisguised. To quote Freud: "I was delighted to survive and I gave expression to my delight with . . . naive egoism. . . . So obvious was it to me that I should not be the one to die." And all this at the time of his very sick friend's "most critical period!"

In September, 1899, Freud had finished the Dream Book. Although he found fault with his work, he knew that it was his *magnum opus*, that from then on the world would never again be the same. On his return to Vienna, he wrote to Fliess: "And now for another year of this extraordinary life in which one's state of mind is the only thing that really matters. Mine is wavering but . . . as it says on the coat of arms of . . . Paris: *Fluctuat nec mergitur* ['It may waver, but it will not sink']."

He sent Fliess another sixty galleys, and announced triumphantly: "The climax of my achievements in dream interpretation comes in this installment. Absurdity in dream! It is astonishing how often you appear in them. In the non vixit dream I am delighted to have survived you; is it not hard to hint at such things?"—We might ask: hard for whom?

How did Fliess take this "killing off?" Why did Freud have to "do away with" Fliess at this time, and why did he have to confess his indiscretion thus leaving himself open to the attack which Fliess was eventually to launch against him?

In 1899, the writing of *The Interpretation of Dreams* overshadowed every other consideration. And yet, Freud's self-analysis was continuing. In this utterly distorted analytic situation, Freud had to hold on to his overevaluation of Fliess, his alter ego, his audience, conscience, and trusted physician. And yet a still submerged part of himself knew that Fliess's theories were figments of the imagination. He knew, moreover, that eventually both men would have to give up the pretense that co-existence was possible for Freud's concept of psychic determinism and Fliess's concept of cosmic determination of human events.

Thus Freud was anticipating that Fliess, too, would soon be left by the wayside to become a "revenant." In the language of infantile wishes, Fliess would be killed off. In Freud's dream and in his triumph over having reached the climax of his achievement his guilt feelings were muted, but eventually they had to come to the fore.

In the correspondence of the next two years, Freud expressed, often in tragic terms, the pain of his struggle. Even when a summer meeting in 1900 left no doubt that the two men were on a collision course which was making a meeting of the minds impossible, the conflict between affection and bitter disappointment continued. Nothing can better describe Freud's pain and the reason for it than a letter of unusual beauty, written in June, 1901, which sounds like his farewell to Fliess.

Dear Wilhelm,

I'm taking advantage of this strange Sunday to write you once again. It is the first Sunday I'm completely free, not reminded by anything that at other times I'm a physician. My aged lady, whom I have been visiting at fixed hours, was taken to the country, and I've been looking at my watch every fifteen minutes to make sure I'm not making her wait for her injection. *Thus we still feel the shackles even after they are removed, and cannot really enjoy our freedom.*

You have reminded me of that beautiful and difficult time when I believed that I was very close to the end of my life, and it was your confidence that kept me going. I certainly didn't behave very bravely or very wisely then. I was too young, my instincts still too hungry, my inquisitiveness still too broad for me to be able to remain detached. I have never shared your optimism. To want to banish suffering and dying from the earth is certainly foolish, and not for this did we do away with our dear Lord God only to shift both of these things from ourselves and our dear ones on to strangers.

I am more humble now and more ready to bear whatever may come. Not all wishes can be fulfilled. Many a thing for which I have striven ardently is already out of the question: why shouldn't I be compelled to bury some new hope each year?

It's true that it is hard to tolerate complainers. This, too, I've learned to understand. I've been quite pleased with my mood for many weeks.

Concurrently with the progress of his self-analysis, Freud's objectivity returned. He still could feel the gratitude which Fliess fully deserved. But his integrity did not permit him to pretend acceptance of scientific theories in which he could not believe. This must have pained Freud deeply and left him with guilt feelings. Freud knew even then, without yet having formulated the concept in these terms, that anticipatory anxiety and guilt were both the privilege and curse of man. He knew that in the end, he could never repay Fliess for the help the latter had given him when he needed it most; he probably foresaw that Fliess, despite all his natural endowment, was heading for a critical period without having Freud's unique ability to engage in self-analysis and without the benefit of a helping friend. As he was to remark in a letter to Ferenczi in September 1910: "A part of homosexual cathexis has been withdrawn and made use of to enlarge my own ego. *I have succeeded where the paranoiac fails.*"

Freud was emerging from their relationship the stronger and richer man. He was now ready to accept loneliness and to travel the next stretch entirely by himself.

Freud might have been able to work through his separation from Fliess without further repercussion if the year 1904 had not brought a violent blast from Fliess accusing Freud of plagiarism. He insisted that Freud had not sufficiently acknowledged his priority in the conceptualization of bisexuality, that Freud had told his patient Swoboda about Fliess's theories, and Swoboda in turn spoke of them to the philosopher Otto Weininger, who made use of the information in a book. Freud's "confession" in the "non vixit" dream had thus come home to roost.

And now I must go from 1898—the year of the "non vixit" dream to 1936. In this year, shortly before his eightieth birthday, Freud published his "A Disturbance of Memory on the Acropolis," written in honor of the 70th birthday of Romain Rolland, the French writer and humanist.

This temporary state of derealization experienced on the Acropolis had occurred under the following circumstances. In August, 1904, Freud had set out on a short trip with his brother Alexander, born in the same year as Romain Rolland. They planned to visit the island of Corfu. Instead, they followed the suggestion of an acquaintance in Trieste to take a boat leaving for Athens. Both men experienced a peculiar feeling that they should by all means forget about embarking on this unexpected adventure. Nevertheless, they *made* the trip, and when they reached Athens and ascended the Acropolis, Freud had an uncanny feeling: "So all this really *does* exist, just as we learned at school." Freud himself interpreted this situation as a case of "it's too good to be true":

And now, here we are in Athens, and standing on the Acropolis! We really *have* gone a long way! So too, Napoleon, during his coronation said to one of his brothers: "What would *Monsieur notre Pere* have said to this, if he could have been here today?"

But here we come upon the solution of the problem. It must be that a sense of guilt was attached to the satisfaction in having gone such a long way: something about it was wrong, and forbidden. It had something to do with a child's criticism of his father, *with the undervaluation which took the place of overvaluation* of earlier childhood. It seems as though to excel one's father was still something forbidden.

Thus what interfered with our enjoyment of the journey to Athens was a feeling of *filial piety*.

What Freud did not mention in his 1936 paper were the events preceding the visit to the Acropolis: that Fliess's blast, mentioned by him, was contained in a letter written on July 26, 1904, only a week or so before Freud started his trip and which was also the date of Martha Freud's birthday, a date only too familiar to Fliess.

We learn more about this trip from a letter written to Jung in 1909. Freud looked upon the younger man as a possible future standard bearer of psychoanalysis. Jung visited Freud in Vienna in March, 1909. We learn from Jung the following facts about this meeting.

Curious to know Freud's general attitude towards "pre-cognition and parapsychology," Jung raised this question with Freud, who allegedly characterized these concepts as "nonsense." While Freud was developing his arguments, Jung had a "peculiar sensation" as though his diaphragm were made of iron which was starting to get red-hot—"a red-hot diaphragm vault." At the same moment, there was such a crash in the bookcase standing beside them that both men became terribly frightened. Jung claimed this as a "catalytic exteriorization phenomenon." When Freud protested against this "explanation," Jung predicted that another crash would follow shortly, and in fact one did. Jung never knew why he felt so sure of his prediction. As for the horror which Freud evidenced, I would suspect that it was occasioned more by Jung's utterances than by the cracking sounds in the bookcase!

A few weeks later Freud sent Jung the following letter from a vacation trip:

Dear Friend,

It is remarkable that on the very evening I formally adopted you as my oldest son and successor you divested me of my paternal rank.

Now I am afraid of falling back into the role of father for you by speaking of my reaction to the "Poltergeist." Your communications and experiment made a strong impression on me. I decided after you left to make some observations, and here are the results. In my first room there is a constant cracking where the two Egyptian steles rest on the boards in the bookcase.

In the second one there is seldom any cracking. At first I would have considered it as evidence if the noise, which was heard in your presence, never made itself heard again after your departure. However, it has since recurred repeatedly, but never when I was preoccupied with you or with this special problem of yours. My readiness to believe, disappeared along with the magic of your presence. It seems to be quite unlikely that anything of this nature should occur. The piece of furniture appears before me stripped of its spirits just as god-forsaken nature appeared before the eyes of the poet after the departure of the Greek gods.

I am therefore putting on the paternal horn-rimmed glasses and warning the dear son to be willing not to understand something rather than make such a great sacrifice to achieve that understanding.

And now I'll tell you of other things "in Heaven and earth" that cannot be understood. Some years ago, I discovered that I had the conviction I would die between the ages of 61–62, which was then a long way off. At that time I went with my brother to Greece. It was really uncanny how the numbers 61 or 60, in conjunction with 1 or 2, kept appearing under all kinds of circumstances, especially in connection with means of transportation, all of which I noted down meticulously. I hoped to breathe easier when a room on the first floor of our Athens hotel was assigned to us. There 61 was out of the question. Well, I got room 31 (with fatalistic license, after all, half of (61–62), and this smarter and more nimble number proved to be more persistent in its persecution than the first one. From the time of my return until quite recently the number 31, in the vicinity of a 2, remained quite faithful to me. Because there *are* areas in my system where I am just thirsty for knowledge and not at *all* superstitious, I have since attempted an analysis, and here it is. It all began in the year 1899, when two events occurred simultaneously: first I wrote *The Interpretation of Dreams*, and second, I was assigned a new telephone number—14362. A connection between the two could easily be established: in the year 1899, when I wrote *The Interpretation of Dreams*, I was *43* years old. What more natural, then, that the other numbers should refer to the end of my life, namely, 61 or 62. Suddenly there was method in the madness. The superstition that I would die between 61–62 showed itself to be the equivalent of a conviction that I had fulfilled my life's work with *The Interpretation of Dreams*, didn't have to produce anything further, and could die in peace. You will admit that with this knowledge the thing no longer sounds so absurd. *By the way, there is a hidden influence of Fliess in all this*: it was in the year of his attack that the superstition erupted. You will find confirmation here once again of the specifically Jewish nature of my mysticism.

It is evident that this preoccupation had the character and intensity of an obsessive compulsive symptom. We may therefore infer that the derealization on the Acropolis was only the culmination of this neurotic episode and that Freud's interpretation of the "undervaluation which took the place of the overvaluation," applied not only to his father, but even more so to Fliess.

Thanks to Freud we know that behind *obsessive* thoughts and concern with other people's death, there mostly lies a hostile wish. We know, too, however, that such wishes are unacceptable to us, especially when they are directed towards persons we also love; so that if they occur in people with a strong conscience, these people may turn their hostile death wishes into a superstitious preoccupation with their own deaths.

In the letter to Jung, Freud alluded vaguely to the "secret influence" of Fliess. A careful study of all the writings of Freud up to 1907 leads me to conclude that at the time of the 1904 episode, Freud was not yet aware of *all* the implications of this "secret influence" and of Fliess's blast. Certainly, the analysis of his number-superstition which he submitted to Jung indicated no such awareness. Specifically, without the element of guilt, there seems to be no reason why Freud should have felt that he had only a limited life span left to him after the publication of *The Interpretation of Dreams*.

However, in his analysis of the "Rat Man," published in 1909, Freud had already asserted that every fear of such nature corresponded to an unconscious wish. Moreover, in answer to his patient's question about how it was possible to wish to kill the person one loved best in the world, Freud remarked that it was "precisely such intense love that was the necessary precondition of the repressed hatred." This statement was followed by the very same quotation from *Julius Caesar* which had figured in Freud's associations to the "non vixit" dream. In a later session with this patient, Freud commented that a "normal period of mourning would last from one to two years, a pathological one would last indefinitely."

In discussing the "non-vixit" dream, I indicated that Freud had treated Breuer and Fliess as "revenants." Though both were still alive, they had been left by the wayside. The guilt of the survivor can also be experienced if one has had to separate oneself dramatically from a beloved-friend-healer-analyst.

Freud not only experienced *guilt* with regard to Fliess; he also mourned for his lost friend. He was to speak in "Mourning and Melancholia" of identification with the dead object as one of the most common phenomena of the mourning process. In Freud's preoccupation with possible dates of his death, he was expressing both his guilt *and* his identification.

After his eightieth birthday, Freud anticipated still another critical period—the age of eighty-one and a half, the limit of life attained by both his father and brother Emmanuel. Yet, it was neither guilt nor a fear of death then which gave rise to such thoughts. Rather, it was a conflict between the wish to live, though experiencing great suffering, and the wish for peace, sweet peace. It was the wish to live which prevailed nearly to the end.

After Freud had formulated his final theory of instinctual drives, he presented in *Civilization and Its Discontents* his most penetrating study of the tragic consequences of aggression and guilt in the life of man. It was written in 1929, a year after the death of Fliess. He included in one of the chapters the same verses by Goethe which he had quoted in his essay "On Dreams" in 1901. He introduced the poem by saying:

> If civilization is a necessary course of development from the family to humanity as a whole, then—as a result of the inborn conflict arising from ambivalance, of the external struggle between the trends of love and death—there is inextricably bound up with it an increase in the sense of guilt, which will perhaps reach heights that the individual finds hard to tolerate. One is reminded of the great poet's moving arraignment of the "Heavenly Powers":

> > Wer nie sein Brot mit Tränen ass
> > Wer nie die kummervollen Nächte
> > Auf seinem Bette weinend sass,
> > Der kennt euch nicht, ihr himmlischen Mächte.

> > Ihr führt ins Leben uns hinein
> > Ihr lasst den Armen schuldig werden
> > Dann überlässt irh ihn der Pein
> > Denn alle Schuld rächt sich auf Erden

> > He who has never eaten his daily bread with tears
> > Who has never spent the nights filled with sorrow
> > Sitting and weeping on his bed.
> > Cannot know you, Heavenly Powers.

> > You guide our entry into life,
> > You let poor man become guilt-laden,
> > Then to agony you abandon him,
> > For every sin is avenged upon this earth.

He concluded the chapter by saying:

And we may well heave a sigh of relief at the thought that it is nevertheless vouchsafed to a few to salvage seemingly without effort from the whirlpool of their own feelings the deepest truths, towards which the rest of us have to find our way through tormenting uncertainty and with restless groping.

References

Freud, S. (1900). The interpretation of dreams. *Standard Edition* 4/5.

———(1901). On dreams. *Standard Edition* 5:633–686.

——— (1909). Notes upon a case of obsessional neurosis. *Standard Edition* 10:155–249.

——— (1917). Mourning and melancholia. *Standard Edition* 14:243–258.

——— (1930). Civilization and its discontents. *Standard Edition* 21:64–145.

——— (1950) *The Origins of Psychoanalysis* New York: Basic Books, 1954.

Schur, M. (1966). Some additional "day residues" of "The specimen dream of psychoanalysis." *In Psychoanalysis—A General Psychology* ed. R.M. Loewenstein et al., New York: International Universities Press.

——— (1972). *Freud: Living and Dying*. New York: International Universities Press.

Chapter 8

THE PROBLEMS OF DEPERSONALIZATION IN

FREUD'S

"DISTURBANCE OF MEMORY ON THE ACROPOLIS"

JULIAN STAMM, M.D.

Depersonalization has been discussed from many vantage points: structurally, topographically, and defensively, as well as in its relationship to crises in identity. It appears not only in so-called normal fatigue states, hypnagogically and states of extreme excitement, but is also manifested in more malignant forms of ego-splitting such as the schizophrenic reaction.

This paper is concerned with one of the original essays on the subject, Freud's "A Disturbance of Memory on the Acropolis" in the form of a letter addressed to Romain Rolland.

In this sensitive analytic communication, Freud makes several important contributions to explain what transpired within himself on that particular occasion. Still, one is left with several questions: Why does Freud select to write about the disturbance of memory on the Acropolis on the occasion of Rolland's 70th birthday? What is the relationship between Freud's letter to his age and state of health at the time it was written? What is the link between his state of feeling at this time and his experience of unreality on the Acropolis? Finally, why does Freud refer to his state of depersonalization on the Acropolis as "a disturbance of memory?"

The following account by Ernest Jones may explain what was uppermost in

Presented, in part, at the May 1967 meeting of the American Psychoanalytic Association, and at the Spring 1968 meeting of The Association for Applied Psychoanalysis.

Freud's mind when he made his journey to Athens in August-September, 1904, and I suggest, may have precipitated the episode of unreality.

Ernest Jones comments on a disagreement that developed between Fliess and Freud which was probably one of the more significant factors culminating in the termination of their intimate friendship:

> In the Christmas Congress at Breslau in 1897 Fliess had expressed to Freud his conviction that all human beings had a bisexual constitution. At their last meeting in Achensee in the summer of 1900, Freud announced it to his friend as a new idea. Whereupon the astonished Fliess replied, "But I told you about that on our evening walk in Breslau and then you refused to accept the idea." [Jones 1953, p. 314]

Freud denied any knowledge of this. However, a week later the memory of it came back to him.

On July 20, 1904, Fliess wrote to Freud that a brilliant young psychologist, Otto Weininger, had just published a book stressing the theme of bisexuality and insisted further that Weininger had gotten his idea from Swoboda, a pupil and/or patient of Freud's to whom Freud had given his (Fliess's) great secret.

Freud had been quite upset about the entire affair and "frankly confessed he must have been influenced by his wish to rob Fliess of his originality, a wish presumably compounded of his envy and hostility."

It is my contention that when Freud left for Athens with his younger brother a few weeks after receiving this bitter recrimination from Fliess, attacking his professional ethics and the origin of one of his basic ideas, that Freud was chagrined, depressed and guilt-ridden, as well as upset over the loss of an intimate friend, father surrogate and colleague.

This was the background of his mood when he set forth to visit the Acropolis—the fruition of a childhood dream. More specifically, he was amazed to have discovered that he had suffered a bit of amnesia himself in entirely repressing his meeting with Fliess in Breslau in 1897 and then claiming originality for himself for the concept of bisexuality expounded by Fliess at that meeting. In short, Freud had repressed the idea in 1900, then came the accusation from Fliess and another bitter reminder from Fliess in 1904, shortly before his trip to the Acropolis where he developed his feeling of depersonalization. May we assume that there is a connection, a connection that even Freud failed to make because of his need to repress the memory of the entire affair? The experience on the Acropolis, a disturbance of memory, represents a return of the repressed in disguised form. The phrase, "can all this really be true," may be viewed as a displacement of his doubts and astonishment in connection with his disturbance of memory related to the Breslau meeting with Fliess.

Thirty-two years later when writing to Rolland, Freud chooses to select this episode on the Acropolis as a disturbance of memory, discusses his oedipal guilt and the fact that he had superseded his father and that his guilt was the key to his experience of depersonalization.

When Freud stood on top of the Acropolis and experienced his feelings of depersonalization ("so all this really does exist," "is this really true?"), he was also re-experiencing doubts about himself and the validity of his own thinking, triggered and reinforced by the letter from Fliess a few weeks earlier. His feelings of guilt toward Fliess were then unconsciously linked with his earlier oedipal guilt in that he was trying to "rob" Fliess of his creativity, his originality, just as in childhood he must have desired to rob, displace, and supersede his father.

I speculate further than when Freud wrote to Rolland thirty-two years later about a disturbance of memory, the power of the unconscious had once more revealed itself because once more at age eighty, he failed to connect the Acropolis episode with the Fliess episode and the Weininger-Swoboda affair.

When he visited the Acropolis in 1904, instead of feeling exalted as he himself says he should have felt, he experienced depersonalization. In other words, he was unable to enjoy his success because of his guilt feelings in respect to Fliess.

He calls it a disturbance of memory because when he visited the Acropolis, there were the unconscious or preconscious memories of Fliess's recriminations and his own self-reproaches: How could I have forgotten Fliess's ideas? And why did I credit myself with the originality of Fliess's ideas on bisexuality? The experience on the Acropolis in which he doubts the truth, the validity of what he is perceiving, unconsciously represented a displacement of and substitute for his anxiety and conflict at that time with Fliess, as well as his wish to defend himself against it.

The Acropolis episode comes to represent in part a symptomatic act, a stage for the unconscious playing out of his infantile wish for power, the struggle with father, and his need for punishment, all precipitated anew by the letter from Fliess.

In addition, we may take some of Freud's comments as disguised associations to his disturbance. These associations are as follows: his analogy of feeling on the Acropolis to standing alongside the monster, Loch Ness; his comments on how King Baobdil felt when he received the news of the "fall of the city of Alhama" which meant the end of his rule; comparing the way he felt as he stood on top of the Acropolis with Napoleon's remark at his coronation: "What would Monsieur notre Père have said to this, if he could have been here today?"; Freud's reference to his feeling of sadness and guilt at the thought of having superseded his father and his feeling that his father lacked the cultural background to appreciate the Acropolis; and his further comments on characters wrecked by success.

The letter was written on the occasion of Rolland's seventieth birthday. Freud himself was eighty at the time, suffering from the agonies of a severe malignancy and approaching death.

Irving B. Harrison in a paper entitled "A Reconsideration of Freud's: A Disturbance of Memory on the Acropolis," calls Freud's experience of unreality on the Acropolis an identity crisis. I would add to this that when Freud wrote to Rolland, the subject of age, his illness, his preoccupation with his own progressive helplessness and thoughts of death also posed a threat to his identity at that time. At the same time, Freud was preoccupied once again with the meaning of his own identity and desired to express to Rolland one of the major contributions to psychoanalysis, namely, the power of the repressed. Once more he was the observer and the observed, confronting another identity crisis—this time at the age of eighty and hence far more threatening. Thus it is not surprising that his still active mind unconsciously raises the identity problem experienced on top of the Acropolis. In addition, these ruminations on the present and on his past contributions may have stimulated a process of temporal regression eliciting childhood memories of exciting trips with beloved relatives. This kind of nostalgic recall of the past one often experiences on important anniversaries, especially if the current reality is a painful one, and the regressive cathexis of the past becomes all the more powerful. It is also significant that in describing his sense of depersonalization on the Acropolis, Freud draws an analogy with the feeling engendered when walking alongside the mythical sea monster, Loch Ness.

My hypothesis is that his preoccupation with his identity precipitated a transient ego and libidinal regression with accompanying loss of self-boundaries and a revival of infantile oral incorporative fantasies such as the wish for union with mother allegorically disguised in the association to the sea monster. Freud's comment on King Baobdil and the coronation of Napoleon designating the end of one reign and the beginning of another may also suggest the ebb in his own reproductive processes as opposed to his creative breakthroughs in the past. (See Lewin 1950, Stamm 1962.)

Freud's visit to Athens in 1904 coincided roughly with the height of his productive powers and a fulfillment of his creative genius. Freud, Harrison (1966) and others have stressed the oedipal conflict motivating the regression and splitting of the ego in the syndrome of depersonalization. Harrison indicates that Freud's visit to the Acropolis represents the emergence of an earlier forbidden oedipal wish with the ensuing guilt leading to depersonalization and expressing the superego interdiction against it. My reference to the Fliess episode as a triggering mechanism would also tend to support the oedipal factor in respect to the process of depersonalization. However, while such psychological content may trigger conflict and defense, resulting in various regressive modes of defense, this does not in itself entirely explain the process of depersonalization per se or an identity crisis. In fact, as is well known, both genital and pregenital conflicts often trigger all kinds of regressive processes, including schizophrenic reactions with or without accompanying manifestations of depersonalization. Many authors have referred to multiple factors on both genital and pregenital levels as well as various factors affecting ego regression that enter into the causality of the syndrome of depersonalization.

For the purposes of this paper, I wish to underscore the vicissitudes of perception experienced in this syndrome. For certainly, regardless of its causation, the phenomenology of depersonalization may also be ascribed to varying degrees of perceptual alteration, so that there is a change in the sensorial interpretation of external phenomena and even more regarding the intactness of one's feeling of self.

In her paper on depersonalization, Jacobson (1959) describes how such states "may be caused by changes to fascinating new surroundings." She attributes this in part to "a narcissistic conflict caused by discrepancies between opposing identifications." In my paper on altered ego states (1962) I also referred to economic shifts in certain fatigue states leading to fluctuations in cathexis and hence to ego splitting and/or various alterations in perception.

In a personal communication, the late Peter Glauber emphasized the economic considerations involved in feelings of depersonalization. He cited the frequent feelings of strangeness one has when flying in a plane or on debarking in a new country. For a moment, the new setting may upset one's identity due to the need to cathect unfamiliar percepts. My views are in accord with Glauber's. In some instances, the hypercathexis of current situations or highly charged memories may so absorb one's attention that the accompanying shift leads to a transient disequilibrium in the sense of self-representations. In the latter instance, an individual may become so intent on his work that he momentarily withdraws interest from his surroundings. When he is suddenly interrupted in the pursuit of his intense concentration, he may be so startled by the intruder as to suffer transient perceptual disorientation in respect to his external surroundings; or the opposite may occur, and he may be so completely absorbed in a beautiful scene that his own self becomes immersed (projected) into his surroundings. Here, I have in mind the frequent fluctuations of attention and alterations in perception often seen among scholars and scientists so absorbed in their work that their environment becomes blurred and they are accused of being "absent-minded professors."

In such instances, the hypercathexis of the particular work creates a withdrawal of attention from other objects and self-representations, at times even modelled on projective and introjective processes; but the feeling of unreality is due in part to the sudden fluctuation in dynamic equilibrium. As a consequence, the steady frame of reference of I-ness is momentarily interfered with, or the pooling of self-identifications that establish a constant frame of reference has been temporarily disrupted (see Spiegel 1959).

I would like to emphasize Spiegel's point of view in this regard. In his paper "The Self and Perception," he states:

> When the objects of the external world which are customarily part of the self as a result of narcissistic identifications are no longer available as a frame of reference and when this is a result of an abrupt change as in traveling, so that oscillations between the familiar framework and unfamiliar can still happen, then alteration of self-feeling may occur. [p. 106]

Jacobson, too, writes of changes in the environment that may lead to feelings of depersonalization:

> We may tend to underrate the extent to which the consistency and homogeneity and hence the stability of our self-image depends on the compatibility, harmonious interplay and collaboration of those innumerable identifications with all the familiar, personal and interpersonal, concrete and abstract objects of our past and present life and environment. [p. 587]

She adds:

> We know that abrupt changes from the familiar to the new, strange and unfamiliar scenes—can bring about fleeting experiences of depersonalization. [pp. 587–588]

Spiegel discusses constancy of frame of reference and oscillation in this constancy as providing an important facet for the perceptual changes observed in depersonalization and feelings of loss of identity:

> To account for the specific quality of depersonalization, we must consider the linkage with a perceptual process. If the concept of the self as a frame of reference for perception of single mental or physical states is accepted, then the intrasystemic conflict described by Jacobson would lay the groundwork for such a linkage with perception. The ego would then have at its disposal not a single steady frame of reference, it would have an alternating framework. The ego would not only defend against pregenitality but would

cathect alternatingly both pregenital and genital positions. . . . It would thus be using two different frames of reference with a consequent disturbance of self-perception. [1959, p. 105]

It is to be noted that in Spiegel's formulation, the main emphasis is placed on an alteration of self-representations leading to transient disturbance in ego stability. The altered ego state is thus a reflection not so much of a particular mental content but rather of the sudden shift in ego identity that these mental contents trigger.

Spiegel explains Freud's feeling of unreality on the Acropolis stating that:

the Acropolis was part of Freud's narcissistic identifications. At one time he must have perceived the Acropolis against the self as a framework as he might have perceived his hand against the external world as a framework. I would make this pulsating oscillation from one framework to another one condition for the emergence of the feeling of unreality which lay behind a singular thought: "So all that really exists just as we learned it in school." [1959, p. 107]

In other words, it is my contention that Freud was so awed by his actual perception of the Acropolis, associated as it was with his fondest dream of childhood, that the hypercathexis at that moment was an important factor in the precipitation of the dramatic alteration in his sense of identity culminating in a feeling of unreality, superimposed as it was on the previous experience with Fliess. In addition to the economic factors, other factors, such as oedipal guilt and conflicting identifications, are also important. I also postulate that many years later, on the occasion of celebrating Rolland's seventieth birthday, Freud once again experienced a threat of self-extinction due to his terminal illness and old age. In the wake of his current representations, the psychological sequelae reawakened reminiscences of his own great achievements and moments of glory, epitomized in his visit to the Acropolis.

Conclusions

In his letter to Rolland, Freud presented one of his major achievements in the evolution of his psychological thinking, namely, the subject of repression and the power of the unconscious.

His preoccupation with death and his past life stirred up once more his infantile conflicts, his oedipal guilt, and need for punishment. His letter to Rolland further represented a kind of symptomatic act in which we observe a magnificent condensation of many chains of thought: his tribute to Rolland; his wish to recall his own great powers of creativity at a time when he was suffering from drastic decline due to severe illness and old age.

Moreover, I suggest that his reference to a disturbance of memory on the Acropolis is a disguise for his repressed guilt in respect to Fliess as a father figure, as well as his desire to atone for his oedipal guilt. Finally, Freud's experience of depersonalization or derealization that he terms a disturbance of memory is greatly overdetermined. In this paper, I have drawn attention to both oedipal and pre-oedipal components, the identity crisis, the ego splitting, the disturbance of perception based on economic considerations, and I have speculated further that his conflict with Fliess shortly before embarking on his trip provided a significant trigger for what ensued.

References

Freud, S. (1936). A disturbance of memory on the Acropolis. *Standard Edition* 22:239–248.

Glauber, Peter. Personal communication.

Harrison, I. B. (1966). A reconsideration of Freud's "A disturbance of memory on the Acropolis" in relation to identity disturbance. *Journal of the American Psychoanalytic Association* 14:518–527.

Jacobson, E. (1959). Depersonalization. *Journal of the American Psychoanalytic Association* 7:581–609.

Jones, E. (1953). *The Life and Work of Sigmund Freud.* Vol. 1. New York: Basic Books.

Lewin, B. (1950). *The Psychoanalysis of Elation.* New York: W. W. Norton.

Slochower, H. (1970). Freud's *déjà vu* on the Acropolis: A symbolic relic of "Mater Nuda." *Psschoanalytic Quarterly* 39:90–102.

Spiegel, L. A. (1959). The self, the sense of self, and perception. *Psychoanalytic Study of the Child* 14:81–109.

Stamm, J. L. (1962). Altered ego states allied to depersonalization. *Journal of the American Psychoanalytic Association* 10:762–783.

Chapter 9

THE PROTOTYPE OF PREOEDIPAL

RECONSTRUCTION

HAROLD P. BLUM, M.D.

Reconstruction has always been an integral part of psychoanalytic theory and therapy. While usually viewed in terms of a specific technical application, reconstruction has actually been a significant tool in the development of theory as well as a check upon theoretical constructions and formulations.*

Emerging from the analytic process, reconstruction and developmental knowledge are mutually explanatory. Reconstruction reciprocally influences understanding and interpretation and may catalyze derivative recollection (Kris 1956, Kanzer and Blum 1967). Reconstructions are tested and remodeled by analyst and patient with increasing refinement of working hypotheses. Greenacre (1975) prefers "construction" to denote the preliminary models of past development and pathogenesis utilized by the analyst, and has elaborated and stressed the importance of reconstruction in psychoanalysis. The careful and continuing evaluation of data and inferences is essential to psychoanalytic investigation and to the elucidation of controversy concerning genetic reconstruction and early development.

This paper will focus upon the early utilization of reconstruction in psychoanalysis and its relation to contemporary preoedipal reconstruction. In addition to conflict and defense, reconstruction now includes archaic ego states and object

*This paper was presented for the Margaret S. Mahler Birthday Celebration of the New York Psychoanalytic Society and Institute on May 10, 1977, and was awarded the Mahler Prize.

relations, reaction patterns and developmental consequences. Articulating with and amplified by the developmental concepts of separation-individuation (Mahler 1966, Mahler et al. 1975b), the reconstructions here are particularly relevant to the origins of structuralization, to preoedipal patterns and their later reactivation or persisting influence.

Freud (1937), having wrestled heroically with the problem of reconstruction, compared psychoanalytic work to the work of the archeologist in discerning, rearranging, and creatively synthesizing meaningful patterns out of the maze of piecemeal evidence provided by the patient in the analytic situation. Psychoanalysis may be said to have begun with an incorrect reconstruction when Freud, believing the stories his patients told him of their childhood seduction traumata, assumed that neurosis was caused by parental seduction. The concept of defense was conceptualized at that time as a repressive force designed to keep painful memories of real traumatic experience outside of consciousness. When Freud made the momentous discovery that the fantasies of the parental seduction were universal oedipal fantasies, he formulated the concept of the oedipus complex, and the analysis of the oedipus complex became a central issue. The libido theory was enunciated with its complex maturational sequences and developmental challenges, with the oedipus complex emerging out of important preceding developmental phases. Although he also uncovered preoedipal conflicts and related them to character formation in such early papers as "Character and Anal Erotism" (1908), the preoedipal contribution to and coloring of character was clinically isolated. The short analyses and techniques of the pioneer days did not permit character analysis. Analysis was symptom oriented, and symptoms and conflicts were mainly determined and evaluated in terms of the oedipus complex. The crucial elucidation of the oedipus complex overshadowed other discoveries. It is of interest that although Freud (1900, p. 245) referred to the preoedipal phase before age three as "the prehistoric period," he incorporated, over the years, the reconstruction of preoedipal reactions and influence, so evident in character, into psychoanalytic theory and technique. Preoedipal determinants and imprints were discerned in psychic structure and oedipal conflict and in the form and content of the infantile neurosis.

But when did preoedipal reconstruction first appear in psychoanalysis and how was it utilized? Most of the preoedipal dimensions of Freud's reconstructions have been overlooked. The extraordinary reconstruction of the primal scene at eighteen months in the Wolf Man case, probably the most famous of psychoanalytic reconstructions, was a preoedipal reconstruction. Freud (1918) gave an extremely detailed reconstruction of this scene, including the age of the Wolf Man, his illness—fever, the time of day, the position of the parents, the child's immediate reaction, and the developmental consequences. Freud regarded this single traumatic experience of the primal scene as a traumatic sexual seduction, but occurring in preoedipal infancy (Blum 1974).

At that time Freud did not regard the primal scene as immediately significant in the mental life of the eighteen-month-old infant. In the magnificent discovery and documentation of the infantile neurosis, such traumata as a protracted life-threatening malaria and a pathological object relation were eclipsed and the focus was placed upon the primal scene. Freud then directly linked the primal scene with instinctual overstimulation, which explained the relation of the primal scene to trauma, but not to trauma that seemed to be tied to a later developmental phase. Invoking the concept of delayed trauma as a possible explanation, Freud proposed that the preoedipal primal scene became pathogenic as a phase-specific oedipal trauma at the time of the Wolf Man's nightmare on his fourth birthday. This preoedipal reconstruction, so daring in its conception and elucidation, was "reconstructed upward" to the oedipal phase. The preoedipal situation and the mode and timing of the reconstruction are often overlooked because of the phallic content, the shift in the significance of the reconstruction from eighteen months to the phallic phase, and the close relation of the primal scene to Freud's discovery of the oedipal infantile neurosis as the precursor of the adult neurosis.

Freud's thinking encompassed developmental issues and the effects of traumatic overstimulation at different levels of development and on different areas of the personality. The unconscious gratifications and the threat of castration associated with the primal scene were evaluated in terms of oedipal progression and libidinal regression. The primal traumatic event of the single primal scene was reformulated as a universal oedipal configuration. The preoedipal primal scene was linked to pathogenic oedipal conflict (Esman 1973, Blum 1974).

Freud's complex discussion of the primal scene engaged different levels of memory, reconstruction, and personality organization. Freud also questioned whether he had reconstructed a phylogenetic memory, a dream equivalent of memory, a primal fantasy, or an actual experience—an animal or a human primal scene—and whether a reconstruction to eighteen months was a retrospective falsification or whether the Wolf Man's nightmare at four years of age reactivated and organized the seduction trauma at eighteen months in terms of the negative oedipus complex (see Eissler 1966).

The puzzling and vexing problems of such early reconstruction can now be understood also if considered in terms of Freud's simultaneous analysis of himself and his patients. Freud's analysis of the Wolf Man touched upon issues in his self-analysis (Kanzer 1972) which were in a continuing process of question, investigation, illumination, and extrapolation. In the Wolf Man analysis, and in his self-analysis, Freud uncovered persistent early infantile influences which had profound consequences for later development.

Oedipal and preoedipal reconstructions actually made their appearance simultaneously, and long before the Wolf Man case. They are to be found in Freud's first analysis—his self-analysis—which can be traced in the Fliess correspondence (Freud 1887–1902). Freud reported his discovery of the oedipus complex to Fliess in September–October, 1897 (Freud 1887–1902, pp. 218–221) and also reconstructed what would now be regarded as important preoedipal influences; most of the reconstructions in the Fliess letters are actually preoedipal reconstructions, e.g., Julius Freud, the one-eyed Doctor, the Czech maid. The presence of the first remarkable reconstruction by Freud (letter 70, October 3, 1897) of the period between eighteen and 24 months—during his separation-individuation phase—has been essentially unnoticed in these terms. Freud reconstructed his relationship at this period of life not only to his one-year-older nephew, but to his one-year-younger brother, whom we now know died on April 15, 1858, after having lived for approximately six months. Freud, then, was approximately one and one-half years of age when his brother was born and just under two at his brother's death. Freud's brother Julius was, therefore, alive only during the rapprochement phase of Freud's preoedipal development. Lacking the sophisticated tools of contemporary analysis, Freud's initial reconstruction of his infancy is uncanny in its authenticity, complexity, and correlation with contemporary analytic and developmental observations. Freud, unraveling screen defenses, has given us an immediate and vivid picture of reconstruction to the period of rapprochement, with a rapprochement crisis complicated by the birth and death of his younger brother Julius.

Later, in the "non vixit" dream of October, 1898 (Freud 1900, pp. 421–425), Freud's nephew John reappears as a revenant, an infantile object important in his own right, but also a screen object for his brother Julius, who is not directly mentioned in the associations to the dream, as Grinstein (1968) and Schur (1972; chapter 7, this volume) have noted. Freud (1900, p. 483) stated: "all my friends have in a certain sense been re-incarnations of this first figure. . . . they have been *revenants*. My nephew himself reappeared in my boyhood, and at that time we acted the parts of Caesar and Brutus together. My emotional life has always insisted that I should have an intimate friend and hated enemy." Referring to Brutus's speech of self-justification in Schiller's *The Robbers*, Freud proceeds to analyze the "prototransference" to Fliess, representing not only his father, but his brother Julius. Fliess, like Julius, was born in 1858 and thus younger than Freud. Brutus slew Julius Caesar, and Freud noted he was playing the part of Brutus in the dream. Freud and John really did act the roles of Brutus and Caesar during Freud's adolescence when John visited Vienna. Freud was identified with Brutus, and carried the "germ of self-reproach" for his death wishes toward Julius. The dream memorial bore the inscription "non vixit," meaning "he didn't live." In the day residue, the monument for the Kaiser Joseph refers to brother Julius (Kaiser-Caesar), father Jacob, and Freud's identification with the Biblical favorite son of Jacob—Joseph the dream interpreter, and the other Josephs who were so important in his life.

The dream parapraxis of "non vixit," or not having lived, rather than "non vivit," not being alive, refers to his baby brother Julius, as do Freud's comments (1900, p. 484): "It serves you right if you had to make way for me. Why did you try to push *me* out of the way? I don't need you. . . ."

Freud utilized familial information in his self-analysis to help organize and test derivative dream reconstruction. In a scene described to him by his father as occurring when he was not yet two years old, Freud had been fighting with his nephew, John. Freud (1900, p. 425) asserted: "It must have been this scene from my childhood which diverted 'non vivit' into non 'vixit' for in the language of later childhood the word for 'to hit' is '*wichsen*'." This is the precise period of the death of Julius, when Freud was not quite two years old (cf. Grinstein, 1968, p. 308). It is the anal phase of psychosexual development with all its problems of sadism, impulse and sphincter control and retention or loss of stool. From an ego orientation, it is also during separation-individuation, the rapprochement subphase, with continuing definition of self and object, animate and inanimate, male and female, with heightened separation anxiety and fears of re-engulfment. The issues of disappearance and reappearance in this preoedipal period of Freud's life might possibly be related to the discovery, loss, and rediscovery of preoedipal influences in the development of psychoanalytic theory.

The enmity toward Julius was associated with the enmity toward his nephew John and his next sibling Anna, who was born in December, 1858, some eight months after the death of Julius. As we now know (Schur 1972), sexual relations, birth, and death occurred in the same room during Freud's preoedipal development.

In *The Interpretation of Dreams* Freud's reactions to Julius and John and their parents are revived in an elaborate disguise in which the early sibling preoedipal material is condensed with oedipal fantasies. In a less disguised reconstructive letter to Fliess, Freud (1887–1902, p. 219) reported, "I welcomed my one-year-younger brother (who died within a few months) with ill wishes and real infantile jealousy, and that his death left the germ of guilt in me. I have long known that my companion in crime between the ages of one and two was a nephew of mine who is a year older than I am and now lives in Manchester; he visited us in Vienna when I was fourteen. We seem occasionally to have treated my niece, who was a year younger, shockingly [see Freud 1899]. My nephew and younger brother determined, not only the neurotic side of all my friendships, but also their depth."

Grinstein (1968, p. 315) has noted the series of deceased figures whom Freud

survived with pleasure and guilt, tracing Freud's guilt over his father's death
to the guilt over the death of his brother. Both Grinstein and Schur have enriched
our understanding of Freud's dreams and the psychobiographical significance
of "non vixit" and Julius Freud, without, however, a contemporary elucidation
of the preoedipal dimension.

Schur (1972, pp. 119, 161, 241) emphasized the "guilt of the survivor" and
documented the significance of this theme in Freud's life and work. In a letter
to Fliess, Freud (1887–1902, p. 171) interpreted the dream, "You are requested
to close the eyes," which he had just after his father's death in October, 1896.
"The dream was thus an outlet for the feeling of self-reproach which a death
generally leaves among the survivors." The request to close the eyes refers to
denial as well as to death wishes and punitive blindness. The "non vixit" dream,
occurring just two years after his father's death, is a richly overdetermined
anniversary dream. On the anniversary of the "request to close the eyes," the
object is annihilated with a piercing look and "non vixit" words. The oedipal
referents are clearly indicated in the associations. Freud has survived Brücke,
Paneth, and Fleischl. A memorial had just been unveiled to Fleischl. Fliess,
represented by "Fl" whose name was similar to that of the dead Fleischl, had
celebrated his 40th birthday and confronted serious surgery. The linkage of these
figures with the series of Josephs, with whom Freud was also identified, is also
clear and includes, ultimately, his father, Jacob, and his brother Julius (Shengold
1971; Chapter 5 of the present volume). Fliess would soon "disappear" as had
the others, and Freud recognized the unconscious childhood equation of separation, disappearance, and death. From the recent past of his professional life,
Freud leaps to the infantile ghosts who return in the "non vixit" dream. In his
early life John had not died, but he disappeared along with Julius, Freud's
nursemaid, his half-brothers Emmanuel and Philipp, and his first home (see
Schur 1972, p. 173). However, Freud's reported affective reaction to the birth
and death of Julius is not yet superego-derived guilt, but, in his own terminology,
"the germ of guilt," or the "seed of self-reproach" (see Schur 1972, p. 164).
The phrase "germ of guilt," translated from letter 70 of Freud's letters to Fliess,
was also translated by M. Schur as "seed of self-reproach." I shall utilize both
translations, as complementary, and emphasizing the affective, cognitive, and
structural processes consistent with the reconstructed infantile phase. (I am
indebted to Drs. Mark Kanzer and Jules Glenn for indicating that the optimal
translation should be "germ of self-reproach." This translation underscores
Freud's avoidance of any confusion of the superego and guilt with the precursors
of the superego and of guilt and self-reproach.) The "germ of guilt" is analogous
to a depressively tinged basic mood, and the "seed of self-reproach" to the
developing sense of self and to a precursor of the superego. The basic mood

and superego precursors develop during the rapprochement subphase of separation-individuation, the developmental period of Freud's "non vixit" reconstruction. Julius did not live, and if his brief life was denied and repressed, it would seem he never "existed": "*. . , people of that kind only existed as long as one liked and could be got rid of if someone else wished it*" (Freud 1900, p. 421). And in the case of Julius, the wish for his elimination became a reality.

The references in the "non vixit" dream to birth, death, and rebirth occur in many forms of appearance and disappearance. The visual annihilation is reminiscent of infantile omnipotence, but also of the archaic primitive superego (Peto 1969). It is also possible, utilizing the developmental level of the Julius reconstruction, to reconstruct the significance of the visual gaze in terms of eye contact and its maintenance, and to wonder about peek-a-boo games and the denial and acknowledgement of object loss. The greater sense of separateness during rapprochement leads to a heightened sensitivity to object loss. As Mahler (1975a) notes, the fear of object loss is then partly relieved by internalization, which includes the beginning internalization of the object's demands and commands. The fear of losing the object's love, now a relatively well-differentiated object, becomes an intensified vulnerability on the part of the rapprochement toddler, which manifests itself in a highly sensitive reaction to the parent's approval and disapproval. By this time the child can already verbally evoke "Mama" during her absence, and can say "bye-bye" in anticipation of separation from mother. The capacity for delay, anticipation, reality testing, and symbolic substitution develops with object relations, and ego advances and drive development occur in the matrix of adequate object response. The achievement of representational thought and language is associated with a more enduring, internalized, and stabilized image of the mother, which permits the shift to active separation experiences characterized by volitional approach and detachment or distancing behavior (Mahler et al. 1975b, McDevitt, 1975).

The reconstruction of the "prehistoric period" of childhood via dreams and screen memories is recorded in the Fliess letters for the first time in history. Transference, the return of "revenants," is codiscovered with reconstruction in *The Interpretation of Dreams* in the context of infantile object relations. In the evolution of the psychoanalytic process, this preoedipal reconstruction (of the rapprochement phase) was an object-relations model which actually preceded libido theory, and which returns as an important dimension of development in modern psychoanalysis. The reconstruction of the maturational phases of libidinal psychosexual development in childhood was one of the great achievements of Freud's analytic work with adults. The preoedipal reconstruction of early ego development and object relations was intimately related to libido theory, to the "libidinal object." Freud introduced dynamic formulations with a genetic viewpoint so that both dynamic and genetic viewpoints were interdependent and interrelated in the origins of psychoanalytic theory.

The "non vixit" dream is often used to indicate the revival and recapitulation of early object relations without indicating that the infantile object relations were indeed from the second year of life, so that such transference would be a preoedipal transference. Further, Freud's statements about his later relationships being determined by his brother Julius and his nephew John merit re-evaluation, just as does his statement that his nephew was his partner in crime at one year of age. In *The Interpretation of Dreams* only John appears as the "inseparable" friend of his childhood until Freud's third year, and the revenants were said to be a series of reincarnations of this friend (Freud 1900, p. 485). How important were these companions, his one-year-older nephew and his brother who died at six months, probably even before he was able to sit up, and certainly before he had language and locomotion? Did not his "friend" represent a composite figure, that is, his brother and other close relatives? As with the reconstruction in the Wolf Man case at eighteen months of age, what may be most important would not be the validity of a specific content, but the methodology of reconstruction and the developmental level to which it pertains. The recapture of the infantile object relations in Freud's first reconstruction is associated with enduring preoedipal influences and a basic affective state. The therapeutic importance of reconstruction in the reorganization of memory and self-representation is implicit in Freud's formulation. The "friend" of his infancy becomes a screen memory.

Just as the primal scene, birth, and death fantasies are so significant in the case of the Wolf Man at eighteen months, so were these issues bewildering infantile realities in Freud's self-analysis. The birth and death of his younger brother may have been at least as significant during Freud's rapprochement subphase as his ambivalent relation to play with John. Moreover, to follow Freud's reconstruction in his letter to Fliess, are the most significant relationships of that period of life likely to be the younger brother and the older nephew, or do these two figures really represent the most significant objects in the toddler's life, namely, the parents? (We do not have the data to indicate how important a mother surrogate and how significant an influence his Czech Catholic maid was, nor do we have data to examine the importance of his half-brothers.) Doubtless, the most important relationship at that period of Freud's life which is not delineated in his 1897 comments or in the analytic literature on his letters or dreams is the (rapprochement) relationship with his mother.

Freud's genius permitted this first reconstruction in psychoanalysis, a preoedipal reconstruction to 18–24 months of age. His "inseparable companion," his partner in life between the ages of one and two was his loving and adoring mother. His relation with his mother remains in the background of the father and brother associations of the "non vixit" dream, and, indeed, of Freud's (1900) dreams in *The Interpretation of Dreams*. The preoedipal mother in the dream book is hidden behind the pale shadow of his oedipal parent, usually the father. On October 15, 1897, Freud analyzed a haunting memory concerning separation from his nursemaid, also representing his beloved mother. "I was crying my heart out, because my mother was nowhere to be found" (1887–1902, p. 222) is a poignant expression of his separation anxiety and infantile grief. (His nursemaid was also used as a probable screen for his mother in the preceding letter [70], where Freud states, ". . . I shall have to thank the memory of the old woman who provided me at such an early age with the means for living and surviving" [1887–1902, pp. 219–220]. Freud, in reconstructing reactions to this obscure preoedipal mother surrogate, also cites her inappropriate mothering and dishonesty [cf. Grigg 1973].) The import of Freud's discoveries would be seen in all later theoretical developments. His (1917) delineation of the predisposition to and mechanisms of depression, consonant with preoedipal reconstruction, took into account regression to orality and narcissistic object relations and pointed to the precursors and consequences of superego development. The loving and beloved superego (Schafer 1960) was also anticipated, along with the formulation of subsequent internalized self-criticism, conscience, and self-punishment.

Freud's nephew and younger brother ostensibly determined the depth of all future friendships. This can be reinterpreted, that is, that his parents were the prototype of object relations and object love. Behind and beyond the ambivalent and complex relations to women which Freud (1913) described in "The Theme of the Three Caskets," his 1897 remarks presage appreciation of the essential ingredient of a mother's love for the infant's development of "confidence" and "basic trust." (Confidence, basic trust, and self-regard were formally introduced and studied much later in psychoanalysis.) Freud (1917, p. 156) later observed: "if a man has been his mother's undisputed darling he retains throughout life the triumphant feeling, the confidence in success, which not seldom brings actual success along with it. And Goethe might well have given some such heading to his autobiography as: 'My strength has its roots in my relation to my mother.' " Freud was identified with Goethe and would be awarded the Goethe Price in 1930; the observations apply to Freud as well as Goethe.

When Freud (1900) states that his emotional life requires an intimate friend and a hated enemy, as he does in association to the "non vixit" dream, ambivalence is apparent. The ambivalence and tendency toward splitting with displacement of anger and projection of aggression so characteristic of the normative rapprochement crisis can be suggestively discerned in his further associations ". . . and it has not infrequently happened that the ideal situation of childhood has been so completely reproduced that friend and enemy have come together in a single individual—though not, of course, both at once or with constant oscillations, as may have been the case in my early childhood'' (1900, p. 483). Freud's description and reconstruction to 18–24 months of age anticipates and is consistent with the modern conceptualization of the process of separation-individuation and the specific features of the rapprochement subphase. From that point on in development, conflicts with the mother and other objects are no longer transitory, but persistent and ambivalent. The mastery of the conflicts of this period will be particularly observable in the wooing of the parent, and intrapsychically, in terms of more cohesive, integrated self- and object-representations with increasing stability and autonomy.

After being "inseparable" until the end of their third year, Freud's independence from his "companion" at that time is fully compatible with the achievement of object constancy (again translating his inseparable companion as his mother). The senior toddler tolerates longer periods away from his mother and demonstrates the capacity to function and play in her absence because of the security of her "constant" mental representation. Julius had a direct influence on Freud, but also on Freud's parents, who reacted to the birth and death of their baby. The birth of a new sibling during rapprochement is not uncommon, and parental reactions impinge upon the toddler just as the toddler also stimulates parental responses.

All development involves challenges and tasks, with normative crises, and progression interrupted by expectable periods of regression. The birth and death of a sibling during rapprochement accentuates and complicates the cardinal conflicts of that period which, as Mahler (1966) delineated, include the additional trauma of toilet training and of the discovery of the anatomical sexual difference. The beginning deflation of the child's impervious narcissism and magic omnipotence is associated with the child's growing awareness of separateness and helplessness, and the beginning of verbal communication. The rapprochement proclivity to a negative affective response and to the feeling of ego helplessness, which Bibring (1953) characterized as the basic cause of depression, is heightened when the mother-child relation is skewed by maternal grief and depression consequent to the illness and death of a baby.

Bibring, consistent with Mahler's formulations, saw the ego helplessness as a narcissistic injury. It is now possible to follow the evolution of affective dispositions during the separation-individuation process, with depression originating during rapprochement and replacing the intoxicated elation associated with the undiminished grandeur of the practicing period. The depressive proclivity may become a structuralized state, which, as Freud implied in his first reconstruction, may be reactivated in later life, depending upon constitution and later development. It is during and after rapprochement that such depressive reactions, differentiated from transitory grief and sadness in infancy, can be structurally related to depression at later ages. Preoedipal disappointments, narcissistic injuries, internalized rage reactions, oral and anal fixations and frustrations were identified in the classical literature on predisposition to depression. The newer formulations of a depressive basic mood proclivity and the development of superego precursors during rapprochement confirm, amplify, and give phase specificity to the more global preoedipal hypotheses.

The "germ of guilt," which becomes guilt after the later consolidation of superego function, may also refer to the differentiation of other related affects. It is analogous to the depressive proclivity and the negative basic mood of the rapprochement period. The feeling of loss at that level of development, when validated by reality, reinforces the affective responses of helplessness, sadness, grief, and the *Anlage* of depression. The "seed of self-reproach" is indicative of the beginning of internalization, of "identification with the aggressor" with turning aggression on the self as a superego precursor which antedates and contributes to the formation of the superego.

That the guilt and self-reproach are triggered not only by the death of Freud's father in the "non vixit" dream, and in the other dreams of the *Interpretation of Dreams*, can be discerned in the specimen dream of psychoanalysis, the "Irma" dream which begins the book. This dream, in which Freud pleads not guilty and confesses guilt at the same time for a variety of sexual and aggressive transgressions, occurred on July 24, 1895, before the death of his father. In his associations, Freud reproaches himself for the deaths of Fleischl and a patient with the same name of his eldest daughter, "Mathilde," and the near death of Irma at the hands of Fliess (Schur 1972). These self-accusations for adult "crimes" conceal the infantile sources of these reactions in his oedipal guilt, and his preoedipal germ of guilt and seed of self-reproach related to his death wishes toward his parents, his sister Anna, and his brother Julius.

The death of Julius when Freud was two years old was the only actual death of a love object during his complicated and turbulent early life. The reconstruction of October, 1897, is augured in letter 23 of April, 1895 (Freud 1887–1902, p. 119). Preoccupied by the "Psychology for Neurologists," Freud writes to Fliess: "My heart is in the coffin here with Caesar." Later, in August of 1898, Freud (p. 261) reports the first understanding of a parapraxis, forgetting a name, that of the poet "Julius" Mosen. ". . . the 'Julius' had not slipped my memory. I was able to prove (i) that I had repressed the name Mosen because of certain associations; (ii) that material from my infancy played a part in the repression. . . ." This example was never published, just as Julius disappeared from Freud's (1900) associations to the "non vixit" dream in *The Interpretation of Dreams*.

While the birth of his first sister, Anna, when Freud was two and two-thirds years old doubtless triggered come complex "ill wishes and infantile envy," neither Freud's nor his parents' derivative grief reactions would be fully accounted for by reconstructing upward from the earlier dead brother to the later live sister. (This does not overlook the importance of later development and of regressive defense against oedipal conflict.) Reaction to the birth of Anna was not reconstructed, was not within conscious memory, as indicated in his paper "Screen Memories" (1899), and could have been displaced backwards to Julius (Schur 1972, p. 123). The hostility to Anna may also represent disguised aggression toward the older brother and father figures, and all the dangerous aggression may be displaced onto the younger weaker brother (Shengold 1971; Chapter 5 of the present volume). But the birth and death of Julius, doubtless with traumatic effects, also colored later reactions. The telescoping of traumatic memories was probably associated with interweaving developmental influences on structuralization and oedipal conflict. Nevertheless, the reaction to the birth of another child is not at all identical to the reaction to the death of a child by the parents and the surviving sibling.

The traumatic infantile loss of Julius and his mother's mourning and new pregnancy appear to be significant roots of Freud's concerns with death and transience (cf. Atkins 1977). Fearing an untimely death, he repeatedly tried to time his death, and told Jones (1957, p. 279) he thought of death every day of his life. The theory of a death instinct is most probably linked to these problems. Further confirmation of Freud's preoccupation with separation and specifically with the death of Julius may be found in his symptoms and self-analysis, that is, the so-called Tilgner episode (Schur 1972, p. 100).

Months before Freud's father's death on October 23, 1896, Freud had written to Fliess (April 16) of a neurotic fear of death, on that occasion based upon an identification with the dead sculptor Tilgner. Schur has detailed a number of possible correspondences between Tilgner and Freud, including the intense longing of both to visit Italy. Reading the details of Tilgner's life and death in an obituary, and writing to Fliess in a letter conveying his great ambivalence and, it might be added, possibly concerned about his father's health, Freud suffered from the dread of death. What was not noticed, however, was the date of Tilgner's death and Freud's letter. Tilgner died on April 15, the same date as Julius Freud. Thus, the dread of dying on April 15 may be understood as an anniversary reaction, just as the "non vixit" dream was dreamt on the anniversary of the death of a love object.

Such "anniversaries" are overdetermined and may also express familial anniversary reactions. Tilgner died before the unveiling of his Mozart statue, and the "non vixit" dream associations refer to the monument to the Emperor and the unveiling of the monument to Fleischl, and unconsciously to the deaths of

Freud's father and his brother Julius. The Rome of Freud's dreams was the Catholic city of the forbidding father and forbidden mother, but also the pre-Catholic city of Julius Caesar. Freud's extraordinary preoedipal reconstruction of the life and death of Julius was instrumental in his self-analysis and led to deepening understanding of his symptoms and inhibitions. An appreciation of formative preoedipal influences was convergent with Freud's discovery of the nuclear oedipus complex and cohesive psychoanalytic theory of neurosis.

Jones (1953, p. 317) recorded Freud's different and isolated levels of interpretation of pertinent oedipal and then preoedipal content. However, Jones did not compare and contrast the different levels of interpretation in different sections of the biography. Freud subjected to critical self-analysis his ambivalent relation to Jung, interpreting his fainting spells in Jung's presence in terms of the positive and negative oedipus complex, as well as his unconscious submission to, rivalry with, and guilty triumph over Jung, Fliess, and his father. It is significant that Freud, having analyzed his fainting, "expressed the opinion that all his attacks could be traced to the effect on him of his young brother's death when he was a year and seven months old" (Jones 1955, p. 146). Freud's giving this age is an interesting error or slip, for it refers to Freud's approximate age when Julius was born, not when Julius died.

Sibling birth, death, and new pregnancy are inevitably potential developmental disruptions in the mother-child relationship, and impose special challenges during the child's second year of life. The experience of intrapsychic loss is here compounded during rapprochement not only by anal-urethral and continuing oral problems and beginning castration conflicts, but by the real illness and loss of Julius. The proclivity to ambivalence will then be increased with abandonment anxiety and rage at the object, and possible splitting of the object world (Mahler 1975a, p. 108). Hostility toward the mother may also be displaced and projected onto other objects or turned on the self. Fearful of aggression and retaliation, the child "survivor" may display more intense separation reactions, defensive reliance on denial, reparative undoing, restitutive ambition, and reactive goodness. A basic negative mood will be accentuated by the effect on both the mother and her toddler of the new baby's birth and death, and the mother's withdrawal, grief, sadness, etc. Mahler (1966) has noted that a negative-depressive mood may persist or may give way to an unchildlike concern which may indicate a precocity of superego structuralization. Freud anticipates and forecasts later developmental research, although what was missing from his knowledge of development at that time would be supplied by his own further research and by the pioneering contributions of his students.

The challenges and crises of rapprochement require maternal acceptance of the child's ambivalence and empathic responses to the child's hostile dependency and separation reactions. The child at this time is easily vulnerable to narcissistic injury and ego and drive regression. Freud (1926) formulated the great danger situations of early childhood, that is, of the preoedipal period, in terms of fear of loss of the object, and fear of loss of the object's love. The abstract "object" was the mother, returned to a pivotal position in psychoanalytic theory. In connection with the infantile separation experience, which he analyzed and reconstructed, Freud (1926) pondered the psychology of pain and mourning and observed of the infant:

> It cannot as yet distinguish between temporary absence and permanent loss. As soon as it loses sight of its mother it behaves as if it were never going to see her again; and repeated consoling experiences to the contrary are necessary before it learns that her disappearance is usually followed by her re-appearance. Its mother encourages this piece of knowledge which is so vital to it by playing the familiar game of hiding her face from it with her hands and then, to its joy, uncovering it again. In these circumstances it can, as it were, feel longing unaccompanied by despair. [pp. 169–170]

This is the first description of the peek-a-boo game in psychoanalysis.

Freud, to buttress and expand his theoretical constructs, utilized and recommended the direct observation of children. Starting from the consideration of traumatic repetitive dreams, he considered the functions of children's play, with the careful scrutiny of his grandson as his research subject. He noted that all the child's toys were used in separation games, for mastery of separation anxiety by turning activity into passivity (1900, p. 461). These observations were of a child at eighteen months of age, the rapprochement period of his Julius and Wolf Man reconstructions. The child could express the concept of separation with the word "gone," one of his first words. Representation in thought, and symbolic play indicative of identification with the mother, convey ego-active modes of dealing with separation distress converging in a more differentiated internalized representation of the mother and the capacity for evocative memory.

The separation-individuation process at this time can be correlated with psychosexual phases with regressive and progressive swings. Psychosexual development and separation-individuation are interrelated developmental processes and frameworks having common roots in Freud's earliest observations and formulations. The concepts of oral incorporation and projection of the part object and retention and expulsion of the fecal object (or narcissistic object) were early correlations of libido and object-relations theory.

I would parenthetically add that I do not believe that Freud's addiction to smoking, his lifelong battle against it, and his reliance on incessant smoking, for example, twenty cigars daily for creative and productive work can be understood mainly in terms of the masturbatory equivalent and father identification he originally implied (Schur 1972, p. 61), or as a nicotine drug habituation. The preoedipal roots of such a literally oral addiction, which led to Freud's oral carcinoma, are today much more clearly defined. In this respect, beginning with the examination of the oral cavity in the Irma dream, a preoedipal dimension can be inferred but not confirmed in many of his dreams and screen memories. Contemporary evaluation of addictive tendencies would include considerations of oral fixation and regression, and archaic ego states, but also of conflicts related to symbiosis and separation-individuation. Such problems, when focal and attenuated, may coexist with many other areas of advanced personality development, and may also spur mastery and sublimation. Freud's unique capacity for developmental mastery and, later, self-analysis, were resources that fostered his insights into both personality formation and psychopathology.

The preoedipal reconstructions in the Fliess letters demonstrate self-analytic reconstructions related predominantly to the period of life before age three. The Freud family left Freiberg when Freud was three, a factor in his designation of the period before age three as "prehistoric," and isolating in time this period of his infancy. His apparent grasp of preoedipal attachment and ambivalence merged with the simultaneous discovery of the oedipus complex. Freud checked some reconstructions with his mother (1887–1902, pp. 221–222), a source of validation with the original object frequently utilized by contemporary analysands. His preoedipal reconstructions contributed to the development of psychoanalytic drive, ego, and object-relations theory, to formulations of preoedipal character traits and patterns, and to the technique of psychoanalysis as a reconstructive therapy.

Reconstruction was always far more than a simple genetic interpretation of one segment of experience. It was a whole piece of mental life, as Freud illustrated in his letters to Fliess and described in "Constructions in Analysis (1937)." This "piece" of mental life can also be considered as a nodal point in development with both important antecedents and certainly significant consequences and ramifications for later development. The early tendency was to understand this in terms of the reconstruction of trauma with pathogenic consequences, but Freud's own reconstruction shows its general importance for the later development of object relations and both affective and character dispositions. What was reconstructed were not simple actual events, but the child's interpretation and reaction to his experience, in other words, the meaning attached to the experience: the ego state and developmental impact became more important than a consideration of actual history.

The historical reconstruction of real experience and of real traumatic episodes remains significant, without diminishing the importance of unconscious irrational conflicts and fantasies which may never have achieved consciousness (Greenacre 1975). The unrememberable and unforgettable (Frank 1969) would then continue to influence further development and the meaning attached to further experience. Even though early trauma might be telescoped into the appearance of the single shock episode, and even though earlier disorder might be overlaid with defensive and adaptive maneuvers and could acquire new meaning, it could be possible under favorable circumstances to reconstruct into the "prehistoric period" of separation-individuation. Analytic interpretation, via reconstruction, can be regarded as a reordering of the infant's misinterpretation of internal and external reality.

Freud's masterful use of dreams and screen memories to reconstruct the infantile past was demonstrated in his own self-analysis long before the development of many other areas of psychoanalytic theory and technique. Prescient of some of the modern debate and controversy about the value and validity of preoedipal reconstruction, Freud (1900) further observed:

It was distressing to me to think that some of the premises which underlay my psychological explanations of the psychoneuroses were bound to excite scepticism and laughter when they were first met with. For instance, I had been driven to assume that impressions from the second year of life, and sometimes even from the first, left a lasting trace on the emotional life of those who were later to fall ill, and that these impressions—though distorted and exaggerated in many ways by the memory—might constitute the first and deepest foundation for hysterical symptoms. Patients, to whom I explained this at some appropriate moment, used to parody this newly-gained knowledge by declaring that they were ready to look for recollections dating from a time *at which they were not yet alive*. [pp. 451–452]

Many analysts were also sceptical, not only of phylogenetic memories or of elaborate fantasy in the first year of life, but of all preoedipal reconstruction. Regarding this controversy, it is clear that tentative preoedipal formulations and converging hypotheses were utilized by Freud and later pioneering analysts in the expansion of psychoanalytic theory. While inferences, especially those regarding the preverbal period have to be extremely cautious and careful, such efforts are consonant with Freud's own models and with continued efforts to trace earlier and earlier verbalized memories to those preverbal and nonverbal phenomena that are isomorphic with the verbalizable clinical material (Mahler et al. 1975b, p. 14). There have been many important examples of such efforts which in the long run have been richly rewarding to psychoanalytic understanding. Perhaps the most classic example of this kind of reconstruction to the earliest period of life is the Isakower phenomenon. This revival of very early ego states and attitudes is also reflected in the reconstructive studies of Greenacre (1950) on acting out, Lewin (1946) on the dream screen, and Spitz (1955) on the primal cavity.

Our expanding preoedipal knowledge and research exemplified in the concepts of separation-individuation should not be misunderstood to mean that initial psychic development and differentiation is accessible to psychoanalysis, that there are no limits or ambiguities to reconstruction, or that the earliest ego disturbances are reversible. The twin problems of the genetic fallacy and of the adultomorphic myth have to be kept in mind. A. Freud (1971, p. 147) expressed reservations about analytic work in the preverbal area of primary repression, but she also stressed the need for both analytic and observational studies:

> Where the imprint of more highly developed functions is superimposed on the remnants of archaic layers, the original simplicity of the primitive picture cannot but be distorted; this is true in particular where regression proceeds from verbal to preverbal phases. . . . with regard to the study of the first eighteen months of life, direct observation is indispensable as a means to complement, correct, and verify the conclusions drawn from the analyses of later stages. [1971, pp. 24–25]

It is not to be expected that reconstructive efforts should be exactly parallel with the data of analytic child observation, but the two sets of data should be consistent, and accurate reconstruction should fit or articulate with our current knowledge of development. The formulations of separation-individuation which organize data derived from analytic reconstruction do not detract from an appreciation of psychosexual development and the role of the Oedipus complex in adult neurotic disorder. Rather, these studies have enriched our appreciation of the epigenetic sequence of development wherein each phase is dependent upon the preceding phase for its impetus and solution; at any point problems of irregular, arrested, or deviant development may occur. Our knowledge of the formative influences that impinge upon oedipal development and solutions have been greatly enriched. Analytic work should take into account all oedipal and accessible preoedipal problems that are encountered in a given case, not excluding the influence of later life. The picture, as we know from our own clinical work and from the dilemmas of many analytic students, can be very complicated and confused. Psychoanalysis is not for those who are looking for an easy solution or the use of some neat oedipal or preoedipal formula, or a conventional mold in which the clinical material can be artificially compressed.

The assessment of preoedipal influences and particularly of preoedipal disorder may be especially noted in the area of the patient's relation to the analyst: the transference, the therapeutic alliance, the attunement to reality, and the quality of object relations. In addition to the clinical history, the patient's use of the analytic process and analytic setting provides valuable information about basic personality function. The more serious the early preoedipal disturbance, with possible structural deficit, the less likely that the patient will demonstrate a classical transference neurosis or that there will be a stable therapeutic alliance. Preoedipal development will influence the formation and form of the oedipal infantile neurosis underlying later transference neurosis. I do not think there is an artificial isolation between preoedipal and oedipal analysis. Though an oedipal transference neurosis is central to analytic work, depending upon the personality structure and depth of regression, varying duration and intensity of preoedipal transference may be discerned or inferred. The analysis of a case of obsessional neurosis will eventually deal with symptoms and character traits related to anal-phase conflicts.

There is no reason to expect that any of the later normal developmental phases of life or pathological states will exactly replicate point by point any of the subphases of separation-individuation or psychosexual development. The early phases of development are not literally recapitulated; various consequences are inferred in terms of residue and influences, of forerunners which undergo further developmental vicissistudes, and which are subject to regressive transformations: "Certain configurations persist in transference or acting-out patterns which seem to be the outcome of unresolved conflicts in the separation-individuation process" (Mahler 1971, p. 415).

In the origins of psychoanalysis, Freud discovered reconstruction and trans-ference, and immediately reconstructed infantile psychological reactions and patterns dating from his second year of life, and returning as "revenants." He returned to these fascinating complexities in his final paper devoted to this topic. In "Constructions in Analysis" (1937) Freud concluded "with a few remarks which open up a wider perspective." Referring to hallucinatory experience, he stated:

sufficient attention has not hitherto been paid that in them something that has been experienced in infancy and then forgotten returns—something that the child has seen or heard at a time when he could still hardly speak and that now forces its way into consciousness, probably distorted and displaced owing to the operation of forces that are opposed to this return. [pp. 266–267]

Psychic history, which for Freud was preserved in its essentials and "present somehow and somewhere," tends to repeat itself. Freud's (1937) last paradigm recapitulates his initial 1897 reconstruction:

> "Up to your nth year you regarded yourself as the sole and unlimited possessor of your mother; then came another baby and brought you grave disillusionment. Your mother left you for some time, and even after her reappearance she was never again devoted to you exclusively. Your feelings towards your mother became ambivalent, your father gained a new importance for you," . . . and so on. [p. 261]

Reconstruction to the nth year (taking into account the most common age sequence in siblings) will often require preoedipal reconstruction consonant with our expanding knowledge of psychological and developmental processes.

Summary

Freud's first reported reconstruction was to the preoedipal period and referred to the psychological meaning and consequences of the birth and death of his younger brother, Julius. In the historical development of psychoanalysis, preoedipal and oedipal reconstruction were simultaneously utilized, and Freud's thinking encompassed preoedipal influences with the oedipus complex.

Reconstruction was one of the earliest discovered methods in psychoanalytic technique, reciprocally contributing to the uncovering of infantile amnesia and the persistent influence of unconscious infantile conflict. Freud anticipated the importance of object relations in contemporary psychoanalytic theory, before formulation of the libido theory. Reconstruction from dreams and screen memories converged in Freud's self-analysis in the discovery of the repression and revival of infantile object relations, leading to the concept of transference.

Freud's self-analytic reconstruction concerning Julius, prototypical of preoedipal reconstruction, was to the protoverbal anal developmental phase, and the rapprochement subphase of separation-individuation. His reconstruction is remarkably consistent with modern knowledge of developmental processes. The integration of psychoanalytic reconstruction and direct child observation promises a deeper understanding of ego development and disturbance, character formation, and preoedipal determinants of oedipal conflict and the infantile neurosis.

References

Atkins, N. (1977). The analyst and transience. Paper presented to the Psychoanalytic Association of New York as the M. Sperling Lecture, February.

Bibring, E. (1953). The mechanism of depression. In *Affective Disorders*, ed. P. Greenacre, pp. 13–48. New York: International Universities Press.

Blum, H. (1974). The borderline childhood of the Wolf Man. *Journal of the American Psychoanalytic Association* 22: 721–742.

Eissler, K. (1966). A note on trauma, dream, anxiety, and schizophrenia. *Psychoanalytic Study of the Child* 21:17–50.

Esman, A. (1973). The primal scene: a review and reconsideration. *Psychoanalytic Study of the Child* 28:49–82.

Frank, A. (1969). The unrememberable and the unforgettable: passive primal repression. *Psychoanalytic Study of the Child* 24:48–77.

Freud, A. (1971). *The Writings of Anna Freud*. Vol. 7. 1966–1970. New York: International Universities Press.

Freud, S. (1887–1902). *The Origins of Psychoanalysis*. New York: Basic Books, 1954.

———— (1899). Screen memories. *Standard Edition* 3:301–322.

———— (1900). The interpretation of dreams. *Standard Edition* 5:339–627.

———— (1908). Character and anal erotism. *Standard Edition* 9:167–176.

———— (1913). The theme of the three caskets. *Standard Edition* 13:289–302.

———— (1917). A childhood recollection from *Dichtung und Wahrheit*. Standard Edition 17:145–156.

———— (1918). From the history of an infantile neurosis. *Standard Edition* 17:3–122.

———— (1926). Inhibitions, symptoms, and anxiety. *Standard Edition* 20:77–177.

———— (1937). Constructions in analysis. *Standard Edition* 23:255–270.

Greenacre, P. (1950). General problems of acting out. In *Trauma, Growth, and Personality*, pp. 224–236. New York: International Universities Press, 1952.

———— (1975). On reconstruction. *This Journal* 23:693–712.

Grigg, K. (1973). "All roads lead to Rome": The role of the nursemaid in Freud's dreams. *Journal of the American Psychoanalytic Association* 21:108–126.

Grinstein, A. (1968). *On Sigmund Freud's Dreams*. Detroit: Wayne State University Press.

Jones, E. (1953). *The Life and Work of Sigmund Freud*, Volume 1. New York: Basic Books.

———— (1955). *The Life and Work of Sigmund Freud*, Volume 2. New York: Basic Books.

———— (1957). *The Life and Work of Sigmund Freud*, Volume 3. New York: Basic Books.

Kanzer, M. (1972). Review of the Wolf Man by the Wolf Man. *International Journal of Psycho-Analysis* 53:419–421.

——— and Blum, H. (1967). Classical psychoanalysis since 1939. In *Psychoanalytic Techniques*, ed. B. Wolman, pp. 93 146. New York: Basic Books.

Kris, E. (1956). On some vicissitudes of insight in psycho-analysis. *International Journal of Psycho-Analysis* 37:445–455.

Lewin, B. (1946). Sleep, the mouth, and the dream screen. *Psychoanalytic Quarterly* 15:419–434.

Mahler, M. (1966). Notes on the development of basic moods: the depressive affect. In *Psychoanalysis: A General Psychology*, ed., R. Lowenstein et al., pp. 152–168. New York: International Universities Press.

——— (1971). A study of the separation-individuation process: and its possible application to borderline phenomena in the psychoanalytic situation. *Psychoanalytic Study of the Child* 26:403–424. New York: Quadrangle.

——— (1975a). On the current status of the infantile neurosis. *Journal of the American Psychoanalytic Association* 23:327–333.

Mahler, M. S., Pine, F., and Bergman, A. (1975b). *The Psychological Birth of the Human Infant*. New York: Basic Books.

McDevitt, J. (1975). Separation-individuation and object constancy. *Journal of the American Psychoanalytic Association* 23:713–742.

Peto, A. (1969). Terrifying eyes: a visual superego forerunner. *Psychoanalytic Study of the Child* 24:197–212.

Schafer, R. (1960). The loving and beloved superego in Freud's structural theory. *Psychoanalytic Study of the Child* 15:163–188. New York: International Universities Press.

Schur, M. (1972). *Freud: Living and Dying*. New York: International Universities Press.

Shengold, L. (1971). Freud and Joseph. In *The Unconscious Today*, ed. M. Kanzer, pp. 473–494. New York: International Universities Press.

Spitz, R. (1955). The primal cavity: a contribution to the genesis of perception and its role for psychoanalytic theory. *Psychoanalytic Study of the Child* 10:215–240. New York: International Universities Press.

Chapter 10

FREUD: THE FIRST PSYCHOANALYTIC GROUP LEADER

MARK KANZER, M.D.

Formation of the Group

The belated appearance of the *Minutes of the Vienna Psychoanalytic Society* provides an opportunity to survey the first recorded instance of analytic group therapy. To be sure, therapy for themselves was not the conscious purpose of the members, but it was a significant instigator and concomitant of their scientific proceedings. This unintended aspect is among the more interesting features, especially as it left a distinct imprint on the development of psychoanalysis itself.

The intimate relationship between the organization of the group and the therapeutic process began when Wilhelm Stekel, who had recently undergone therapy with Freud, proposed regular meetings at which other followers could discuss analysis with the founder of the movement. Thus the Wednesday Evening Society came into being. The exact date of Stekel's treatment is uncertain, but it presumably began in 1901 and may well have continued after the meetings were initiated. In any event, the fantasies now so common among patients—to engage in work with the analyst and ultimately to become an analyst oneself—thus achieved their first gratification.

Presented in part as the seventh Nunberg Lecture, 1970: "Sigmund Freud: Group Leader and Educator."

These fantasies, oedipally motivated, usually extend to the wish to eliminate the analyst and take his place. Such a wish may well have entered into Stekel's constant rebelliousness and ultimate break with the Freudian school. The same constellation was even more marked in the case of Alfred Adler. He also underwent treatment with Freud, a significant fact little noted in the commentaries on their relationship. This information seems to have been divulged only in later years, when it came to light among the posthumous papers of Freud, which were not published until 1960.

In the early days, the analytic procedure was rudimentary as compared with later standards. Indeed, until 1918 it was not considered necessary for an analyst to have undergone a preliminary phase of treatment himself. In January 1907, for example, Max Eitingon, the first analytic candidate, arrived for a two-week visit and was "analyzed" by Freud as they strolled through the streets together. In the evening, Eitingon attended meetings of the society, where he questioned Freud critically about his doctrines and elicited clarifications that are still important.

Psychoanalytic education and treatment thus went hand in hand, as had been the case since Freud's own clinical insights and self-analysis had reinforced each other to create a new dimension in psychology. This mutual interaction did not come to an end at any precise time; indeed, it continued throughout Freud's life. Until 1901, he intuitively used Wilhelm Fliess as his "analyst," sending him letters that were actually sessions combining explorations of personal and scientific problems. After a break with Fliess, these activities were carried over to the meetings with the group and into transferences toward the individual members.

The nature of transference was still obscure, however, and was especially difficult to recognize beneath the facade of educational, scientific, and organizational enterprises that engaged the growing society. Moreover, Freud's own status, actual and psychological, underwent rapid change after the group was formed, complicating the task of self-analysis. Where previously he had been predominantly a disciple and "son" learning from such older men as Brücke, Meynert, Charcot, and Breuer and had even placed himself in a filial position toward the somewhat younger Fliess, he was now a prominent figure and an older man sought out by pupils and "sons" of his own. He was distinctly the oldest in the group, and Otto Rank and Fritz Wittels were actually young enough to be sons. His external position also changed markedly as he emerged from the isolation, hostility, and derision that had surrounded him as the first analyst and as he gained recognition from an increasing number of followers.

The first group was very different from a modern psychoanalytic society. For several decades now, members of psychoanalytic societies have been required to prove their eligibility by completing their own analyses, demonstrating an ability to analyze others, and providing certification as to the soundness of their education. None of these preconditions was possible in the beginning. The early followers were drawn largely from nonmedical circles, few possessed therapeutic experience, and none except Freud himself had been subjected to more than a modicum of personal analysis. There could be little debate about the principles of the young science. They might be accepted or rejected, but Freud alone had used the necessary investigative tools and was the only authority in the field.

Indeed, analytic knowledge itself was in its infancy. Even by 1906, when the membership had risen to nineteen and the first formal minutes were being recorded by Rank, the indispensable background for the discussions was to be obtained from a few works, whose essence might easily have been limited to *Studies on Hysteria, The Interpretation of Dreams*, and the consolidation of the libido theory in *Three Essays on the Theory of Sexuality*.

Educational And Scientific Aspects

Freud, searching in 1914 for the causes of the many withdrawals and painful schisms in the previous few years, wondered whether matters might have turned out more favorably had he organized his following along the lines of an educational institution rather than as a society of ostensible equals. The fact is, however, that inevitably the group had functioned as an educational enterprise from the beginning, although the therapeutic and personal aspects were never far from the surface.

The early followers, representing varied professional backgrounds, had in common a devotion to intellectual and cultural advancement. It was a period of rapid change, but progress in the physical and industrial sciences was not matched by corresponding achievements in the mental sphere. Laborious attempts by neurologists to explain psychological activity in terms of brain functions were doomed to failure and had been abandoned by Freud himself in 1895. More was to be learned about human motivation and behavior from contemporary writers like Ibsen, Strindberg, and Gide than from the neurologists. Freud was able to place the writer's insights within the framework of a scientific psychology.

His own vision of psychoanalysis extended beyond the boundaries of the clinical. He recognized that the abnormal could be encompassed and treated only within a total perspective of human behavior. *The Interpretation of Dreams* had already sought to eschew the neuroses as source material and to fashion the outlines of a normal mental apparatus from a study of thought processes during sleep. Freud's research thereafter produced in rapid succession insights into behavior in everyday life, wit, religion, literature, and the normal maturation of sex life.

In the selection of prospective members for the group, Freud deliberately sent invitations to representatives of nonmedical specialties—musicologists, teachers, a publisher, etc. When Max Graf, a music critic, was invited to join the circle, he expressed his astonishment and was told that Freud wished to include experts in other fields who could discuss his theories from their own viewpoints. Later, Graf was assigned the task of investigating the psychology of great musicians and the process of musical composition. An important study of Wagner's *The Flying Dutchman* resulted. Freud definitely intended to use his group not only for the members' own education but beyond that to propagate psychoanalysis among the most diverse elements and thus spread the psychoanalytic movement. He was a crusader, and this group was the first of his legions of educators.

Within the group of physicians in the society, few had psychiatric training—the specialty at that time was virtually unknown—and Freud drew from each what he had to contribute to psychoanalytic insight. The pediatrician was especially welcome, for child observation was already recognized as particularly crucial for the confirmation and future development of Freud's postulates. Thus it may be said that the membership of the society was calculated, so far as possible, to be an assembly of the widest range of cultural representatives available and to lend social reality-testing to Freud's clinical perspectives.

Although dissensions within the group have received great stress, the fact is that the conflict-free area of growth was far more significant than the dissensions. The experiment launched in 1901 was, despite Freud's misgivings after the painful schisms of 1911 to 1913, a tremendous success. These pioneers were participating, and may well have sensed it, not only in a struggle for a new key to themselves and all humanity but in one of the greatest intellectual and therapeutic experiments of all times—the realignment of man's vision to include areas of his mental processes hitherto excluded from consciousness. In this sense, they were actually speeding the progress of biological evolution, which has allied the specifically human with the dominance of conscious control over the forces that make for individual as well as group survival and enjoyment in life.

Therapeutic Aspects

The therapeutic aspects of the learning process were inherent in Freud's teachings. His clinical experience provided the inner core of his data and insights, which inevitably extended to the deepest motivational levels within his followers. The recognition of one's own neurosis, at least in projected form, lies latent even in the unenlightened or normal person, and Freud's adherents tended to belong to neither category. Many of them, Jews like himself in a world that was destroying even their traditions, were also rejected by or alienated from the institutions that lend the individual a sense of relatedness to his culture. Their search for an acceptable identity was individual and social, therapeutic and adaptive.

His followers often made their acquaintance with him through his books, and their reports display an intermingling of intellectual enlightenment with hopes of cure and even the sense of a religious experience. The contemplation of Freud's work on dreams was, according to Hanns Sachs, like "a moment of destiny for me."

A. A. Brill made his adherence to Freudianism conditional upon a scientific trial that may be more justly compared to an ordeal of faith. Unable to recall the name of a patient, Brill invoked the method of free association, about which he had recently read, to pry the secret from the unconscious. It was in vain. Later he wrote: "I became discouraged and thought to myself, 'If that is the way I find a thing through the Freudian method, I shall never be a Freudian.' " Awaking toward morning the next day, he wrestled with the problem for another hour and was rewarded with the recollection he sought. "If I had not been able to find it, I probably would never have continued to take the slightest interest in Freud" (Brill 1938).

Freud would doubtless have concluded that the outcome of this self-devised act of faith was determined neither by chance nor by divine intervention but was an inner decision, already made, that was gradually, like a hypnotic command, given access to consciousness.

The twenty-year-old Rank also sought out Freud after he felt a sense of revelation while reading *The Interpretation of Dreams*. He was impelled to present himself to the inspired author and consult with him about a manuscript on art that he was writing. Rank's true purpose—to be accepted as a disciple—was accomplished. Freud was so impressed that he undertook to advise Rank about his studies and finally in 1906 brought him into the society both as a potential contributor to the nonmedical side of psychoanalysis and as the paid secretary of the organization. This latter position not only helped support the youth but resulted in the valuable minutes that he kept for nearly ten years.

The traditional myth of Ulysses and Telemachus suggests itself in this connection, the search of the father for the son and the son for the father. Rank, who at sixteen had repudiated his own alcoholic father, did so passively by refusing to speak to him and by retiring into a troubled schizoid world of diaries, art, and contemplated suicide. The new vision that he sensed in Freud's explanation of the meaning of dreams made possible an outward turning to an object world where he found actual contact with a more encouraging father. Later both men collaborated in scientifically evolving the concepts of the family romance, birth anxiety, and the myth of the birth of the hero.

The aura of the legendary adhered also to Freud's recruitment of other young men, such as Tausk and Sachs. Their recruitment into the society followed along similar lines and made the group a vehicle for the establishment of father-son relationships. To study and crusade with Freud was no mere educational exercise. It meant friends, financial aid, a cause, and a career. There would be patients, aid in writing papers, and positions as teachers, editors, and officers in organizations as Freud's spell conquered the outer world as remarkably as it established dominance over the unconscious. "I am a conquistador!" Freud exclaimed in a triumphal moment. Even the dissenters made their way by breaking with him and lending themselves as spokesmen and witnesses for the opposition.

The therapeutic aspects of the society's sessions were further heightened by the fact that the meetings were held in his office. Wittels reminisced in 1924 that "The couch and the armchair behind it were the arena of Freud's Nibelungen labors. For us, each article was laden with symbolism." Some members had literally stretched out on the couch and would never be entirely freed from the symbolism.

Wittels' natural recourse to the epic and the myth to describe the atmosphere of the sessions was shared by other members of the group. On Freud's fiftieth birthday, May 6, 1906, they presented him with a medallion which bore his portrait on one side and on the other a line from Sophocles hailing Oedipus as one "who divined the famous riddle and was a man most mighty." Jones tells of the emotion with which Freud confessed his own youthful daydream of seeing his bust among similar tributes to famous professors and engraved with just that line. The transferences and countertransferences operating within the group could scarcely be better epitomized than through this episode.

Certain parallels between the conduct of the meetings, as devised by Freud, and the investigative techniques of psychoanalysis also intensified the therapeutic aspects of the proceedings. Freud's own personality was probably a common factor in both the educational and the therapeutic situation.

Freud always presided, so distance was established between himself and his followers. His position as chairman, reinforced by his authority as the foremost analyst, ensured that all remarks were ultimately addressed to him. Correspondingly, he is said to have preferred addressing a particular person, real or fancied, so that, as in analysis, a one-to-one relationship was established, despite the group setting.

An aspect of free association was used for the regulation of the discussions. After a presentation, each member of the group was called on in turn and obliged to speak when his name was drawn from a Greek urn, which stood in their midst like the embodiment of psychic determinism if not of fate. The resistance of patients to verbalization under such circumstances found its counterpart in the anxiety experienced by members who were prone to escape on one pretext or another before the drawings began. The imperatives of the urn were to become the targets of more open rebellion as group resistances to Freud mounted.

The themes of the unconscious and of sexuality were always in the foreground and in themselves provided natural bridges between the educational and the underlying therapeutic aspects of the discussions. Nunberg describes the tendency of the meetings to drift from the analysis of patients to self-analysis of the members themselves, of their sexual difficulties, memories, fantasies, and personal lives. The conditions for modern group therapy had been created and were to be partly resolved empirically and with scientific insight by Freud and the other participants. Large areas proved insurmountable through self-analysis, so they required other measures of control.

In the discussions that followed the presentation of a paper, Freud alone had the privilege of intervening at will. The lucidity of his expositions, as impressive in spontaneous utterances as in his writings, led to a summing-up that possessed the impact of an interpretation. Graf, Wittels, and Reik remember him as always speaking last. Actually, this was by no means the case, and Wittels is probably correct in surmising that, after Freud had spoken, a subject was closed for them.

Submissive acceptance, the product of awe and relative ignorance, was, of course, countered by ambivalence, negativism, and increasingly informed and independent judgments. The working-through processes, after the interpretations, were diffused through channels of education, therapy, scientific achievement, acting out, dropping out, neurosis, and—in some instances—suicide. Freud naturally became the focal point and mediator among the various strivings that sought expression. When his mediations were successful, he promoted the differentiation of aims and the transformation of instinctual into neutral energy; when they were unsuccessful, the opposite was the outcome. His own personality, however, was at the center of the entire system.

Freud's actual personality was revealed to his followers only gradually as it crystallized out from the aura of genius, first encounters, and structured settings for scientific debate. This crystallization was never complete, no matter how long they knew him and no matter how close they came to his inner circle. There is much agreement that central to this inaccessibility was a certain aloofness. Andreas-Salome wrote: "He enters the class with the appearance of moving to the side. There is in this gesture a will to solitude, a concealment of himself within his own purposes, which by his preference would be no concern of his school or his public" (1964). Similarly, his published self-analyses tell us more of his life than any autobiography has ever revealed, yet one does not really discover in them the inner self of Sigmund Freud.

Only Stekel, according to Ernest Jones, who was not quite accurate, ever dared to address him more familiarly than as "Herr Professor." It is notable that, even after many years, followers were apt to refer to themselves as his pupils or, with a note of deeper reverence, to call him "the Master." Letters addressed to and from his oldest associates were scarcely less formal. Graf spoke of the meetings in terms that compare Freud with a Moses presiding over a religious sect that was sometimes provoking in its insubordination, and Tausk alluded earnestly to psychoanalysis as a "scientific religion."

Yet Freud does seem to have unbent, as far as he was capable, with the group. He appreciated their enrichment of his intellectual and social life after his years of isolation as the first psychoanalyst. He played the part of host, serving coffee and cigars and bringing back gifts from abroad for the "Wednesday gentlemen." The minutes show him engaging in jokes, such as that all cooks were paranoid, especially his own, or crying out unguardedly that a certain patient was an "absolute swine." In contrast to earlier statements, in letters to Fliess, which have been construed as indicating a premature end to his potency, he remarked on November 18, 1908, at the age of 52, that he would write on love when his sex life was extinguished. The human side of Freud and his personal opinions were also revealed when he chided a young colleague, Wittels, for views derogatory to female physicians. Nevertheless, he himself was rather dubious that medicine was a proper field for women, although he joined in welcoming them to the society in 1910.

Still, a deep chasm remained between Freud and his followers. Here one must take cognizance of Freud's unique intellectual qualities and of an orientation that has been called rigid but that was probably another manifestation of the same firmness of commitment and adherence to scientific reality-testing that had led to the discovery of psychoanalysis and was continued into its development and defense. Graf recalls Freud as a brilliant speaker to whom words came readily: "On the most difficult subjects he spoke as he wrote, with the imagination of an artist, using comparisons from the most varied field of knowledge. His lectures were enlivened with quotations from the classics, especially from Goethe's *Faust*" (1942).

In the minutes, illustrations from case histories and dreams follow in unending and fascinating succession as new ideas were constantly adumbrated. A stream of publications bore out the promise of these ideas. Views that his students had laboriously acquired were swept away by the latest bursts of insight. Such a man, as Nunberg pointed out, was an impossible ideal, beyond emulation or identification, and a source of constant frustration to such ambitious followers as Adler and Tausk.

Many felt that he was overly critical in his judgments and intolerant of opposition, yet the minutes rarely bear out this impression. His efforts to teach the correct analytic approach to the inexperienced were unremitting, it is true, and the contributions that others made did not always seem to him as important or as valid as they were to their exponents. Yet he was mild and scientific in most interchanges, accepted with little challenge and even with admiration the consistent opposition of Adler, and seems to have gained his reputation for severity more because of his role as a superego figure than because of his actual conduct. He was no doubt sincere in his statement in later years that he was disposed to tolerate the shortcomings of his followers in view of their courage in accepting psychoanalysis. Yet these followers seem to have understood and resented this tolerance as well as the conscientious and unremitting efforts to educate them.

Freud's reminiscences, his letters to friends, his fantasies, and his behavior indicate that the tolerance often wore thin and merged into resentment at the unending forms of resistance he encountered. Educational ambition as well as therapeutic ambition can be self-defeating to all concerned. Freud's self-image seems to have been that of a patriarch conveying visions of the truth to bickering and unworthy followers, a man for the ages lost among lilliputians who sought to usurp his accomplishments rather than benefit from them. He inquired of Andreas-Salome why they could not all be like Rank, the dutiful son, although he already sensed the delayed rebellion that would assail him from even that quarter. He was indeed a tormented titan. However, Freud's greatest opponent came from within himself—from the beleaguered ego that sought to be freed from the same patriarchal superego and, still incompletely analyzed, had to be projected through unconscious sympathy into a counteridentification with his own critics in the society.

The Group's Proceedings

The ferments which took place within the group during the educational process may be followed with almost autosymbolic accuracy in the first volume of the *Minutes of the Vienna Psychoanalytic Society* (1962–1976), covering the period from October 1906 to June 1908. This volume opens with a presentation in which Rank dutifully applies the teachings of Freud to a new field, mythology, and closes with a full-fledged challenge to Freudian theories and personal leadership by Adler and his paper on aggression.

Rank's study, "The Incest Drama and Its Complications," was the forerunner of his classical work, *The Incest Motif in Poetry and Saga* (1912), which Freud himself considered the foremost contribution of his students during this period. Freud's own commentaries could not have been more painstaking, systematic, impartial, or helpfully intended. However, the young man, appearing for the first presentation before the group and the awe-inspiring father figure, may well have felt rejected. In any event, although Rank had anticipated an early publication of this work, its appearance was delayed for five years, as he noted in the introduction, because of inner inhibitions rather than external difficulties.

Freud first took up the manner of Rank's presentation, finding it loose, as did other discussants, and offering concrete suggestions for a more coherent organization of the material. Then he carefully reviewed the contents, citing clinical studies that would have bearing on inferences derived from literary themes and their assumed connections with the personal lives of authors. Such measures, aimed at limiting speculation, were further buttressed by Freud's insistence on a multidisciplinary approach that did not claim for psychoanalysis a disproportionately important share in the total constellation of events. Thus, where Rank wished to approach the madness of Orestes as a psychological reaction to the murder of his mother, Freud reminded him of the need to trace in the legend the ascendancy of a patriarchal over a matriarchal form of society.

Similarly, Freud took exception to the inclusion of the Titans Uranus and Cronus among the examples of beings with incestuous dispositions. After all, he pointed out dryly, there was no one outside their family with whom they could have had sex. In the course of his discussion, Freud casually introduced the concepts of the family romance and the antithetical meaning of primal words, concepts that were not to appear in his published works for several years.

The distance in grasp and style of exposition that separated Freud from his followers at this point indicates the vast scope of the educational task that lay ahead. Some withdrew from the group, especially under the pressure of the remorseless urn, which did not permit temporizing. Among the early drop-outs was Phillip Frey, a schoolteacher who had written on analytic subjects but who on this occasion felt it appropriate to complain that Rank had interpreted everything "according to the Freudian method." Frey could see no reason for regarding the poetic image of a shackled hero as the psychic projection of an inner inhibition. He also took exception to interpreting as a castration the removal by Oedipus of a sword and belt from his father's body. After all, Frey pointed out, the hero did not even know that the victim was his own father.

For the most part, the comments of other participants were similarly naive or unrestrained, evoking from Freud only patient explanation. Adolf Deutsch, a physiotherapist, simply made the point that a previous speaker, in some brief remarks, had already anticipated what he himself had to say. Edward Hitschmann, who was to become a great analytic biographer, considered Rank's work on mythology a superfluous extension of Freud's discoveries about the Oedipus complex and predicted that such one-sided incest-hunting would bring the speaker to a sad end. This all-too-prophetic remark was fulfilled only after Rank had given up the Oedipus complex for an equally one-sided devotion to the birth trauma.

Paul Federn was already sufficiently advanced to take a more favorable attitude toward Rank's research, but he was surprised at the ubiquity of incestuous tendencies. Adler went even further in supporting Rank, citing clinical experiences to confirm several of his interpretations of sexual imagery. Nevertheless, he gave a hint of future divergences with the remark that attempts to explain criminal acts by tracing them to their sexual roots explained nothing—a contention that, put in less drastic form, would have coincided with Freud's treatment of Orestes. Stekel, as was to be the case regularly, couched his criticisms on a personal level and found Rank's paper schoolboyish. At the same time, with a slap at "the Master" himself, Stekel, like Frey, complained that the myth had been "seen through spectacles colored by Freudian teachings" but without going beyond Freud. Certainly this attempt to go beyond Freud was Stekel's own consistent aim.

The minutes do not confirm the notion that Freud was surrounded by sycophants or that he showed resentment of their criticisms. The interchanges after Rank's presentation were typical of later meetings, with Freud offering brilliant and thorough appraisals of the material and seeking to find his way constructively to differences between himself and other members of the group. Stekel and later Sadger and Wittels made it difficult to keep the exchanges on a purely educational level. Sometimes personalities presented problems; at other times persistent intellectual disagreements cloaked negative transferences or approaches that were genuinely incompatible with psychoanalysis.

From 1906 to 1908, the group showed impressive progress in understanding by the members and in the level of the discussions. On the other hand, emotional attacks on each other increased in frequency and intensity, and a particular charge—plagiarism—became rampant. In the plagiarism charges, there is the appearance of a resistance that has crystallized. Hostilities, displaced from Freud to one another, found intellectualization in the idea that these others sought to deprive them of their claims to originality. These recurrent charges revealed an inner resentment of their own need to borrow from Freud and their wish to identify with his envied originality. In time, the hostility and the accusations of stealing their ideas were turned against Freud himself.

Stekel and Adler lend themselves especially well as examplars, respectively, of the frankly emotional displays of transference difficulties and of the more subtle manifestations hidden behind intellectual exchanges.

The note of sibling rivalry that prompted Stekel to greet new members with a notable lack of charity, already apparent in relation to Rank, was duplicated a few months later when Wittels made his first presentation, on the psychology

of female assassins. Wittels concluded with the injudicious remark that he did
not like hysterics, and Stekel, opening the discussion, retorted that this remark
was a projection of the hysterical tendencies Wittels shrank from recognizing
in himself. The charge was probably true. Wittels, like Stekel himself, had a
gift for promoting the appearance of regressive trends within the group.

Charges of plagiarism were especially apt to emanate from Stekel, as when
he played an important part in driving Alfred Meisl out of the society after
Meisl's presentation of "Hunger and Love" on January 23, 1907. Although
Meisl's differentiation between sexual and nonsexual instincts was approved by
Freud himself on this occasion and the speaker was bringing to the fore the need
of the analyst to give more heed to the self-preservative tendencies, ultimately
the ego, Stekel rejected Meisl's claim to priority with the sneer that "no one
else would want to use Meisl's few novel ideas." As he had done with Wittels,
Stekel proceeded to turn from the substance of the presentation to an analysis
of the speaker himself, interpreting the argument that non-sexual instincts required consideration as a sign that Meisl was sexually repressed. Freud took the
occasion to support Meisl's contentions and made the important observation that
both sexual and nonsexual instincts join in guiding the infant to its first love
object—a formulation that anticipates the later concept of narcissism and even
Hartmann's descriptions of the undifferentiated phase and the inborn apparatus
of the ego.

Stekel was the most vocal in his personal criticisms of others and the most
sensitive to criticism directed against him or his ideas. Freud was fond of Stekel
as a good companion but objected not only to his ill-considered attacks on others
and his intuitive and superficial approach to analytic problems but also to his
lack of scientific conscience—that is, to Stekel's disregard for the truth, as Jones
sets forth. Stekel and Freud's ultimate break, expectably enough, came during
a tilt that mixed personal, scientific, and administrative motives. After Freud
made Stekel an editor of the *Zentralblatt fuer Psychoanalyse*, he requested him
to permit Tausk to write reviews for the journal. Enraged at this sign of favor
to a sibling rival, Stekel refused and was unmoved by the argument that his
own appointment involved responsibility to a psychoanalytic organization and
should not be used for personal motives detrimental to science. Freud had to
withdraw his support, and their break followed.

Stekel's special qualities provided assets as well as liabilities for the development of psychoanalysis. His free use of intuitive judgments without consideration of methodology and theory placed him in a position to recognize—though
with typical overgeneralizations and distortions—the elements of bisexuality,
fears of death, and symbolism in dreams. Insights—and dangerous overgeneralizations—also appeared in his early recognition of characteristics of the ag-

gressive drives at a time when Freud found himself unable to regard them as other than particular manifestations of the libido. As one of three members who opened a discussion on suicide (all three—Tausk and Federn were the others—would one day become suicides themselves), Stekel could deliver himself of the striking statement that "the suicide is tormented by a deep sense of guilt: no one kills himself who has not wanted to kill someone else."

Moving away from his pansexual position as he became more aware of the death drive—a term he introduced but did not use in quite the same sense as Freud—Stekel proclaimed that hate was older than love, aggression deeper than sex. The jumble of half-baked and ill-considered propositions that poured from his pen moved Freud and other members of the society to plead in vain that he restrict his output and not bring psychoanalysis into disrepute. Stekel retorted that he was accustomed to finding that his contributions met with little understanding but were ultimately taken up into the writings of others, not least of all by the Herr Professor.

With a rising tide of discontent discernible among the disciples toward the end of 1907 and the beginning of 1908—a collective adolescence, one might say, that reflected emergence from antecedent dependency but with a continuing need for Freud's guidance, which was now galling—Freud himself began to show dismay and a longing to pass on the leadership to someone else. Roazen reports that Freud wrote, in a self-analytic mood: "What personal pleasure is to be derived from analysis I obtained during the time when I was alone . . . an incurable breach must have come into existence at that time between me and other men" (1968).

The growth of a psychoanalytic group in Zurich and the proposal that a first international meeting be held in Salzburg in April, 1908, made Freud turn hopefully to Jung on February 18 with the suggestion that Bleuler preside. "My Viennese colleagues would behave better," he predicted.

Two stormy meetings of the Vienna society on February 5 and 12 supply background to Freud's complaints against his own group. At the first of these meetings Adler brought forward a recommendation that a change be made in the usual methods of conducting the sessions. The urn and its coercive authority came under attack in a particularly transparent displacement from the leader himself. Next, Federn suggested that measures be taken to curb "intellectual communism"—that is, plagiarism. Sadger, so often the victim, wished the chairman to take more definitive steps to suppress personal invectives and attacks.

With these proposals, the long-standing discontents were finally brought to the surface of group consciousness for discussion. It remained for Graf to go more deeply into the subject and indicate that the proposals "stem from a feeling of uneasiness." Tactfully, he related this feeling to the fact that the group was on the way to becoming a full-fledged organization rather than simply the invited guests of the Herr Professor. Graf suggested that the meetings be transferred from Freud's office to a different site.

Freud responded that he was opposed to using his powers as chairman to suppress any utterances except those conversations that might disturb the speaker. For himself, he waived the right to protect his remarks from plagiarism—a deeply ironic statement. Then, confronting the underlying issues more directly, he expressed the opinion that, if the members could not stand each other or freely express scientific opinions, perhaps the entire enterprise ought to be abandoned. However, he had hopes that deeper psychological understanding might yet appear and assist in overcoming the difficulties. Clearly, he was referring to some advance in self-analytic insight.

Freud's stand, expressed with restraint and dignity, seems entirely correct from both the educational and the therapeutic viewpoints. He took as the basis of his views the contention that the meetings were an educational situation in which chairman and participants were expected to maintain an alliance directed to promoting the scientific and educational aims that constituted the purpose of the meetings. Self-analysis, promoted by these meetings, should be used to correct divergences from the announced aims.

That Freud would transmute the experiences of this session into scientific and self-analytic terms was to be expected, and the echoes of those experiences are heard in references of later years to "the uncanny and coercive characteristics of group formation. . . . The group wishes to be governed by unrestricted force; it has an extreme passion for authority. . . . The primal father is the group ideal, which governs the ego in the place of the ego ideal" (1921, p. 57).

The destiny of the primal father to be overthrown and replaced by one of the sons was further elaborated in *Totem and Taboo* and was reasserted, despite better scientific knowledge, in *Moses and Monotheism*. Freud seems to have perpetuated, in his appraisal of group dynamics, unanalyzed fragments of his own family romance.

On February 12, a committee headed by Adler and appointed to consider the proposals put forward at the last meeting, recommended the abolition of the urn, a widening of the educational process by including book reviews on a more regular basis, brief case presentations by individual members, and a request for more notice about longer papers to be presented so that all concerned could be better prepared. The sense of these changes was to formalize the meetings, to give the members a greater share of the responsibility, and to reduce the overshadowing personal influence of Freud. There was no real solution to the problem of the "ill humor in the empire," as members put it euphemistically, and even the proposal to abolish the urn was blocked, probably out of deference to Freud. This fetish, however, was stripped of some of its authority: it could still be used to summon members to speak, but they were within their rights if they decided to ignore its call.

Certainly the meeting at Salzburg in April, 1908, was not conducive to greater harmony. Freud unmistakably favored Jung and the Zurich group. When he went to America the next year, he took none of the Viennese in his retinue. With his increasing inner and outer withdrawal from the Vienna society, a gap had to be closed.

A counter claimant for the leadership of the Vienna group, Alfred Adler, had long been on hand, pursuing a relationship to Freud that was governed by a curious process. Adler brought to the fore precisely the areas of the personality that had found representation in the Freudian system with the greatest difficulty—aggression, the ego, and social adaptation. Freud, aware of these shortcomings, found in Adler a constant reminder and stimulus to consider these problems, so he welcomed Adler's contributions and treated him with marked respect. The antipathy with which he could react to Stekel and Sadger was almost never in evidence with Adler—but neither was there any warmth. The same might be said of Adler's own behavior toward Freud.

The evolution of the Adlerian system of psychology may be followed in considerable detail in the minutes of the group. His interests were centered successively on organic inferiority, aggression, and the masculine protest. With less self-consciousness than Freud's scrutiny of his own dynamics, Adler was doubtlessly reflecting his personality structure as it unfolded under the impact of transference and analytic teachings. Adler was fourteen years younger than his eventual arch-rival, and the key to his personality may be found in early rickets, which prevented him from walking until the age of four. Thereafter, he repeatedly fell and was involved in street accidents because of the unsteadiness of his legs. Inhibited in his motor activity, he read a great deal and was well versed in many cultural topics, like Freud himself. His interest in becoming a physician was also an outgrowth of his ailments during childhood. Lifelong jealousy of an older brother paved the way for the ambivalence he showed toward Freud.

On November 7, 1906, Adler presented a paper, "On the Organic Bases of Neuroses," in which both his potential contributions to analysis and his inevitable future divergences from Freud were apparent. This prime motivating power of the mind, he held, was to be found in inherently defective organs, which influence the psychic superstructure so that it becomes a medium for cultural adaptation to the defect. Certain points of correspondence to Freud's instinct theory may be discerned. If the Adlerian and Freudian systems were to be reconciled, however, a bridge was needed to the concepts of infantile sexuality and repression. This bridge was not created on this occasion nor on later ones.

Freud's responses were at first cautiously favorable. But when, on March 5, 1907, Adler implemented his theoretical outline with a case presentation, a minor but distinct cleavage between the two men became observable. Where Adler assumed that a patient had developed talent as a speaker in order to overcompensate for initial stuttering, Freud held that the stuttering was an inhibition of earlier powers of speech. It became increasingly apparent, as Freud repeatedly pointed out, that Adler's use of analytic tools and inferences was very limited and that he took the leap from biological assumptions to social adjustments through a rarefied psychological atmosphere.

The implication of the organic in all behavior, as construed by Adler, began to approach mysticism and yielded dogmatic obsessions rather than empirically derived conclusions. Adler looked for speech defects in singers, visual defects in dramatists, abnormal palatal reflexes in cooks, etc. He saw in symbols the representation of inferior organs striving for a certain degree of perfection. Few of the members responded favorably to these constructions, and complaints were common that Adler was dragging organic inferiority into every situation to the detriment of a truly analytic grasp and to the boredom and irritation of the group.

Adler's interest was obsessively displaced to the instinct of aggression, which became the instrument for his most useful contributions to psychoanalysis. He made the valid point that rage was the emotion corresponding to aggression, just as love corresponded to the sex instinct. Many useful clinical observations and theoretical formulations were later added. The concepts of turning against the self and of reaction formations to aggression proved permanent additions to instinct and ego psychology and a nucleus for formulations about the superego. Adler saw in the fear of death a self-reproach for wishing the death of another person, in altruism a defense against sadism (as in the choice of medicine for a vocation), and in the Marxist concept of the class struggle (Adler was an active social democrat) an opportunity to sublimate aggression constructively and make history consciously. When he sought to combine Marxism and Freudianism in a single framework, Freud repudiated the effort, perhaps a little too peremptorily. Adler saw culture as expanding the self, Freud as limiting the self.

Freud did not so much reject the contentions of Adler on the subject of aggression as insist that aggression was merely an aspect of the libido. Nevertheless, under the prodding of his opponent, Freud accepted Adler's ideas of a "confluence" of sex and aggression, but applied it to a fusion of sex and ego instincts. Significantly, many of Freud's early comments on the ego came about under the impetus of discussions with his adversary.

In general, Freud's appraisal of Adler's system was correct and even admiring.

The rival framework, he repeated over and over again, represented an excellent contribution to insight into the surface of the personality—the ego, consciousness, social adaptation. But it did not reach down into the unconscious, it avoided the sex instinct, and its concepts of the neuroses and therapy drifted further and further from the Oedipus complex and the indispensable doctrine of repression. This appraisal of Adlerian psychology was equally correct.

There was little acrimony or even impoliteness in these exchanges over the years, and it is difficult to reconcile the even tone of the exchanges with the traditions of Freud as a despot embattled in defense of his analytic principles. His sharp words are usually to be found directed toward coarse and provocative personal behavior or toward slipshod presentations of analytic thought, like Stekel's, rather than toward the honest and consistent exposition of a different viewpoint. Freud's likes and dislikes of his followers were often apparent and had little to do with their analytic orthodoxy. Rank, the good son and loyal disciple, seems to have been neither more nor less favored than Wittels, a perennial naughty boy whom Freud found amusing. Sadger, who made quite important contributions to classical analysis, was distinctly disliked because of his personality by Freud—and by most other members of the group.

Transformation of the Group

The personal side of the relationship between Freud and Adler was at first obscured behind their polite intellectual discussions, but it figured increasingly in the rifts that grew between them and accompanied a crisis within Freud himself. Adler's boldness in reaching out for intellectual and political dominance of the group was complementary to Freud's increasing withdrawal from the Vienna group and his preference for the Zurich contingency. Freud reasoned that the academic status and Aryan backgrounds of the Swiss offered a greater guarantee for the future of psychoanalysis than did his Viennese colleagues, although it is to be doubted that such rationalizations provided the true motives. As the second International Psycho-Analytical Congress, to be held in Nuremburg on March 30 and 31, 1910, drew nearer, Freud pushed plans to transfer the leadership of the psychoanalytic movement to Jung and its headquarters to Zurich.

Ferenczi, who had been chosen to convey this message to the Viennese in Nuremberg, succeeded only in uniting the angry delegation behind Adler and Stekel. Freud then decided to resign from the presidency of the Viennese group and to recommend that Adler succeed him. That he should select the man who was the greatest threat to analysis as his successor, even if he regarded him as the most able member of the society, seems to require explanations that have not been forthcoming. Perhaps, as Adler indicated, the choice was not Freud's alone to make. A hint of deeper psychological motives appears in a letter to Ferenczi on April 3, in which Freud refers to himself as a "dissatisfied and unwanted old man." An inner bond with the rebel against the father and the paternalistic aspects of psychoanalysis seems to have been present.

The stage was set for a remarkable group confrontation on April 6, 1910, after the return to Vienna. With the contemplated transition in power from one leader to the other on the agenda, the group meeting was a veritable occasion for a totem meal involving Freud and his "primal horde." Before the assembled group, Freud undertook to carry through his intentions of politely ceding the leadership to Adler, who would have none of this evasion. He criticized Freud for his behavior at Nuremburg and spoke—almost in the language of *Totem and Taboo*, published two years later—of the banding together of the group against the founding father of psychoanalysis. Adler then offered a program that clearly promised to replace Freud's administrative and intellectual leadership with his own. The membership was to be widened, as it soon was to admit more of Adler's friends; the society would remove from Freud's office; it would publish a journal, which in time Adler and Stekel edited; and Freud himself, while retaining leadership, would be relieved of administrative duties. Later, Adler used publications of the society and educational courses to make psychoanalysis a cover for his own views.

Stekel, as first commentator, could not imagine how the group would exist without Freud, whom he nevertheless accused of harboring a deep hatred against Vienna. He suggested that Freud remain as president, Adler be made vice-president with administrative duties, and the forthcoming publication be used to prove, despite the leader's apparent doubts, that Vienna and not Zurich held the key to the future of psychoanalysis. Others joined the discussion in much the same vein. A note of sadness dominated, not the bitterness and readiness to sweep aside Freud that Adler alone had sounded. Local patriotism emerged repeatedly in the feeling that Freud had mistakenly prized the Zurich analysts as offering a better soil than the Viennese for the future. Wittels commented that his countrymen possessed, as the Swiss did not, "a neurosis which is necessary for entry into Freud's teachings." Sadger added—in graceful enough fashion for once—that, although Freud had been fed up with the Viennese for two years, they were still ahead of the Zurich group because of his "steady leadership, instruction and advice." A solution was found when, in response to vigorous demands that he at least accept an honorary presidency, Freud agreed to retain a scientific chairmanship while the presidency went to Adler.

At the next meeting, April 13, the transition was sealed symbolically with the total abolition of the urn and the agreement to move the meeting place from Freud's office. The transformation of the Wednesday Evening Society of guests invited to discuss psychoanalysis with the professor into the Viennese Psychoanalytic Society was complete.

Although the occasion had its melancholy aspects for both Freud and the group, it actually marked the successful completion of a phase in which their mutual purposes had been achieved. Psychoanalysis was no longer a one-man discipline, and, although Freud would remain the intellectual leader throughout his life, the society had become a congregation of scientists with varying views and degrees of competence; it was no longer an assemblage of students who sat at the feet of a master. His faults could now be discerned, tolerated, and understood, just like their own. The children had grown up. The former students, like former analysands, had become sufficiently detached to form new object relationships that still left Freud realistically a teacher and prophet.

What lay ahead for Freud himself at this point was a relapse into temporary isolation and inner scrutiny, from which he emerged strengthened, the guilt for primal parricide shifted from himself to his successor, and free to rid himself and the movement of a truly incompatible element. It is scarcely a coincidence that the topic chosen for his own presentation at the Nuremburg congress dealt with the problem of countertransference. Throughout 1910, this subject was on his mind. In October, after some months of rest and a period of travel with Ferenczi, he wrote this latest favored disciple and former analysand (whose future revolt was already discernible), conveying some of the thoughts that had been distilled from the experiences and temporary setback with the group: "I am not the psychoanalytic superman that you construed in your imagination, nor have I overcome the countertransference" (E. Freud 1960). Ferenczi had evidently been engaged in reversing the analytic procedure and exploring the psychology of Freud himself. The master confessed to difficulty in revealing his secrets and acknowledged that his disciple was correct in attributing this difficulty to a permanent incapacity to reach out to others, which was a residue of the traumatic termination of his relationship with Fliess. Freud's disposition to terminate close relationships traumatically went back much further, however. He diagnosed himself, in this letter to Ferenczi, as having regressed to healthy narcissism rather than to paranoia.

As for Adler, once the reins of power were in his hands, he abandoned caution and quickly gave scope to views that carried him increasingly farther away from the Freudian school. The members of the society, educated by Freud and chastened by their guilt toward the rightful leader, found this departure intolerable, and Adler was forced to resign after a few months in office. This act, too, was part of the group's progress in becoming an educational organization, confident of its own purposes and judgment. When Freud turned toward the group again after a period of self-scrutiny, it received him gladly.

On the personal side, Freud, like Adler, had an ambivalent relationship with an older ''brother''—his nephew John, who was a year older than Freud—and guilty memories of a younger brother, Julius, for whose death he felt responsible. With John, he liked to take turns in playing Julius Caesar and Brutus, thus alternating in the murder and revival of a ''brother.'' Adler himself emphasized in his clinical studies the importance of birth order in a family, and his ambivalence with respect to his own brother may well have complemented Freud's. In accepting the opportunity to be Caesar, Adler seems to have opened the way to Freud's long pent-up desire to enact Brutus.

The educational aspects of these meetings promoted an ultimate dominance over the therapeutic, but they also seem to have fostered the emergence of repressed transferences long hidden beneath the cool intellectual exchanges between Freud and Adler. Observers like Graf and Wittels supply pictures of Freud and Adler sitting side by side at the meetings, puffing furiously at cigars. In 1911, the year of the break between them, Freud described, in an addendum to the Schreber case, which helped to precipitate their estrangement, a commentary on the myth that the eagle (Adler) establishes its lineage by looking into the sun without blinking. If it does not, the father casts it out of the eyrie. One eagle apparently failed the test. Adler found a similar image and told Freud that he did not propose to stand in his shadow forever. But Bottome relates that Adler confessed, toward the end of his life, that he had not, after all, caught up with his older brother.

Conclusion

The group that gathered about Freud for instruction in psychoanalysis had multiple functions to perform. It provided a means for continuing his self-analysis and initiating him into group dynamics. It also seems to have provided an impenetrable haven for some resistances. The ostensible educational aims of the other members were all but swallowed up at times by therapeutic needs, aspirations for a career, and a climate that made them into propagandists or antagonists of a revolutionary new concept of the human mind. The triumphs and failures of the group found dramatic expression in the intertwined and opposing personalities and ideas of Sigmund Freud and Alfred Adler.

References

Andreas-Salome, L. (1964). *The Freud Journal*. New York: Basic Books.
Bottome, P. (1957). *Alfred Adler*. New York: Vanguard Press.
Brill, A. A., ed. (1938). *The Basic Writings of Sigmund Freud*. New York: Random House.

Freud, E., ed. (1960). *Letters of Sigmund Freud.* New York: Basic Books.

Freud, S. (1887–1902). *The Origins of Psychoanalysis.* New York: Basic Books, 1954.

———— (1914). On the history of the psychoanalytic movement. *Standard Edition* 14:7–66.

———— (1921). Group psychology and the analysis of the ego. *Standard Edition* 18:69–143.

Graf, M. (1942). Reminiscences of professor Sigmund Freud. *Psychoanalytic Quarterly* 11:465–476.

Jones, E. (1953–1957). *The Life and Work of Sigmund Freud.* 3 vols. New York: Basic Books.

Nunberg, H., and Federn, E. (1962–1975). *Minutes of the Vienna Psychoanalytic Society.* 2 vols. New York: International Universities Press.

Rank, O. (1912). *The Incest Motif in Poetry and Saga.* Leipzig, Vienna: Deuticke.

Reik, T. (1942). *From Thirty Years with Freud.* London: Hogarth Press.

Roazen, P. (1968). *Freud: Political and Social Thought.* New York: Alfred A. Knopf.

Sachs, H. (1945). *Freud, Master and Friend.* London: Imago.

Wittels, F. (1924). *Sigmund Freud.* New York: Dodd, Mead.

Chapter 11

THE FREUD/JUNG LETTERS

LEONARD SHENGOLD, M.D.

When Carl Jung, then an old man, was asked about the project of publishing his correspondence with Sigmund Freud, he said that he felt the letters were not of great scientific interest. In the sense that these letters contain no new exposition of thought, he was right. There is important dialogue about psychosis and narcissism (areas which are still being explored and defined). The reader gets a sense of the two men learning from each other and of the development of their ideas. Jung had the access to hospitalized schizophrenics that Freud lacked, and it was from Jung that Freud derived the supposed "*fact* that these patients reveal their complexes without resistance and are inaccessible to transference" (21J, p. 35; my italics), which Freud used as a basis for some of his theorizing. Freud was at work on several of his basic concepts during these years. But this collection of letters is in marked contrast to the Fliess correspondence which contains a much more active exchange of ideas.

Both sets of letters permit the study of the relationship between scientific ideas and the "complexes" (Jung's term for unconscious clusters of ideas) that, as Freud had discovered, determined them. We see what the two men meant to each other and how their major relationships were mutually invoked. The themes of rivalry with father and with brothers, and of homosexual love, predominate

This is an expanded version of a book review first published in the *Journal of the American Psychoanalytic Association*.

in the Freud-Jung correspondence. For Freud, there is a coming to life in relation to Jung of all of his *revenants*: father, older brother, younger brother, mother, sister, early playmate, and, above all, of Wilhelm Fliess, the arch-revenant (Schur 1972). Fliess was Freud's closest friend during the years of Freud's great discoveries. The neurotic relationship to Fliess served as subject matter for Freud's self-analysis, and Fliess was a kind of auxiliary analyst for him. As he had done before with Fliess, Freud re-lived his earliest years in relation to Jung, but with a difference. Jung came into his life after Freud had achieved his initial mastery of psychoanalysis and written *The Interpretation of Dreams*, and after he had worked at his self-analysis with a resultant partial transcendence of his transference to Fliess. Jung was to attain *his* mastery only after the end of the relationship with Freud and the breakdown that followed it. We know less of Jung's early life than of Freud's, but in these letters we see his crucial relationships come into focus on Freud, "thanks to," as Freud writes his younger friend, "the universal human tendency to keep making new prints of the clichés we bear within us" (p. 98).

Jones, who had read these letters in preparation for his biography of Freud, compares Freud's attachments to Fliess and to Jung, noting similarities, but stating that the intensity of Freud's feeling was far less toward the much younger man. This is obviously so, yet the intensity revealed by these letters is much greater than Jones leads his readers to expect. Indeed, one wonders if, as Jones implies, the greater involvement was always Jung's. Clearly Jung was *left with* the greater involvement: Freud seems able to contain and reduce his wishes toward his "son and heir" while Jung ends things in a near-paranoid blaze of hatred that introduces a period of intense psychic pathology. Freud found in Jung, as he had in Fliess, something he longed for—the promise of magic—which corresponded to something Freud mistrusted in his own personality and felt as a deficiency that would be supplied by another man: "I have always felt that there is something about my personality, my ideas and manner of speaking, that people find strange and repellent, whereas all hearts are open to you" (Freud [to Fliess] 1887–1902, p. 82). It is also important to recall that Jung entered Freud's life at a time when oedipal conflicts can center around a son—a son, too, can promise magical solutions.

It was part of Jung's family romance fantasy, communicated to Freud early in their relationship, that he was the grandchild of an illegitimate son of Goethe. The great man nourished both men's fantasies and influenced their ideals; they were steeped in *Faust*, and their works (including these letters) abound in *Faust* quotations. To Freud, so conscious of his fifty years and still (a trace of the Fliess legacy) half-expecting an early death, this supposed offspring of Goethe, his very name connoting youth*, suddenly appeared as a kind of Mephistopheles, promising magic and beckoning the "old man" out of his comparatively provincial Viennese-Jewish isolation toward the wide world of official scientific and intellectual acceptance. Jung, as Fliess had done before him, showed himself full of self-confidence and surrounded by the aura of success. He promised the marvelous—his first publication was about the psychological implications of the occult, and he had a lifelong interest and belief in it. Under the influence of "the magic of [Jung's] personal presence" (p. 218), Freud allowed himself temporarily and intermittently to share in Jung's belief. Jung had corresponding feelings toward Freud; he writes him in an early letter: "Anyone who knows your science has veritably eaten of the tree of paradise and become clairvoyant" (p. 56). Jung was the son of a minister and as a youth had been obsessed with God and the Devil, both roles he eventually would assign to Freud.

The figure of the devil or the demon was a recurrent metaphor for Freud (Kanzer 1961). Fliess had appeared in this guise: "Demon," Freud addressed Fliess in 1895, "you Demon! Why don't you write to me? How are you? Don't you care at all anymore what I'm doing?" (Schur 1972, p. 87). Here Fliess is reproached for not answering letters, as Freud was so often to reproach Jung. The devil is mentioned dozens of times in the Freud/Jung letters; he was called up by their relationship. The devil is used as a metaphor for the instinctual, for the bad father, for the homosexual seducer, and for the guide toward wisdom (like Mephistopheles), for the creative daemon of the unconscious, and for each other. The relationship between the two during these years can be seen as a love story—a love story with a bad ending. One man transcends the homosexuality and learns from it; the other finds it too much for him, denies it, and breaks down.

The twenty-year difference in the men's ages is a meaningful one for Freud, whose twenty-year-older brother Phillip was a bad father-figure. Jung was young enough for Freud to be his father. In one letter, Freud assumes the role of Philip of Macedon, calling Jung "dear son Alexander" (p. 182), and reassures his appointed successor that he has left him much to conquer. The correspondence starts with a Moses-like invocation of a successor (Freud later calls Jung his Joshua [p. 196]). in which the motif of age addressing youth is first sounded: "in view of my age (50), I hardly expect to see the end of the struggle; but my follower will I hope . . ." i.e.:[p. 6]. Freud was always seeking a comrade as well as a successor—a spiritual brother or son, the one elect person, who, like

---

*Jung is, of course, German for "young": Letter 23F: "Don't take the burden of representing me too hard. You are so enviably *young* and independent" (p. 42; my italics).

Fliess, would appreciate him. Jung, for his part, was looking for a father. His father, who had died in 1899, had been a minister, the man in black who haunts his autobiography. The two men quickly took to each other, and cemented a master-disciple relationship so that after several months of correspondence Jung talked of colleagues moving "closer to *our* side" (p. 9; my italics).

In the early letters, partly in relation to a kind of confessional on Jung's part (a form of communication that recurs), conflicting and unpleasant aspects of Jung's character are revealed: he displayed ambivalence toward authority—the need to defy and the need to submit. Also revealed was the tendency to sacrifice truth to court acceptance: "As you rightly say, I leave our opponents a line of retreat, with the conscious purpose of not making recantation too difficult for them. . . . If I appear to underestimate the therapeutic results of psychoanalysis, I do so only out of diplomatic considerations" (7J, pp. 10–11). Freud, for whom equivocation and diplomacy were so alien, plays the role of analyst, gently and tolerantly underlining Jung's failings. Jung is alternately apologetic and righteous, writing in terms that seem to express blunt honesty: "I speak of things as I understand them and as I believe is right" (p. 15). Freud inclined to see the "diplomacy" as practical know-how. Here was another man with those qualities of assurance and practicality that Freud felt he lacked. (Freud, to Fliess: "I read through your draft in a single breath. I liked tremendously its easy assurance, the natural, almost self-evident way in which each point leads to the next, its unpretentious unfolding of riches . . ." [Freud 1887–1902, p. 42]. The draft mentioned was about the relationships between the nose and sex, and this letter shows the infatuated Freud's credulity [see Jones 1953].) And surely this new man who could so inspire him with confidence could never be a confidence man. Freud expected that his influence would banish Jung's waverings and need for a diplomat's psychology. Jung, after all, had spontaneously affirmed Freud's request "to trust me for the present in matters where your experience does not yet enable you to make up your own mind. . . . I believe I deserve such trust" (8F, p. 13). Nevertheless Freud wrote Jung that "in our special circumstances, the utmost frankness is the best diplomacy" (p. 18). In retrospect, Jung's reply to this seems significant: "I am still young, and now and then *one* has *one's* quirks in the matter of recognition and scientific standing. . . . (my italics; note the shift from the first to the third person that evades responsibility). "I shall never abandon any portion of your theory *that is essential to me*" (p. 20; my italics). Here the confidence man seems to be speaking. I have been told by an analyst who met Freud in the 1930s and asked him about Jung that he would never forget how Freud grimaced in disgust and muttered, "Bad character!" (personal communication from Dr. Robert Fliess). Right or wrong, such a judgment was far from Freud's feeling in 1907. After the first meeting in Vienna on March 3, 1907, Jung wrote Freud rapturously of "the tremendous impression you have made on me. . . . I hope my work for your cause will show you the depths of my gratitude and veneration. I hope and even dream that we may welcome you in Zurich. . . . a visit from you would be seventh heaven for me personally" (p. 26). And Freud replied that Jung had "inspired me with confidence for the future. . . . I now realize that I am as replaceable as everyone else and that I could hope for no one better than yourself, as I have come to know you, to continue and complete my work" (p. 27). Freud was not aware that in choosing his successor he was stirring up what Schur (1972) calls the guilt of the survivor—the feelings in relation to the one-year-younger brother who had died shortly after birth: the successor who, Freud himself said, was one of the two people from his childhood who "now determine the neurotic element, but also the intensity of all my friendships" (1887–1902, p. 219).

As with a new analysand who has transferred positive feelings onto his analyst, Jung felt temporarily that he had conviction: "The last shreds of doubt. . . . about the rightness of your theory. . . . were dispelled by my stay in Vienna" (p. 26). But his ambivalence is quickly evident. When Freud proposes sending Jung a patient he has seen—the "boy from Gorlitz . . . (who) loves his mother, hates his father. . . . he is the first case we shall both have been able to observe directly" (p. 33), Jung uneasily states that there is no room for the boy at the clinic "at present" (p. 35). Freud then sends a theoretical dissertation on paranoia, which includes his famous saying that "anyone who gives more than he has is a rogue" (p. 40). Freud learns from Jung about the "lack of resistance and the fragility of transference" (p. 42) in dementia praecox and shares with him his concept of the psychosis as a regression to auto-erotism. Freud is re-expressing ideas and concepts (e.g., the use of projection in paranoia) that he first wrote about to Fliess in the 1890s. Freud's remarks on paranoia evoke "a long pause" (p. 43) from Jung. The closeness is telling on the younger man; he has trouble understanding Freud's thinking about the linkage of homosexual feeling and paranoia. Jung makes an analogy to dementia praecox patients which those who have read of his childhood religious obsessive struggles can see applies to himself: "The following analogy has always struck me as enlightening: the religious ecstatic who longs for God is one day vouchsafed a vision of God. But the conflict with reality also creates the opposite for him: certainty turns into doubt, God into the devil, and the sublimated sexual joy of the *unio mystica* into sexual anxiety with all its historical spectres" (p. 44).

Freud begins to crave Jung's letters and to reproach him for his delays: "My personality was impoverished by the interruption of our correspondence" (p. 76). Jung brings to Freud, as Fliess had, the promise of the future—the son will make the father immortal. He responds to Jung's praise ("Your *Gravida* is magnificent—I gulped it at one go" ᵂp. 49ᴱ) with "To tell the truth, a statement such as yours means more to me than the approval of a whole medical congress; for one thing it makes the approval of future congresses a certainty" (p. 52; my italics). And Jung replies in ecstatic language: "I rejoice every day in your riches and live from the crumbs that fall from the rich man's table" (p. 56).

As their positive feelings intensify, the concomitant hostility is directed onto their mutual opponents. Freud sends Jung "two bombshells from the enemy camp" (p. 53). Jung is a master of vituperation: "these pachyderms just can't understand anything unless you write it out as big as your fist on their hides" (p. 49). Freud at times reflects Jung's coarseness, and the two gleefully continue to vilify their enemies until enmity breaks out between them.

In the summer of 1907, a new figure appeared who was to bring triangular complications: Karl Abraham. Jung was immediately jealous of Freud's interest in Abraham, and tried to master his hostility toward him. Abraham distrusted Jung, having been with him at Burghölzli since 1904, but Freud would not listen to Abraham's warnings. Jung criticized Abraham, attributing to him character traits of his own—"highly adaptable"—and declaring that Abraham was"totally lacking in psychological empathy, for which reason he is usually very unpopular with the patients" (p. 78). But Jung admitted his jealousy and bias. Freud was interested in Abraham's name, and whether he was Jewish: "Is he a descendant of his eponym?" (p. 79). Jung replied that Abraham "is what his name implies" (p. 81). (See Shengold 1972, for the connection between Freud's and Jung's forgetting of Abraham's *name*, death wishes toward the father, and Freud's fainting fits.)

In September of 1907 Jung sent what sounds like a lover's request for a "photograph of you, not as you used to look but as you did when I first got to know you." Jung wanted it "dearly. . . . I would be ever so grateful because again and again I feel the want of your picture" (p. 86). The men exchange pictures which seems "almost absurd" (p. 93) to Jung: the honeymoon is at its height. Jung inveighs in his coarse fashion against Eitingon and Gross for their supposed sexual immorality; he is feeling the pressure of his own increased homosexual libido with its "undeniable erotic undertone" (p. 95).

In October, 1907, a year and a half after the correspondence began, there was a confessional letter from Jung which marked a high point of personal insight for him, and a watershed in the men's relationship. In it Jung made a confession (committing a slip of the pen on the word "honestly" *redlich* which he attributed to an "evil spirit that. . . . bedevils my pen"): his "boundless admiration" for Freud has the nature of a " 'religious' crush. . . . though it does not really bother me, I still feel it as disgusting and ridiculous because of its undeniable erotic undertone. This abominable feeling comes from the fact that as a boy I was the victim of a sexual assault by a man I once worshipped." Jung added that he was hampered by finding "relations with colleagues who have a strong sexual transference to me downright disgusting. I therefore fear your *confidence*. I also fear the same reaction from you when I speak of my intimate affairs" (p. 95; my italics). In making his own confidences to Freud Jung was increasing his homosexual involvement and ultimately his "disgusting," hostile feeling. The "man [he] once worshipped," whoever he was, must have had the significance for the boy of his pastor father and of the Christian God with whom Jung was so ambivalently obsessed in his youth. (He had a repetitive fantasy associating God with a giant turd.) Jung's confession showed that he had actually lived out the requirements of Freud's early theory of neurosoge nesis—he had been seduced as a child by a father-figure.

At first the confession cleared the air. Freud clearly had good expectations and drew closer to Jung, changing the salutation of his letters to "Lieber Freud und College": "What you say of your inner development sounds reassuring; a transference on a religious basis would strike me as most disastrous. It could only end in apostasy . . ." (p. 98). Here the future of the relationship is outlined. In fact, the confession was followed by its suppression, and not by a "working through." The story was never referred to again in these letters or in Jung's autobiography. Jung continued to fear and court a re-enactment, and the resistance appropriate to this burst out years later.

Freud started seeing with increasing clarity the links between paranoia and homosexuality: in patients, in the Schreber *Memoirs* he was to read at Jung's suggestion, and in the relationship with Fliess, whom he designated as paranoid. But he did not see it in his relationship with Jung to whom he expresses his affection (and underlying erotic wishes) as toward a son: ". . . spirit of my spirit, I can say with pride, but at the same time something artistic and soft, lofty and serene . . ." (p. 115). This sentiment seems bound to provoke Jung's disgust, and it is hardly surprising that Jung did not reply for several weeks following the receipt of this letter.

Jung wrote that he wanted to establish a relationship different from that between Freud and Fliess: "let me enjoy your friendship not as one between equals but as that of father and son. . . . this distance [sic] appears to me only fitting and natural" (p. 122). This letter was written only four months after Jung's confession and shows no awareness that it is the oedipal feelings between "unequals" that imply the opposite of "distance"—feelings that for Jung involved a combination of parricidal and homosexual wishes that could lead to paranoia. Jung ended his letter in language that suggests unconscious pregnancy fantasies: "your views on paranoia have not *lain fallow*" (p. 122; my italics).

Jung then became overinvolved with a kind of equal. Like the "boy from Gorlitz," the psychiatrist Otto Gross had first consulted Freud. He lost his colleague status for Jung when he was certified into Burghölzli for drug addiction. Jung wrote Freud that he thought he had completed Gross's analysis (a miracle cure of two weeks!); he had been working intensively and had been analyzing Gross's homosexuality. At first Jung did not see that Gross was psychotic: "I have let everything drop and have spent all my available time, day and night, on Gross, pushing on with his analysis. . . . whenever I got stuck, he analyzed me" (p. 153). Gross could not stand the intensity of this reversible father-son relationship (which mirrors Jung and Freud) and ran away from the hospital. *Then* Jung recognized his patient's psychosis and something of his identification with the brilliant Gross: "he often seemed like my twin brother" (p. 156). But brother Jung had gotten too close by pushing to be father or son. Freud wrote flatly that Gross was paranoid in a letter whose concluding "by the way" sentence was not calculated to discourage Jung's fear of homosexuality: "In conclusion, a little peculiar item; I recently came across your birthday in a medical dictionary: 26 June. . . . it's my wife's birthday" (p. 160).

In the spring of 1909, there was a marked infusion of the devil motif into the correspondence. Freud was anxious over another gap in communication (evoking Fliess, and unconsciously symbolizing the female genital). Jung had delayed because he had something to confess—a serious countertransference involvement (the full details are withheld for a while) with a female patient. Jung complained that his patient had been spreading rumors about his alleged sexual misconduct. He asked Freud not to scold him "for [his] negligence" (p. 209)—consciously he was referring to not writing. Freud reassured him about the rumors, quoting Goethe's Mephistopheles: "And another thing: 'In league with the Devil and yet you fear fire?' Your grandfather said something like that" (p. 211). Jung was then just about to visit Freud. He wrote back his own reassurance which turned out to be a self-fulfilling prophecy, negatively presented: "You may rest assured, not only now but for the future, *that nothing Fliess-like is going to happen*. . . . it's just that for the last fortnight the *devil* has been tormenting me in the shape of *neurotic ingratitude*" (p. 211; my italics). Here the identity of the devil shifts from Freud to the dispensable and seemingly-disposed-of Fliess.

But something Fliess-like does happen in Vienna in April, 1909: the theme of "spookery" blasts forth. Jung felt impelled to demonstrate his independence by, Mephisto-fashion, summoning up a poltergeist to prove to Freud the reality of the occult and the possibility of predicting the future. The incident, described most tellingly by Schur (p. 251), ought to have shown Freud the depths of Jung's "crazyness." Freud was obviously very worried. Both men recognized what

Jung calls "the Fliess analogy" (p. 216). Freud apparently had been acting as analyst and had made some remarks about Jung's pregnancy fantasies, which may have precipitated the "neurotic ingratitude" (see above) of the analysand and the rebellious supernatural demonstration. Jung wrote to repudiate Freud as father: "That last evening with you has, most happily, freed me from the oppressive sense of your paternal authority. . . . I hope I am now rid of all unnecessary encumbrances. Your cause must and will triumph, so my pregnancy fantasies tell me, which luckily you caught in the end . . ." (p. 218). Freud responded, sadly and fondly, in a marvelous letter, telling Jung that he didn't believe in the occult: "My credulity. . . . vanished with the magic of your personal presence" (p. 218). Freud provided a natural explanation of the strange phenomena; he warned Jung against superstition* and linked him with the numerologically obsessed Fliess by giving a long account of his own superstitious feeling about numbers which he then analyzed, removing any need for supernatural explanation.

For a while this exchange seemed to clear the air. Jung wrote Freud of the dangers of closeness in relation to his patient-colleagues Gross and Spielrein: "[They] are bitter examples. To none of my patients have I extended so much friendship and from none have I reaped so much sorrow" (p. 229). Freud used Jung's reactions to demonstrate to him the power of countertransference: "a permanent problem for us" (p. 231), but neither saw the parallels to their own relationship.

The project of a trip to America in response to invitations from Clark University helped distance the unpleasantness about the "spookery." The adventure of a journey to the new world together (evoking the fantasy common to adolescents of two men "on the road" that is presented in so many picaresque novels) helped to discharge and to sublimate the mutual temptations toward hostility and homosexuality. But the balance was precarious. Freud and Jung met in Bremen, and Freud suffered the first of his fainting fits in Jung's presence. This symptom had first appeared during Freud's meetings with Fliess, evoked by what Freud years afterward called "an unruly piece of homosexual feeling" (Jones 1953, p. 317). Freud fainted after he and Jung had had an argument about Bremen's famous "peat-bog corpses" which both men felt involved a fantasy of father-murder (see Shengold 1972, pp. 138–140). On the liner bound for

---

*According to Jung (1961) during a meeting in Vienna in 1910 (apparently a mistake for 1909), Freud warned him "never to abandon the sexual theory" which would be needed "as a dogma. . . . a bulward ʷby the two men, but obviously Freud meant by Jungᴇ against the *black* tide of *mud* of occultism" (p. 150; my italics). Jung regarded this as a demand for his faith, as his minister father had demanded it. The story links sexuality, anality ("mud"), the *black* man (father, devil) of Jung's fantasies, and occultism.

America, Freud, Ferenczi, and Jung analyzed one another's dreams. (It would appear that there was some discussion of homosexual impulses). However, it was Ferenczi's passivity that was discussed in these letters! Most of the dream interpretations apparently related to fathers, but (as is to be expected when homosexuality is associated to) the dreams also led to women: wives, sisters, mothers. The getting rid of fathers, wishes to love women, and the telling of the truth are themes interwoven in Jung's narrative (written long after the event):

> We were together every day and analyzed each other's dreams. . . . I regarded Freud as an older, more mature and experienced personality, and felt like a son in that respect. But then something happened which proved to be a severe blow to the whole relationship. Freud had a dream—I would not think it right to air the problem it involved. I interpreted it as best I could, but added that a great deal more could be said about it if he would supply me with some additional details from his private life. Freud's response to these words was a curious look—a look of the utmost suspicion. Then he said, "But I cannot risk my authority!" At that moment he lost it altogether. That sentence burned into my memory; and in it the end of our relationship was already foreshadowed. Freud was placing personal authority above truth (Jung 1961, p. 158).

After this righteous pronouncement about truth, Jung tells of a dream of his that Freud tried to interpret. It was the famous dream that Jung wrote of elsewhere about the many layers of "my house" (Jung 1911–1912). In the course of the interpretation, Jung decided to lie to Freud:

> What chiefly interested Freud in this dream were the two skulls. He returned to them repeatedly. . . . I knew perfectly well, of course, what he was driving at: that secret death-wishes were concealed in the dream. "But what does he really expect of me?" I thought to myself. Toward whom would I have death wishes? I felt violent resistance to any such interpretation. . . . [but]. . . . I submitted to [Freud's] intention and said, "My wife and my sister-in-law"—after all, I had to name someone whose death was worth the wishing! I was newly married at the time and knew perfectly well that there was nothing within myself which pointed to such wishes—[so much for a belief in the unconscious!]—. . . . I did not feel like quarreling with [Freud], and I also feared that I might lose his friendship if I insisted on my own point of view. On the other hand I wanted to know what he would make of my answer and what his reaction would be if I deceived him by saying something that suited his theories. And so I told him a lie. I was quite aware that my conduct was not about reproach, but *à la guerre, comme à la guerre*!" [pp. 159–160].

Apparently for Jung victory in "la guerre" was also to be placed "above truth."

Some of the hidden meaning of this quoted exchange has been revealed (whatever the "truth" of it is) in an interview with Jung that took place in 1957, shortly before Jung wrote the above account. The interview was undertaken by Professor John M. Billinsky who published it in the *Andover-Newton Quarterly* in 1969; its contents were picked up by national news magazines. Jung told Billinsky that when he and his young wife Emma first visited Freud in 1907, Freud was apologetic about his hospitality, saying "I have nothing at home but an elderly wife" (p. 42). Jung continued:

Freud's wife knew nothing about psychoanalysis. . . . [but] soon I met Freud's wife's younger sister. She was very good-looking and she not only knew enough about psychoanalysis but also about everything that Freud was doing. When, a few days later, I was visiting Freud's laboratory, Freud's sister-in-law asked me if she could talk with me. She was very much bothered by her relationship with Freud and felt guilty about it. From her I learned that Freud was in love with her and that their relationship was indeed very intimate. It was a shocking discovery to me, and even now I can recall the agony I felt at the time. . . . From the very beginning of our trip [to America] we started to analyze each other's dreams. Freud had some dreams that bothered him very much. The dreams were about the triangle—Freud, his wife, and wife's younger sister. Freud had no idea that I knew about the triangle and his intimate relationship with his sister-in-law. [p. 42]

Jung's display in his autobiography of his relationship to the "truth" in regard to the telling of these dreams related to wives and sisters-in-law and sexual triangles does not inspire confidence. The unlikelihood of "Aunt Minna" making such a confession to a young man she had never met before hardly needs pointing out, and the notion of Freud having had an affair with his sister-in-law has been dismissed as absurd by many who knew both; (e.g., personal communication from Max Schur). What, if anything, Jung saw or was told in 1907 we cannot know. But the fantasy was there in the mind of the old man who wrote his recollections, and it does supply some basis for Jung's suggestion of "wife and sister-in-law" to the question about the two skulls.

I suggest that the triangle fantasy represents a projection back into the past onto Freud of Jung's own situation. By the time of this interview Jung had had an "intimate" relationship for forty years with a woman (Antonia Wolff) whom he had invited to share his home alongside his wife. Billinsky (1969, p. 43) quotes Jung as saying, "It was my knowledge of Freud's triangle that became an important factor in my break with Freud." The intimacy on the trip to America in 1909 prefigures the break between the two men in relation to fantasies about women: Em *ma*, (Ir *ma*—see Kanzer, Chapter 12 of the present volume), *M*artha,

Minna—all suggest mama and *Amme* ("nurse"); Toni (Antonia Wolff's nickname) has other connotations.

All the stress was covered over; the relationship had its more positive later moments, but it was really deteriorating. Freud and Jung both continued to deny that Jung was incapable of mastering his conflict about paternal authority, and the men alternatively provoked and defused the conflict. Freud intermittently even tried to share Jung's belief in the occult in order to preserve the relationship. (Freud's ambivalent interest in the occult is an expression of a lifelong conflict—and it remained, partly as identificatory residue, long after the breaks with Jung and Fliess.)

Freud's main failing in relation to Jung was his wish to have him be an extension of himself—the part of his self-image he felt was inhibited. As fathers so often look to their sons, Freud wanted Jung to share in and fulfill his wishes—narcissistic as well as libidinal. Freud's narcissistic claim (which formerly had been extended to Fliess) did threaten Jung's separate identity. Since Jung not only feared but also longed to be swallowed up, he sensed the danger and temptation early; but he could not control the intensity of his reactions. Freud was less threatened by his predominant role of father in the relationship than was Jung by the more passive role of son; but Freud knew too little about how deeply involved he was with Jung and insisted on defining a fantasy-Jung in the service of denying the emotional facts and the theoretical differences based on them. It is clear from Emma Jung's letters to Freud that she saw the dangers for both men in her husband's role as "son and heir." Jung's struggle for a separate identity is clear throughout the correspondence. It is intertwined with the central thematic thread of the relationship—the oedipus complex.

Freud discovered oedipal wishes when he was analyzing patients and doing self-analysis in the 1890s. He announced his findings in a letter to Fliess of October 15, 1897. The universality of the sexual desire for the parent of the opposite sex and the murderous hostility toward the parent of the same sex was recognized and described in *The Interpretation of Dreams* (1900). But it was in the years covered by the exchange of letters with Jung that Freud's insight deepened and the oedipus *complex* (as he first called it in 1910, borrowing a word from Jung) was seen as central in human behavior. At a time when his sons were nearing manhood, Freud had been reliving his own oedipus complex, much of it in relation to Jung: the father/son struggle with its inevitable intimations of homosexual surrender (the negative oedipus complex) or elimination of the rival. These letters document Jung's need to run away from his emotional involvement with the "father creator" (p. 279), Freud, by concomitantly repudiating the concept of the oedipus complex. Jung defended against his feelings by abstraction—in his writings he treated incest as symbolic; he defended against the current situation in relation to Freud by displacing to the past—he began to study mythology. Meanwhile Freud in his writings was able to sublimate his involvement by understanding: he saw the connection between homosexuality and paranoia (the Schreber case, 1911); he competitively followed Jung's lead into mythological and historical studies but found there a basic oedipal theme (*Totem and Taboo*, 1913).

Both men were led to study the importance of the mother, and Freud was no longer calling the oedipus complex the "father complex" (as he had in his early works). Indeed, the final break between Freud and Jung occurred in relation to the mother/child confrontation, rather than the father/child confrontation. Analysis of homosexuality as well as of heterosexuality always leads to the mother. Freud in 1937 said that a man's need to repudiate his femininity provides the "bedrock" (p. 252) of his resistance to change. But most specifically, I think, the hardest task is facing the feminine strivings in relation to the *feelings* toward the mother. Jung recognized the problem. In February, 1912, he apologized for yet another delay in answering letters by explaining he had been absorbed in his work: "Essentially it is an elaboration of all the problems that arise out of the mother-incest libido, or rather the libido-cathected mother-imago. This time I have ventured to tackle the mother. So what is keeping me hidden is the *katabasis* ("descent") to the realm of the Mothers . . ." (p. 487). (Here is another descent to Hell.) But then Jung was impelled to attempt to desexualize libido. It is the *experiential* quality of incest that Jung must attenuate to "primarily a fantasy problem" (p. 502) and ultimately to the symbolic and the mythical. The seduction by the father-figure from childhood was suppressed, but the possibility of feeling sexual desire for the mother had to be denied. Shortly after Jung announced he was "tackl(ing) the mother" the "Kreuzlingen gesture" misunderstanding occurred (Jung projected a slip of his own onto Freud). Jung neglected his official duties as the President of the International Psycho-Analytic Association, and as an editor—as Karl Abraham kept reminding Freud. Then Jung gave a series of lectures in America dissociating himself from many of Freud's ideas. In November, 1912, there was a very short-lived reconciliation at Munich where Freud had another fainting fit. In December Jung's brutal letters bring an end to the relationship. Faust concludes with the Eternal Feminine, and these two spiritual sons of Goethe end their ties over the mother and incest.

In one of these last letters, Jung dismisses Freud in a manner familiar to those who watch the vicissitudes of the oedipal struggle. In his spite (his worst character traits are evident in these letters), Jung still could not face the loss of a father; in order to get rid of Freud, he first reduced him to a brother:

I am objective enough to see through your little trick. You go around sniffing out all the symptomatic actions in your vicinity, thus reducing everyone to the level of sons and daughters who blushingly admit the existence of their faults. Meanwhile you remain on top as the father, sitting pretty. . . . You see, my dear Professor, so long as you hand out this stuff I don't give a damn for my symptomatic actions; they shrink to nothing in comparison with the formidable beam in my *brother* Freud's eye." [p. 535; my italics]

In 1920, long after Freud saw clearly what had been going on to cause the break with Jung (or at least Jung's part in it), he added a note on the oedipus complex to his *Three Essays on Sexuality* (originally published in 1905):

It has been justly said that the oedipus complex is the nuclear complex of the neuroses, and constitutes the essential part of their content. It represents the peak of infantile sexuality, which, through the after-effects, exercises a decisive influence on the sexuality of adults. . . . With the progress of psychoanalytic studies the importance of the oedipus complex has become more and more clearly evident; its recognition has become the *shibboleth* that distinguishes the adherents of psycho-analysis from its opponents. [1905, p. 226; my italics]

Jung was an opponent in 1920; Freud dismisses him here as would an Old Testament judge, making use of a favorite word, "shibboleth," with its connotations of murderous rage (see Judges 12:6).

These letters are a record of the relationship of two men of genius that is as fascinating and dramatic as any great novel. Their scientific split was predetermined by the vicissitudes of their oedipal conflicts. Jung could not master his; Freud struggled in relation to Jung, as he had with Fliess, to consolidate the most difficult of all his insights. He was continuing his "interminable" self-analysis, a process he compared in a 1900 letter to Fliess (p. 323) to an exploration of an "intellectual hell" (evoking Dante, another good hater)—a hell in which his parents and himself were the demons frozen at the center. Freud discovered that he was Mephistopheles as well as Faust; the devils were not without but within. For Jung, Freud had become the externalized black devil. And in Jung's struggle to achieve exorcism, Freud's insight—the fruit of the "tree of paradise"—was also cast out.

References

Billinsky, J. (1969). Jung and Freud (the end of a romance). *Andover-Newton Quarterly* 10:39–45.

Freud, S. (1887–1902). *The Origins of Psychoanalysis*, ed. M. Bonaparte, A. Freud, E. Kris. New York: Basic Books, 1954.

———— (1900). The interpretation of dreams. *Standard Edition* 4/5.

———— (1905). Three essays on the theory of sexuality. *Standard Edition* 7:125–245.

———— (1906–1914). *The Freud/Jung Letters*, ed. W. McGuire. Princeton: Princeton University Press, 1974.

———— (1911). Psycho-analytic notes on an autobiographical account of a case of paranoia (dementia paranoides). *Standard Edition* 12:3–86.

———— (1913). Totem and taboo. *Standard Edition* 13:1–161.

———— (1937). Analysis terminable and interminable. *Standard Edition* 23:216–254.

Jones, E. (1953–1957). *The Life and Work of Sigmund Freud*. 3 vols. New York: Basic Books.

Jung, C. G. (1911–1912). Symbols of transformation. In *Collected Works*, vol. 5. Princeton: Princeton University Press, 1952.

———— (1961). *Memories, Dreams, Reflections*, ed. A. Jaffé. New York: Vintage Books.

Kanzer, M. (1961). Freud and the demon. *Journal of Hillside Hospital* 10:190–202.

———— (1976). The correspondence of Emma Jung with Sigmund Freud. This volume.

Schur, M. (1972). *Freud: Living and Dying*. New York: International Universities Press.

Shengold, L. (1972). A parapraxis of Freud's in relation to Karl Abraham. *American Imago* 29:123–159. (Chapter 13 of this volume.)

Chapter 12

THE CORRESPONDENCE OF EMMA JUNG WITH

SIGMUND FREUD:

October 30–November 24, 1911

MARK KANZER, M.D.

In the thick and important volume of letters between Sigmund Freud and Carl Jung (McGuire 1974), there are seven from Emma Jung, Carl's wife, to Freud. Three are routine in nature, transmitting messages from her husband. Four are personal, and though unlisted in the table of contents and printed merely as appendages to the numbered correspondence of these famous men—the lot of many a wife, without a separate "number" of her own—they impress the reviewer as of great interest and importance. The four in question were written within a period of a month, October 30 to November 24, 1911, as the relations between the two analysts were heading toward a crisis—indeed, they were prompted by the crisis. A deeper reason seems obvious—Mrs. Jung's transference to Freud. Even transference, however, is not a final explanation: she wished somehow to figure as a person in her own right instead of being permanently condemned to the background. Little known to any of the three, Emma did indeed figure in the interplay between the men in the form of dreams about her that Jung submitted to Freud for interpretation. The latter's success with the first can be shown to have gained Jung's confidence, his "failure" with a later one to have lost it. We have Jung's statements in the matter to guide us and our judgment with respect to Freud's approach. Emma seems to have been the third partner in an oedipal triangle and to have evoked, in part, Jung's characterization of the oedipal triangle as merely "symbolic."

Unfortunately, Freud's responses to Emma do not seem to have been preserved and we must infer their nature from her share of the correspondence. In letters to Carl, Freud referred to her (on July 21, 1911) as "your charming, clever and ambitious wife"—words no doubt carefully chosen, and hints at the latter's advantage (Emma was wealthy) in enabling him to be less dependent on his practice (p. 436). On September 1, he spoke of "your dear wife, well known to me as a solver of riddles" (p. 441), in response to Carl's statement that he and Emma felt that Freud's last letter (268F) had been enigmatic and they had been puzzled by it. All three were being enigmatic; the real problem lay in Jung's ambiguity about where he was heading with respect to the libido theory and Freud's ambiguity as to how he would take the apparent drift from his own positions by a disciple. For the most part, however, Emma and Mrs. Freud rarely assumed any individuality in the letters. Oddly enough, the children of both men do. Emma scarcely figures in Jung's book of reminiscenses *Memories, Dreams, Reflections* (1965); the single reference leads us to a footnote and he comments, apparently somewhat peevishly, that his wife's "life task," a book dealing with the Holy Grail, had kept him from intruding on territory that would otherwise have been of great interest to him (p. 215). Though Emma presumably had sought to find a common path along which she could walk with her husband, collaboration had not been achieved.

The deepening and uncomfortable "riddle" to which Jung and Freud were referring (both bringing Emma into their field of observation for once) did not prevent external harmony at the Third Psychoanalytic Congress in Weimar on September 21–22. In October, Freud was preoccupied with a final confrontation with the Adler group; Jung was away on military service and their correspondence no longer reflected the ardent mutual enthusiasm of an earlier day. By November 14, however, Jung was broadly hinting at incompatibility of their views on the Schreber case (p. 461). Freud announced on the same day the founding of the *Imago*, which excluded Jung from the editorial board and in fact loomed as a rival to his *Jahrbuch* (p. 463). By November 30, Freud was ready to take cognizance of Jung's challenge and confirmed, though good-temperedly, the incompatibility (p. 471).

It was against such flashes of lightning in a stormy sky that Emma addressed herself on October 30 to "Dear Professor Freud" and declared that she had found "the courage to write you (by) following the voice of my unconscious, which I have so often found was right and which I hope will not lead me astray this time." She described herself as "tormented" by the feeling that something had come between her husband and himself. This she attributed (correctly) to a disagreement over the libido theory. They had not discussed the disagreement forthrightly—would it not be better if they did? Then on a more personal note, and with obvious reference to her own conversations with Freud, she suggested other motives for his changing behavior. She hoped he would confide in her "for I cannot bear to see you so resigned and I even believe that your resignation relates not only to your real children (it made a quite special impression on me when you spoke of it) but also to your spiritual sons; otherwise you would have so little need to be resigned." She closed with the assurance that the letter was entirely between Freud and herself—her husband had no part in it (pp. 452–453).

Some of Mrs. Jung's impressions are borne out by a letter to Carl from Freud on November 2 picturing himself as depressed, beset by "hungry nestlings" both within and outside the household (confirming Emma's equation of the real with the spiritual sons), and plagued with publishers, deserting followers, and a meager practice. "Old age is not an empty delusion," he declared (at fifty-five). "A morose senex deserves to be shot without remorse" (p. 453). As for his children, Ernst had recovered from an intestinal ailment but Sophie was ailing from an undiagnosed condition. If the multiplicity of complaints had a single underlying and unspoken determinant, however, it was probably the disappointment of his hopes with respect to Jung himself.

Carl answered on November 6 with a basically bland letter whose most important line was probably the casual remark that he was too busy to work further on the libido theory at this time. However, on the same day, Emma sent Freud her second letter thanking him for his kindly reception of the first. Then she proceeded to admonish Freud for his own good, perhaps as no one had done before or would do again. She recalled their conversation on the first morning after his arrival—he had visited the Jungs in September prior to the Weimar meeting: "You said then that your marriage had long been 'amortized', now there was nothing more to do except—die. And the children were growing up and then they become a real worry, and yet this is the only true joy. This made such an impression on me and seemed to me so significant. . . . I fancied it was intended just for me because it was meant symbolically at the same time and referred to my husband."

Emma was a determined riddle-solver and the equation of the spiritual with the real son was one that she would not let go. Now she turned to some riddles she found in connection with Freud's real children. Why did he not prescribe psychoanalysis for them, she asked. Readers of the correspondence will learn that Ernst had been suffering from a duodenal ulcer or fistula (p. 256) and Martin had sustained a broken leg earlier in the year in a skiing accident in which his father had acknowledged probable psychological factors. Two of the daughters were intermittently ill.

"One certainly cannot be the child of a great man with impunity," she continued. "And when this distinguished father also has a streak of paternalism in him, as you yourself said! . . . You said you didn't have time to analyze your children's dreams because you had to earn money so that they could go on dreaming. Do you think this attitude is right?'' she demanded. Then switching back to the ''spiritual son,'' she added that she didn't think the ''spiritual father'' was right either. ''You cannot imagine how overjoyed and honoured I am by the confidence you have in Carl, but it almost seems to me as though you were sometimes giving too much—do you not see in him the follower and fulfiller more than you need? Doesn't one often give much because one wants to keep much?''

''Why are you thinking of giving up already instead of enjoying your well-earned fame and success?'' she inquired with respect to Freud's plans to give up the leadership of the psychoanalytic movement in favor of Jung. ''After all you are not so old that you could speak now of the 'way of regression,' what with all these splendid and fruitful ideas you have in your head! Besides, the man who has discovered the living fountain of ps.a. (or don't you believe it one?) will not grow old so quickly.'' He should expand his own life, she suggested, and ''not think of Carl with a father's feeling: 'He will grow, but I must dwindle,' but rather as one human being thinks of another, who like you has his own law to fulfill.'' She closed with a plea to Freud not to be angry with her and signed herself ''With warm love and veneration'' (pp. 455–457).

Whether or not the recipient of this letter in Vienna still regarded Emma as clever or ambitious, her riddle-solving seems to have had little charm for him on this occasion. She had already spent all her effort to emerge from the background and the next two letters were anticlimactic apologies, defenses, personal complaints—and withdrawal. On November 14, she wrote in response to a lamentably missing reply: ''You were really annoyed by my letter, weren't you?'' It had never occurred to her but, she stated, she must now agree with Freud that her last letter had really been addressed to her father imago. However, it is to Freud himself that she must address defenses against ''the way you take my 'amiable carpings,' as you call them.'' She protested that she had not meant to convey that ''Carl should set no store by your opinion'' or recognize Freud's authority. Probably Freud was correct, however, in suggesting that Carl's problems over his work were due to his resistances to his own self-analysis rather than to a fear of Freud's reactions. (This contention receives strong support when we turn to Jung's reactions to the interpretations by Freud of his dreams—about Emma!)

Referring again to the ''real'' children, she maintained that ''You have also completely misunderstood my admittedly uncalled-for meddling in your family affairs. Truthfully I didn't mean to cast a shadow on your children. I know they have turned out well and have never doubted it in the least. I hope you don't

seriously believe that I wanted to say they were 'doomed to be degenerate.' ''
She had merely meant to suggest that their physical complaints might be in some
fashion psychically conditioned, since "I have made some very astonishing
discoveries in myself in this respect and do not consider myself excessively
degenerate or markedly hysterical.'' She concluded with the earnest request,
''Please write nothing of this to Carl; things are going badly enough with me
as it is'' (pp. 462–463).

Emma's active interventions with Freud had come to an end and her last letter
merely elaborated the hint of unhappiness with her husband. She apologized on
November 24 for the despondency of her recent communication and expressed
relief that Freud was not angry with her. Now she was ''tormented by the conflict
about how I can hold my own against Carl. I find I have no friends, all the
people who associate with us really only want to see Carl. . . . Naturally the
women are all in love with him, and with the men I am instantly cordoned off
as the wife of the father or friend.'' Carl himself ''says I should stop concen-
trating on him and the children, but what on earth am I to do.''

By now, she continued, Jung had discovered something of their correspondence but, while astonished, seemed little inclined to pursue the matter further—a
dubious note of discretion, perhaps! The tenor of the letter becomes all the more
reminiscent of a patient seeking analysis when she concludes: ''Will you advise
me, dear Professor, and if necessary dress me down a bit? I am ever so grateful
to you for your sympathy. With warmest greetings to you *and yours*'' (my
italics). If Freud ever did respond to this request, there is no record in these
letters. By November 30, Freud was set to take cognizance at last of Jung's
hints of a widening chasm between them and the relations between the two men
openly deteriorated. On January 10, 1912, Freud (in an appendage to a letter
to Jung) thanked Emma for an article she had sent him about a lecture at the
Keplerbund (p. 481). On February 15, in the space at the end occasionally
reserved for mention of Emma, Jung informed Freud that she ''is working
conscientiously at etymology'' (p. 484).

Emma emerged from the background of Jung's dreams to become the occasion
for beginning the warmly enthusiastic phase of his relationship with Freud when
the latter interpreted the dream about the ''failure of the rich marriage'' (Letter
9J, December 29, 1906). She was then only twenty-four, the mother of two
children and seven years younger than her husband. Freud had celebrated his
fiftieth birthday earlier in the year and welcomed warmly the manifestations of
support outside Vienna and especially in academic circles that came with Jung's
interest.

In his book, *The Psychology of Dementia Praecox* (1906), Jung had described
a dream of a powerful brown horse that was tied by straps and being hoisted

aloft. The cable broke and the dreamer thought it must have been killed. However the animal leaped up and gallopped away despite a heavy log that it was dragging. A rider on a little horse stood in its pathway and seemed in danger until a cab drove up between them and the brown horse moderated its pace. Then the danger seemed over (McGuire 1974, p. 14). In a missing letter, Freud had apparently indicated the limitations put on his powers of interpretation, which had apparently been solicited, by the paucity of dream background and dream thoughts supplied. Now Jung was constrained to admit that the dreamer had been himself. "My wife is rich," he went on. "For various reasons I was turned down when I first proposed; later I was accepted and I married. I am happy with my wife in every way (not merely from optimism), though of course this does nothing to prevent such dreams. So there has been no sexual failure, more likely a social one." The dream, however, he conceded, hides "an illegitimate sexual wish that had better not see the light of day. One determinant of the little rider. . . . is the wish for a boy (we have two girls)." He envied his chief, Bleuler, who had two boys.

Freud responded on January 1, 1907, that he had indeed surmised Jung to be the dreamer and suggested that the log was a penis. He thought Jung might have stressed further the "alternative gallop"—the forbidden sexual wish as infidelity after the marriage bonds were broken. In a response on January 18, Jung now apologized for "having played hide-and-seek with my dream" and attributed some of the indirectness to the circumstance that it was Emma who had written out for him the description of the dream (!). He expressed now his hope of visiting Freud at Easter; on March 3, the Jungs did in fact call on the Freuds.

Thus Emma figured in the dream (and problems?) that opened up a friendship and ardent intellectual contact between the two men (had Freud himself become the "alternative gallop"?) and was destined to figure in another that was the turning point in the decline of their relationship. (Was it again a repetition of the theme of the cable snapping and the brown horse careening madly away?). The year was 1909 and Freud and Jung were apparently cementing their friendship and futures by their trip together to America. The substratum of their relationship was already eroding however, for in Bremen, before the ship departed, Freud had a fainting spell during dinner which Jung attributed to the fact that he had been speaking of peat-bog corpses, ancient men whose bodies had been mummified in the marshes where they had been dug up. According to Jung, Freud was annoyed at him for bringing up the topic and accused the startled Jung of harboring death wishes against him (Jung 1965, p. 156). (Jung also recounts a similar incident in 1912 when the topic turned to the pharaoh Akhenaton and the question of whether his actions in systematically obliterating the name of his father were due to hostility. It was while Jung maintained that this need not be the case that Freud, according to his version, again fainted [p. 157].)

On board ship, the two associates exchanged dreams, each interpreting the other's. Jung became disillusioned with Freud as a man and an analyst as the exchanges continued. Freud declined to give personal details that Jung felt necessary, protesting "But I cannot risk my authority." Jung felt his mentor was placing authority above truth and at that moment lost his authority. (It is interesting, of course, to note how this reverses their first interchanges on dreams in which Freud showed such tact and forbearance when Jung played "hide-and-seek" with the facts.) Jung also submitted a dream, one which was to be of such fundamental importance for him that "it led me for the first time to the concept of the 'collective unconscious' and thus formed a kind of prelude to my book, *Wandlungen and Symbole der Libido*" (1912–1916), the publication of which was to occasion the final break between the two men. The dream, which thus provided an experience of revelation as an antidote to the personal and intellectual ascendancy of Freud, concerned "a house I did not know which had two stories. It was 'my house'." Briefly, the dreamer descended from the top story, furnished in rococo style, to the ground floor, fitted out in medieval fashion. Descending further to the celler, he recognized the walls as dating from Roman times. A staircase then led deeper still to a low cave cut into the rock and, amid scattered bones and broken pottery, he "discovered two human skulls, obviously very old and half disintegrated" (p. 159).

Freud concentrated on the skulls and asked whose they were and what wishes might be connected with them. Jung realized that Freud was trying to get him to acknowledge death wishes and felt "violent resistance" (a measure of these very death wishes toward Freud which, in the two-story house, descended from the civilized behavior between them to the oedipal death wishes toward both parents at the bottom—an assumption which will draw support from further Jung dreams to be presented). To throw Freud off the track, Jung opined that the skulls belonged to his wife and sister-in-law. "After all, I had to name someone whose death was worth the wishing" (!), he explains (p. 160).

"I was newly married at the time and knew perfectly well that there was nothing within myself which pointed to such wishes," he continues. Actually, he had been married for some six years and now had three children, the hoped-for boy having arrived. At the beginning of his relationship to Freud, he had similarly denied the evidence that he wished to break up his "rich marriage." How could he, in 1909, and prospective heir to the Freudian "fortune," have absorbed even the first principles of psychoanalysis if he thought that the occurrence to him of his wife's name as "someone whose death was worth the wishing" was to be dismissed as merely a joke to be perpetrated on Freud? To be sure, his reminiscences were dictated after the age of eighty.

"And so I told a lie," Jung avows. "I was quite aware that my conduct was not above reproach." (Was he aware that this metaphor led back to the Holy Grail which so engrossed him?) "*A la guerre, comme a la guerre,*" he concluded. He had started the colloquy allegedly with the deepest respect for Freud: at what point had it become a war justifying any means? If he had lost his respect for Freud for frankly withholding highly personal data, did this entitle him to self-respect for deliberate lies?

With neither humor nor insight, Jung concluded that Freud was now mistakenly satisfied that he understood the dream: it seems more likely that he understood Jung. The latter himself felt that the many-storied house of the dreams represented the mind, as it descends ever-deeper into the unconscious and the individual comes upon the primitive within himself. This would then provide, he stresses, "an altogether *impersonal*" (his italics) picture of the psyche itself: thus the mind too is designed to withhold confidential information!

We are a little curious at discovering in the same book an "earliest dream" that is not only very similar to the above but far more personal and confirmatory of Freud's ideas about sexuality. At the age of three he, Jung, again descended to a "stone-lined hole in the ground" in which, behind a curtain, was a king's throne upon which sat an enormous phallus. He heard his mother's voice cry out, "That is the maneater" and awoke in a state of horror with the feeling that the phallus would creep toward him (pp. 11–12). We may note a similar pattern with the dream of the "rich marriage" in which the horse falls—descends—and rushes toward the boy on the little horse—a typical phobic structure with the horse as phallus. The rationalization that Jung wanted a son would probably have carried the reverse meaning.

A similar repetitive pattern suggests itself as operative in a metaphor conveyed to Freud in a letter from Jung on February 25, 1912, when their relationship was being only formally preserved. He reports enigmatically, to explain his failure to communicate, that his work on the "symbolic" libido has led him to descend to "the realm of the Mothers" (an allusion to Faust), "where, as we know, Theseus and Peirithoos remained stuck, grown fast to the rocks. But in time I shall come up again. These last days I have clawed my way considerably nearer to the surface" (pp. 487–488).

There is in this allegorical account of his withdrawal from the Freudian influence (the realm of the father?) the familiar images of a deep descent below the ground to an enclosure with two incumbents. According to legend, Theseus and Peirithoos were twins who descended below the earth to demand of the underworld god Hades that he turn over to Peirithoos his consort Persephone; it is apparently related to the Orpheus-Eurydice myth. In response, Hades clapped them into chairs of forgetfulness where they grew fast to the rocks. Eventually Heracles attempted to rescue them but not before he had torn away pieces of flesh which adhered to the chairs. Theseus survived but Peirithoos did not. Freud is apparently being requested not to play the role of Heracles

One may surmise that the mythology echoed a discussion by Freud on October 13, 1911, in which, fresh from his triumph over the Adlerians, he discoursed on twins and remarked that in legends "one is always weaker than the other and dies sooner" (p. 448). One tends to be noble, the other base, he continued. This observation arrived at a time that the Jungs were concerned with his enigmatic behavior. Perhaps we find a relevant predecessor to these "symbolic" exchanges with a letter from Jung on February 20, 1910 (after the America trip and probably as a withdrawal into his own system of psychology was taking place), in which he stated: "My dreams revel in symbols. For instance, my wife had her right arm chopped off" (p. 296). He proceeded to the day residue: "I had injured my thumb the day before, thus lending a hand to self-castration." Jung at this time was still capable of good Freudian insight for he offered the interpretation that his resistance to writing Freud stemmed from the father complex and doubted that he could come up to Freud's expectations (to be his right-hand man?). "One's own work is garbage, says the devil!" (p. 297). It was unnecessary for Jung to remark further that his symbols spoke "volumes." Once again, Emma served as symbol for the changing relationship between the two men.

Summary

The brief correspondence of Emma Jung with Sigmund Freud in the fall of 1911 adds an interesting touch to her husband's far more weighty letters. Her efforts to avert a break between the two men evoke images of both as they appeared in her eye, while she in turn justifies Freud's description of her as charming, clever, ambitious and a solver of riddles. Her search for an independent identity has poignant and modern aspects which led her eventually to etymology and studies of the Holy Grail.

Unsuspected importance attaches to Emma as a figure in her husband's dreams, which he offered Freud for interpretation. These apparently marked turning points in their relationship and perhaps also in Jung's turning away from a sexual to a "symbolic" understanding of the oedipus complex.

A repetitive pattern is noted in Jung's dreams and likewise suggests an oedipal pattern to his early enthusiasm and then alienation from psychoanalysis.

References

Jung, C. G. (1907). *The Psychology of Dementia Praecox*. New York: NMD
   Publishing.
———— (1916). *The Psychology of the Unconscious (Transformations and Symbols of the Libido*, 1911–12). New York: Moffat and Yard.
———— (1961). *Memories, Dreams, Reflections*. New York: Random House.
McGuire, W. ed. (1974). *The Freud-Jung Letters*, Bollingen Series 94. Princeton
   University Press.

Chapter 13

A PARAPRAXIS OF FREUD'S IN RELATION TO

KARL ABRAHAM

LEONARD SHENGOLD, M.D.

In the writings of and on psychoanalysis—scientific, hagiographic, icono-clastic—there is very little about or by Karl Abraham that does not make us admire him. His character exhibits the uprightness, courage and candor of the hero of a romantic novel: a sophisticated Adam Bede or an intellectual Ivanhoe (Jones called him a *"preux chevalier* of science, *sans peur et sans reproche"* [1927, p. 41]).

Abraham was the ablest of Freud's followers—and if not the most beloved, was probably the most respected by Freud. In his obituary notice of the much younger man, Freud paid tribute to Abraham's honesty and upright character, applying to him Horace's *integer vitae scelerisque purus* ("he whose life is blameless and free from guilt") (Freud 1960, p. 363). Perhaps so much virtue was intimidating—frequently a certain holding at distance on Freud's part is perceptible in their letters. This was noted by others. Jones said: "[Abraham's] distinguishing attributes were steadfastness, common sense, shrewdness and a perfect self-control. However stormy or difficult the situation he retained his unshakable calm. . . . [He] appeared to have no need for any specially warm friendship. . . . One would scarcely use the word 'charm' in describing him; in fact, Freud used sometimes to tell me he found him '*too Prussian.*' But Freud

Presentation to Psychoanalytic Association of New York, March 20, 1972. Reprinted from *American Imago*, vol. 29, no. 2, Summer 1972.

had the greatest respect for him" (1955, p. 159). Wilhelm Reich: "[Freud] also liked Abraham very much, but not very personally. He respected him" (1967, p. 68). Throughout the years, the disciple was often in the thankless position of admonishing his leader. The vicissitudes of their relationship can be followed in their published correspondence. Despite occasional disputes, there is on Abraham's side little envy and on Freud's side much respect.

Abraham was in the second generation of analysts. He first met Freud in 1907 when he was thirty and Freud fifty-one, but he had been studying the older man's work since 1904 (Jones 1955, p. 38). Their friendship lasted until Abraham's death in 1925. His writings not only supplemented but also inspired Freud's work. While Freud called himself, somewhat zestfully, a good hater, it has been said of Abraham that although he could fight, he could not hate (Grotjahn 1968, p. 10). Abraham's fairness and calm made him a guide and helper in many distressing factional quarrels, particularly in the defections of Jung and Rank. Freud was generally not as good a *Menschenkenner* (a "judge of people") in his personal life as was Abraham (Grotjahn 1968, p. 10; Glover 1965, pp. xii, xv).

Abraham's great intellectual abilities are not those of a towering genius, like Freud, whose character is heroic in the Aristotelean sense—full of conflict, defects and quirks. Yet, like the milder and more consistent Abraham, Freud is dedicated to searching for the truth—no matter where it might lead. This quality of mind is part of what makes Freud the greatest as well as the first of psychoanalysts. But human failings show, in Freud's work and in his life. (We know less about Abraham.) Inevitably, there were transferences and identifications that influenced Freud's reactions to Abraham. Jones writes: "At times Abraham almost assumed the attitude of an analyst towards Freud who did not want to admit a painful truth" (1957, p. 54)—and the analyst draws onto himself feelings from all the important figures in the patient's life. Freud was about twenty years older than Abraham— old enough to regard him as a son (Abraham was, after Jung's defection, Freud's chosen successor as the leader of the psychoanalytic movement). Abraham could also appear as a younger brother (like Julius Freud who died when Sigmund was one and a half). In his roles of advisor and arbiter, Abraham could be seen as an older brother (there was the same twenty-year age difference between the men as there was between Sigmund and his half-brother Phillip, to whom, partly because he was just the age of Sigmund's own mother, he had at age four attributed the responsibility for engendering his unwanted younger sister Anna). Abraham could be a father-figure (the Biblical Father Abraham evoked by his name). Mother and sister could be involved for Freud too—not only in relation to rivalry *for* them, but also by way of (feminine) identification, rivalry *with* them—in part because of Abraham's reliance in his last illness on the man who had evoked more of the "feminine side" (Freud 1887–1902, p. 302) of the adult Freud than any other man—Wilhelm Fliess.

I was led to this study of the Freud-Abraham relationship by a surprising and totally uncharacteristic omission on Freud's part in his *Moses and Monotheism* (published in 1939) of a paper by Abraham, written in 1912, in which some of Freud's conclusions about Moses and monotheism are pre-figured (see Shengold 1971; chapter 5 of the present volume).

Bisexuality and the Struggle for Priority

Freud was scrupulous about assigning priorities and crediting others, and there are many citings of Abraham's contributions to, and initiation of his ideas (for example: Freud 1911, pp. 40, 70, 76; 1914, p. 18; 1917, pp. 249, 250; 1925, p. 61; 1931, p. 25) especially in relation to dementia praecox, female sexuality, and melancholia. There is one significant exception, though a transient one, in relation to acknowledging priority which Freud himself described:

> One day in the summer of 1901 [really 1900] I remarked to a friend [Wilhelm Fliess] with whom I used at that time to have a lively exchange of scientific ideas: "These problems of the neuroses arc only to be solved if we base ourselves wholly and completely on the assumption of the original bisexuality of the individual." To which he replied: "That's what I told you two and a half years ago at Br. [Breslau] when we went for that evening walk. But you wouldn't hear of it then." It is painful to be requested in this way to surrender one's originality. I could not recall any such conversation or this announcement of my friend's. One of us must have been mistaken and on the "*cui prodest?*" principle it must have been myself. Indeed, in the course of the next week I remembered the whole incident, which was just as my friend had tried to recall it to me; I even recollected the answer I had given him at the time: "I've not accepted that yet; I'm not inclined to go into the question." But since then I have grown more tolerant when, in reading medical literature, I come across one of the few ideas with which *my name* can be associated, and find that *my name* has not been mentioned." [1901, pp. 143—44; my italics]

The theme of bisexuality will reappear in relation to Freud's not mentioning Abraham's *name*.

Abraham's Akhenaten Paper

Abraham's work was "Amenhotep IV: A Psycho-Analytical Contribution

Towards the Understanding of his Personality and of the Monotheistic Cult of Aton" (1912). Freud must have "forgotten" Abraham's paper which he had greeted in his letters to Abraham in 1912, had discussed with other colleagues, and to which he referred as late as 1923 (Freud and Abraham 1965, p. 334). It was after Abraham's death that he made the "slip"—a complicated mental event whose many meanings cannot be completely known without the cooperation of the perpetrator. But I am going to attempt a speculative analysis in the hope of arriving at some of the complex meaning that one person (Abraham) can have for another (Freud). In the process, I hope to illustrate the importance of Freud's use of Biblical metaphor.

Abraham was confident of Freud's involvement in his work on Amenhotep because he had been influenced by Freud's fascination for Egypt as evidenced by his collection of Egyptian statues and objects. (The Wolf Man describes Freud's office in 1910: "I can remember, as though I saw them today, his two adjoining studies, with the door open between them and with their windows opening on a little courtyard. There was always a feeling of sacred peace and quiet here. The rooms themselves must have been a surprise to any patient, for they in no way reminded one of a doctor's office but rather of an archaeologist's study. Here were all kinds of statuettes and other unusual objects, which even the layman recognized as archaeological finds from ancient Egypt. Here and there on the walls were stone plaques representing various scenes of long-vanished epochs" [Wolf Man 1971, p. 139].)

Abraham referred to Freud's interests in his letter of January 11, 1912, announcing the new paper:

> I know its theme will interest you: it is about Amenhotep IV and the Aton cult. The subject has a *peculiar attraction* for me—to analyze all the manifestations of repression and substitute formation in a person who lived 3,300 years ago. The Oedipus complex, sublimation and reaction formation—all exactly as in a neurotic of the present day. I did the preparatory work in the Egyptian department of the Berlin museum and was reminded more than once of the *first introduction to Egyptology that I enjoyed in Vienna in 1907.* [Freud and Abraham 1965, pp. 111–112; my italics]

The "peculiar attraction" for Egypt, derived from the father-figure Freud, must have contributed to Abraham's motivation to write his historical essay about an Egyptian father-son conflict in which the son breaks away from the father's beliefs (especially relevant at a time when there was a struggle over the succession for the leadership of the psychoanalytic movement). Freud responded to Abraham's announcement with great excitement: "Just think of it, Amenhotep IV in the light of psychoanalysis. That is surely a great advance in orientation" (1965, p. 112). The progress of the work was discussed in several more letters; Freud suggested including a portrait of "the interesting king" (p. 116) and told Abraham that *Imago*, the psychoanalytic magazine for applied analysis, was "eagerly awaiting your Amenhotep" (p. 116). In his reply, Abraham accepted the suggestion about the photograph and added that he would also print a picture of the sun-worshipper's mother, Queen Tiy (thereby bringing up the third figure in an oedipal triangle).

Freud as Akhenaten

In his paper, Abraham described Amenhotep IV as the "first great man in the realm of ideas in recorded history" (1912, p. 263). The young Pharaoh rebelled against polytheism and especially the old god Amon, the chief god of Amenhotep's father, and put Aton, the sun god, in Amon's place. At the age of seventeen, Amenhotep changed his name to Akhenaten: ("he who is agreeable to Aten"), and established the sun god as the *only* god. He had Amon's name effaced, even from the monuments of his own father Amenhotep III (this involved erasing his father's name). When his mother Queen Tiy died, Akhenaten put her body not in his father's tomb but in one meant for himself. Abraham had told an oedipal story of a son who wanted to efface his father's identity and replace him. Freud could have identified with the young Egyptian when he read Abraham's paper (as he identified with Moses whom he called an Egyptian in his last book). Akhenaten was, like him, an intellectual who had turned away from war and conquest. Freud once said, "I am nothing but by nature a *conquistador*" (Jones 1953, p. 348).* Akhenaten's renunciation had come when he was seventeen, Freud's age when, according to Jones (1953, p. 348), *he* turned away from military ideals and toward understanding the life of the mind. Akhenaten also was a writer; that he described himself as "the king who lives for the truth" would have enhanced Freud's feelings of identification. Freud's involvement can be seen in a letter written after he received the manuscript of Abraham's paper: "I have read your Egyptian study with the pleasure that I always derive both from your way of writing and your way of thinking"; Freud went on to make two "criticisms or suggestions for alteration." He wondered about Abraham's generalization that "when the mother is particularly important

---

*On Freud's ambition expressed in Biblical metaphor (letter to Martha of Feb. 2, 1886): "[Breuer] told me he had discovered that hidden beneath the surface of timidity there lay in me an extremely daring and fearless human being. I have always felt as though I had inherited all the *defiance* and all the passions with which our ancestors defended their Temple and could gladly sacrifice my life for one great moment in history. . . ." (Freud 1960, p. 202; my italics)

the conflict with the father takes milder forms. I have no evidence of this.''
(Freud could have been thinking of himself here.) The other criticism, well-
founded though it is, reflected Freud's thinking of himself in relation to Akhenaten. He had ''doubts about representing the king so distinctly as a neurotic,
which is in sharp contrast with his exceptional energy and achievements, as we
associate neuroticism. . . . with the idea of inhibition. *We all have these complexes*, and we must guard against calling everyone neurotic. . . .'' (Freud and
Abraham 1965, pp. 118–119; my italics). Abraham accepted the suggestions:
''I shall revise it. . . . I shall only *compare* Akhenaten with the neurotic patient. . . .'' (Freud and Abraham 1965, p. 119).

The Sun

Freud could have been affected by Abraham's references to the relations
between Akhenaten and the father as symbolized by the sun. In his paper on
the Schreber case (1911) Freud had written about Schreber's defiance of the sun
by staring into it. This had been referred to by Abraham in the letter expressing
his intention of including in his paper a picture of Tiy, ''the sun-worshipper's
mother'' (1965, p. 117). Abraham had seen two patients who, like Schreber,
could ''stare into the sun without flinching. The photophobia (sic) proved to be
directly connected with the father. . . . the paternal sun'' (1965, p. 117). Freud
had written: ''And when Schreber boasts that he can look into the sun unscathed
and undazzled, he has rediscovered the mythological method of expressing his
filial relation to the sun, and has confirmed us once again in our view that the
sun is the symbol of the father'' (1911, pp. 81–82). The ''delusional privilege''
of being able to gaze at and defy the father-sun with open eyes is to be contrasted
to Freud's attitude to his own father as expressed after the latter's death (in
1896) in ''a very pretty dream on the night after the funeral: I found myself in
a shop where there was a notice up saying:

> You are requested
> to close the eyes'' (1887–1902, p. 171).

Freud called the dream ''an outlet for the feeling of self-reproach which a *death*
generally leaves among the survivors'' (1887–1902, p. 171). The ''request'' is
also a mild statement of the terrible reproach and punishment that drove Oedipus
to blind himself. Freud's preoccupation with his vision and insight, his father's
eyes and his own, light and blindness, is amply documented in the *Interpretation
of Dreams* and in Jones' biography (see also Shengold 1966 Chapter 4 of this
volume).

In his paper, Abraham compared Akhenaten to Phaeton, son of the sun god Helios, who "had the temerity to seek to drive the chariot of the sun across the heavens in the place of his father" (1912, p. 290) and, unable to hold the horses, fell and was killed. Abraham ends his paper with this parable, saying that Akhenaten, like Phaeton, "in striving to reach the height of the sun . . . dropped the reins which his forefathers had held with a strong hand, and so shared the fate of many an idealist: living in their world of dreams, they perish in reality." This was a strong warning to the son who wanted to climb higher than his father. One is reminded of Freud's reaction on climbing the hill of the Acropolis. According to Jones (1955, p. 147), Freud compared the "curious attack of obfuscation" on the Acropolis in 1904 to his fainting attacks of 1906–1912. For the relevance to Abraham see below.

Moses

Freud's interest in Egypt started in childhood, as part of his "early familiarity with the Bible story at a time almost before I had learnt the act of reading . . . [which had] . . . as I recognized much later, an enduring effect upon the direction of my interest" (1925, p. 8). In *The Interpretation of Dreams*, he presents a dream with obvious oedipal meaning and an Egyptian setting "from my seventh or eighth year, which I submitted to interpretation some thirty years later . . . I saw my beloved mother, with a peculiarly peaceful, sleeping expression on her features, being carried into the room by two (or three) people with birds' beaks and laid upon the bed. I awoke in tears and screaming, and interrupted my parents' sleep. The strangely draped and unnaturally tall figures with birds' beaks were derived from the illustrations to Phillipson's bible. I fancy they must have been gods with falcons' heads from an ancient Egyptian funerary relief" (1900, pp. 583–584). (In *Moses and Monotheism*, Freud writes of the *falcon* as a sign of the old sun god, Amon; the use of such signs was proscribed by Akhenaten. [1939, p. 24].) Freud associated to the German "street" word for sexual intercourse—*vögeln*," derived from *Vogel* ("bird"), that he had learned from a boy named Philipp; Freud did not mention him, but his brother Phillip was obviously involved. He remembered waking up afraid that his mother was dying or dead. Freud attributed the anxiety in the dream to "an obscure and evidently sexual craving" (p. 584). The funerary relief from an illustrated Bible which provided the scenario for this dream might well have been evoked again by Abraham's writing of the burial of Queen Tiy in the tomb destined for her son.

Abraham wrote that "Tiy's embalmed body was not interred beside that of her consort, but in a new mausoleum near the city of Aten, in which Akhenaten himself one day wished to rest . . . his rivalry with his father for the possession of his mother was to extend beyond the grave. *So he realized with her dead what he was unable to achieve with the living.* In this respect he particularly reminds us of the behaviour of neurotics'' (1912, p. 274; my italics). One might add—and particularly of the *dreams* of neurotics.

Freud had a lifelong involvement with Moses, sometimes as an *alter ego* (''the man who dared to challenge God and [was] punished'' [Kanzer 1969, p. 197]); sometimes as ''the formidable father-imago'' (Jones 1955, p. 364). Freud wrote that sometimes when he entered the church of S. Pietro in Vincolo and approached the statue of Michelangelo's *Moses*, he felt that the eyes of the statue were looking at him scornfully, as if he were one of the rebellious multitude (1914a).

The Moses of Michelangelo

Freud first saw Michelangelo's *Moses* in 1901 and responded to it with a ''flash of intuition'' (Jones 1955, p. 20). *After* the correspondence with Abraham about Akhenaten in 1912, Freud went to Rome again and wrote his wife (letter of September 20, 1912) that he was ''visiting Moses daily and might write a few words about him'' (Jones 1955, p. 108). This grew into a paper, published anonymously at first, *The Moses of Michelangelo* (1914a). Jones (1955) says that ''this essay is of special interest to students of Freud's personality. The fact alone that this statue moved him more deeply then any other of the many works of art with which he was familiar gives his essay on it a peculiar significance. . . .'' (p. 407). An identification can be seen in Freud's interpretation of the statue. Instead of seeing Moses as about to start up and punish the disobedient people below him, as most commentators had, Freud said the statue represented the moments afterwards when the desire to preserve the tablets of the Commandments that had been slipping out of his hand, forced Moses to control his wrath. ''So that the great frame with its tremendous physical power becomes only a concrete expression of the highest mental achievement that is possible in a man—that of struggling successfully against inward passion for the sake of a cause to which he has devoted himself'' (1914a, p. 233). (In *Moses and Monotheism* Freud interpreted the breaking of the tablets of the law in the Bible as symbolic of the *murder* of Moses by his followers, connecting it with death-wishes towards the father.) Freud did not want to publish his essay: he finally did so in 1914, but anonymously, and he did not acknowledge it as his until 1924. The reasons he gave in a letter to Abraham seem inadequate. He called the anonymity ''a pleasantry,'' said he was ashamed of the essay's amateurishness and that his doubts ''about the findings are stronger than usual'' (Freud and Abraham 1965, p. 171). A neurotic inhibition is suggested by Jones, who felt that some of Freud's doubt about his conclusions was based on the strain over the quarreling that was going on in 1913 and 1914 with and about Jung; Freud was uncertain, in relation to *his* followers, "about whether he would now succeed in self-mastery as Michelangelo's Moses did" (1955, p. 367). The quarrel with Jung, his chosen successor, involved a father-son confrontation; it also brought out hostility towards a younger man like Freud's earliest "successor," his brother Julius.

Freud commented on the fact that Michelangelo's statue was originally designed for the tomb of the great Pope Julius II. Julius II was a strong-willed man who could use violence to further his ends. Michelangelo, Freud said, "felt the same violent force of will in himself. . . . And so he carved his Moses on the Pope's tomb, not without a reproach against the dead pontiff, as a warning to himself, thus in self-criticism rising superior to his own nature" (1914a, p. 230). It was the early death of his brother Julius (Julius I?) that, he had written to Fliess, "left the germ of guilt in me" (1887–1902, p. 219), and Freud had a continuing need to struggle with death-wishes (see Schur 1964, 1969). In his "non vixit" dream, Freud had expressed death-wishes towards Wilhelm Fliess as what he called a "revenant" of people who had died—like Julius and his recently dead father (1900). And Pope Julius—*Il Papa*—would connote both Julius and father for Freud. It is interesting also to note Freud's uninterpreted dream—inserted into *The Interpretation of Dreams* in 1914 (!): as a reaction to hearing church bells early on a Sunday in the Tyrol he dreamt: "The Pope is dead" (1900, p. 232).

Moses and Bismarck

In *The Interpretation of Dreams*, Freud connected Moses with another "Prussian" besides Karl Abraham, in fact an Arch-Prussian: Otto von Bismarck. The reference to Moses was made in relation to a dream of the Chancellor's, analyzed by Hanns Sachs and interpolated in Freud's book in 1919. The dream contained a scene "of a miraculous liberation from need by [Bismarck's] striking a rock and at the same time calling on God as a helper; [this] bears a remarkable resemblance to the biblical scene in which Moses struck water from a rock for the thirsting Children of Israel. . . . It would not be unlikely that in this time of conflict Bismarck should compare himself to Moses, the leader, when the people he sought to free rewarded him with hatred, rebellion and ingratitude . . ." (1900, p. 380). Freud went on to point out the masturbatory fantasy involved both in Bismarck's dream and in the biblical story of Moses seizing the rod. Bismarck, Freud said, identified himself with Moses in the dream and even went beyond Moses by being permitted to enter the Promised Land.

What makes this linkage interesting is that Bismarck fascinated Freud (according to Jones), and that "Freud's father had been such an ardent admirer of Bismarck, on the grounds of German unification, that when he had to translate the date of his birthday from the Jewish calendar into the Christian one he chose that of Bismarck . . . [both men had been born in 1815]. . . . Freud once asked his friend Fliess whether his numerical computations could predict which of the two men would die first." In the 1880's, Freud had written to his fiancée that "Bismarck like a nightmare (*Alp*) weighed heavy on the whole continent: his death would bring universal relief" (Jones 1953, p. 192).

Moses and Monotheism

In at least three places in his paper, Abraham links *Moses* and *monotheism* to Akhenaten who is described as a predecessor of Moses: "Akhenaten's teachings not only contain essential elements of the Jewish *monotheism* of the Old Testament, but are in many ways in advance of it. . . . Akhenaten does not imagine [God] as corporeal, like the old gods, but as spiritual and impersonal. He therefore forbids all pictorial representation of this god, thus making himself in this respect a forerunner of *Moses* the lawgiver" (1912, p. 275; my italics). "The belief in a single divine being, invisible to man, would certainly not have conquered the minds of the people. This fact . . . also explains why the *monotheism* of *Moses*, which chronologically came soon after the Aten cult, appealed so little to the people" (p. 285; my italics). (The last statement could lead to thoughts on Michelangelo's *Moses*.) Towards the end of his paper, Abraham said that Akhenaten made Aten "the one and only god, in transparent imitation of the uniqueness of the father. He thereby became the precursor of *Moses and his monotheism*, in which the one and only god unmistakably bears the features of the patriarch, the sole ruler of the family" (p. 287). Abraham himself bears the name of the first patriarch.

Moses and Abraham

These allusions to Moses and monotheism must have been suppressed by Freud when he was writing his Moses book and identifying Moses as a follower of Amenhotep IV. Freud in his 1939 book reviewed the entire story of Amenhotep IV, his rebellion against the god of his father, the establishment of the monotheistic worship of Aten—all without mention of the paper that had impressed him so in 1912. Freud believed that Moses was Akhenaten's follower and perhaps had been in contact with him. By declaring that Moses was an Egyptian, Freud deprived the Jews of one of their culture-heroes.

Freud had forgotten that—as with Moses—an "Abraham" had preceded him in Egypt. Indeed, there is neglect in Freud's book of the Biblical Abraham too. Moses is regarded by Freud as an historical figure while the patriarchs Abraham, Isaac and Jacob (Freud's father's namesake) are called legendary inventions, introduced after the time of Moses. One of the arguments Freud advanced in his claim that Moses was an Egyptian has to do with his assertion that Moses introduced circumcision to the Jews. Since historians, such as Herodotus, claimed that circumcision was an Egyptian custom, then it was derived *from* the Egyptians by the Jews. In making this case, Freud dismissed as a later "clumsy invention" (p. 45) the attributions in Genesis to circumcision as part of the covenant that God made with Abraham. If one starts out with assuming the historical validity of Abraham, then a consistent argument could be made for the story of Abraham dwelling in Egypt representing some historical truth—then the Egyptians could have derived the custom *from* the Hebrews at a time long before Moses. Freud's view dissociates circumcision from Abraham and from Jacob, but only by depriving them of their historical existence. Moses is made the true father of the Jewish people. The Egyptian-Hebrew confrontations in the Bible represented a lifelong passionate issue for Freud; he was sometimes on one side, sometimes on the other. The ambivalent meaning of Egypt is also there in Freud's lifelong identification with Joseph (son of Jacob). (See Shengold 1971, Chapter 5 of this volume.) Slochower (1972) has made the significant observation that Abraham is not only the first patriarch, but the first *Jew* and that therefore Freud's guilt over denying Moses' Jewishness might have led him to displace his guilt to his namesake, Karl Abraham.

The Name Abraham

The name *Abraham* would seem a superficial factor in the Freud-Abraham relationship. But Akhenaten's patricidal impulse was directed, Abraham said, against the *name* of his father. It was in part due to Abraham's short 1911 paper, "On the Determining Power of Names," that Freud became aware of "the importance of names in unconscious mental activities" (1913, p. 56). With Freud's intense childhood interest in the Bible stories, the early impact of the patriarch Abraham can be safely assumed. Abraham had written, confirming Stekel's observation, that "the bearer of a particular name often feels he has a duty to it," adding, "certainly one finds that a boy who has the same. . . . name as a famous man tries to emulate him, or shows an interest in him in some other way" (1911, p. 31). There is scant evidence, however, that Abraham saw *himself* as the patriarch's namesake. The name itself, according to the Torah means "the father of a multitude" (p. 26). When Yahweh grants the name Abraham to his favorite Abram he tells him, "And you shall no longer be called

Abram, but your name shall be Abraham, for I make you the father of a multitude of nations'' (Genesis 17:3). This is followed by the covenant about circumcision: ''the covenant which you shall keep, between me and you and your offspring to follow: every male among you shall be circumcised'' (Genesis 17:10). This was the covenant described as a later invention by Freud in *Moses and Monotheism*. Father Abraham is mentioned elsewhere in Freud's writings, in relation to the sacrifice of Isaac (1909, p. 65–66). Perhaps the association of this primal father with circumcision and filicide conditioned some of Freud's hostile attitudes to Karl Abraham.

Jung

As this paper continues its meandering *fugato*, the reader may not be aware that a chronological sequence is being followed. At this point in time, shortly after the publication of Abraham's Akhenaten paper (1912), Carl Gustav Jung makes his entrance. Freud had met him in 1907, shortly before his first meeting with Abraham; Jung, like Abraham, had been interested in Freud's ideas for several years prior to the meeting. A regular correspondence between the two began in 1906, and Freud felt ''elation'' (Jones 1955, p. 35) that his ideas were finding acceptance at the famous Psychiatric Clinic at Zurich where the great Bleuler was the Professor, and Jung his chief assistant. Together with the favorable impression Jung made in person, it was very hard, Jones says, for Freud to maintain a detached view of their relationship:

> for two or three years . . . Jung's admiration for Freud and enthusiasm for his work were unbounded. His encounter with Freud he regarded as the high point of his life, and a couple of months after the first meeting he told him that whoever had acquired a knowledge of Psycho-analysis had eaten of the tree of Paradise and attained vision. Freud on his part was not only grateful for the support that had come to him from afar, but was also very attracted by Jung's personality. He soon decided that Jung was to be his successor and at times called him his ''son and heir.'' [Jones 1955, pp. 35, 37]

Jones quotes from an unpublished letter from Freud to Jung of February 28, 1908, in which the older man said that ''Jung was to be the Joshua destined to explore the promised land of psychiatry which Freud, like Moses, was only permitted to view from afar'' (Jones 1955, p. 37). In his autobiography Jung tells that, as a boy, his ''schoolmates hung the nickname 'Father Abraham' on me. . . . [I] could not understand why. . . . yet somewhere in the background I felt the name had hit the mark'' (Jung 1961, p. 66). We do not know if Freud knew about this Abraham identification of Jung's, but it is possible since, according to Jung, the two men spent some weeks in 1909 when "we [met] every day and analyzed each other's dreams" (1961, p. 178). In 1910, Freud had appointed Jung as the President of the International Psycho-Analytic Association, which was resented by many of Freud's Viennese followers.

Abraham had worked in Zurich for three years (1904–1907) under Bleuler and Jung, and this long look apparently gave him a less favorable impression of the Swiss group and, specifically, of Jung. Very soon there was a good deal of mutual hostility between the psychoanalysts from Vienna (mostly Jewish) and the Swiss (mostly gentile); Freud was obliged again and again to make peace, although his feelings were more often with the Swiss than with the Viennese; Adler was particularly disliked. Abraham, from Berlin, was for a while outside the quarrel and was called upon by Freud to help patch things up. But at the Salzburg Congress in 1909 Jung and Abraham had clashed, personally and over scientific matters. Freud at first did not want to recognize Jung's differences with major psychoanalytic assumptions. By 1912, Abraham and Freud were in disagreement about Jung, and Freud was extremely worried about his followers' differences and the future of the psychoanalytic movement. It was in this setting that the penultimate meeting between Freud and Jung occurred, and its most dramatic happening was connected with Karl Abraham's Amenhotep paper. Five of Freud's chief followers had been called to a meeting in Munich in November of 1912 to consider the idea of founding a new analytic magazine. The matter was settled quickly. Freud and Jung then had a long walk before lunch in which they discussed their differences and, according to Jones:

Freud . . . had steam to let off and did not spare him a good fatherly lecture. Jung accepted all the criticisms and promised to reform. . . . Freud was in high spirits at the luncheon, doubtless elated at winning Jung round again. There was a little discussion about Abraham's recent paper on the Egyptian Amenhotep . . . in which Abraham traced the Egyptian King's revolution to deep hostility against his father. . . . Jung protested that too much was made of Amenhotep's *erasing of his father's name* and inscriptions wherever they occurred; any such death wishes were unimportant in comparison with the great deed of establishing monotheism . . . then Freud started to criticize the Swiss for their recent publications in Zurich where his work and *even his name* were being ignored. [Jones 1955, pp. 146–147; my italics; note the reappearance of the theme of offending the name]

Jung defended himself, and Jones had the impression that Freud was taking the matter rather personally: "Suddenly, to our consternation, [Freud] fell on the floor in a dead faint. The sturdy Jung swiftly carried him to a couch in the lounge where he soon revived. His first words as he was coming to were strange: 'How sweet it must be to die' " (1953, p. 317).

This was the third fainting fit that had taken place in the same room in the Park Hotel in Munich. The earlier two had occurred in 1906 and 1908. There had also been one in 1909 in Bremen when Jung was present. "On both occasions with Jung there had just been an argumentative discussion on the topic of death wishes, and on both occasions Jung had reproached [Freud] for attaching too much importance to them" (Jones 1955, p. 147).

Jung described the two fainting attacks that he witnessed in his autobiography. In 1909, in Bremen, Jung had kept discussing "peat-bog corpses"—bodies of prehistoric men drowned or buried in peat marshes of Northern Europe whose bodies had been perfectly preserved by the chemicals in the bog water: "a natural mummification" (1961, p. 156). (There is an obvious link to Egypt here.) Jung continues:

> this interest of mine got on Freud's nerves. "Why are you so concerned with these corpses?" he asked me several times. He was inordinately vexed by the whole thing and during one such conversation, while we were having dinner together, he suddenly fainted. Afterward he said to me that he was convinced that all this chatter about corpses meant I had death-wishes towards him. I was more than surprised by this interpretation. I was alarmed by the intensity of his fantasies—so strong that, obviously, they could cause him to faint. [1961, p. 156]

Freud's interpretation is perhaps supported by Jung's confusion about the locality of the "peat-bog corpses" which were not in Bremen at all. He states ingenuously, and not like an analyst, that he had thought about them "when we were in Bremen, *but being a bit muddled*, confused them with the mummies in the lead cellars of that city" (1961, p. 156; my italics).

Here is Jung's version of the second attack at Munich. It is fascinating that in his account of the argument about the significance of the son's erasing the name of the father, he completely fails to mention the name of Karl Abraham. The name of this brother-figure with whom he was in conflict is not, in fact, mentioned anywhere in "Father Abraham's" autobiography:

> Someone had turned the conversation to Amenophis IV (Akhenaten). The point was made that as a result of his negative attitude towards his father he had destroyed his father's cartouches on the steles, and that at the back of his great creation of a monotheistic religion there lurked a father complex. This

sort of thing irritated me, and I attempted to argue that Amenophis had been a creative and profoundly religious person whose acts could not be explained by personal resistances toward his father. On the contrary, I said, he had held the memory of his father in honor, and his zeal for destruction had been directed only against the name of the god Amon, which he had everywhere annihilated. [1961, p. 157]

Jung goes on to describe how Freud slid off his chair in a faint:

Everyone clustered helplessly around him. I picked him up, carried him into the next room and laid him on a sofa. [This recalls Freud's Egyptian dream of his mother being carried—here Freud himself is the "mummy."] As I was carrying him, he half came to, and I shall never forget the look he cast at me. In his weakness he looked at me as if I were his father. Whatever causes may have contributed to this faint—the atmosphere was very tense—the fantasy of father-murder was common to both cases. [1961, p. 157]

Freud analyzed his own fainting attacks and came to two conclusions that he mentioned to Jones. One was that all "his attacks could be traced to the effect on him of his young brother's [Julius] death when he was a year and seven months old" (Jones 1953, p. 317). I have already mentioned that in association to his "non vixit" dream, Freud talks of the far-reaching consequences of his fulfilled death-wishes toward his younger brother Julius and the "germ of guilt" (1887–1902, p. 219) that remained. One of the *revenants* of Julius, who was the main current target of Freud's death-wishes in the "non vixit" dream, was Wilhelm Fliess who was just about as much younger than Freud as brother Julius had been (see Grinstein 1968, p. 297). Jones says that shortly after the November, 1912, Munich attack, Freud wrote him an explanation: "It was a repetition . . . he wrote to me:

I cannot forget that six and four years ago I suffered from very similar though not such intense symptoms in the *same* room of the Park Hotel. I saw Munich first when I visited Fliess during his illness and this town seems to have acquired a strong connexion with my relation to that man. There is some piece of unruly homosexual feeling at the root of the matter. . . . "I [Jones] visited Freud in Vienna a month after this and my memory is that he told me that the final quarrel with Fliess took place in the same room. But I cannot completely vouch for this point since it is possible that he only said that the room was associated with Fliess, which it certainly was." [Jones 1953, p. 317]

Freud's fainting apparently involved both sides of the Oedipus complex: punishment for death-wishes toward rivals for the exclusive possession of the mother, and homosexuality associated with passive surrender to them—in short, the basic bisexuality of man, here associated with the person whose *name* he had once forgotten in the struggle to claim originality for discovery of the concept—Fliess.

Fliess and Freud and Abraham

We must go back in time at this point to interpolate Abraham's meeting with Fliess in 1911 before his writing to Freud of his Amenhotep paper in 1912.

Freud had had an intense neurotic and dependent relationship to Fliess from 1887 to 1902 (Freud's ages 31 to 46); Jones calls it "a passionate friendship for someone intellectually his inferior" to whom he subordinated his judgment and opinions (Jones 1953, p. 287). The contrast of this subordination to the liberating pioneer effort of Freud's self-analysis (conducted in part in relation to Fliess as a kind of analyst-figure) Jones calls "extraordinary in the highest degree" (Jones 1953, p. 287). The two men met for the last time in 1900, their correspondence broke off in 1902, and there was an irreparable break in 1906 with a public quarrel in which Freud was attacked by Fliess in a nasty pamphlet for having furnished information about Fliess's views on bisexuality to others. The charge was not without foundation; the conflict over priority in relation to bisexuality was still affecting Freud. Freud felt that the publication of his private apologetic letters was unforgivable, and he obviously considered the tone of Fliess's attack as revealing paranoia. He replied in 1906 with two angry letters to the press, characterizing Fliess as ambitious and overbearing. That was the end of the relationship. Although Freud had largely freed himself from his dependence on Fliess (see the renunciatory letter of March 23, 1900 [1887–1902, pp. 313–314]), the separation left a scar. The fainting fits show this; so does Freud's continuing (although greatly diminished) interest in periodicity and numerology—although it is clear that he was aware of the pathological basis for Fliess's interest in numbers.

When Abraham set up practice of psychoanalysis in Berlin in 1907 (a year after the public quarrel over bisexuality), he had asked Freud for referrals. Freud replied: "That you have my sympathy and best wishes in setting out on your new path is obvious, and if possible I should like to offer you more than that. If my close friendship with Dr. Fliess of Berlin still existed, the way would be levelled for you, but now unfortunately the road is completely blocked" (Freud and Abraham 1965, p. 9). Fliess was a very popular and successful medical practitioner in Berlin. Abraham was aware of what had passed between the two men, and in 1911 he wrote a letter which involved sharing an idea of Fliess's, almost asking for Freud's permission to meet him: "At the moment I find myself in a dilemma. The other day I mentioned to a colleague that I had, in a case of circular psychosis, been struck by the appearance of masculine and feminine periods. She spoke of this to Fliess, with whom she is friendly, and a few days later told me of Fliess's request that I should visit him" (1965, p. 99). This motivated Freud to an immediate reply, one marked "in haste"!:

I am replying by return of post because of what you say about Fliess, and am taking the liberty of giving you my advice unasked, that is, telling you my attitude in the matter. I cannot see why you should not call on him. In the first place you will meet a remarkable, indeed fascinating man, and on the other hand you will perhaps have an opportunity of getting scientifically closer to *the grain of truth that is surely contained in his theory of periodicity*, a possibility that is denied to me for personal reasons. He will certainly try to side track you from psychoanalysis (and, as he thinks, from me) and to guide you into his own channel.

But I am sure you will not *betray* both of us to him. You know his complex, and are aware that I am the centre of it, and so you will be able to evade it. You know in advance that he is a hard man, which I took years to discover. . . . [1965, pp. 100–101]

Two weeks later Abraham describes the meeting:

Now I must tell you about Fliess. I had a very friendly reception. He refrained from any attacks on Vienna; he has closed his mind to the new results of psychoanalysis since the conflict, but showed great interest in all I told him. I did not get the fascinating impression that you predicted.* Fliess may have changed in the last few years but, nevertheless, I did get the impression of a penetrating and original thinker. In my opinion he lacks real greatness, and this is borne out in his scientific work. He starts off with some valuable ideas, but all further work is concentrated merely on proving their correctness and on their more exact formulation. He met me without prejudice, has meanwhile visited me in turn, and I must admit that he made no attempt to draw me over to his side in the way you feared. I have learned many interesting things from

---

*Jones mentions this letter of Abraham's in his description of Fliess: "Of those who knew him, with the exception of the level-headed Karl Abraham, *who was not impressed*, everyone speaks of his "fascinating personality" (1953, p. 289; my italics). This is a distortion based on only part of what Abraham said after the first meeting, and it leaves out the evolution of Abraham's opinion away from "level-headedness" which will be followed below.

him, and am glad to have made his acquaintance, perhaps the most valuable
I could make among colleagues in Berlin: [1965, p. 103]

Freud replied: "You must not think Fliess so crude as to betray any intention
in the first hour. Unfortunately, he is the opposite, subtle or even cunning. You
will certainly come across his complex. Do not forget that it was through him
that both of us came to understand the secret of paranoia. . . . What you say
about the nature of his work strikes me as remarkably true; I once loved him
very much and therefore overlooked a good deal" (1965, p. 103). Fliess then
disappears for a while from the correspondence which goes on to deal with the
quarrels about Jung, and then in January of 1912 with Abraham's Akhenaten
paper. By 1913, after the fainting fit episode, Freud was able to see the depth
of Jung's disturbance, as he had Fliess's. He wrote Abraham: "Jung is crazy,
but I have no desire for a separation and should like to let him wreck himself
first" (1965, p. 141). Freud paid tribute to Abraham as a "Menschenkenner":
"since being taken in by Jung, my confidence in my practical judgment has
greatly declined" (p. 141).

Later in 1914, Jung resigned as president of the International Psycho-Analytic
Association, and Freud proposed Abraham to take his place. "He was called
to lead," Grotjahn says: "As had his Biblical namesake, he accepted his fate"
(p. 9). Freud wrote to Abraham: "So we are at last rid of them, the *brutal*,*
sanctimonious Jung and his disciples. I must thank you for the vast amount of
trouble, the *exceptional clear-sightedness*, with which you supported me and
our common cause. All my life I have been looking for friends who would not
exploit and then *betray* me, and now, not far from its natural end, I hope I have
found them" (1965, p. 186; my italics). The last quoted sentence is again
reminiscent of the "non vixit" dream of 1898. In his associations, Freud told
of his deeply ambivalent feelings toward his older nephew John: "I have already
shown how my warm friendships as well as my enmities with contemporaries
went back to my relations with a nephew who was a year my senior; how he
was my superior, how I early learned to defend myself against him, how we
were inseparable friends, and how, according to the testimony of our elders, we
sometimes fought with each other and—made complaints about [*betrayed*] each
other. All my friends have in a certain sense been re-incarnations of this first
figure . . . they have been *revenants*. . . . My emotional life has always ins
isted that I should have an intimate friend and a hated enemy. I have always

---

*Freud had used this word to characterize Fliess in relation to the pamphlet on bisexuality (in
1906) which Freud had described as a result of "the overbearing presumption of a *brutal* personality. . . ." (Jones 1953, p. 316; my italics).

been able to provide myself afresh with both, and it has not infrequently happened that the ideal situation of childhood has been so completely reproduced that friend and enemy have come together in a single individual . . .'' (1900, p. 483). In 1898, the single individual was Wilhelm Fliess. In 1914, Jung had become a *revenant* of Fliess for Freud.

In his letter, Freud praised Abraham for his clear-sightedness; he had need to use Abraham's eyes, undazzled by the sun, as auxiliaries of his own. (''You are requested / To close the eyes,'' his dream had said). Thus it was of special importance to him that Abraham share his view of Fliess. Tragically, as Abraham became ill and finally dependent on Fliess as his physician, the view of Fliess that he shared was that of Freud at the height of his neurotic dependence.*

Illness: The Re-appearance of Fliess

In World War One, Abraham served in the German Army. He contracted chronic bronchitis and went to Wilhelm Fliess as a patient. Grotjahn comments: ''He always maintained that Fliess sent him the most suitable cases for psychoanalysis, and his trust in Wilhelm Fliess as a capable diagnostician endured to Abraham's last illness'' (1968, p. 3). Freud, too, had been a patient of Fliess's and even had his nose operated on by him on several occasions. When Freud became ill in 1923, there is evidence that the wish to be treated by Fliess was revived.

Freud noticed trouble with his jaw in February of 1923, and in April an operation was performed to remove a growth. It turned out to be cancerous, and this illness was to torment Freud for the rest of his life and finally to kill him. The operation was a terrible one; Freud nearly died from bleeding, and it was followed by x-ray and radium treatment. Although Freud was not at first told he had cancer, he knew it. A few months after the operation, Freud's beloved grandson Heinz died. This was the only time that Freud was seen to shed tears,

---

*I am indebted to Dr. Richard Sterba for pointing out to me when discussing a short version of this paper at the December, 1971, meetings of the American Psychoanalytic Association that the English translation of this passage from the letter of July 26, 1914, does not correspond to the German text printed in ''Sigmund Freud-Karl Abraham Briefe, 1907–1926'' published by S. Fischer Verlag, Frankfurt am Main, 1965. Specifically the key words ''extraordinary clearsightedness'' are the translator's (Hilda Abraham) rendition of *ausserordentliche zielbewusste Tätigkeit*—the literal meaning, ''extraordinary methodical activity,'' has nothing to do with imagery involving the eye (although it is connected with Freud's view of Abraham as ''Prussian''). I would assume the German version is correct—although one can only be sure if the original is checked. I have not rewritten the passage since it is still true that Freud used Abraham to supplement his *eyes*. But the moral should be drawn that any student of Freud who doesn't know German thoroughly and who works from another language cannot be the most ''clear-sighted'' guide to Freud's use of imagery.

and he said that he found the blow unbearable, much worse than his own cancer. In September, 1923, a much more radical operation was performed, and it became necessary to wear a painful prosthesis over his palate.

Just before the cancer was found, there was an exchange of letters between Abraham and Freud which again touch on Egypt and Akhenaten. The occasion was the much-publicized discovery of the tomb of Akhenaten's successor, Tutankhamen. Abraham had sent a number of newspaper clippings about it to Freud, who replied: "It now seems certain that they will soon find the mummy of the king and perhaps also that of his consort, a daughter of *our analytic Pharoah*" (1965, p. 334; my italics). There was no amnesia of Abraham's paper in 1923. In his reply, Abraham seriously proposed that they visit Egypt together the following summer. Freud answered that he was "neither rich nor well enough," and added, ominously, "You must gradually get used to the idea of my mortality and frailty" (1965, p. 365).

"Betrayal" by Rank

In addition to his illness, another worry for Freud was the behavior of Otto Rank (apparently in part brought on by his reaction to Freud's illness). Abraham found himself again in the position of criticizing a beloved disciple of Freud's, pushing Freud toward an undesired loss. Abraham wrote that he felt forced "to my deepest sorrow, and not for the first time in the 20 years of my analytic life to sound a warning. . . . [We see] the manifestations of a regression in the scientific field, the symptoms of which agree in every small detail with those of Jung's secession from psycho-analysis. . . . Do you remember that at the first Congress in Salzburg I warned you about Jung? At the time you dismissed my fears and assumed my motive was jealousy. Another Salzburg Congress is before us and once more I come to you in the same role—a role which I would rather not play" (1965, p. 349). Indeed, all was repeated, Freud once more distrusting Abraham and accusing him of stirring up trouble. Abraham responded: "Your letter expresses a distrust of me that I find extremely painful, and, at the same time, strange . . . I must state that your letter has not evoked even a shadow of guilt in me . . . I [knew] I was exposing myself to a similar reaction from you as in the past, when I drew your attention to unwelcome facts . . . now the reaction has set in after all" (1965, p. 356). Again Abraham turned out to be correct and things were set to rights between the two men after Abraham had once more drawn down on himself the anger focused on those who play the role of Teiresias, teller of unwelcome truth.

Numerology

Later in 1924, there was a strange sequence of letters in which numerology—Fliess's obsession (he thought that in relation to the "masculine" number 23 and the 'feminine' number 28 he had found the secret of all periodicity in life)—came up between Freud and Abraham. Freud was ill and very aware of his cancerous condition. He felt, as he had a year previously, that his (68th) birthday might be his last. Abraham, in an unpublished letter of April 26, 1924, had mentioned his intention to carry out a study (which he never did) of the significance of the number 7 in myths and customs. Freud referred to this in a letter of August, 1924:

in re 7: I am putting at your disposal an idea the value of which I cannot judge myself because of *ignorance*. I should like to take a historical view and believe that the significance of the number 7 originated in a period when men counted in sixes. (Here *ignorance* sets in). In that case seven would not be the last of a series as it is now in the week, but the first of a second series and, like first things, subject to taboo. The fact that the initial number of the third series, that is to say 13, is the unluckiest of all numbers would fit in with this. The origin of my idea was a remark in a history of Assyria that 19 was also one of the suspect numbers, which the author explains with reference to the length of the month by the equation $30 + 19 = 49$, or 7×7. However, $19 - 13 + 6$, the beginning of a fourth series of sixes. This system of sixes would thus be pre-astronomical. One should investigate what is known of such a system, of which enough traces remain (dozen, gross, division of the circle into 360 degrees). Moreover, it is notable how many prime numbers appear in this series: 1, 7, 13, 19, 25 is an exception but is followed by 31, 37, 43, 49 which is again 7 x 7. [1965, p. 365; my italics]

Here, Freud sounds so much like Fliess that I postulate that a longing to be taken care of by his old doctor is expressed by an identification with him; the last sentence of the letter shows awareness of the link to Fliess.

"The craziest things can be done with numbers so be careful" (Freud and Abraham 1965, p. 365).

Ignorance and Needing Not to Know

There had come a time in Freud's relations with Fliess when he could no longer believe in his mathematics and could only disclaim knowledge (or proclaim *ignorance* as in the above letter). Kris writes:

The less the observed facts fitted in with [Fliess's] theoretical requirements, the more strained became his calculations. So long as the time intervals in which he dealt could be explained as parts or multiples of 23 and 28, Freud followed him, but Fliess soon found himself obliged to explain the intervals with which he was confronted by combinations of four figures and to use not only 23 and 28 but 5 (28 − 23) and 51 (28 + 23). Freud refused to accompany him in this step, excusing himself on the ground of his lack of mathematical knowledge" (Kris 1954, p. 10). "You know that I lack the slightest mathematical ability," Freud had written apologetically when Fliess accused him of not believing in the period theories, and Freud called himself "a friend who because of his *ignorance* can never be dangerous" (1887–1902, p. 336; my italics). To keep Fliess in 1901, Freud had to cover his eyes.

Freud and the Number Seven

The number 7 had specific associations with Fliess for Freud. When he had been a believer in Fliess's period theories, Freud would consult him about the future, almost as if he were a numerologist-fortune teller. In 1899, Freud wrote him about a current dearth of productive work: "According to an earlier calculation of yours, 1900–1901 ought to be a productive period for me (every *seven*-and-a-half years)" (1887–1902, pp. 300–301). On January 8, 1900, Freud reproached Fliess for not writing sooner: "Now do not let another long interval like this happen again (Dec. 24th–Jan. 7th = 14 = 28/2)" (p. 308). Here Freud's longing for Fliess was expressed in terms of *parts* (see above) of the "feminine" period 28 which involves a series of seven. The longing for Fliess would involve the passive "feminine" side of Freud's nature. Freud wrote to Fliess (May 7, 1900): "No one can replace the intercourse with a friend that a particular—perhaps feminine—side of me requires" (1887–1902, p. 302). He had triumphed over this in his self-analysis, but this (like all analyses as Freud was going to make explicit in *Analysis Terminable and Interminable* [1937]) had been incomplete and Freud was left with some dependence and yearning. It was a "piece of unruly homosexual feeling" in relation to Fliess to which Freud had traced his fainting fit ("How sweet . . . to die") at Munich in 1912.

In 1913, after the fainting fit, Freud wrote a numerologic letter to Ferenczi which again evidenced wishing for Fliess; he was about to make another visit to Munich. One sees how much he still holds with the period theory, and how important seven is. The occasion of the letter was Ferenczi's fortieth birthday:

Your nostalgic letter moved me very much, first because it reminded me of my own 40th birthday, since when I have changed my skin several times, which as we know, occurs every *seven* years. At that time [1896] I had reached the peak of loneliness, had lost my old friends and hadn't acquired any new ones. [Here astonishingly, Fliess is left out—in 1896 the relationship with him was at its height.]

No one paid any attention to me and the only thing that kept me going was a bit of defiance and the beginning of *The Interpretation of Dreams* . . . Abraham is to visit us at the end of August and will probably accompany us to Munich. Your hope of my being able to tell you something new by then I cannot as yet support. *My good ideas actually occur in 7 year cycles*: in 1891 I started work on aphasia; 1898 / 9, the interpretation of dreams; 1904 / 5, wit and its relation to the unconscious; 1911 / 12, totem and tabu; thus I am probably in the waning stage and won't be able to count on anything of importance before 1918 / 19 (provided the chain doesn't break before) . . .'' (my italics: p. 300).

Fliess is present here not only because of his ideas but above all because his existence as a friend in 1896 is erased. Freud's creativity and death are brought in relation to periods, here of seven years. The year of Freud's fortieth birthday—1896—was the year of his father's death. When he wrote Fliess about his father's death, Freud said, according to Schur (1969; Chapter 7 of the present volume) in an unpublished part of the letter, that it had all happened during his "critical period."

I feel that following his cancer operation, the loss of his grandson and the repetition of the loss of an analytic "son" (Rank), there was an intensification for Freud of the conflicting wishes to kill and replace the father, and to submit to him with the attendant expectation of castration and death. The losses of the "sons" could have been regarded as punishment for the death-wishes against the father and brothers. Much of Freud's conflict with his father was (as it generally is) displaced onto his siblings, more dispensable and less dangerous. For Freud this had begun with Julius and John and Phillip, culminating in Fliess. Fliess continued to have the power to appear as a *revenant* of the beloved and hated brothers and father of the past. Freud's illness and suffering in the years before Abraham's death in 1925 made for an upsurge of regressive passive feeling which the indomitable man was fighting successfully and heroically in his behavior and in his continuing power of creative thinking. But the longing for Fliess must have been fed by the tragic illness of another "son" and younger brother-figure—Karl Abraham—and by Abraham's increasing involvement with, and passive surrender to, Fliess.

According to Schur there was a similar period in 1904, following the beginning of the quarrel with Fliess over priority for bisexuality. This led to the disturbance on the Acropolis with its fainting-like episode, and was also connected with a Fliess-inspired preoccupation with numbers. To document this, Schur quotes the following letter to Jung, written in 1909:

> Some years ago [1904] I discovered that I had the conviction I would die between the ages of 61–62, which was then a long way off. . . . At that time I went with my brother to Greece. It was really uncanny how the numbers 61 or 62, in conjunction with 1 or 2, kept appearing under all kinds of circumstances. . . . Being in low spirits I hoped to breathe easier when a room on the first floor of our Athens hotel was assigned to us. There 61 was out of the question. Well, I got room 31 (with fatalistic licence, after all, half of 61–62), and this smarter and more nimble number proved to be more persistent in its persecution than the first one. . . . Because there *are* areas in my system where I am just thirsty for knowledge and not at all superstitious, I have since attempted an analysis, and here it is. It all began in the year 1899, when two events occurred simultaneously: first I wrote *The Interpretation of Dreams* and second, I was assigned a new telephone number which I still have—14362. A connection between the two could easily be established: in the year 1899, when I wrote *The Interpretation of Dreams*, I was *43* years old. What more natural then that the other numbers referred to the end of my life, namely 61 or 62. Suddenly there was method in the madness. The superstition that I would die between 61–62 showed itself to be the equivalent of a conviction that I had fulfilled my life's work with *The Interpretation of Dreams*, didn't have to produce anything further, and could die in peace. You will admit that with this knowledge the thing no longer sounds so absurd. By the way, there is a hidden influence of Fliess in all this; it was in the year of his attack that the superstition erupted. [1969, pp. 28–29]

Schur says that the preoccupation with numbers "had the character and intensity of a severe compulsive symptom" (p. 29).

Relevant to this is another meaning of *seven* for Freud that is furnished by Jones. On the night before the final decision about whether he would be chosen to be the one to receive a travel grant (which he did and used to study with Charcot) in 1885, "Freud dreamed that his representative, who was none other than Brücke, told him he had no chance because there were *seven* other applicants with more favorable prospects. Since there had been seven brothers and sisters besides himself in the family it is not hard to perceive the reassurance in this simple little dream" (Jones 1953, pp. 75–76).

An enigmatic use of *seven* comes up in a letter to Ferenczi of 1921, quoted by Jones. It links seven with death prediction, and shows Freud's ability to transcend the temptation connected with superstition: "On March 13th of this year I quite suddenly took a step into real old age. Since then the thought of death has not left me, and sometimes I have the impression that *seven* of my internal organs are fighting to have the honor of bringing my life to an end. . . . Still I have not succumbed to this hypochondria, but view it quite coolly . . ." (Jones 1957, p. 79). Schur (1964) feels that Freud was paraphrasing the Greek pentameter that goes, "Seven cities are competing for the honor of being the birthplace of Homer." This is convincing; by evoking it Freud equates birth with death. The death wishes against the seven brothers and sisters whose birth followed his (especially the fulfilled ones against Julius), and the retaliation for those wishes might, if we follow Jones' interpretation of seven above, be involved in Freud's fanciful paraphrase of a Greek original. If so, another seven may be relevant—the "Seven against Thebes" with its fratricidal theme.

The Riddle of the Sphinx

There was a numerologic mystery which concerned Freud for a good part of his creative life: the riddle of the Theban Sphinx. Graves states it thus:

> "What being, with only one voice, has sometimes two feet, sometimes three, sometimes four, and is weakest when it has the most?" Oedipus' answer: "Man—because he crawls on all fours as an infant, stands firmly on his feet as a youth, and leans on a staff in his old age." [1955, p. 10]

Freud interpreted the riddle as "the great riddle of where babies come from which is perhaps the first problem to engage a child's mental powers" (1909, p. 133), thereby connecting it with the child's sexual curiosity. With his interpretation Freud transformed instinct-ridden numerologic superstition to psychic analysis. The sublimation of the sexual wish to see and know into a passion to understand was so much a part of Freud's mastery that his followers were inspired to present him with a medallion of Oedipus reading the riddle of the Sphinx. (The Sphinx was a creature derived from Egypt, and was bisexual—part of its mystery is the mystery of bisexuality.)

On October 25, 1924, Abraham wrote the final communication between the two men on the number seven, in which he dismisses Freud's half-serious historico-numerologic suggestions for a psychological explanation that involves the oedipus complex and the riddle of the Sphinx:

> The investigation into the number seven has been completely put aside for the time being . . . I see that one cannot attack the problem either from the angle of astronomical significance or from that of numerical systems. The

basic psychological phenomenon seems to me to lie in the ambivalent attitude
of mankind to the number seven. This must represent the thing to which one
is most ambivalent and I thus come back once more to the Oedipus complex.
Seven is the number of abstinence (Sabbath, etc.) everywhere, it expresses
the taboo and is at the same time the number of many rites compulsively
performed. I see in this double significance the justification for assuming a
fusion of two other numbers in this one, and believe that the significance of
the three equalling father and the four equalling mother (three patriarchs and
four matriarchs mentioned in the Bible etc.) will have to be retained. . . .
[1965, p. 370]

The Sphinx also has been seen as an image of the parents in intercourse and as
a bisexual fusion of mother and father.

The Surrender to Fliess

The numerological letters about *seven* prefigure the fateful reappearance of
Fliess in the correspondence between Freud and Abraham. Eight months after
the sensible letter which represents a repudiation of the "Fliessian" approach
to number seven, Abraham became ill. It was to be a fatal illness. In a letter
of June 7, 1925, he complained of a persistent feverish bronchitis. This had
started with an injury to the pharynx caused by a fishbone which went on to a
septic bronchopneumonia, lung abcess and finally to a terminal sub-phrenic
abcess. The course of the illness was variable: "[It] took the typical course of
septicaemia, prior to the introduction of anti-biotics with swinging temperatures,
remission and *euphoria*. Abraham's previous emphysema had doubtless made
him susceptible to such infection" (1965, p. 382; editor's note). The *euphoria*
implies mental disturbances which might account for the adherence to Fliess and
his systems that became part of the pathological dependence of a dying man on
his physician.

Freud continued to worry about Abraham's health, and the two compared
illnesses, Freud noting the twenty-one-year-old age difference between them.
On Sept. 8, 1925, Abraham wrote that he had been exhausted and *euphoric*
(he speaks of a "new manic phase"): "I shall in any case have to undergo some
treatment for my nose and throat from Fliess. If this letter were not already
unduly long, *I would tell you how my illness has most strikingly confirmed all
Fliess's views on periodicity*" (1965, p. 395; my italics). Freud must have been
appalled at this: because of his concern about what was going on in Abraham—in
mind and body; and because he had more than once had *his* nose treated by
Fliess when *he* had believed in Fliess! Abraham was identifying with Fliess. In
his short reply to the above letter, Freud simply expressed his concern about

Abraham's continuing to be physically ill. Several weeks later, Abraham wrote about *his* worry over Freud's health. He himself was feeling "very much better. . . . I am so sorry to hear that you are continuously troubled by certain discomforts. . . . I have been wondering whether a stay in a very dry climate might be beneficial. But I do not know whether you still need to be near your surgeon. You may be interested to hear that Fliess, who heard about your illness two years ago, has repeatedly asked after your health with warmest interest. As far as I am concerned, I must repeat here once again that I owe him the utmost gratitude" (1965, p. 397). Abraham here contrasts Freud's relation to his surgeon, Pichler—in whose near presence Freud was obliged to remain, with the relationship that Abraham has with Freud's old surgeon, Fliess, whose care deserves "the utmost gratitude." Fliess is portrayed as "warm" and interested in Freud. Abraham sounds euphoric in this letter.

The last months' exchange of letters concerns a strange conflict over the project of a commercial film to be made under psychoanalytic auspices (it was finally filmed under the title "Secret of the Soul"). Abraham supported the idea, but Freud was very reluctant and others objected strongly, expressing themselves and behaving in a way that made Abraham disapprove. Freud again accused the younger man of intolerance (apparently this was one of the times that Freud found him "too Prussian" [Jones 1955, p. 159]). But the unfortunate acerbity of the last letters must also have to do with unconscious rivalry for the other Berliner (and Prussian), Fliess. A film project called "Secret of the Soul" would inevitably connect with the eyes and the forbidden, invoking Oedipus and the Sphinx. Abraham writes:

You know, dear Professor, that I am very unwilling to enter once again into a discussion of the film affair. But because of your reproach of harshness (in your circular letter), I find myself once more in the same position as on several previous occasions. In almost twenty years, we have had no differences of opinion except where personalities were concerned whom I, very much to my regret, had to criticize. The same sequence of events repeated itself each time: *you indulgently overlooked everything that could be challenged* in the behavior of the persons concerned, whilst all the blame—which you subsequently recognized as unjustified—was directed against me. In Jung's case your criticism was that of "jealousy"; in the case of Rank "unfriendly behavior" and, this time, "harshness." Could the sequence of events not be the same once again: *I advanced an opinion which is basically yours as well but which you did not admit into consciousness.* All the unpleasure linked to the relevant facts is then turned against the person who has drawn attention to them. [1965, p. 398; my italics]

Abraham here speaks as "the analyst" who tells the patient to open his eyes to unwelcome truth; but there is another meaning in the italicized words. Abraham had been advancing his favorable opinion of Fliess which Freud consciously did not, and did not want to, share—but which was still present in his unconscious. It is not surprising that this counterpoint brings out in Freud's last letter to Abraham the "harshness" with which he had charged the latter. It must be remembered that Freud had no idea that Abraham was dying and that he was writing a farewell letter:

Dear Friend,

I note with pleasure that your illness has not changed you in any way, and am willing to regard you as having again recovered. That takes a great load off my mind.

It does not make a deep impression on me that I cannot convert myself to your point of view in the film affair. There are a good many things that I see differently and judge differently.

Let us not give too much play to repetition compulsion. You were certainly right about Jung, and not quite so right about Rank. That matter took a different course, and would have passed over more easily if it had not been taken so very seriously in Berlin. It is still quite possible that you may be even less right in the matter with which we are concerned now. You are not necessarily always right. But should you turn out to be right this time too, nothing would prevent me from once again admitting it.

With that let us close the argument about something that you yourself describe as a trifle. Such differences of opinion can never be avoided, but only quickly overcome.

What matters more to me is to hear whether you intend to stay in Berlin or spend the winter in a milder climate. I am not quite sure in my mind what to wish for you, but in any case let the outcome be that you cause us no more worry.

With cordial greetings to you and your wife and children

Yours,
Freud [1965, p. 399]

Abraham died on December 25, 1925, at the age of forty-eight. Freud wrote to Abraham's widow:

Since my telegram on receiving the news of your husband's death I have put off writing to you. It was too difficult, and I hoped it would become easier.

Then I fell ill myself, became feverish, and have not yet recovered. But I already see that putting it off was useless, it is just as difficult now as it was then. I have no substitute for him, and no consolatory words for you that would be anything new. That we have to submit with resignation to the blows of fate you know already; and you will have guessed that to me his loss is particularly painful because, with the selfishness of old age, I think he could easily have been spared for the probable short duration of my own life. [1965, p. 399]

The death was, he wrote to Jones, "perhaps the greatest blow that could have struck us. Who would have thought when we were all together in the Harz that he would be the first to leave this senseless life! We must work on and hold together. No one can replace the personal loss, but for the work no one must be irreplaceable. I shall soon fall out—it is to be hoped that the others will do so only much later—but the work must be continued, in comparison with whose dimensions we are all equally small" (Jones 1955, p. 364).

This loss was another great blow for Freud—part of a gauntlet of fate that he was traversing. His letters to Mrs. Abraham and to Jones have the characteristic heroic, oedipean note of the man who can face *Ananke*, bitter Necessity. And he was able to go on—to fifteen more years of creative work of the highest order—defying cancer, old age, and finally the Nazis who drove him out of the land as Moses had been driven out of Egypt.

Summary

This paper has resembled a detective story—the riddle being why Freud erased from his mind Karl Abraham's name and his Amenhotep paper when he wrote *Moses and Monotheism* many years after the younger man's death. The answer I have suggested is that Abraham had become another of Freud's beloved and hated ghosts—"victims" of his death wishes, the most important of whom were Freud's father and his younger brother Julius. The transference was accomplished mainly by way of Abraham's association with the chief "re-incarnation" of all for Freud's adult life, Wilhelm Fliess. Even after Freud's break with him, Fliess continued to evoke a concentrate of wishes attached to the important people from Freud's childhood—father, mother, brother. This kind of transference permitted Freud to make use of Fliess as an analyst-figure during his self-analysis. Abraham too sometimes played the part of an analyst—pointing out unwelcome truths and urging renunciation. Both men drew the death-wishes directed toward the parent-analyst, as well as those displaced onto the rival sibling. The first and greatest of "detective stories"—*Oedipus Rex*—is involved, as are all the motive forces expressed in the Family Romance. We know from Freud's dream at seven of his dead mother and from his lifelong identifications with Joseph and Moses that Freud's family complexes were expressed and lived out in metaphors derived from the Bible and from Egypt. In attempting to write a Family Romance of the Jews, Freud dismissed Father Abraham and his name-sake Karl Abraham. The beloved and lost disciple is forgotten insofar as he is connected with Egypt, the Bible and the oedipal struggle between father and son over the body of the mother that is the essence of the story of Amenhotep IV.

But perhaps the most basic answer to the puzzle involves passive wishes and the castration complex in relation to the *revenants*. Death-wishes toward the father evoke submission to the father. This vicious cycle—seeking castration to avoid castration, engendering hatred while trying to escape hatred—was called by Freud, in a work written after *Moses and Monotheism* (*Analysis Terminable and Interminable*), the bedrock beyond which analysis cannot go: "the attitude proper to the opposite sex which has succumbed to repression . . . the repudiation of femininity [that] can be nothing else than a biological fact, a part of the great riddle of sex" (1937, pp. 250, 252). We come again to the Riddle of the Sphinx and are back full circle to Fliess and the concept of bisexuality which was the subject of Freud's first publicly acknowledged erasing of a name.

The oedipus complex and the castration complex have supplied for this paper a *grundbass* against which various themes have appeared, faded and re-appeared like leit-motifs: Abraham and Moses; Israel and Egypt; betrayal; the struggle for succession; numerology and superstition; the sun and sight; Prussianism—these are various images for Freud that, to continue the musical analogy, combine polyphonically while expressing what is present in the *Grund bass*. The leit-motifs evoke and are evoked by the major figures in Freud's life. Listening for themes and patterns in the form of metaphors is part of the art of psychoanalysis (see Kanzer 1958, 1969; Slochower 1972) although there the music is, so to speak, for two players. I have tried to portray the counterpoint of Freud's living out his passionate involvements in the metaphor of the Old Testament stories that had absorbed him so early.

References

Abraham, K. (1911). On the determining power of names. In *Clinical Papers and Essays on Psycho-Analysis*, pp. 31–33. London: Hogarth Press, 1955.
——— (1912). Amenhotep IV: a psycho-analytical contribution towards the understanding of his personality and of the monotheistic cult of Aton. In *Clinical Papers and Essays on Psycho-Analysis*, pp. 262–290. London: Hogarth Press, 1955.

Freud, S. (1887–1902). *The Origins of Psychoanalysis*. New York: Basic Books, 1954.

———— (1900). The interpretation of dreams. *Standard Edition* 4/5.

———— (1901). The psychopathology of everyday life. *Standard Edition* 6.

———— (1909). Analysis of a phobia in a 5 year old boy. *Standard Edition* 10:5–149.

———— (1911). Psycho-analytic notes on an autobiographical account of a case of paranoia (dementia paranoides). *Standard Edition* 12:9–82.

———— (1913). Totem and taboo. *Standard Edition* 13:1–161.

———— (1914a). The Moses of Michelangelo. *Standard Edition* 13:211–238.

———— (1914b). On the history of the psycho-analytic movement. *Standard Edition* 14:7–66.

———— (1917). Mourning and melancholia. *Standard Edition* 20.

———— (1925). An autobiographical study. *Standard Edition* 20:7–74.

———— (1931). Female sexuality. *Standard Edition* 21:225–243.

———— (1936). A disturbance of memory on the Acropolis. *Standard Edition* 22:239–248.

———— (1937). Analysis terminable and interminable. *Standard Edition* 23:216–253.

———— (1939). Moses and monotheism. *Standard Edition* 23:7–137.

———— (1960). *The Letters of Sigmund Freud*, ed. E. Freud. New York: Basic Books.

———— and Abraham, K. (1965). *The Letters of Sigmund Freud and Karl Abraham*, ed. H. Abraham and E. Freud. New York: Basic Books.

Glover, E. (1965). Introduction. In *Letters of Sigmund Freud and Karl Abraham*, ed. H. Abraham and E. Freud. New York: Basic Books.

Graves, R. (1955). *The Greek Myths*. Vol. 2. Baltimore: Penguin Books.

Grinstein, A. (1968). *On Sigmund Freud's Dreams*. Detroit: Wayne State University Press.

Grotjahn, M. (1968). Karl Abraham, the first German psychoanalyst. In *Psychoanalytic Pioneers*, ed. F. Alexander et al., pp. 1–14. New York: Basic Books.

Jones, E. (1927). Introductory memoir. In *Selected Papers of Karl Abraham*. London: Hogarth Press, 1949.

———— (1953). *The Life and Work of Sigmund Freud*. Vol. 1. New York: Basic Books.

———— (1955). *The Life and Work of Sigmund Freud*. Vol. 2. New York: Basic Books.

———— (1957). *The Life and Work of Sigmund Freud*. Vol. 3. New York: Basic Books.

Jung, K. (1961). *Memories, Dreams, Reflections*. New York: Random House.

Kanzer, M. (1958). Image formation during free association. *This Quarterly* 27:465–484.

———— (1969). Sigmund and Alexander Freud on the Acropolis. *American Imago* 26:324–354.

Kris, E. (1954). Introduction. In *The Origins of Psycho-Analysis: Letters, Drafts and Notes to Wilhelm Fliess*, pp. 1–50. New York: Basic Books.

Reich, W. (1967). *Reich Speaks of Freud*, ed. M. Higgins and C. Raphael. New York: Farrar, Straus and Giroux.

Schur, M. (1964). The problem of death in Freud's writings and life. Paper presented as the 14th Freud Anniversary Lecture of the New York Psychoanalytic Society.

———— (1969). The background of Freud's "disturbance" on the Acropolis. *American Imago* 16:303–324.

Shengold, L. (1966). The metaphor of the journey in *The Interpretation of Dreams*. *American Imago* 23:316–331.

———— (1971). Freud and Joseph. In *The Unconscious Today*, ed. M. Kanzer, pp. 473–494. New York: International Universities Press.

Slochower, H. (1972). The psychoanalytic approach to literature. Some pitfalls and promises. *Literature and Psychology* 21:107–111.

Torah, The Five Books of Moses. Philadelphia Jewish Publication Society of America, 1962.

Wolf Man. (1971). *The Wolf Man.* New York: Basic Books.

Chapter 14

DISCUSSION OF CHAPTER 13 (I)

MARK KANZER, M.D.

It is indeed remarkable, as Shengold points out, that in writing *Moses and Monotheism*, Freud did not make the slightest reference to Karl Abraham, who had discussed the apparent influence of Amenhotep on the Jewish leader and his ideas about a single god. To be sure, this connection had been made by Breasted, the American historian, in 1906. Both Freud and Abraham quoted him on this subject and the illustrations to Abraham's article were reproduced by permission from Breasted's *History of Egypt*. It is also true that Freud's further propositions about Moses—that he was an Egyptian, a deputy of Amenhotep, and that he introduced circumcision among the Jews—were all entirely original and almost certainly reflected a private family romance. Through this series of propositions, the patriarchs Abraham and Jacob (the namesake of Freud's father) were eliminated as ancestors, and Moses, with whom Freud identified, took their place as the spiritual father of his people.

Nevertheless, there was ample opportunity for such a courteous and appreciative note on Abraham. I believe Shengold's explanations have much to recommend them. While it is true that he offered us a self-styled speculative analysis, speculation can follow scientific lines and stimulate the discovery of confirmatory evidence. I will try to offer such validation, some speculative, some more substantive.*

Speculatively, it strikes me that the omission of Abraham's name is counter-

*This paper was presented at the Psychoanalytic Association of New York, March 20, 1972.

balanced by significant references in *Moses and Monotheism* to Otto Rank. These recall earlier and happier days of collaboration between them and suggest that the *Moses* is a continuation of their joint research. Oddly, this is precisely what might have been said of its relationship to Abraham's "Amenhotep" and suggests a reversal of the decision he had reluctantly made at one time to favor Abraham over Rank.

The theme of the patriarch bestowing his blessing on one of two sons is in the tradition of the Old Testament. Actually, Abraham and Rank had long vied, especially in the field of mythology, to win Freud's approval and had been stimulated by his interest in this subject. Both had induced him in this way to take a hand in their writings. Both had presented their first contributions almost simultaneously, Abraham's "Dreams and Myths" coinciding with Rank's study of the birth of the hero. When Rank offered the latter in outline form at the Vienna Psychoanalytic Society on November 25, 1908, Freud had first hinted that the name Moses was associated with Egyptian kings and that the legend of his birth was characteristic of monotheistic beliefs (Nunberg and Federn 1967, p. 69).

While Abraham won out over Rank and for that matter over Jung and Ferenczi, as contending brother figures, becoming Freud's acknowledged heir in the psychoanalytic movement, he seems never to have gained the personal affection of the leader to the extent that the others did. His "Prussianism" and "talmudistic thinking," to which Freud would refer, contrasted with the charm which often determined the latter's preferences. Perhaps also Freud, who never seems entirely to have lost his boyhood ardor for alternately playing Caesar and Brutus with a "revenant," felt attracted to or unwittingly instigated the latent rebelliousness against himself which was so often forthcoming. Abraham, however, was stalwart and uncomfortably reminded Freud that he must adhere to his own image and teachings. He was a superego and an analyst to be respected but not loved.

Nevertheless, it is not surprising that the rebelliousness which became overt in the others should be found in Abraham's apparent fantasies as revealed by his writings. His choice of Amenhotep as a subject was avowedly stimulated by figurines in Freud's study. He was perhaps adding another figure—and ultimately himself—to the household of a new father in the tradition of the family romance, but then was it entirely without significance that he chose a king who had erased the name of his father? More direct evidence of hostility may be found in 1912 when, in thanking Freud for kindness shown him as a guest, he took the occasion to point out that critics sometimes accused his host of treating his followers like patients (Abraham and Freud 1965, p. 129). This none-too-welcome information was then followed by a remarkable comparison of himself with a spoiled patient in whom kindness has aroused guilt that can turn into hostility. The hostility was already in evidence, perhaps exacerbated in a need to overcome feelings of dependency that had been gratified.

Dependency was also overcome when Abraham would take the lead in "rescuing" Freud from other followers who showed hostility—and in 1922, he wrote a paper on the aggression that underlies the rescue-of-the father fantasy. For this purpose, he selected the myth of Oedipus, so closely associated with the triumph of Freud's insights, and really went beyond Freud in his detailed analysis of each symbol in the narrative. Of special interest is the apparent unconscious communication between the two men achieved by the use of imagery, such as Shengold has shown in the case of their use of sun symbolism. A related use, however, appears to have involved the image of run-away horses.

It was in the *Psychopathology of Everyday Life* that Freud (1901) revealed a rescue-of-the-father fantasy that he had evolved in his loneliness in Paris when he pictured that he might heroically stop a carriage whose horses were running away and receive a reward for thus saving an important man. Abraham, in concluding his essay on Amenhotep, compares the king's downfall to that of Phaeton who, driving the chariot of his father, the sun god, plunges to his doom. Here, both the sun and the run-away horses are united in a father-son cautionary tale. In the analysis of the death of Laius, father of Oedipus, Abraham supplies an intermediate link to show that the son kills (rather than rescues) the father before he gains possession of the chariot (representing the mother) and control over the horses (sexual power). In a way, perhaps, he was analyzing the daydreams of young Freud in Paris as well as hinting at his own.

In his further analysis of the Oedipus myth, Abraham takes up the theme of the cross-roads where the slaying occurs (the mother's genitals). In 1922, when the rescue-of-the-father fantasy was analyzed to show the hidden aggression, Abraham was involved once again in rescuing Freud from rebellious sons and found himself at the cross-roads of his career through the opposition he was encountering from the none-too-grateful father. Now the rebels were Ferenczi and Rank, and the struggle continued over the next two years. Ferenczi asserted that Abraham was motivated by "limitless ambition and jealousy" (Jones 1957, p. 65). Freud himself put most of the blame for the dissension on Abraham and accused him of blowing up minor matters into a crisis of disunity. When logic and the reactions of his fellows forced him to recognize that the points at issue were by no means so minor, he admitted that his defense of his errant "sons" was motivated by fondness for them. This argument would seem to have had converse significance as far as Abraham was concerned. When, in 1924, the latter was to be elected president of the International Psychoanalytic Association, Freud had last-minute qualms. However, once the event had taken place, Freud apologized for his campaign against the chosen heir, attributing it to his illness (cancer) and "a sort of senile depression" (Jones 1957, p. 68).

Under the circumstances, when Abraham turned to Fliess for care in his own illness, it is hard to escape the impression that he was affiliating himself with another old friend turned enemy. We must go beyond speculation to mysticism to find meaning in the fact that Abraham, like Freud, had cancer which required multiple operations, or that he died on Christmas day which by tradition marks the death of the old and the birth of the new sun—the very theme of Amenhotep and the change in religion he introduced into Egypt. Freud's reactions, on the other hand, leave more scope for the application of inferences made by Shengold. He specifically linked the illnesses of Abraham and himself with the remark, "Who would have thought he would be the first to leave this senseless world?" (Jones 1957, p. 116). Although the *Internationale Zeitschrift für Psychoanalyse* was about to come out with a special Festschrift in honor of his seventieth birthday, he insisted that this be postponed until a memorial number for Abraham had been issued: "One cannot celebrate any festival until one has performed the duty of mourning." In effect, the death of the younger son was followed by a rebirth celebration and Freud himself became the revenant of Abraham, just as he had once been of Julius. Similar endeavors to ward off his own death by an exchange of identities with a "younger brother" were not uncommon (Kanzer 1969; Chapter 16 of the present volume).

Thus, the pattern of the relationship between Freud and Abraham, as traced by Shengold, is by no means "speculative" if we place it in the context of the writings of the two men and the line of development of Freud's personality from earliest days as revealed by his own self-analysis and verified by continued studies since his death.

References

Abraham, H. C. and Freud, E. L., eds. (1965) *The Letters of Sigmund Freud and Karl Abraham. 1907–1926.* New York: Basic Books.

Abraham, K. (1909). Dreams and myths. In *Clinical Papers and Essays on Psychoanalysis*, pp. 153–209. London: The Hogarth Press, 1955.

———: (1912). Amenhotep IV. In *Clinical Papers and Essays on Psychoanalysis*, pp. 262–290. The Hogarth Press, 1955.

——— (1922). The rescue and murder of the father in neurotic fantasy-formations. In *Clinical Papers and Essays on Psychoanalysis*, pp. 68–75. London: The Hogarth Press, 1955.

Breasted, J. (1906). *A History of Egypt.* London: Scribner.

Freud, S. (1901). The psychopathology of everyday life. *Standard Edition* 6.

———— (1939). Moses and Monotheism. *Standard Edition* 23:7–137.

Jones, E. (1957). *The Life and Works of Sigmund Freud.* Vol. 3. New York: Basic Books.

Kanzer, M. (1969). Sigmund and Alexander Freud on the Acropolis. *American Imago* 26.324–354. (Chapter 16 of this volume.)

Rank, O. (1912). *The Myth of the Birth of the Hero.* New York: Robert Brunner, 1952.

Nunberg, H. and Federn, E. (1967). *The Minutes of the Vienna Psychoanalytic Society.* Vol. 2. New York: International Universities Press.

Chapter 15

DISCUSSION OF CHAPTER 13 (II)

ROY LILLESKOV, M.D.

Shengold has presented us with a speculative analysis of a symptomatic act by Freud. Whereas Freud was usually so careful to credit others, especially his co-workers, with priority when it was due, in *Moses and Monotheism*, while discussing Akhenaten he did not mention Abraham's 1912 study of Amenhotep IV who became Akhenaten. Sterba, discussing this paper at the midwinter (1971) meeting of the American Psychoanalytic Association, felt that this omission amounted to unconscious plagiarism. Examination of the Abraham paper and the Freud book do not bear this out. Freud's references to Akhenaten derive directly from J. H. Breasted's *A History of Egypt* (1906) and *The Dawn of Conscience* (1934) and other historical texts. Abraham also used Breasted as a source. Freud does not rely on or even refer to Akhenaten's father complex, which was the theme of Abraham's paper. But Abraham did consider Akhenaten's monotheism a precursor of Mosaic monotheism and thus touched on one of Freud's essential assumptions. The omission of any reference to this is uncharacteristic and does amount to a parapraxis.

From the rich pattern of Freud's biography, correspondence, and work, Shengold has pointed out a striking figure in the background. He links the ambivalence toward Abraham, shown by the omission, to Abraham's relationship with Fliess

*Presented before the Psychoanalytic Association of New York, March 20, 1972.

in terms of his Oedipus and Cain complexes. In this, Dr. Shengold follows the lead of Max Schur (1972), who had discussed at length the influence of the Fliess relationship on Freud's neurosis in published papers that were summarized in his book *Freud: Living and Dying.* I find Shengold's analysis ingenious and plausible, though subject to all of the risks that the analysis of a historical personage entails. Here, too, Shengold is in good company, for the two works in question in this symptomatic act are both exercises by Abraham and Freud of just that kind of analysis of historical personages. Without the benefit of the analytic process as a constant corrective, it is difficult to know what weight to assign to subjective factors or intrinsic determinants of any act. Working with much more reliable data than Freud and Abraham had at their disposal, Shengold has further minimized the risks by staying close to Freud's own interpretation of his various symptoms. Perhaps it would be in order to review some of the other possible determinants of this parapraxis.

Moses and Monotheism was written and rewritten between 1934 and 1938. In its first title—*The Man Moses, a Historical Novel*—Freud acknowledged its speculative nature. Apparently inspired by an attempt to understand the problem of anti-Semitism, this book traced the hostility back to the origins of Judaism but betrays the conflicts of the author. Composed of three unequal parts, it is full of recapitulations and repetitions and a preface at the beginning, two more prefaces before part three and a fourth preface inserted in the middle of part three. If it were not for the remarkable clarity and precision of the *Outline of Psychoanalysis* which was to follow, one would suspect that Freud was showing the effects of his age. He was, after all, seventy-eight years old when he began the book and eighty-one when portions of it were first published. For over eleven years he had been waging a painful struggle with cancer and the effects of treatment. In a letter to Arnold Zweig in December, 1934, Freud wrote, "I think my memory for recent events is no longer reliable" (1970, p. 98). Perhaps this reflected the organic component that would have to be considered in further accounting for his slip. In that case, a subtitle for Shengold's paper might have been taken from one of Abraham's titles—"An Octogenarian's Mistake" (1922).

But Freud's account of his conflicts over this book seems to indicate that other factors were of far more importance. He repeatedly wrote to Zweig and stated also in the prefaces that he had internal and external reasons for not publishing the work. The latter concerned the political situation and the fear of antagonizing the Catholic authorities in Vienna and thus jeopardizing psychoa nalysis. The internal conflicts were expressed in terms of doubts about his thesis. Thus in September, 1934, he wrote to Zweig: "in addition there is the fact that the work doesn't seem to me sufficiently substantiated . . . (1970, p. 92). In November he wrote, "I need more certainty and I should not like to endanger the final form of the book, which I regard as valuable, by founding it on a base of clay" (1970, p. 97). Finally, in December he wrote that the *Moses* had failed because "I was obliged to construct so imposing a statue upon feet of clay, so that any fool could topple it" (1970, p. 98). Schur (1972) attributes this conflict to a resurgence of guilt over having surpassed and survived his father and brother and connects it to a renewal of the obsessional concern at eighty-one and a half, a "critical period," according to the Fliess-Freud calculations (see here also Freud, 1936).

Yet I do not think these conflicts general to the book *Moses and Monotheism*, or the period during which it was written, explain the specific symptom (paraphasia) under examination on this occasion. They form the conditions under which the symptom occurred. In reading the Freud-Abraham correspondence (1965), I was struck by one feature in particular. That was the quality of *mutual* though unequal stimulation between the two men in clinical and theoretical work. Though many of Freud's disciples were stimulated by him and inspired to brilliant work, one rarely got the feeling of Freud's being inspired by them in return. When this occurred, it appeared in reaction against ideas which were uncongenial to Freud, as in the case of Jung's formulations about psychoses and later Rank's idea of the birth trauma. But with Abraham it was otherwise. The most noteworthy examples of this process were in the area of orality, depression and mourning.

Furthermore, there is frequent reference to plagiarism in their correspondence with each offering the other free title to shared observations and findings and encouraging the other's investigations. In Freud's second published letter to Abraham, dated July 5, 1907, he wrote, "My dear colleague, I have read your acute and, what is more important, conclusive observations with quite special interest. Before I deal with them there is one possibility that I should like to clear out of the way, namely that you should regard remarks of mine such as 'that we knew already' or 'I came to a similar conclusion' as making any claim to priority. Please also consider yourself at liberty to make use of my observations in any way you wish . . ." (1965, p. 1). Abraham's interest in Egypt derived in part from a gift of two small figurines which Freud gave him after a visit in December, 1907. On January 8, 1908, Abraham offered Freud dreams of himself and his wife for the new edition of the *Interpretations of Dreams*, an offer which Freud readily accepted. Abraham asked for, received, and used advice in treating his patients. On July 11, 1908, Freud wrote "your idea about marriage between close relatives is certainly correct and worth describing. It has already been mentioned in our group but you need take no notice of that" (1965, p. 43). The relationship grew and, even in the midst of their dispute about Jung, Freud wrote admiringly of Abraham's paper on dementia praecox and hysteria, and added:

"May I say that it is consanguineous Jewish traits that attract me to you? We understand each other" (1965, p. 46). In the same letter regarding "Dreams and Myths" Freud added, "I am more and more convinced that you are right and that we share the honour of explaining mythology" (1965, p. 47). On February 24, 1910, Freud responded to a request of Abraham by putting some notes on fetishism at his disposal—"please make any use of it you wish" (1965, p. 86). Working on the Schreber case Freud wrote to Abraham on October 24, 1910: "I am in the thick of the work, and have penetrated somewhat more deeply into paranoia along the path you trod" (1965, p. 95). On finishing, Freud declared on December 18, 1910: "when I worked out these ideas at Palermo I particularly liked the proposition that megalomania was the sexual overestimation of the ego. In Vienna I found that you had already very trenchantly said the same thing. I have of course had to plagiarize you very extensively in this paper" (1965, p. 97). In May of 1912, Freud wrote, "your paper on melancholia was very intelligently criticized by Federn, and all sorts of things dawned on me which may lead further" (1965, p. 116). Then on December 8, 1913, Abraham apologized for an "unconscious plagiarism" which he planned to correct in the proofs (1965, p. 159). In 1915, Abraham wrote Freud on March 31st regarding an "outline of a theory of melancholia." He reviewed his own previous work on the subject and advanced some criticisms. In his next letter, May 4th, Freud replied: "your comments on melancholia were very useful to me, and I unhesitatingly incorporated in my paper those parts of them that I could use" (1965, p. 220). There were many more examples of mutual influence until Abraham's death. I will only quote one more, which Freud wrote March 4, 1923, thanking Abraham for some newspaper cuttings on the discovery of the tomb of Tutankhamen. He added: "It now seems certain that they will soon find the mummy of the King and perhaps also that of his consort, a daughter of *our* analytic Pharoah" (1965, p. 334; my italics).

I have quoted all of these examples to show how close was the intellectual collaboration between these two men, a collaboration which had large elements of mutual identification and frequently led to unconscious plagiarism. One is reminded of the ideas shared by Freud and Breuer in their early collaboration (1893–1895), and the later sharing of ideas by Freud and Fliess as seen in their correspondence (1887–1902). Freud's relationship with Abraham, though more distant and possibly more sublimated, certainly showed elements of the same ambivalence he had toward the earlier figures. In fact, similar features are found in a number of his close friendships as reflected in his correspondence. These friendships include some which antedate Fliess, as for example the one with his friend Silberstein who moved to Rumania after they graduated from gymnasium (Stanescu 1971). Therefore, I think that tracing his symptom to his conflicts with father and brother by way of those with Fliess may be too specific. According to this view the seeds of the later symptom would have been sown before Fliess entered the picture and would have been part of the total relationship between Abraham and Freud.

It appears to me that a full explanation would have to concern itself with a study of the special characteristics of Freud's friendships. It would have to take into account the ease and intensity of major identifications and the struggle against these identifications. It would further have to explain his intense idealizations and their fate. In short, it would have to come to terms with certain narcissistic features of Freud's object relations. Freud himself commented upon his need for a loved friend and a hated enemy who often came together in the same person. He traced this phenomenon to his relationship with his nephew and boyhood playmate John. Analyzing this further, he concluded that there was a "piece of unruly homosexual feeling at the root of the matter" (Jones 1953, p. 317). As Shengold has stated, this involved both the positive and the negative oedipus emphasis. Though Shengold points out that this implies passive feminine urges, the feminine identifications embodying these wishes have not been developed further.

Freud often behaved toward his ideas and words as if they were children. The most dramatic instance of this is in the letter to Fliess of November 14, 1897, in which he writes "It was November 12, 1897; the sun was in the eastern quarter, and Mercury and Venus in conjunction—no, birth announcements do not begin like that any more. It was on November 12th a day under the influence of a left-sided migraine on the afternoon of which Martin sat down to write a new poem and on the evening of which Oli lost his second tooth, when, after the terrible pangs of the last few weeks, a new piece of knowledge was born to me" (1887–1902, p. 229). He was referring, of course, to infantile sexuality.

An interesting exchange between Freud and Arnold Zweig forty years later is suggestive (1970). Freud had been trying to convince Zweig that Shakespeare's plays had really been written by an aristocrat, probably Edward de Vere, 17th Earl of Oxford. Zweig wrote on March 21, 1937: "[Oxford] is not the author of Shakespeare's works, but the begetter. . . . The feminine element in the poet thus comes into its own. He is able to conceive it, make it vibrate and by way of the short cuts of the imagination he lives through the life of others. Even Shakespeare's aristocratic element is 'begot' in this way. It is not inborn but implanted in him." Freud replied that "it is quite inconceivable to me that Shakespeare should have gotten everything second hand. Hamlet's neurosis, Lear's madness, MacBeth's defiance and the character of Lady Macbeth, Othello's jealousy, etc. It almost irritates me that you should support the notion. . . . (1970, p. 138). That Freud, who had told us so much about identification, should have been so "irritated" by the idea that Shakespeare got his ideas by identification, by "conception" as Zweig had suggested, seems to indicate a conflict over such an idea of impregnation and may be relevant to the parapraxis under discussion.

Of course this, too, is speculative. Freud did not tell of pregnancy fantasies in the glimpses he gives us of his self-analysis. It may be, however, that his self-analysis did not progress that far. Max Schur has argued (1972) that Freud's relative underestimation of preoedipal conflicts was due to the limitations of his self-analysis. He attributes this to the intense traumatic atmosphere of Freud's first three years in a one-room household, witness to primal scene, birth and death. Perhaps under any conditions it is difficult for a self-analysis to penetrate that far.

Shengold has previously given us a beautiful paper on the Joseph theme in Freud's life (chapter 5 of the present volume) and with the "Parapraxis" paper he has touched upon Freud's identification with Akhenaten and Moses. I hope that he continues in his exploration of Freud's identifications so that one day we will be closer to a full explanation of the creative richness of Freud's work.

References

Abraham, H. and Freud, E., eds. (1965). *The Letters of Sigmund Freud and Karl Abraham*. New York: Basic Books.

Abraham, K. (1912). Amenhotep IV. In *Clinical Papers and Essays on Psychoanalysis*, ed. H. Abraham, pp. 262–290. New York: Basic Books, 1955.

———— (1922). An octogenarian's mistake. In *Clinical Papers and Essays on Psychoanalysis,* ed. H. Abraham, p. 80. New York: Basic Books, 1955.

Breasted, J. H. (1906). *A History of Egypt*. London: Scribners.

———— (1934). *The Dawn of Conscience*. London: Scribners.

Breuer, J. and Freud, S. (1893–1895). Studies on hysteria. *Standard Edition* 2.

Freud, E. (1970). *The Letters of Sigmund Freud and Arnold Zweig*. New York: Harcourt Brace Ovanovich.

Freud, S. (1887–1902). *The Origins of Psychoanalysis*. New York: Basic Books, 1954.

———— (1939). Moses and monotheism. *Standard Edition* 23:7–137.

Jones, E. (1953). *The Life and Work of Sigmund Freud*, Vol. I. New York: Basic Books.

Schur, M. (1972). *Freud: Living and Dying*. New York: International Universities Press.

Stanescu, H. (1971). Young Freud's letters to his Rumanian friend, Silberstein. In *The Israel Annals of Psychiatry*, Vol. 9, pp. 195–207.
Sterba, R. (1971). Discussion at the Midwinter Meeting of the American Psychoanalytic Association, December.

Chapter 16

SIGMUND AND ALEXANDER FREUD ON THE ACROPOLIS

An experience of Freud's on the Acropolis (1936) has attracted increasing attention in recent years both as a contribution to ego psychology and as an autobiographical document that bears on the relevance of his personality and self-analysis to the attainment of scientific insights. Since many valuable studies are now available, we shall direct our attention especially to one aspect of the experience, the part played by his brother Alexander, his only companion during the experience. This "figure in the background" is generally overlooked but has a very important bearing, we suggest, on our understanding of two crises that Freud encountered, and indeed on his travel phobia and life history generally.

The Letter to Rolland

The first crisis occurred in 1904, when the experience on the Acropolis took place; the second in 1936 when it was described in a letter to Romain Rolland. The "Letter," as we recall, constituted a gift to the French writer on the occasion of his seventieth birthday—a seemingly strange gift, as it treats so exclusively of an episode in Freud's own past that had come to trouble him increasingly in recent years. Moreover the spirit of the letter is scarcely in keeping with a birthday celebration, since Freud laments the decline of his own powers as he approaches eighty and implicitly holds out the same prospects for his correspondent, though the latter is still hailed for his "youth" and vigor.

To be sure, there is also homage to Rolland as a great writer and humanitarian— characteristics which both men shared and had discussed in previous correspondence between them (E. Freud 1960; Letters 217, 241, 242, 261). Indeed, the point of departure for the letter lies in a comparison of the ways in which they serve humanity, corresponding essentially to the differences between art and science (E. Freud 1960, p. 364). Implicit, too, is the continuance of earlier exchanges on religion and Freud's rejection of the comforts it offers an aging man to seduce him from the bleak paths of reason (Freud 1929, p. 64–68). The background is thus vast, worthy of the occasion and the theme—an experience on the Acropolis—and becomes significantly personal in relation to two eminent men who can now look back on long lives successfully dedicated to advancing the frontiers of civilization that are so impressively symbolized by the Acropolis itself.

In an important and specific sense, the letter is also a contribution to humanity and is thus openly addressed to the public. There may be something incongruous and even egotistic in Freud's choice of a self-analytic theme and the revelation, even confession, of a troublesome personal problem on this occasion. Nevertheless, his career offers powerful support for the reason he gives: psychoanalysis, as a science, derives from his own self-analysis, and what he can offer Romain Rolland and advancing civilization is most appropriately a specimen of psychoanalytic work that modernizes the ancient Greek aphorism "Know Thyself!" A novelist also transmutes his experiences and personal insights into benefits for his fellowmen, though as a rule with less obligation to discover or reveal the innermost recesses of the self.

Romain Rolland is now tendered an even greater honor: in effect, he is permitted on this occasion to become the analyst of Sigmund Freud himself, for we regard the entire letter that follows as a self-analytic session. In this respect, Rolland is the heir to Wilhelm Fliess and the correspondence that was such an important factor in Freud's analysis some forty years earlier (Freud 1954). The "resurrection" of Fliess in connection with these reminiscences about the Acropolis is by no means accidental, as we shall learn, and to a considerable extent pervades the letter, although no specific mention is made of the man who once commanded the loyalty and admiration of Freud even more than did Rolland.

If the French writer thus becomes the analyst, it is also true that Freud now becomes the writer—a first exchange of identities in a gem of literature that will reveal many more. Another crucial exchange occurs almost immediately thereafter as Freud, having thus set up the analytic situation, yields to free association and becomes a patient. His associations concern the holiday excursion to Athens—a suitable birthday theme, to be sure!—that Sigmund had undertaken with Alexander in 1904. At this point, an unexpected connection occurs—a widening of consciousness which is a forerunner of insight: "My brother is ten years younger than I am, so he is the same age as you—a coincidence which has only now occurred to me" (E. Freud 1960, p. 240; all subsequent quotations from this letter will be indicated only by page numbers in parentheses). "Coincidence" will continue to be a travelling companion on this venture; together with constitution (the two brothers), it determines man's fate (the complemental series of psychic motivations) (Freud 1912, p. 99).

Actually, Freud now takes leave of Romain Rolland except for a fleeting and impersonal farewell at the end, such as occurs on leaving the analyst's office. He has merely served as a transference vehicle for the analytic process, just as real people lose their individual identity in the artist's work. Alexander, on the contrary, emerging from beneath the façade of Rolland, steps increasingly from the shadows of virtual non-identity until, at the climax of the "session," it is he who, both as brother and analyst, becomes the recipient of a creative new insight attained by Freud. In effect, it is the younger brother who is placed in the position of the analyst in a further progression of the identity reversals.

The theme of the session, as it unfolds, is a "little problem" that cannot be contained within the dramatic unities of time, place and person that ostensibly frame the Athenian holiday jaunt. Man's control over his destination must yield to the unexpected, and we realize increasingly that the journey is an allegory that begins with a birthday and ends at the threshold of death. First it is Alexander's business needs and then advice from his business acquaintance that lead to a change in their plans, so that Athens is suddenly substituted for another travel goal. This aspect receives no special emphasis but it is tantamount to equating the brother's presence with the influences that modify Freud's travels, or life. The experiences of eighty years are under review in this session.

The rational façade of the trip soon gives way to an element of mystery (the unconscious intrudes further) as Sigmund and Alexander both react with depression and uncertainty (can they land in Greece without passports?) at the prospect of thus unexpectedly making their way to the ancient capital. For hours they wander about Trieste, at the gateway to the Adriatic, and then "without bothering in the least about the supposed difficulty and indeed without having discussed with one another the reasons for our decision," book passage for Athens without further hesitation. "Such behavior," Freud underlines, "was most strange" (p. 240).

Allegorically, we see in this the beginning of the birth process, as especially represented in fantasies about the hero and his travels to a distant land where he finds new and more exalted parents. This "family romance" (Freud, 1909a) was especially significant in relation to Freud's travel neurosis, which we learn so much about in a self-analysis of the prolonged difficulties that beset his path to Rome (1900, pp. 193–198). We shall learn more about it it Athens. In a more limited sense, a moment of hesitation after undertaking analysis again and a period of trial (wandering for hours in depression and uncertainty) is followed by the forging of a therapeutic alliance as initial misgivings are overcome.

Thereafter, the journey speeds ahead with the characteristics of magical thought and the brothers find themselves on the Acropolis. Again mystery (the unconscious) intrudes. The elation that might be expected is replaced by a "surprising thought" as Freud surveys the scene: "So all this really does exist, just as we learnt at school" (p. 241). It is a reaction of doubt and denial which had already begun with the "experience" in Trieste. On the Acropolis, it has become a full-fledged symptom—a rejection of the outer world in the form of a "dérealization" that appears when a danger, long warded off by phobic avoidances, is directly confronted. We need to learn more about the meaning of this danger.

This Freud now endeavors to determine both for himself and for us. The initial outcome is a theoretical exposition in which a splitting of the ego is postulated: "the first person" within himself seemed "obliged, under the impact of an unequivocal observation, to believe in something, the reality of which had hitherto seemed doubtful." The "second person" was astonished because he was unaware that such doubt had existed. Two alternative hypotheses follow: could Sigmund, as a schoolboy, have disbelieved in the real existence of Athens? Or was it more likely, as he decided, that the correct phrasing, as apparent already in Trieste, might be: "I could really not have imagined it possible that I should ever be granted the sight of Athens with my own eyes." Our insight into an irrational element in his train of thought deepens: "Fate"—now directly invoked—would never permit him to visit this lovely place, for it "is a materialization of our conscience, of the severe superego within us, itself a residue of the punitive agency of our childhood" (p. 243).

The dimensions of the problem now become clearer for the analyst; uncanny feelings and mysticism are yielding to insight and metapsychology. A city with special charm for Freud, the lover of antiquity, lies open before him, but an inner danger threatens—the fate which, as he often stated, is a derivative of the father figure of infancy. The oedipal triangle is discernible in transparent disguises within the manifest content of the travel phobia—indeed, the Oedipus legend itself, whose hero's footsteps were directed against his will to a "strange" city that was after all his own home. Could the recent decipherer of the fate of Oedipus have contemplated his arrival in Greece with indifference? In later years, according to Hanns Sachs, the city of Athens drew him in the same fashion that Rome had done in his youth (1944, p. 85).

We become aware, as the session progresses, that Freud alternates between a narrative style adorned with metaphors (free association is inherently the matrix of poetic imagery) and more elaborate and expository statements. We recognize in this the alternation between "analysand" and "analyst" forced upon him by the requirements of self-analysis. There is a split between free expression and critical commentaries, between the experiencing and the observing egos, such as had arisen between the "first person" and the "second person" in reacting to the scene on the Acropolis. It is the second person who is probing the first under the conditions made possible by the analytic situation. We may expect a further interplay of the two in consequent manifestations of resistance and transference.

Metaphors, during the analytic process, possess much of the structure of dreams as compromise-formations between more primitive and more mature thought (Kanzer 1958). We find that Freud's theoretical comments on his adventures and their background are constantly interspersed with comparisons that are highly individual and imaginative in nature. Like a number of other analysts who have remarked upon this tendency in the letter to Rolland (Harrison 1966; Slochower 1970; Stamm 1969), and in accordance with Freud's own methodology in interpreting many written works, we shall survey these "comparisons" for the amplification that the preconscious may bring to the conscious communication.

Thus, the opportunity to visit Athens is likened to the surprise on hearing good news, such as the winning of a prize "or when a girl learns that the man whom she has secretly loved has asked her parents for leave to pay his addresses to her" (p. 242). Both images are readily combined to offer a third partly described by Freud himself: Fate (the father) has unexpectedly granted a girl permission to receive a suitor. Shengold (1966, p. 326) has remarked on Freud's feminine identification here. Certainly such passivity was also to be noted in relation to the coincidences that steered him toward the Acropolis. However, there are defensive possibilities that by no means exclude positive trends. Perhaps Freud was the suitor who received the permission. We do learn from Ernest Jones that he put on his best shirt for the occasion and was later given to enthusiastic descriptions of the beautiful scene (1955, p. 24). His own equation of landscapes with the features of the body is particularly pertinent here (1900, p. 399).

The sense of unreality which pervaded and overcame the elation (the forbidding voice of the father opposing voyeuristic and incestuous pleasures), next elicits from Freud a revealing metaphor as he compares his feelings to those of a traveller who "walking besides Loch Ness, suddenly caught sight of the famous monster stranded upon the shore and found himself driven to the admission: 'so it really does exist—the sea-serpent we've never believed in!' "

The displacement here seems obvious as the Aegean sea gives way to Loch Ness, whose monster was much in the news in 1936. Efforts at control and detachment are apparent—time, setting and person are all shifted and an absurd monster, a current joke, obscures the original terror of a nightmare. Childhood memories seem to be rising to the surface and the travel phobia—now that avoidance mechanisms were dropped in Trieste—gives way to a still earlier animal phobia: the danger threat from within is materializing on the outside as an immediate threat.

New defenses must be mobilized through inner changes in the representation of the self and the object, with concomitant symptoms of depersonalization and derealization. The "serpent," in the tradition of a nightmare and totem, is (we assume) the father (and particularly his phallus), while the lake, in the language of equally universal symbolism, is the mother and her womb. We confirm here the impressions of Slochower (1970) and others who have implicated the primal scene in Freud's reactions on the Acropolis, equating the sea itself with the mother and connecting the travel phobia and the derealization with the sight of the mother's nudity when little Sigmund was travelling in an eerily lit train (Freud 1954, p. 237). The meaning of the journey has now widened to include themes of sex as well as of birth—the traditional preoccupations of the inquiring child. Since we have also undertaken to trace the course of mental events through the same symbols, we shall also interpret the monster arising from the lake as the warded-off memory that seeks to enter consciousness again.

Along with the beginning emergence of the repressed, certain new insights for Freud, the scientist, also make their appearance. As the inner danger begins to undergo a shift to the outer world in which it originated before internalization—that is, the actual confrontation with the mother's nudity and the primal scene—his "critical ego" discusses the mechanisms of disavowal that were invoked to withdraw from reality. Concomitantly, he widens the outlook of psychoanalysis which—derived from earlier stages of his own self-analysis—had dwelled too exclusively on the inner boundaries of the ego. "Repression," he points out, "was the starting point of the whole of our deeper understanding of psychopathology." With the advance of ego psychology, defenses against outer reality had been receiving greater recognition. His immediate discussion of derealization extends the horizons of psychoanalysis along this border.

"My daughter, the child analyst," he adds, is presently engaged in clarifying the entire scheme of defenses (p. 245). It is also Freud himself, we suggest, who is contributing to this expansion of horizons but—with the well-known tendency of the creator (so often demonstrated in his own works) to ward off guilt and punishment by projecting the responsibility for the inspiration to God, the muse or another person (Erikson 1954)—he is here again showing a disposition to defer to the younger generation.

The altruistic aspects of such renunciation of personal ambition were especially meaningful during the Acropolis trip, for Freud had recently been confronted with a bitter charge of plagiarism by Wilhelm Fliess (Schur 1968). This charge could be indirectly answered by the repudiation of credit for his own work, a tendency which actually may be demonstrated in another instance through his deference at this same time to the Greek philosopher Empedocles as the originator of certain of his own theories (Freud 1937, pp. 244–245). Similarly, he renounces the analytic function in favor of Rolland and Alexander as a defense against charges of ambition. We have also been able to show elsewhere how another important step in the development of ego psychology coincided with the lifting of certain inhibitions within Freud at the end of a journey to Rome (Kanzer 1966, p. 527–528). The arrival at a destination is registered as the fulfillment of goals both in the inner as well as the outer world. The guilt attached to external discoveries has roots in the curiosity attached to the primal scene and the desire to take father's place with mother. Later, this is carried over into the scientific sublimation of curiosity and experimental problem-solving (Prometheus).

We also learn more about these processes when, immediately following the theoretical exposition on disavowal, a supplementary train of thought is contributed by the unconscious, a "comparison" to illustrate the operation of this defense mechanism. Freud recalls in this connection the lament, "Alas for my Alhama," which tells how Baobdil, the last Moorish ruler of Spain, received the news of the fall of his citadel and with it the end of his rule. In a final exercise of such authority as was left to his ego, he burned the letter and had the messenger put to death. Significantly, Freud terms this defense of undoing *non arrivé*—the event had not "arrived!"

Displacement from the Greek to the Spanish citadel is apparent, as well as some inner link between Baobdil and Freud himself.* Pursuing the assumption that the primal scene continues to be operative in shaping the choice of the material in this "session," we observe progress and continuity from the Loch Ness image comparable to the sequence in two dreams of the same night. In the one, a monster emerges from the water; in the second, evil news is burned and the bearer put to death. Combining these details, we see the threat that has emerged from the water as disposed of by throwing it back into the fire. The "undoing" is now achieved through the antithetical symbolism of water and fire, which played an important part in Freud's own habitual metaphors, his self-analysis of ambitious traits (1900, p. 216) and his scientific research (1932).

---

*Although we are unable to follow the important theme of Freud's Jewish identity in this analytic fragment, it may well be of significance that the Semitic Baobdil had deposed his own father and was the last obstacle to the establishment of Catholic rule in Spain (Webster 1958, p. 162).

The loss of the Alhama, which precipitates the king's despair, may be correlated with the loss of the primal scene mother and points to a similar meaning for the Acropolis as the consecrated site of the temple of Athena, the virgin goddess who protected and gave her name to the city. It also suggests still earlier relations to the mother (Amelia Freud) and a Catholic nurse ("Amme") who played a very important part in Freud's earliest memories (1954, p. 219).

With such alternations between the insights of the critical ego and the discharge facilities permitted the experiencing ego, the analytic process now enters a new phase as Freud refocuses once more the research problem set by this "session." Perhaps the sense of unreality had been derived not from doubts about the existence of Athens, or as to whether he would actually see it, but rather from the more specific question: Would he ever be able to "go such a long way?" (formulation three). This last phrasing brought him closer to the travel neurosis and opened the way by means of a pun, a "verbal bridge" to a fended-off idea, closer to the core of the neurosis, that would now, after preliminary foreshadowings, come to the surface in this letter.

"To go such a long way" correlates an outer journey with a more subtle and abstract inner equivalent, to attain fulfillment of ambitious strivings. This newly opened channel of thought now carries Freud back to a wider view of his own childhood when doubts about the ability to reach the Acropolis ("the city on the heights") could well arise from the "limitations and poverty of our conditions of life." However, he quickly passes from such external realities to more fundamental psychological motives. "My longing to travel was no doubt also the expression of a wish to escape from that pressure, like the force which drives so many adolescent children to run away from home. I had long seen clearly that a great part of the pleasure of travel lies in the fulfillment of early wishes [and] that it is rooted . . . in the dissatisfaction with home and family" (p. 247).

This is, of course, again the concept of the family romance and its specific application to the background of Sigmund Freud himself. While the emphasis here is on adolescence, the deeper material would assuredly reach further back to far earlier phases of relatedness to the family. Freud now connects travel goals with the recapture of feelings of infantile omnipotence: "When first one catches sight of the sea, crosses the ocean and experiences as realities cities and lands which for so long had been distant and unattainable things of desire"—(surely the mother transmuted into typical geographic symbols!)—"one feels oneself like a hero who has performed deeds of improbable greatness." Sublimation itself is illustrated by this fusion, in such terse and beautiful language, of the critical expositor and the experiencing poet in Freud who have differentiated from the same background as the hero and the anxious traveller. Each offshoot of the common stem has maintained connections with the common matrix.

Next, the train of associations between the past and present seizes on Alexander as a real link and a suitable transference object for mediating the return of the ultimate image that is sought. "I might that day on the Acropolis have said to my brother," Freud continues, " 'Do you still remember how, when we were young, we used day after day to walk along the same streets on our way to school, and how every Sunday we used to go to the Prater or on some excursion we knew so well? And now, here we are in Athens, and standing on the Acropolis! We really *have* gone a long way' " (Freud's italics). What thus finds verbal expression at last is an exultant inner reality that could not be acknowledged originally and had to be warded off by anxiety, avoidance and depersonalization: the experience of the journey as worthy of a hero's reward—an incestuous reunion with the mother in this incomparable setting.

The fantasies then gain force in a remarkable illustration that immediately follows: "So too, if I may compare such a small event with a greater one, Napoleon, during his coronation as Emperor in Notre Dame, turned to one of his brothers—it must no doubt have been the eldest one, Joseph—and remarked: 'What would *Monsieur notre Pére* have said to this, if he could have been here today?' " (Freud's italics). This striking image is the culminating point of the hero fantasy which the experiencing ego was so belatedly permitted to enjoy in the person of Napoleon, while the critical ego, as the "elder brother," Joseph, was reduced to the role of a subordinate and passive observer, precisely like the analyst.

Freud's interests in Napoleon (1900, p. 198; Jones 1957, pp. 368, 463–464) and the Biblical Joseph (1900, p. 484) were long standing and need concern us here only insofar as they have reference to our immediate comprehension of the remarkable comparison between the Freud and Bonaparte brothers involved on this occasion. The links were by no means as strange and startling as may be assumed. The Corsicans and the Hebrews were alike patriarchal clans with many sons—which was true also of the Freud family. Joseph was the son of Jacob; Sigmund and Alexander were sons of Jacob Freud. Joseph and the younger Benjamin were full brothers among many half-brothers; so too were Sigmund and Alexander Freud.

Napoleon and Joseph were brilliantly successful and turned sibling rivalry into opportunities for ignoring feuds and altruistically serving their families. Sigmund Freud has recorded the aggressive side of his own childhood and conflicts with brothers and a nephew, but the deepest impression was a guilt reaction to the death of a younger brother, Julius, which "left the germ of guilt" in the surviving child, himself only nineteen months old (Jones 1953, p. 219). By the age of ten, Sigmund knew that death wishes would not dispose of his latest newborn sibling and, in consonance with the superego formation that had now taken place, he delegated his own military ambitions (identifications with Hannibal and Napoleon's Marshall Massena) (Freud 1900, pp. 147–148) to the newcomer by suggesting that he be named Alexander after the Macedonian conqueror (1901, p. 21). When the suggestion was accepted, he could settle down to unconscious paternity and protection toward his "name-child."

In "The Psychopathology of Everyday Life," Freud tells of a memory disturbance which he attributed to a desire to be the son of an elder brother rather than of his father (1901, pp. 219–220). Perhaps the interpretation that he wished to be father rather than elder brother to Alexander was the more deeply repressed possibility. (The presumptive role of a similar identification with an older half-brother Phillip, when a sister Anna was born, constitutes a ramification that we shall not explore here [1954, pp. 222–223]; see however Shengold [1969]. Philip of Macedonia was the father of Alexander the Great.)

The Napoleon and Joseph sagas were linked in the coronation metaphor by the figure of Joseph Bonaparte, another "bridge" who consciously preoccupied Freud in long-standing fantasies (Jones 1957, pp. 191, 368). These received a new edition in 1936 when the latter suggested, in a letter to Thomas Mann, that Napoleon's feelings toward his brother Joseph had drawn him to undertake a military campaign in Egypt, home of the Biblical Joseph, and had been a determinant of his marriage to Josephine (Jones 1957, pp. 463–464). Thus the "coronation scene" that climaxed the analysis of the experience on the Acropolis intertwined three family romances which had long been related in Freud's fantasies.

The parents as well as the brothers are represented in the "coronation scene" (see also Harrison 1966). "Notre Dame" is conspicuously paired with "Notre Pere" to bracket the sons. The Acropolis has found a new image that moves it closer than in the preceding displacements to the temple of the virgin goddess whom Freud failed in this letter to associate with the Athenian experience. Later, she received isolated consideration in an article which stressed the significance of the Medusa head as a protective charm of her shield (Freud 1940)—a guarantor of safety from male penetration. Athena, a mother goddess, was transformed into a virgin with the transformation from Greek matriarchy to patriarchy, and bore an inverse position to that of the Virgin Mary in the later Christian culture. In such roles, she receives occasional mention in Freud's writings (1900, p. 233; 1939, pp. 22, 46).

Of interest is the apparent fact, cited by Strachey, that Freud may have shown a "disturbance of memory" in citing the French cathedral as the scene of the coronation in which the exchange between the Bonapartes took place (p. 247). This presumably occurred in another setting, in Milan. However, Notre Dame was a favorite resort of Freud's himself when he visited Paris in 1885 at the end of another journey. Here, too, his experiences were memorable: "My first impression on entering was a sensation I have never had before: This is a church" (p. 183).*

If the access to memories and desires connected with the mother still had to be made through the indirect superego symbols and controlled feelings associated with cathedrals and virgin goddesses, the return of the father to express his opinions about the son's coronation was less ambiguous. He had already made his appearance symbolically as a churlish fate whose permission to visit the Acropolis was suspect. In the Loch Ness imagery, he was a monster, and in the Alhama dirge, he became a messenger to be put to death. Now summoned at the moment of the coronation—the passing of the head through the crown that consummates the oedipal triumph of the son—he becomes a veritable figure of the Last Judgment, Monsieur ("my Lord") notre Père returning as a ghost to haunt the son who had destroyed him and seized the mother for himself. (Elsewhere we have dwelled on a comparable hidden meaning of "Signor" as the God of the Last Judgment in Freud's incomplete analysis of the Signorelli painting (1901, pp. 4–5) on the occasion of another journey [Kanzer 1968].)

The critical intervention of the father is felt at once in the sequel to the coronation fantasy; a mood of sombre confession and regret swallows up the momentary elation of the preceding self-indulgence as hero. Insight and desexualization accompany each other; "It seems as though the essence of success was to have got further than one's father, and as though to excel one's father was still something forbidden." It is a sad and infirm man, one who has "grown old and stand[s] in need of forbearance and can travel no more" (p. 248), who brings the letter to a close. Identification with the father has invoked its own punishment in the form of the ultimate identification, the passage to death which adds the last dimension to the symbolism of the trip to Athens. If the analytic session failed to bring relief, the depressing confrontation with old age was no longer neurotic but realistic. We find the same imagery in a letter that Freud wrote to his son Ernst on the eve of departing for the last journey to England: "I sometimes compare myself with the old Jacob who, when a very old man, was taken by his children to Egypt. . . . It is high time that Ahasuerus came to rest somewhere (pp. 422–443). We shall return to this image later.

---

*Many references throughout this letter point to the Catholic nurse of Sigmund's childhood as a force operative in shaping the experiences on the Acropolis. She would take the little boy to church and apparently introduced a dichotomy into his sense of identification with the religion of his parents (1954, p. 219).

Alexander Freud

Our remaining task will be to follow the thread from the figure of Joseph Bonaparte in the coronation scene along the lines that reveal its connections with the real figure of Alexander and provide otherwise unsuspected clues to inmost fantasies that underly the travel neurosis of Sigmund Freud himself. The younger brother, as we have noted, emerged briefly from the shadows of Romain Rolland amid hints that his appearance had disturbed the travel plans—the ambitions and the destiny—of the older one, and then was promptly swallowed up again into a mysterious "we" as the narrative proceeded (see also comments on this "we" by Slochower 1970). "We" were both in remarkably depressed spirits at the prospect of visiting Athens: "we" wandered discontent and irresolute through Trieste until the conflict was suddenly solved and "we" went up to the counter and booked our passages for Athens as a matter of course. There had been no consultation about this simultaneous decision which, as Freud himself points out, was "most strange" (p. 240).

In reconstructing the experience at Trieste, Sigmund attributes to Alexander his own sense of incredulity (which would also have been most strange, if true). As the analysis progresses, Freud comes to recognize that despite their apparent harmony, a certain sense of reserve had entered into the silence between them both in Trieste and on the Acropolis. This is never fully explained—any more than the strange unity assumed to exist between them. A clear differentiation between the brothers begins at the climactic moment when insight will dawn through the verbalization of their mutual guilt, part of the "strange reserve," at surpassing the father. Sigmund still assumes that Alexander had undergone all his own experiences and will also be relieved by his insights. Thus, Freud asks his brother to recall with him the beginnings of the pleasure in travel in a tone that warmly shares memories of their companionship: "Do you still remember how, when we were young, we used day after day to walk along the same streets on our way to school, and how every Sunday we used to go to the Prater or on some excursion we knew so well?" Now both are in Athens together: "We really *have* gone a long way" (p. 247).

There is something a little odd about this fellowship. One might get the impression of an exchange between comrades of the same age—but in what sense could they have walked along the same streets on the way to school when the seven-year-old Alexander was in his earliest classes while Sigmund was already attending the university? Did they really go to the Prater and on excursions every Sunday together? A family picture of 1876 shows a frail and immature ten-year-old Alexander against the background of a bearded and decidedly mature Sigmund (p. 216). I have found nothing in published material, including the biography by Jones, to indicate that after the eventful naming of the newborn, there had been any close relationship such as Freud seemed to invoke both in his reminiscences and the freedom with which he felt he could answer for the thoughts of Alexander.

The comparison with the Bonaparte brothers, which immediately follows the differentiation of the Freuds, brings certain suggestive and challenging aspects to bear on the puzzling "identity." Immediately after the exultant cry, sharing triumph with his brother: "We really *have* gone a long way"—and with the mental reservation pending, "and like the brother horde have destroyed our father"—the amplification splits the partners, just as the experiencing and the critical egos are split by the same reservation. Sigmund then compares himself to Napoleon, while Alexander is equated with the lesser Bonaparte. In essence "we" have gone a long way together, but "I" have gone much further! Ambition and conquest have eliminated the rival brother, just as they have the rival father.

This last statement may seem too radical: Alexander still shares in part the triumph of his brother, it may be said. In the same way, the dead father is granted amnesty: he may return to life just long enough to witness the son's celebration—provided he is a passive spectator (the critical ego) only, precisely the same part allotted to Joseph Bonaparte at Napoleon's coronation. Is there an ominous note for Alexander in thus being coupled with the dead father? The infantile experiencing ego, Napoleon, is really not altruistic and brooks no infringement on its complete power. Has a hidden aggression, sheltered by the "we," broken through at the critical point which obscured sibling rivalry for so long behind the name of a conqueror delegated at birth by the elder, but now withdrawn on the Acropolis? Did the re-emergence of primary narcissism bring the ego back to the point at which sibling rivalry had been resolved magically so many years ago by the death of Julius?

Max Schur, in "The Guilt of the Survivor" (1968; see also Chapter 7 of the present volume) adopts the thesis (partly promulgated by Freud himself, 1954, p. 219) that a series of figures in the life of Sigmund were "revenants," reincarnations of Julius, resurrected through guilt and slain again in periodic alternations with the emancipation of the ego from this guilt. Wilhelm Fliess had been such a revenant, "slain" at the end of Freud's analysis, but recently returned to accuse Freud of plagiarism, of usurping his identity as the originator of the concept of bisexuality. The shadow of Fliess hung heavily over the Athenian trip (see also Stamm 1969).

There were intricate relationships between the analysis with Fliess and the travels with Alexander. In another pertinent study, Schur describes the impact on the positive transference when, in the spring of 1895, Freud discovered a scandalous instance of malpractice which connected Fliess with one of his own patients, "Irma." Freud resolved part of the problem brilliantly through sub-limation, with rich yields for the science of psychoanalysis when he was inspired, through a dream about Irma, to resolve basic problems in dream interpretation (Schur 1966; chapter 6 of the present volume).

We ourselves suggest another line of development taken by Freud (in addition to the one above) to resolve the same trauma. On August 16, 1895, he wrote to Fliess to break off preliminary arrangements for a meeting between them during the summer (events that ordinarily had the greatest significance for Freud) and announced instead his intention to proceed to Venice with "my little brother" (now well into his thirtieth year!), motivated by an unspecified concern for the younger man (1954, p. 122). We are inclined to believe that—as at an earlier period of life—Freud resolved the disruption of his own dependency on Fliess by adopting a protective attitude toward a person dependent upon himself, that is, by identification with the "good parent" and good older brother whom Fliess could no longer represent. (Fliess was in fact younger than Freud and his pro-motion to a father figure represented the type of reversal we find so frequently in this letter. Freud's relation to a nephew older than himself may have been a factor [1900, p. 424].) For this purpose, he could readily re-establish earlier relations with the "little brother." Moreover, analysis was now replaced by "travelling together" toward the goal of therapy: two alternative routes toward the unconsciously desired reunion with the mother.

Alexander, who figured in Freud's life first as a replacement for Julius through whom he might expiate his lasting sense of guilt, and now as a replacement for the "revenant" of Julius, Wilhelm Fliess, henceforth became part of a mystic travel ritual. "Every year at that time, toward the end of August or the beginning of September, I used to set out with my younger brother on a holiday trip, which . . . would take us to Rome" or some other southerly destination (1936, p. 240). These ritualistic travels with Alexander occurred nearly every year from 1895 to 1905. They are to be regarded as substitutes for a continuance of self-analysis as conducted with the assistance of the involuntary transference-figure, Wilhelm Fliess. Thus the emergence of Alexander as the "analyst" and critical ego of his older brother Sigmund finds determinants in his substitution for Fliess.*

---

*Related to the reversals of identity so common in this "session," we may also note Freud's disposition to name his own sons after heroes (as with Alexander) and respected teachers—Oliver Cromwell, Jean-Martin Charcot, Ernst Brücke. His daughters also received names associated with his teachers and friends (Breuer, Paneth, Hammerschlag). Unconsciously, the desire to reverse the relationship to the father and to acquire the mother and sisters may be assumed.

We venture the interpretation that weekly walks with his father, which figured in Freud's self-analysis, were fused in memory with the weekly excursions with Alexander, thus permitting another

If Alexander ultimately, as we would expect, is not only Julius but the arch-rival of the later oedipal period, father himself, then his coupling with the father not only portends their equation as death objects but also the tacit reconsignment of the revived analyst Fliess to final oblivion. The "end of the journey" si-multaneously concludes the analysis (as we have followed it in our interpretation of the symbolism) and assumes (in addition to the birth and sex motives) the form of the third of the three intertwined figures of fate: man's death.

We turn now to another of the "disturbances of memory" which are so abundantly illustrated in the recall of the Acropolis experience and reach a crescendo in the equation of Alexander and Joseph in one of the most cryptic messages ever delivered by the unconscious: the coronation scene that "oc-curred" to Freud and is described as resolving the "little problem" not only for himself but for Alexander as well. In addition to a presumptive blunder as to place (Milan or Paris) there is now apparent, though quickly covered over and never elucidated, confusion as to person. "Napoleon turned to one of his brothers—it must no doubt have been the eldest one." Freud's "free associa-tions" run on.

The gap here we interpret as a momentary hesitation, a resistance. Certainly a false element in the equation must be calling for some awareness on the part of the critical ego, the analyst, at this point. Freud, submerging himself in the experiencing Napoleonic ego, brushes past the reservation that Alexander is, after all, the younger, not the elder brother, reverses identities once again during this session and adds with telltale and delusional conviction ("It must no doubt have been the eldest") that through the equation and regression to infantile omnipotence, he has become the younger brother. The last of the displacements in the drama has occurred—not only through place and person but in temporal order as well. This daydream—as we shall argue—has achieved the inmost of the hidden wishes that the session fulfills.

The context of the letter or session is, after all, the welcoming of a birth and is customarily associated with friendly wishes for a long life. Quite the opposite had been the case when Sigmund greeted the birth of Julius and magically achieved his early death. Perhaps, there is some residue of this early hostility as Freud begins his congratulations of Rolland by informing him of the delay

---

reversal of identities (1900, p. 197). They may even have been the model for his travel urges and travel neurosis; perhaps they were an acting out of the ambition to "keep pace with father." The recollection of these walks is associated with the humiliation of the Jewish father and a line of alternative idealized identifications that carry Sigmund from Hannibal to Napoleon.

The easy reversibility of identities, dating back perhaps to early relationship with Julius, may well have contributed to the empathies with patients that disposed Freud to such success as an analyst.

and difficulties he had encountered in bringing himself to the point of such a communication. Links between them are then forged in the sphere of the humanities (reaction formations against aggression!), but Freud had sensed in the past a deeper bond, certainly ambivalent, that he could not fathom: "I have rarely experienced that mysterious attraction of one human being for another as vividly as I have with you; it is somehow bound up, perhaps, with the awareness of being so different" (p. 406). There is apparently a transference operative here; much the same sentiments had been directed to Fliess. The allusion to the differences with Rolland had special reference to the religious faith of Rolland which Freud, the scientist, felt compelled to reject.

Freud next proceeds to eliminate Rolland permanently in the letter and to subtly acquire the characteristics of his "alter ego." His beautifully written essay displays the full inventiveness of his own genius still advancing toward new frontiers. He is a hero with all the vitality with which he had equipped Rolland at the start of the letter and instead of attaining the "end" awaiting himself, as he predicted in the beginning, he has become the Emperor of the French and even usurped the religious faith of Rolland as well as his nationality: it is he himself who is the supreme figure in the cathedral of Notre Dame. He has won the last of his arguments with the French writer, for the comforts of self-analysis in allaying guilt and offering a reassuring daydream for the dying man have been demonstrated as effective competition for the comforts of religion.

It is our contention that in this context—and we shall adduce further evidence—Freud once again wrested identity from a "younger brother," consigning him to the death confronting the older one (the aged Freud) and regaining for himself the position of "last-born" that he had once inherited after Julius had been magically eliminated. We believe this thesis finds direct support in an analysis elsewhere which reveals Freud's latent hostility and aspects of his travel relationship to Alexander.

In "The Psychopathology of Everyday Life," which contains so much of Freud's self-analysis as well as his most profound attempt to replace mysticism within himself by the firmest commitment to the doctrine of psychic determinism, he raises the "little problem" to be solved in one particular "session" the question, "How did I come to read in a newspaper one day: *Im Fass* ("in a tub") across Europe, instead of *Zu Fuss* ("on foot")?" The first associations led to the tub of Diogenes and then to the celebrated remark of the Macedonian conqueror, "If I were not Alexander, I should like to be Diogenes" (pp. 107–108).

An inner obstacle imposed itself on the further unravelling of the problem until, on a later occasion, Freud read of the strange means of transportation that people were using to get to Paris for the International Exhibition of 1900 (which helps us to place the time of the analysis with fair exactitude as in the midpoint of the travel decade which corresponded so remarkably to the actual temporal difference between the brothers). One man, it appears, proposed to be rolled to Paris in a tub. Freud's thoughts went on scornfully to the lengths that people went to fulfill pathological ambitions to attain publicity. Then Alexander of Macedonia came to mind, "One of the most ambitious men that ever lived," and immediately thereafter the clarifying association, "How could I possibly have failed to recall that there is another Alexander who is closer to me, that Alexander is the name of my youngest brother? I immediately found the objectionable thought about this other Alexander that had to be repressed."

Other references to Alexander the Great in Freud's works that may be of some pertinence to the Alexander Freud "complex of associations" include his conquest of Tyre with the aid of a dream interpreter (1900, p. 99); an odd debate as to whether psychoanalysis is as credible as the existence of Alexander or Moses (another favorite figure to represent Freud himself), (1915–1916, pp. 18–19) and a very ambiguous paper, with possible personal significance, which refers to the legend that the temple of Diana (a virgin goddess) was destroyed by fire on the night that Alexander the Great was born (1911, p. 342).

Alexander Freud, it seems, had become such an authority on tariffs and transportation (evidence pointing in fact to longstanding participation in a travel identity with his brother?) that it seemed likely he would receive the title of professor before Sigmund himself attained it. (As readers of *The Interpretation of Dreams* will recall, the twin ambitions—to reach Rome and to obtain a professorship—were dominant in the older brother at the moment.) To make matters worse, "our mother expressed her surprise that her younger son was to become a professor before her elder." The word *Beforderung*, which can mean transportation or promotion, had been the medium on this occasion for permitting competitive ambition to be hidden behind the desire for travel.

We are struck by the many connections between the reactions to Alexander revealed by this fragment of self-analysis and its successor, as we have interpreted it, so many decades later. The brother, so close at hand, emerges unexpectedly from behind the identity of another person. Travel and ambition are related themes in both and are connected by a verbal bridge during the self-analysis. A split of identities along very similar lines is found: the conqueror Alexander is set in contrast to the philosopher Diogenes as representatives of the experiencing and critical egos and a wish for the reversal of identities. The recollection of the existence of Alexander, the immediate competitor for a professorship and mother's admiration, emerges conveniently from behind the self and must take on the accusation of pathological ambition to see oneself in print. It was in 1900 that Freud, with considerable trepidation, exposed so much of himself to the public in *The Interpretation of Dreams* and awaited signs of interest that were long delayed.

Another common feature will require us to proceed further in depth in our comparison of the two "sessions": both are permeated with birth imagery that gives more detailed meaning to the travels of the brothers and the neurosis of the older one. The scorn, envy, and secret identification with the public exposure of the "man in the tub" have familiar connotations as reactions of the older sibling to the inhabitants of the mother's womb during her pregnancy. With this thought in mind, we shall elaborate further upon the introduction of Alexander into the birthday greetings to Rolland and the consequent disturbance in Sigmund's own "travel plans."

This begins with the statement: "Every year at that time, towards the end of August or the beginning of September, I used to set out with my brother on a holiday trip" (pp. 229–230). This would bring them to their destination, preferably some seaport along the Mediterranean, during the ninth month of the year; Rome was reached on September 2nd, Athens on September 4th. Alexander accompanied Sigmund on the successful mission to Rome, where Freud experienced feelings of awe and was inclined to worship at the ruins of the temple of Minerva (the Roman virgin goddess who was the counterpart of Athena) (1954, p. 335). Later he confronted a terrifying Moses of Michelangelo who, he feared, might start up wrathfully at any moment (1914, p. 220)—that is, the dead father returned to life again in the unlikely setting of a church in the heart of Christendom. There is little reason to suppose that this journey marked the true end of Freud's neurosis or his analysis. In a letter to Fliess recounting his visit to Rome with a stress on its disagreeable aspects, and already disputing the charge of plagiarism on the subject of bisexuality, Freud describes an attack of gastroenteritis during the ninth day in the city and reports its continuance even to the time of his return to Vienna (1954, pp. 335–356).

There is a well-known aspect of travel neuroses that we now find pertinent. They can be partly overcome by the companionship of a person, usually the mother whom analysis reveals as the object of the aggression that the traveller fears will ultimately befall himself (Deutsch, 1929). Infantile identity with the mother and separation anxiety provide the prototype. Thus, on the trip to Athens with Alexander—as reconstructed in terms of birth imagery—the split within Freud may be seen as related to identifications on the one hand with the pregnant mother, on the other with the child to be delivered. The undifferentiated "we" attains new dimensions from this aspect. Through the identification with the birthday child, Freud renews the intimate contacts with the mother's body before the birth process and usurps the brother's position later.

The unwelcome news that they must go to Athens, invoking anxiety and depression, now corresponds to the onset of birth pangs. The trip from Trieste along the narrow strait of the Adriatic which widens into a view of the sea from the top of the Acropolis, becomes a passage through the birth canal. This ends with the "oceanic experience" that was part of the total reaction on the Acropolis and interpreted by Freud as recapturing the earliest identity with the mother—an experience which he explains psychologically rather than from a religious view-point, as did Rolland (1930, pp. 64–68): "When I stood for the first time on the hill of the Acropolis, looking out over the blue sea . . . a feeling of aston-ishment mingled with the joy" (1927, p. 25). Oddly, this joy does not find its way into the 1936 letter, unless we find it represented in the coronation (head presentation) this is rudely interrupted by the apparition of the dead father.*

Freud captured for himself some part of a universal reaction to the view of the Acropolis. Here, according to legend, Aegeus, bequeathing his name to the sea, leaped from the heights when Theseus, his son, on returning from Crete, "forgot" to raise the white flag as a signal that he had survived his encounter with the Minotaur. This hero's "disturbance of memory" was literally lethal to his father and may be interpreted as the murder of the old by the new king in the presence of the Medusa-mother, Athena, from whose temple on the summit the father at the foot of the cliff is forever separated.

Freud tells us the rest of the story through the multiple meanings of the imagery that punctuates his narrative. "Fate" has consented to his birth and he puts on his best shirt (strips) for the occasion. A monster emerges from the lake (the unwanted brother) and is destroyed in the Alhama episode. As in the typical fairy tale, there is success on the third try: it is Sigmund who is reborn as the youngest, while the reproaches of conscience are momentarily stilled at the festivities by the evidence of the brother's presence, along with that of the dead father. The passage of the head through the crown is the consummation of the birth process. He is once again the infant with life ahead of him, while the senior males of the family are pushed correspondingly closer to death.

The "youngest son" is invoked in Freud's writings in contexts that show a long-standing preoccupation with this particular fantasy, which finds its way into some of the more speculative passages even of his scientific works. In *Group Psychology and the Analysis of the Ego*, the youngest son becomes the "mother's favorite," the poet who invents the heroic myth, leads the group toward individual differentiation and takes the place of the slain father (1921, pp. 124, 136). The mother's favorite son is an optimist and potential hero (1900, p. 398). Christianity is the religion of the younger son, closer to the Great

*The coronation as a challenge to the dying father was remarked upon by Freud with reference to Prince Hal and brought into connection with his own ambitions on an earlier occasion (1900, p. 484).

Mother-Goddess (1939, pp. 88–89), Judaism that of the father's favorite, Moses, the first born (1939, p. 91).

Thus Freud distinguishes a mother-oriented from a father-oriented sense of reality both in individual and group development. This he came to formulate variously in terms of the primary and secondary processes, the distinctions between the pleasure and the reality principles, and in postulated advances from animistic to scientific thought. Correlated with the evolving sense of reality are representations of the self and objects whose vicissitudes were experienced in the mental events attending the journey to the Acropolis and its subsequent recall in the letter.

Freud's own thinking processes, we suggest, are well represented autosymbolically in the image he repeatedly used, the metaphor of Athena springing fully armed from the forehead of Zeus. The earlier mother-child world of reality is no longer repressed but comes to life in the form of creative insights permitted by the watchful father, the intellect subserving the critical ego. The patient and analyst form a team that demonstrates the various shades of reality-testing operating within the psychic apparatus. Free association and freely wandering attention co-operate to permit the intrusion into consciousness of warded-off ideas, personified as Athena who bears on her shield the reminder of her origins in the Medusa of the sexual mother.

The analyst, with the "courage" of his masculine reality-testing, reconstructs the past oedipal world of the patient from these neutralized memories, while the writer continues the neutralization in controlled fantasies that teach the reader, like himself, to reconcile if not fully integrate the past with the present. Freud's own creative insights drew upon the imagination of the writer as well as the discipline of the scientist, but he showed distinct envy as well as affection for this more youthful "brother," closer to the pleasure principle, who could invent wishful endings rather than feeling compelled to renounce them and live so exclusively in the realm of contemporary reality.

Freud's ambivalence to the writer is more clearly understood from our reconstructions about the ambivalence to his younger siblings. It was not a "coincidence," we believe, that birthdays proved occasions for the display of mixed feelings and a desire for exchange of identities as conveyed in congratulatory messages on such occasions. Thus, a letter to Thomas Mann on the latter's birthday in 1935 brings to the fore attitudes and themes we have ascertained in the communication to Rolland the following year. There is a quick substitution of thoughts about the self for thoughts about the recipient: ("I am one of your 'oldest' readers") and a note of envy ("and admirers") (E. Freud 1960, p. 426).

Then a singularly ungracious tone is taken: "I could wish you a very long and happy life, as is the custom on such occasions. But I shall refrain from doing so." The ostensible reason is a reminder of his own suffering, which is to cloud the joy of the birthday for this "brother": "My most personal experience tends to make me consider it a good thing when merciful fate puts a timely end to our span of life."

If Freud finally does concede that it is Mann who is "the hero of the day," he nevertheless feels his friend should be spared "speeches which overwhelm him with praise" and instead instructs him in the duties of a hero's life: to fulfill the "confidence that you will never do or say anything that is cowardly or base, and that even at a time which blurs judgment you will choose the right way and show it to others."

Interestingly, Freud was preparing this letter to Mann just before his own birthday and describing his own mental state at the same time in a communication to another writer, Arnold Zweig, on May 2, 1935. Here he mourns his inability to travel to the Holy Land (where Zweig is residing), identifies with Oedipus (referring to his daughter as "my Anna-Antigone") and clinging to his Moses identification as the one fantasy channel open as a substitution for other pleasures: "I can no longer smoke freely, I no longer want to write. . . . Moses won't let go of my imagination" (pp. 424–425). Doubtless the sufferings of old age intensified the claims of the pleasure principle and affected the habitual dominance of the reality principle as he turned during this period to works about the heroic Moses and (in his own conceptions) the anti-heroic Wilson, who violated the mandate to "choose the right way and show it to others."

The letter to Rolland closes in the vein that characterizes the "real self" of these later years, with a yielding to the "fate" that requires him to relinquish the joys of past conquest and shows mercy only by terminating the life of an infirm old man who could "travel no more." The end of the journey has narrowed in its connotations to the last of all possibilities. Nevertheless, even in confronting the stark finality with courage and adherence to his principles of truth, secret gratifications through unconscious wish-fulfillment may still be discerned: through identification with the dead father as a guide and companion to the after-life—the ancient spur to the invention of religions which gratify the refusal of psychic reality to accept the existence of death; guilt is relieved not only by identification with the father but by shifting the oedipal blame to the more youthful survivor: "we both," Sigmund assures Alexander pointedly at the end, "desired to surpass our father" (and brothers—a desire from which the altruistic Joseph could not escape); helplessness itself conveys the meaning of a regression to the infantile state and the care of the mother ("Antigone"). There is still a hidden reserve of brilliant mental powers and expanding insights that can be invoked to warn the younger generation not to take the plea of failing powers too literally—the old man can still assert his leadership if he chooses to do so.

The themes of the letter to Rolland were by no means exhausted by this analytic session and we may follow them further in Freud's later writings. In another letter to Thomas Mann later in 1936, in which he elaborated further upon the themes of Napoleon and Joseph Bonaparte, he now turned his attention to Jerome, younger brother of the Emperor, his "Benjamin," and "worthless" recipient of fraternal favors (p. 433). On the occasion of Alexander's seventy-second birthday, Freud took leave of his erstwhile travel companion on the eve of his own final great journey to England: "I would like you to take over the good cigars which have been accumulating with me over the years, as you still can indulge in such pleasures, I no longer" (p. 442). Did the older brother link his own fatal cancer with the smoking of these cigars?

The last line to Alexander is taken directly from Hamlet's final words to his alter ego, Horatio: "The rest—you will know what I mean—is silence." Tacit understanding will be maintained until death—then the story may be told by the survivor. Hamlet's true alter ego, Shakespeare, lent him the desired immortality, while Freud's own alter ego was the creative poet within him which gave birth to and granted matchless expression to his scientific thoughts.

A note from Freud to his son Ernst immediately before the departure for England gives us a glimpse of the anticipated journey in a wish fulfillment without shadows of separation anxiety. The model is that of the child trusting to the care of good parents. "I am sitting inactive and helpless," while his daughter prepares for the trip and arranges clearance with the authorities.

We turn now to a passage in this letter, previously mentioned which we can now amplify: "I sometimes compare myself with the old Jacob who, when a very old man, was taken by his children to Egypt, as Thomas Mann is to describe in his next novel" (*Joseph, the Provider*). Freud had become the father-hero and had found his Horatio, indeed the Homer for whom Alexander the Great had longed. Thus, he may transcend the boundaries of individual identity to take his place in the ever-recurrent cycles of the racial prototype: "Let us hope that it won't also be followed by an exodus from Egypt. It is high time that Ahasuerus [the Wandering Jew] came to rest somewhere" (pp. 442–443).

A protective angel is sent ahead—the figure of Athena, the favorite of his famous collection (Holland, 1969). She had been entrusted to a worthy guardian, Princess Marie Bonaparte of Greece. A final image represents the trip as a rebirth of the eternal phoenix from the fire: "The whole thing reminds me of the man trying to rescue a bird's nest from the burning house" (p. 443). Was there also a recollection of Aeneas fleeing from burning Troy, his father on his back, his goddess mother leading the way, to become the founder of Rome? Freud's own inner destination was assuredly the world of the myth!

Princess Bonaparte, a modern Nausicaä, sheltered Freud as he passed through Paris and returned this prized statue to him. He wrote from London that her hospitality "restored our good mood and sense of dignity; after being surrounded by love for twelve hours we left proud and rich under the protection of Athena" (Jones 1957, pp. 227–228). How remarkably fact and fantasy blended in transferring the scene of the Acropolis first to a Bonaparte palace and then to the new home in England!

Summary

We have approached Freud's "experience on the Acropolis" as a self-analytic session which brings to the fore a long-standing and obscure relationship with his companion on that occasion, his younger brother Alexander. Analysis of the relationship shows Alexander as endowed from birth with an extension of Sigmund's own self-image, which protected him from death-wishes directed to a decreased intermediate brother Julius and beyond that to the father. Alexander is also intimately associated with Freud's travel neurosis, especially during the decade 1895–1905 when it became involved with his self-analysis. The trip to Athens, and its later analysis in the course of a congratulatory birthday epistle to Romain Rolland, is followed on the basis of the continuity of associations and a series of metaphors examined in four frameworks relating to birth, sex, death and the progress of an analytic session. The deepest motive to be discovered emerges as the wish to be reborn (regain access to mother), withdraw the self-cathexis from Alexander and permit the latter, through a reversal of identities, to take his own place on the road to death, as Julius once had done. Interrelationships between the emergence of repressed fantasies and the formation of scientific ideas are repeatedly demonstrated during the "session." Creative impulses become symbolized for Freud himself as Athena, the virgin goddess, springing fully armed from the forehead (intellect) of her father-son (husband) Zeus. (The physical side of Athena is expressed by the forbidding Medusa on her shield.) Scientific thinking, the demand for truth, becomes a counterposed and morally censoring father. Freud uniquely combined both elements in his works, the imaginative aspect disposing especially to a deep sense of identity with poets and travellers.

The usual equilibrium within Freud could be shifted by three interrelated mechanisms: (1) Travels which changed the outer scene; (2) Self-analysis which changed the inner scene; (3) Creative thought which combined inner and outer worlds into new designs. In pathological aberrations, such attempts at creative re-designing gave rise on the Acropolis to errors of memory and recognition of the self and objects. The harmonious resolution of the conflicting force is brilliantly illustrated in a self-analytic session that produced not only advances in science and health but a work of art.

Addendum

Richard F. Sterba has alerted the author to a number of errors in the *Standard Edition* translation of Freud's "A Disturbance of Memory on the Acropolis" (1936).

On page 240, Strachey's translation reads, "As we walked away from this visit, we were both in remarkably depressed spirits." Sterba states that the original German, *Als wir den Triestiner verlassen hatten, waren wir beide in merkwürdig übler Stimmung* (p. 11),* should be rendered as "When we left the Triestian we were in a particularly bad mood." *Merkwürdig*, he adds, means strange, noteworthy, peculiar; *übler Stimmung* refers to a bad or grumpy mood, but not necessarily depressed.

In addition, Freud's final sentence is poorly translated as: "And now you will no longer wonder that the recollection of this incident on the Acropolis should have troubled me so often since I myself have grown old and stand in need of forebearance and can travel no more" (p. 248). The German is: *Und jetzt werden Sie sich nicht mehr verwundern, dass mich die Erinnerung an das Erlebnis auf der Akropolis so oft heimsucht, seitdem ich selbst alt, der Nachsicht bedürftig geworden bin und nicht mehr reisen kann* (p. 21). Sterba observes that Strachey's translation of *mich heimsucht* as "troubled me" is incorrect: *Heimsuchen* is "visiting." The translation should be: ". . . why the memory of the experience on the Acropolis so often *occurs to me* (or *visits with me* or *looks me up* or *comes to mind*) since I am old. . . ."

Sterba continues, "There is another significance to *heimsuchen*, referring to disasters, 'acts of God' like earthquakes or the plagues of Egypt in the Bible. For this meaning—which is certainly not applicable to the above sentence—the word 'trouble' is much too weak; therefore Freud can only have meant 'comes to mind.' Even 'haunts me' is too strong. There is no negative feeling in this *heimsuchung*. It would rather be an experience of nostalgia."

Finally Sterba notes that Freud's comments on his feeling that the news of his going to Athens was "too good to be true" was inadequately translated as: "It is an example of the incredulity that arises so often when we are surprised by a piece of good news . . . [as] when a girl learns that the man whom she has secretly loved has asked her parents for leave to pay his addresses to her" (p. 141). Actually the German *für ein Mädchen, dass heimlich geliebte Mann bei den Eltern als Bewerber aufgetreten ist* (p. 13) should read, "when a girl learns that the man whom she has secretly loved has asked her parents for

---

*Page references for the original German are to Freud's article, (1937) *Eine Erinnerungsstörung auf der Akropolis*, as it appeared in the *Internationaler Psychoanalytischer* Verlag Wien, pp. 9–21.

permission to marry her.'' We are grateful to Dr. Sterba for this valuable information.

References

Deutsch, H. (1929). The genesis of agoraphobia. *International Journal of Psycho-Analysis* 10:51–69.

Erikson, E. (1954). The dream specimen of psychoanalysis. *Journal of the American Psychoanalytic Association* 2:5–56.

Freud, A. (1937). *The Ego and the Mechanisms of Defence*. London: Hogarth Press.

Freud, E. L. ed. (1960). *The Letters of Sigmund Freud*. New York: Basic Books.

Freud, S. (1887–1902). *The Origins of Psychoanalysis*. Ed. M. Bonaparte, A. Freud, E. Kris. New York: Basic Books, 1954.

—————— (1900). The interpretation of dreams. *Standard Edition* 4/5.

—————— (1901). The psychopathology of everyday life. *Standard Edition* 6.

—————— (1909a). Family romances. *Standard Edition* 9:237–241.

—————— (1909b). Notes upon a case of obsessional neurosis. *Standard Edition* 10:158–249.

—————— (1911). 'Great is the Diana of the Ephesians.' *Standard Edition* 12:342–344.

—————— (1912). The dynamics of transference. *Standard Edition* 12:99–108.

—————— (1914). The Moses of Michelangelo. *Standard Edition* 13:211–238.

—————— (1915–1916). Introductory lectures on psychoanalysis. *Standard Edition* 15/16.

—————— (1921). Group psychology and the analysis of the ego. *Standard Edition* 18:69–143.

—————— (1927). The future of an illusion. *Standard Edition* 21:3–56.

—————— (1930). Civilization and its discontents. *Standard Edition* 21:64–145.

—————— (1932). The acquisition and control of fire. *Standard Edition* 22:187–193.

—————— (1936). A disturbance of memory on the Acropolis. *Standard Edition* 22:239–248.

—————— (1937). Analysis terminable and interminable. *Standard Edition* 23:216–253.

—————— (1939). Moses and monotheism. *Standard Edition* 23:7–137.

—————— (1940). Medusa's hair. *Standard Edition* 18:273–274.

Harrison, I. B. (1966). A reconsideration of Freud's "A Disturbance of Memory on the Acropolis" in relation to identity disturbance. *Journal of the American Psychoanalytic Association* 14:518–527.

Holland, N. (1969). Freud and H. D. *International Journal of Psycho-Analysis*

50:309–315.

Jones, E. (1953–1957). *The Life and Work of Sigmund Freud.* 3 Vols. New York: Basic Books.

Kanzer, M. (1958). Image formation during free association. *Psychoanalytic Quarterly* 27:465–484.

———— (1966). The motor sphere of the transference. *Psychoanalytic Quarterly* 35:522–539.

———— (1968). Freud, fate and free will. *Bulletin of the New Jersey Psychoanalytic Society* 1.

Sachs, H. (1944). *Freud, Master and Friend.* Cambridge, Massachusetts: Harvard University Press.

Schur, M. (1966). Some additional "day residues" of "the specimen dream of psychoanalysis." In *Psychoanalysis—A General Psychology,* ed. R. M. Loewenstein, L. M. Newman, M. Schur, A. J. Solnit, pp.44–85. New York: International Universities Press. (chapter 6 of this volume.)

———— (1969). The background of Freud's disturbance on the Acropolis. *American Imago* 26:303–323. (chapter 7 of this volume)

Shengold, L. (1966). The metaphor of the journey in *The Interpretation of Dreams. American Imago* 23:316–331. (chapter 4 of this volume)

———— (1970). Freud and Joseph. In *The Unconscious Today,* ed. M. Kanzer, pp. 473–494. New York: International Universities Press. (chapter 5 of this volume)

Slochower, H. (1970). Freud's "deja vu" on the Acropolis: a symbolic residue of *Mater Nudam. Psychoanalytic Quarterly* 39:90–102.

Stamm, J. (1969). Freud's "Disturbance of Memory on the Acropolis" and the problems of depersonalization. *American Imago* 364–372. (chapter 8 of this volume)

Webster's Biographical Dictionary. (1958). Springfield, Massachusetts: G. & C. Merriam.

Chapter 17

FREUD AND HIS LITERARY DOUBLES

Freud's feeling of affinity for creative writers was often attested. Indeed, we find in his own writings gifts of imagination, exposition and style which may be recognized even before he entered the University of Vienna. His frequent references to literature and the arts attest to deep-seated cultural interests and appreciation, while even in his most scientific writings there is an admixture of metaphors and allegories which are not only an inherent part of their teaching value but arise from his very processes of thought. His works show a revealing alternation, hitherto insufficiently studied, between clinical and metapsychological works on the one hand and applied analysis on the other. His metapsychological essay "On Narcissism" (1914b), his clinical study of the Wolf Man (1918), and his semi-autobiographical article on "The Moses of Michelangelo" (1914a) were written almost simultaneously and reveal related aspects of a personal as well as scientific reorientation through which he was passing at the moment (Kanzer 1966).

It is sometimes held that Freud discovered the significance of dreams through the revelations of his patients, but in fact he was already collecting and appraising his own dreams scientifically long before he was practicing psychotherapy (E. Jones 1953; E. Freud 1960). His fundamental application of the principle of determinism to psychic events probably owed as much to such self-observations and critical appraisals of literature (see especially the letters to his fiancée,

Martha Bernays [E. Freud 1960]) as to his observations of patients or, more generally, his schooling in the doctrines of physical determinism. Indeed, his introduction of this principle was in metaphorical language as he described how "A most important piece of information is often announced as being a redundant accessory, like an opera prince disguised as a beggar" (Breuer and Freud 1893–1895, pp. 279–280). The patient wishes to ignore the disguised beggar as "unimportant" and "irrelevant" to the proceedings but this is no more true than that a brushstroke by Leonardo or a word chosen by Shakespeare is irrelevant. Attention to such cues is the foundation of psychoanalysis both as a science of the mind and an instrument of psychotherapy.

The creative gifts of his schoolboy days were submerged for some years in the neuropathology laboratory, but his work with patients first through hypnosis and then free association found him mobilizing his poetic insights in his attempts to understand them. It was not without misgivings that he noted: "It still strikes me as strange that the case histories I write should read like short stories." Then, with the independence and self-confidence which made his unique course of investigations possible, he commented:

> I must console myself with the reflection that the nature of the subject is evidently responsible for this, rather than any preference of my own. The fact is that local diagnosis and electrical reactions lead nowhere in the study of hysteria, whereas a detailed description of mental processes such as we are accustomed to find in the works of imaginative writers enables one, with the use of a few psychological formulas, to obtain at least some kind of insight into the course of that affection. [Breuer and Freud 1893–1895, pp. 160–161]

Ultimately he would establish the "primary process" of thought, prominent in dreams, creativity, and neurosis, as deeper and more universal than the rational "secondary process" of logic.

It is doubtful if any scientist but Freud would have felt it corroborative of his theories to cite Sophocles and Shakespeare, as he did (1954, pp. 223–224). When he taught psychoanalysis to his cultured disciples at the Wednesday Night meetings that anticipated the formation of the Vienna Psychoanalytic Society, applied analysis was constant fare and the membership drew freely on intellectuals as well as physicians. In raising the status of a none-too-important novel by a none-too-important writer to a scientific work worthy of analysis, he hailed writers as "valuable allies" because, through self-observation and artistic expression, they could give immediate shape to unconscious fantasy while the scientist would have to follow more laborious routes to come to the same conclusions (Freud 1906).

One would suppose that Freud, especially after his own self-analysis, could easily have placed himself in either category, but this does not seem to have been the case. Thus in the same year (1906) in which he penned the lines distinguishing between the modes of insight available to the writer and the scientist, he wrote to Arthur Schnitzler, the famed Viennese playwright, that "I have often asked myself in astonishment how you came by this or that piece of secret knowledge which I had acquired by a painstaking investigation of the subject, and I finally came to the point of envying the author whom hitherto I had admired (E. Freud 1960, p. 251)."

Fellow-scientists like Bleuler might remark, perhaps ambivalently, that Freud wrote and thought like an artist (Grotjahn 1967); Freud would, in time, be awarded the Goethe Prize and be nominated for the Nobel Prize in literature by others less ambivalent, but the distinction that Freud made between himself and the artist—before whom the analyst must lay down his arms—was sincerely meant and leads into areas of his thinking that seem in some respects to have eluded self-analysis. We hope to bring some clarification to these areas.

Thus in 1907 he wrote to Carl Jung whose capacities he scarcely knew but was already advancing in his mind to supplant himself as leader of the psychoanalytic movement, that "you will be spared a part of the opposition" that he himself aroused for "I have invariably found that something in my personality, my words and ideas strike people as alien, whereas to you all hearts are open. . . . I must claim for myself the class 'obsessive,' each member of which lives in a world shut off from the rest" (E. Freud 1960, p. 256).

Freud's opinion of the success of his self-analysis could not have been very great at that moment despite his increasing renown and demonstrable acquisition of new followers. His scientific imagination had never been more creative. He must also have known how withdrawn into their own worlds were many writers and artists who nevertheless stirred a deep response from the public.

A second letter to Arthur Schnitzler (E. Freud 1960, pp. 334–340, letter 197), written on the occasion of the latter's sixtieth birthday on May 15, 1922, offers features related to the riddle of the renunciation of poetic gifts and also—it would appear—claims to popularity and leadership. Freud had celebrated his sixty-sixth birthday on May 8 and had as yet no sign of the cancer that would end his life more than seventeen years later. I have italicized, in excerpts from the letter, features which recur under other circumstances, especially in the form of birthday congratulations to younger writers, usually on the occasion of the completion of a decade of their lives.

"Now you too have reached your sixtieth birthday, while *I, six years older, am approaching the limit of life and may soon expect to see the end of the fifth act of this rather incomprehensible and not always amusing comedy.*" (Freud's expectation of the imminent end of his life may be traced backward through the decades and is certainly related to the proposal to make Jung his heir and successor in 1907. The birthday letter begins with a self-reference on a note quite unlikely to add to the jubilation of the recipient.)

The gloom imposed on the recipient is scarcely alleviated by the information that Freud has so far renounced the "omnipotence of thoughts" that he will refrain from sending the birthday child *the warmest and heartiest good wishes for the years that await you. I shall leave this foolish gesture to the vast number of your contemporaries who will remember you on May 15.*" (Again the note that had been struck with Jung—the lonely isolate on the one hand, the acclaimed of many on the other.)

"*I will make a confession which for my sake I must ask you to keep to yourself.*" (The stage is being set for a self-analytic communication which will be more clearly labeled in other such letters; see E. Freud 1960, pp. 339–340).

"*I think I have avoided you from a kind of reluctance to meet my double. . . . whenever I get deeply absorbed in one of your beautiful creations I invariably seem to find beneath their poetic surface the very presuppositions, interests and conclusions which I know to be my own.*" (Freud cites here their common determinism, scepticism, pessimism, preoccupation with the unconscious and the instincts, etc., so that "all this moves me with an uncanny feeling of familiarity." Again he reiterates the message of 1906, that Schnitzler knows by intuition what Freud learned "from laborious work on other people." (Has the part in his insights gained by self-analysis been forgotten?)

The avoidance of which Freud speaks is related to isolation and repression. A part of himself must be avoided—a part spared from self-analysis. This is projected onto the writer—partly himself, partly another person. And now a shadow drifts between them as the boundary becomes blurred and the letter ends: Schnitzler, he avers, is at heart an honestly impartial and undaunted psychological explorer (tacitly, like himself)—qualities for which he had paid, however, by some sacrifice that would have given him a greater appeal to the masses. Was this not in turn Freud's own secret and rejected dream?

Scarcely a year later the picture becomes more clearly defined as he opens correspondence with another younger writer, Romain Rolland, who will become a "Double" (E. Freud 1960, pp. 341–342, Letter 200). The occasion is not a birthday but the sentiments are familiar: (1.) "I am ten years older than you." (Why was it necessary to mention that?) (2.) I am Jewish, you are Catholic. (Has this something to do with a comparison of identities?) (3.) You create illusions, I destroy them. (4.) As a result Rolland is the more popular: "My writings cannot be what yours are: comfort and refreshment for the reader." In token of his own limitations he sends Rolland the copy of a "not . . . particularly successful" book, *Group Psychology and the Analysis of the Ego* (1921).

This book contains a rather interesting passage which we find recurrently in Freud's works—an idea which, we suggest, belongs in the realm of the family romance rather than deriving its strength from demonstrable scientific data. It is the idea that the younger son is the mother's favorite and that this in turn gives the former an optimism that will be transmuted into real success in life. It is this idea, we suggest, that leads to the contrasts we have noted between the writer, still wrapped in the joys of omnipotence of thought and finding acceptance readily, and the displaced older one, morose, and left to work out the mysteries of life for himself.

The primal father, as Freud delineates him, was "probably" replaced after his murder by the younger son "who had up to then been a member of the group like any other" (1921, p. 124). He became *"the first epic poet"* (my italics), disguised the truth (unlike the scientist!) and invented the heroic myth that the father was slain by the hero alone, the youngest son who was the mother's favorite. "In the lying poetic fancies of prehistoric times the woman, who had been the prize of battle and the temptation to murder, was probably turned into the active seducer and instigator to the crime" (1921, p. 136). The persistence of the seduction theory, here attached to the mother, and the bitterness against the favored son as a liar, are noteworthy here. While Freud acknowledges Rank's work and fairy tales as evidence for these assumptions, he now advances beyond *Totem and Taboo* (1913) to suggest that the liaison between mother and youngest son may have anteceded the establishment of the Father God—a step that we will have occasion to give further consideration in another of Freud's works so largely informed by the family romance—*Moses and Monotheism* (1939).

By 1926, Romain Rolland had been enrolled in the list of younger authors who received the standard birthday greeting:

> Unlike you I cannot count on the love of many people. I have not pleased, comforted, edified them. Nor was this my intention; I only wanted to explore, solve riddles, uncover a little of the truth. . . . It seems to me a surprising accident that apart from my doctrines, my person should attract any attention at all. But when men like you whom I have loved from afar express their friendship for me, then a particular ambition of mine is gratified. [E. Freud 1960, p. 370]

We shall learn more of this ambition, and briefly append some of the very brief 1931 "congratulations" to Rolland: "Approaching life's inevitable end, reminded of it by yet another operation and aware that I am unlikely to see you again, I may confess to you that I have rarely experienced that mysterious attraction of one human being for another as vividly as I have with you. It is

somehow bound up, perhaps, with the awareness of our being so different"
(E. Freud 1960, p. 406). The sense of uncanniness, the mixture of the familiar
and the unfamiliar in the "alter ego" have still eluded self-analysis.

Another candidate for birthday honors was Thomas Mann, whom Freud added
to the list in June, 1935, on the occasion of the latter's sixtieth birthday, greeting
him with "I am one of your 'oldest' readers and admirers" (the usual notes of
admiration and contrast between the birthday celebrant and the infirm older
person heading for eclipse). Freud refrains from anything so "trivial" as to wish
him "a very long and happy life, as is the custom of such occasions." This
would smack too much of "omnipotence of thought." It is better indeed "when
merciful fate puts a timely end to our span of life" (E. Freud 1960, p. 426–427).
No doubt Freud had reason to think so—but must the birthday recipient be
reminded of it? Or was it necessary to remind the "hero of the day" that it was
unthinkable that he would ever do anything cowardly or base—i.e., weaken in
his fight with the Nazis?

We are prepared now to examine Freud's article on "The Uncanny" (1919)
as a preliminary to following clues that will begin to accumulate rapidly in 1936,
when Freud attains the age of eighty. His father and an older brother had died
at eighty-one. To survive them had an element of effrontery smacking of murderous oedipal wishes left over from childhood which an episode recorded in
this essay elucidates. Freud's survival was a miracle—the prospects of his people
dismaying as he was "pursued" by the ghost of Moses, demanding a new
account of his life and origins. Moses had long been an alter ego of Freud
himself.

We learn in the *Standard Edition* that the article on "The Uncanny" had its
roots in "an old paper [dug] out of a drawer" which he decided to rewrite. The
discovery was mentioned in a letter to Ferenczi on May 12, 1919, in which
Freud's birthday on May 6 is mentioned. (Jones 1957, p. 521, actually cites
May 6 as the date of the letter!) The uncovering of the old paper corresponds
to the evocation of a forgotten memory and—while the *Standard Edition* surmises
that the paper dated back to 1913, certain of the contents seem related more
recognizably to 1904 and the background to Freud's remarkable experience on
the Acropolis. In any event, Freud was rewriting the paper in 1919. He approached the uncanny from the standpoint of aesthetics, the senses of the beautiful and ugly. He sought to elucidate particularly the admixture of the familiar
and unfamiliar, of attraction and repulsion, which had played so large a part in
his feelings toward the writer-doubles. He became personally reminiscent as he
recalled walking on a hot summer afternoon in an unknown and deserted provincial town of Italy and finding himself drawn back again and again unwittingly
to the red light district. On another trip the number sixty-two seemed to crop
up wherever he went: he had reached that age the previous year. (A study by

Max Schur [1964; Chapter 6 of the present volume] will prove enlightening on this point.)

Freud reflected upon the mechanisms which writers use to create a sense of the uncanny. Perhaps we will be surprised by his comments on the admired Arthur Schnitzler in this respect. The latter had written a story, *Die Weissagung* ("The Prophecy") which flirted with the supernatural. It used the writer's prerogative to arrange the material so that the reader is betrayed "to the superstitiousness [he had] ostensibly surmounted" and leaves the reader with "a kind of grudge against the attempted deceit" (1913, pp. 250–251). The writer on the uncanny has acquired the ability to master his own residual sense of omnipotence by reproducing it at will in the reader. Such mastery, related to hypnosis, had been at least partially repudiated by psychoanalysis with its ultimate dependence on reason. Residual resorts to magic were eschewed, but did not lose their attraction for Freud.

Such a residue adhered to the periodicity theory of Wilhelm Fliess who, while not a writer, figured in a chain of transference figures to father and brothers which came to be attached to the writers also. An early trip to Greece in 1904 was made under the spell of malevolent wishes from Fliess that made Freud find the number sixty-one everywhere in Athens, which he took to be premonitory of death at that age. While this was sufficiently far off to be reassuring (Freud was then forty-eight, it placed him in a dismal mood for the culmination of the journey, the ascent of the Acropolis (Schur 1969; Chapter 7 of the present volume and Stamm 1969; Chapter 8 of the present volume). (We may note at this point that the number sixty-two, his then-current age, which figured in "The Uncanny," may already have been a falsification of memory and that the letter to Ferenczi on his sixty-third birthday may have signified his survival of Fliess's dreaded curse.)

Now in 1936, with his own eightieth birthday impending, the spell of Fliess and a prediction that he would die at eighty-one (as had his father and older brother) were reawakened (Schur 1969) in the form of reminiscences of the trip to Greece and the Acropolis so many years ago. This background is set for the most remarkable of the anniversary letters to alter ego writers—now to Romain Rolland again on the occasion of his seventieth birthday (Freud 1936). The familiar characteristics are present: (1.) Freud finds great difficulty in penning a suitable letter for this great occasion: "I am ten years older than you are and my powers of production are at an end" (1936, p. 239). (2.) As a "gift of an impoverished creature," he will recall and analyze the curious experience when, viewing the glorious scene from the Acropolis, he momentarily doubted the reality of his experience in being there (a derealization doubtlessly linked with a momentary recrudescence of a long-standing travel phobia).

Quickly and subtly Rolland has been displaced from his possession of the birthday gift and it is Freud himself who takes and remains in the foreground thereafter despite further pleas about his waning powers—which are scarcely illustrated by this supreme testimonial not only to his analytic but also to his literary powers. Two Freuds, in fact, now figure—Sigmund, and his younger brother Alexander who, in fact, is, like Rolland, ten years younger than Sigmund. I have elsewhere (1969; chapter 16 of the present volume) made a study of the role of Alexander as Freud's travel companion during the trip to Greece and about the fact that he was named after the Greek conqueror by no other than his ten-year-old brother Sigmund. A particularly benevolent attitude to this son-brother, Benjamin to Sigmund's "Joseph" (both sons of one of the wives of Jacob), had always prevailed. Ambivalence is present, however, since I have also discussed how Alexander was a replacement and screen for Julius, an intermediate brother, for whose death Freud had always borne guilt. On the Acropolis, facing death himself at the age of eighty, a desire to exchange identities with Rolland and Alexander comes to the fore, carrying with it the promise of ten years more of life for Sigmund while the younger, now older brothers, are sent to their death in his place. Such an exchange of death wishes with Wilhelm Fliess had prevailed in 1904. Other important aspects of the Acropolis experience that have been brought out by Fisher (1976), Harrison (1966), Niederland (1969), Slochower (1970), Stamm (1969; Chapter 8 of the present volume) et al., need not occupy us in this context.

With the interpositioning of Alexander Freud into the chain of younger writers, doubles, with whom identity was both experienced and repudiated, a key to the recurrent features of the birthday letters to writers is offered. They often mark decades: Freud was ten years old when Alexander was born. They speak of the birth of a hero, the mother's favorite who effortlessly wins her heart, while the displaced favorite finds little consolation in his greater intellectual equipment. Freud recognizes in the creative writer the perpetuation of the primal dream—the happiness of being the perpetual younger child, the only child who, as in the fairy tales, may look forward to solving all his wishes magically with the aid of a favoring goddess.

In his self-analysis of the Acropolis experience, Freud compares his success in reaching his destination (both through travels and, no doubt, as the discoverer of psychoanalysis) with the moment in the life of Napoleon when, during his coronation as Emperor in Notre Dame cathedral ("our Lady-Mother") he "turned to one of his brothers—it must no doubt have been the eldest one, Joseph—and remarked: "What would *Monsieur notre Pere* have said to this, if he could have been here today?" (1936, p. 247). The triumph of the younger brother over both father and older brother is indicated (Kanzer 1969; chapter 16 of the present volume) as the mother (crown and cathedral) now becomes a possession of the youngest son. Quite possibly there is an allusion here in the French setting to Romain Rolland as well, the birthday hero with whom Freud (as Joseph, the dream interpreter) would have liked to switch identities.

Neither self-analysis nor exchanges with younger writers had been concluded for 1936. To Thomas Mann he wrote on November 29 (E. Freud 1960, pp. 432–434, Letter 287), suggesting that he take as a theme for a story the influence on Napoleon Bonaparte of his older brother Joseph. Pointing to apparent historical sources, he suggested that the latter had first been a hated rival who later became excessively admired and exercised a baleful influence on the younger Bonaparte. A rather strange interpretation of Napoleon's life follows. Freud was burgeoning forth as a poet of the family romance and loosening the restraints that strict scientific discipline had always imposed upon him. 1936 also saw him preoccupied with the family romance of Moses in a study which he at times subtitled "a historical novel." In his correspondence with Arnold Zweig, the last of his Fliess figures and reduced in stature to a son and pupil, there is an especially valuable account of the creativity of Freud's mind even when, as he himself declared, his powers were failing not only because of age but because of interminable suffering. It was Moses now, not Zweig, who had become the alter ego: he spoke of the book (*Moses and Monotheism*) as "probably my last creative effort—the man and what I wanted to make of him pursue me everywhere" (E. Freud 1970, p. 98). As he reconstructed the Biblical narrative he denied that Aaron, the brother of Moses, could ever have existed. (At the same time he adopted a new theory that the Earl of Oxford was the true author of Shakespeare's works.)

Within *Moses and Monotheism* we find a recapitulation of the older thesis that "for natural reasons, youngest sons occupied an exceptional position. They were protected by their mother's love, and were able to take advantage of their father's increasing age and succeed him on his death. We seem to detect echoes in legends and fairy tales both of the expulsion of the elder sons and of the favoring of younger sons" (1939, p. 81). Actually, within the Bible, this would have applied both to Isaac, favored over Ishmael, and Jacob, favored over Esau.

The relationship between older and younger son received a new elucidation by Freud. It is used to account for the hatred of the ages directed at the Jew by the Christian. "I venture to suggest that jealousy of the people which declared itself the first-born, favorite child of God the Father, has not yet been surmounted by other peoples even today" (1939, p. 91). An older son favored by the father is set up against a younger one who is the mother's favorite. Now the former is the one who is envied. A son of the superego, he is more intellectual and moral than the younger brother. "The religion of Moses knew none but these positive feelings (admiration, awe, thankfulness) towards the father-god." This older brother was unquestioningly obeyed—the reaction formations were too great to permit acknowledgment of the hostility to God. Pauline Christianity recognized, however, that God the Father had been killed (as was Moses by the Jews, according to Freud's reconstruction). This permitted the Christian to atone while reproaching the Jew for having killed God, now portrayed as identical with the son.

The trend in the last works to recognize and identify with the role of the older son, the father's favorite, seems to have been a new development in Freud's decades-old analysis. It may be examined in relation to Freud's experience of derealization on the Acropolis, which he attributed to a sense of guilt for having surpassed the real father in life. It appears in a heightened sense of Jewishness as the Nazis close in to drive him from Vienna. It appears also in relation to the "good sons" as writers favored by himself as the father and inspired by him to new and creative works. The last he renounced for himself, recapitulating the father role he assumed to younger brother Alexander rather than the murderous sibling-rivalry to Julius, the one who had displaced him as the mother's favorite. To revert to the latter goal was dangerous and was warded off by assigning to the "double," the creative writer, the ability to regress without the superego control required of God's favorite son.

Summary

Despite clear evidence of his literary and creative gifts, Freud firmly classified himself as a scientist and permitted his imagination to receive recognition only indirectly through projection onto writers and artists toward whom he experienced a sense of "doubles" that evoked uncanny reactions. Such defenses against accepting responsibility for creative inspirations, with their oedipal aspects, are well known. Freud often avoided these doubles and further isolated them from himself with the declaration that analysis must lay down its arms before the problem of art.

Aspects of non-application of self-analysis emerge through a study of characteristics of typical birthday messages to writers with whom he established "doubles" relationships such as Schnitzler, Rolland and Mann. A prototypical relationship to his younger brother Alexander is adduced and a characteristic fantasy intruding into his scientific works pointed out. The birth of Alexander when Sigmund was ten launched a reaction in which the privilege of being the mother's favorite son was reluctantly replaced by superego pride in being the father's favorite son. Acceptance of the hostility to father and brother covered up by the latter defense was noticeable in the self-analytic material of Freud's final years.

References

Breuer, J. and Freud, S. (1893–1895). Studies on hysteria. *Standard Edition* 2.

Fisher, D. J. (1976). Sigmund Freud and Romain Rolland. *American Imago* 33:27–62.

Freud, E. ed. (1960). *The Letters of Sigmund Freud.* New York: Basic Books.

Freud, E. ed. (1970). *The Letters of Sigmund Freud and Arnold Zweig.* New York: Harcourt, Brace and Wald.

Freud, S. (1906). Delusion and dream in Jensen's "Gradiva." *Standard Edition* 9:7–95.

———— (1913). Totem and taboo. *Standard Edition* 13:1–161.

———— (1914a). The Moses of Michelangelo. *Standard Edition* 13:211–238.

———— (1914b). On narcissism. *Standard Edition* 14:73–102.

———— (1918). From the history of an infantile neurosis. *Standard Edition* 17:7–122.

———— (1919). The uncanny. *Standard Edition* 17:219–252.

———— (1921). Group psychology and the analysis of the ego. *Standard Edition* 18:69–143.

———— (1936). A disturbance of memory on the Acropolis. *Standard Edition* 22:239–248.

———— (1939). Moses and monotheism. *Standard Edition* 23:73–137.

———— (1954). *On the Origins of Psychoanalysis.* New York: Basic Books.

Grotjahn, M. (1967). Sigmund Freud and the art of letterwriting. *Journal of the American Medical Association* 200:13–18.

Harrison, I. (1966). A reconsideration of Freud's "A Disturbance of Memory on the Acropolis." *Journal of the American Psychoanalytic Association* 14:513–527.

Jones, E. (1953). *The Life and Work of Sigmund Freud.* Vol. 1. New York: Basic Books.

Jones, E. (1957). *The Life and Work of Sigmund Freud.* Vol. 3. New York: Basic Books.

Kanzer, M. (1966). The motor sphere of the transference. *Psychoanalytic Quarterly* 35:522–539.

Kanzer, M. (1969). Sigmund and Alexander Freud on the Acropolis. *American Imago* 26:324–354. (chapter 16 of this volume)

Niederland, W. (1969). Freud's disturbance of memory on the Acropolis. *American Imago* 26:373–378.

Schur, M. (1969). The background of Freud's "disturbance" on the Acropolis. *American Imago* 26:303–324. (chapter 7 of this volume)

Slochower, H. (1970). Freud's deja vu on the Acropolis. *Psychoanalytic Quarterly* 29:90–102.

Stamm, J. (1969). The problems of depersonalization in Freud's "Disturbance of memory on the Acropolis." *American Imago* 26:364–372. (chapter 8 of this volume)

Chapter 18

NARCISSISTIC ASPECTS OF FREUD AND HIS

DOUBLES

JULES GLENN, M.D.

The universal core of narcissism in scientific and artistic creativity manifests itself in Freud's conceiving of certain illustrious men as his doubles. As Kanzer (1976; chapter 17 of the present volume) documents, Freud bore certain similarities to Arthur Schnitzler, Thomas Mann and Romain Rolland. However, Freud in correspondence with these men modestly underrated his own creative imagination which actually matched or surpassed that of his "double."

Although in his letter to Schnitzler (E. Freud 1960, pp. 339–340, Letter 197) he overlooked the inner sources of his own scientific insights, self-observation was a key to his brilliant achievements, as he recognized in a paper dedicated to Rolland (Freud 1936). Although Freud contrasted the artist's easy access to the unconscious with his own hard work in exposing its contents, in fact the complex reorganization of data necessary for scientific and artistic achievement requires labor as well as inspiration. Obviously Freud idealized the alter egos he admired and envied.

Kanzer demonstrates certain aggressive, libidinal and defensive currents in Freud's relationships with these authors. At the same time that he praised the artist for his unusual capacities, Freud at times accused him of hiding the truth, thus achieving popularity through deceit. The artist, Kanzer discovers, represents the envied younger brother who is mother's favorite. Hence Freud's disguised attack on his younger double protects him from conscious awareness of his childhood rivalry and its adult derivatives. Further, defending himself against the guilt inherent in the scientist's fantasied stealing of knowledge from the gods, Freud invokes the double as the true creator and diminished his own achievement.

In this essay, I will place greater emphasis on the narcissistic regression involved in imagining oneself a double and its adaptive value for the creator. The reconstructions that follow will be based for the most part on the applications of our knowledge about doubles and narcissism rather than on detailed knowledge of Freud's early infancy, information about which is scanty.

In his classic article, *The Double* (1925), Rank mobilized evidence that the double reflects a narcissistic preoccupation. The double represents an extension of the self (Freud 1914) and can be traced back to the early mother-child symbiosis (Mahler, Pine and Bergman 1975). The baby in the symbiotic phase feels one with its mother. Later, in a derivative of this early sense of merging, he feels as if his mother were a mirror image (Eisnitz 1961, Kohut 1971), an alter ego, a double. His ability to differentiate his self-representation from that of his mother leads to the wishful fantasy of having a twin as a double (Glenn 1974). In later years these images attain new meanings. A boy's wish to fuse with his mother, be one with her, may retain pre-oedipal desires when fantasies of oedipal genital joining or penetration become dominant. The double appears once more as identification with the oedipal father comes to the fore. Freud in fact wrote to Martha Bernays that "he was the duplicate of his father physically and to some extent mentally" (Jones 1953, p. 2). Primitive identification with diffusely perceived pre-objects conceived of as omniscient can grow into mature identification with powerful real or mythic persons, again conceived of as doubles.

Concomitantly, early self-cathexis can develop into mature ability for self-observation so valuable to the psychoanalytic pioneer and into mature self-confidence and self-esteem.

As is true of all creative men, Freud's narcissism was essential for his achievement. The reader will recall his fierce ambitious pride when he predicted that a plaque would be erected to celebrate his discovery of the interpretation of dreams and his suggestion as a teenager that his friend save his letters which would become valuable. This pride manifests itself in picturing himself the double of esteemed artists, a specific instance of identifying with great men. Freud also identified himself with Joseph, the interpreter of dreams, Moses, the truth giver who led men to the promised land but could not enter himself, and Prometheus, who robs fire from the gods (Shengold 1966; chapter 4 of the present volume).

Freud's narcissism provided a motive for his great achievements. We can see this force at work when he competes with Rolland, producing a masterpiece of scientific and artistic import which he offers as a birthday gift (Freud 1936).

Identifying with his double, he does not merely acquire his creative ability; using his own innate talent (which justifies and stimulates his pride), he over-shadows Rolland.

The fantasied double forms a reassuring presence adding strength to the weak child. Castration, maternal deprivation, and other narcissistic losses need not be feared as the double, representing a penis, mother, or other narcissistic object, substitutes for that which may be lost (see Burlingham 1952 and Rank 1925). Feigelson (1975) has proposed that the specific defense here utilized be called *duplication*. This maneuver can be used adaptively in artistic creation; the novel or story or painting contains more or less disguised replicas of the lost objects. Winnicott's (1953) suggestion that art forms are derivatives of transitional objects is relevant to this point.

Feigelson observed that duplication is operative as a defense against primal scene traumata and the fantasies of destruction that develop. This finding is supported by observations by Eisnitz (1961) and Isay (1975). We may wonder whether Freud's alter egos derived from early primal scene experiences. Schur (1972) has discovered that Freud's family occupied a single room in Freiberg and that he must have been subjected to such experiences repeatedly in his early days. The memories of these events seem to have been completely repressed. They may have appeared in screen memories of fires while on a childhood journey from Freiberg to Leipsig (Jones 1953–1957). Arlow (1978, 1979) has observed the appearance of fires following primal scene imagery in literature. Grinstein (1968) has found references to the primal scene in a number of Freud's dreams (Count Thun, Goethe's attack on Herr M., Hollthurn, Frau Doni, His Father like Garibaldi, the Open-Air Closet, His Mother and the Bird-Beaked Figures) but no *direct* associations (Freud 1900).

Regression to narcissism creates a state that facilitates creativity. Such regression produces a fluidity of ego boundaries essential to artistic work in general and analytic work specifically. Freud's empathy with patients and, his bold recognition that his inner conflicts and fantasies were shared with his patients were achieved because projection and identification (which involves temporary confusion of self- and object-representations) were available for adaptive purposes, tempered by reality testing and impulse control.

Kanzer observes that Freud must have recognized that creative persons need not be fully aware of the dynamics they brilliantly portray. It would appear that Freud's stated belief that they do understand with ease what he must struggle laboriously to achieve is an idealization of his doubles who are narcissistic objects. It will be recalled that he also idealized Fliess to the point that he had to overlook that man's grievous errors (Schur 1966, Chapter 6 of the present volume).

A typical narcissistic configuration comprises idealizing the object while retaining a sense of grandiosity (Kohut 1971). Idealization may be followed by a fantasy of gaining the imagined power of the admired one. The early belief that mother is omnipotent and that her power can be attained through fusion and the later wish to acquire father's power (including his penis) are thus repeated in condensed form.

Paradoxically, although authors may describe and depict complex and subtle human relations, dynamics and fantasies, they frequently fail to appreciate the significance of their astonishing insights. With few exceptions artists do not welcome analysts' interpretation of their work. Thomas Mann, one such exception, expressed gratitude for explanations of his work which he had failed to realize (Mann 1961). Other artists, when confronted with their own stated insights, are appalled and deny that they intended them. In a panel on his play *Equus*, Peter Shaffer (1975) disclaimed any intellectual or analytic understanding of the characters of his play. He proclaimed that the psychological explanations of the panel members were a "sea of words" which he could not comprehend. In addition, I am reminded of a celebrated author whom I saw in conjunction with a consultation for his daughter. In his short stories he had described relationships between a fictional father and daughter in a moving manner and with great clarity. When I tried to show him that he was engaged in interactions exactly like those he deemed pathological in his writings, he was surprised by what I had said. He could not agree with my characterization of the family in his stories. He astonished me by revealing that he did not consciously realize what he had written, had not consciously perceived what was obvious to his readers.

Although Freud may have failed to note the obvious, that authors are generally blind to their most telling insights, I cannot fault him for this. His idealization of them and consequent creative activity depended in part on the achievement of narcissistic states which may result from regression. By idealizing these men he could fantasy borrowing their power, avoid full guilt and responsibility for his own creative genius, and, through regression and reversal (replacing hate with love), hide his antagonism to his rivals.

References

Arlow, J. (1978, 1979). Pyromania and the primal scene: a psychoanalytic comment on the work of Yukio Mishima. *Psychoanalytic Quarterly* 47:24–51, and Downstate 25th Anniversary Series, Volume 4. New York: Jason Aronson.

Burlingham, D. (1952). *Twins: A Study of Three Pairs of Identical Twins*. New York: International Universities Press.

Eisnitz, A. (1961). Mirror dreams. *Journal of the American Psychoanalytic Association* 9:461–479.

Feigelson, C. (1975). The mirror dream. *Psychoanalytic Study of the Child* 30:341–355.

Freud, E. ed. (1960). *The Letters of Sigmund Freud.* New York: Basic Books.

Freud, S. (1900). The interpretation of dreams. *Standard Edition 4/5.*

—— (1914). On narcissism: an introduction. *Standard Edition 14.*

—— (1936). A disturbance of memory on the Acropolis. *Standard Edition* 22.

—— (1954). *The Origins of Psychoanalysis.* New York: Basic Books, 1954.

Glenn, J. (1974). Anthony and Peter Shaffer's plays: the influence of twinship on creativity. *American Imago* 31:270–292.

Grinstein, A. (1968). *On Sigmund Freud's Dreams.* Detroit: Wayne State University Press.

Isay, R. A. (1975). The influence of the primal scene on the sexual behavior of an early adolescent. *Journal of the American Psychoanalytic Association* 23:535–554.

Jones, E. (1953–1957). *The Life and Work of Sigmund Freud.* 3 vols. New York: Basic Books.

Kanzer, M. (1976). Freud and his literary doubles. *American Imago* 33:231–243.

Kohut, H. (1971). *The Analysis of the Self.* New York: International Universities Press.

Mahler, M. S., Pine, F., and Bergman, A. (1975). *The Psychological Birth of the Human Infant.* New York: Basic Books.

Mann, T. (1961). *The Story of a Novel.* New York: Alfred A. Knopf.

Rank, O. (1925). *The Double.* Trans. H. Tucker, Jr. Chapel Hill: University of North Carolina Press, 1971.

Schur, M. (1966). Some additional "day residues" of "the specimen dream of psychoanalysis." In Loewenstein, R. L., et al. *Psychoanalysis—A General Psychology.* New York: International Universities Press.

—— (1972). *Freud: Living and Dying.* New York: International Universities Press.

Shaffer, P. (1975). Panel discussion on *Equus* at the Association for Applied Psychoanalysis, June, 1975.

Shengold, L. (1966). The metaphor of the journey in *The Interpretation of Dreams. American Imago* 23:316–331.

Winnicott, D. W. (1953). Transitional objects and transitional phenomena: a study of the first non-me possessions. *International Journal of Psycho-Analysis* 34:89–97.

INDEX